Radical Diplomat

Radical Diplomat

The Life of
Archibald Clark Kerr,
Lord Inverchapel,
1882–1951

Donald Gillies

BLOOMSBURY ACADEMIC
LONDON · NEW YORK · OXFORD · NEW DELHI · SYDNEY

BLOOMSBURY ACADEMIC
Bloomsbury Publishing Plc
50 Bedford Square, London, WC1B 3DP, UK
1385 Broadway, New York, NY 10018, USA
29 Earlsfort Terrace, Dublin 2, Ireland

BLOOMSBURY, BLOOMSBURY ACADEMIC and the Diana logo
are trademarks of Bloomsbury Publishing Plc

First published in Great Britain by I.B. Tauris 1999
This paperback edition published by Bloomsbury Academic 2022

Copyright © Donald Gillies, 1999

Donald Gillies has asserted his right under the Copyright,
Designs and Patents Act, 1988, to be identified as author of this work.

For legal purposes the Acknowledgements on p. vii constitute
an extension of this copyright page.

All rights reserved. No part of this publication may be reproduced or
transmitted in any form or by any means, electronic or mechanical,
including photocopying, recording, or any information storage or retrieval
system, without prior permission in writing from the publishers.

Bloomsbury Publishing Plc does not have any control over, or responsibility for,
any third-party websites referred to or in this book. All internet addresses given
in this book were correct at the time of going to press. The author and publisher
regret any inconvenience caused if addresses have changed or sites have
ceased to exist, but can accept no responsibility for any such changes.

A catalogue record for this book is available from the British Library.

A catalog record for this book is available from the Library of Congress.

ISBN: HB: 978-1-8606-4296-8
PB: 978-1-3501-8245-5
ePDF: 978-0-7556-3242-8
ePub: 978-0-7556-3243-5

Typeset in Palatino by Dexter Haven, London

To find out more about our authors and books visit
www.bloomsbury.com and sign up for our newsletters.

Contents

Acknowledgements vii

Introduction – From a Far Country ix

Maps xi

Genealogy xiv

1 Shore 1882–1900 1

2 Upland 1900–15 8

3 Foothills 1915–22 20

4 Outcrop 1922–25 30

5 Corrie 1925–37 68

6 Ridge 1938–42 85

7 Mountain Top 1942–46 120

8 Pinnacle 1946–48 181

9 Cairn 1948–51 219

Notes on the Text 229

Index 245

Acknowledgements

My principal thanks are to Sir William ('Tony') and Lady Lewthwaite for making many private papers available to me and for their help and kindness throughout the years of research. Sir William also undertook the onerous task of editing the first draft of this biography, a task which he had all but completed at the time of his death late in 1993. His advice and suggestions were always helpful and sensible and I am particularly sorry that he did not live to see the project through to fruition. I am also grateful for the advice of Sir Geoffrey and Lady de Bellaigue.

Several other individuals assisted me greatly. I must thank Her Majesty, Queen Elizabeth, the Queen Mother, and her private secretaries, Sir Martin Gilliat and Alistair Aird, for answering my enquiries. Lady Boothby allowed me access to her late husband's papers and was a most hospitable hostess during my time working on them. Struan Lamport of Sydney, NSW, gave me invaluable assistance regarding the Clark family's Australian history. Similarly Ray Clark of Boggabri, NSW, provided information regarding Ghoolendaadi sheep station. Dr Kessler and Professor Wolgast of Heidelberg University carried out research for me into university archives. Lesley Callaghan and Margaret Wenger both helped with German translation. J. Richard Thackrah, who had earlier done much work on Lord Inverchapel's career, directed me to several important sources. M. Joyce of Bath Library identified useful material and Jill Grey was a most efficient researcher of those sources. James Murray of the Public Record Office at Kew kindly carried out some initial research for me which helped me make best use of my time there. Similarly Gregory Quinn and P. Donougho of the Records Branch of the Foreign and Commonwealth Office provided information and directed me to useful sources. Captain D.J. Archibald of the Scots Guards researched the regimental archives for me and answered my queries. Margaret Kirk of Inverchapel Lodge also gave me useful information. Sir Robert Rhodes James directed me to profitable sources.

Javier Diaz Lira of Santiago gave me some information about his aunt, Lady Inverchapel. Kenneth Harington and Lord Colyton were helpful in providing information about the Stockholm legation. The following individuals were helpful in answering my inquiries regarding Lord Inverchapel's time in China: L.H. Lamb; Sir Berkeley Gage; Lord Alport; Ian Mackenzie; J.F. Ford. Major Ian Westmacott kindly read over Chapter 6 and made some helpful suggestions.

Thanks are also due to those who assisted me in researching Lord Inverchapel's period in the USSR: G.H. Bolsover; Sir Edward Tomkins; Sir John Lawrence; Sir Michael Hadow; Sir Isaiah Berlin; Sir Frank Roberts; Lord Brimelow. I should also like to acknowledge the help of King Michael of Romania. Mr Frank Giles assisted me regarding Lord Inverchapel's mission to the Dutch East Indies.

The following individuals answered my queries about Lord Inverchapel's period in Washington: Michael Foot; Sir John Barnes; Sir Nicholas Henderson; Bill Edwards; Lord Sherfield; Sir Ernest Sabben-Clare; Sir P. Pares; Sir Frederick Everson; Arthur Maddocks; Sir George Middleton; the Marquis of Anglesey; Walter Bell; Lord Mayhew; John Hersey; ex-Senator J.W. Fulbright. The staff of Alfred Knopf also answered my questions.

I should also like to thank Helen Langley of the Bodleian Library, Oxford, and Colin Harris and staff of the Modern Papers Reading Room there. St John's College, Oxford, enabled me to carry out research in most pleasant surroundings thanks to their excellent Schoolteachers Study Periods. Other libraries and staff who assisted me are also due thanks: the Mitchell Library, Glasgow; the University of Glasgow Library; the National Library of Scotland; the District Library, Dunoon; the Scottish Records Office; the Public Record Office, Kew; Hamilton District Library; the James Watt Library, Greenock. In Canada, R. Calvin Best of the Provincial Archives of Newfoundland and Labrador answered my enquiries as did D. O'Keefe of the Department of Health. Deborah L. Jeans Snow efficiently carried out research for me in Newfoundland.

The following individuals from the 1950 Inverchapel Campaign Committee were also helpful: Donald Dickson; Patrick Hooper; M.A. Tinney; Isabel Mackenzie.

Finally I must thank my wife Lorna who remained positive and stoically supportive during the obsessions and depressions which researching this book entailed.

Donald Gillies
Glasgow

Introduction –
From a Far Country

If you take the road north from Dunoon, travelling inland beyond the shores of the Holy Loch, and continue past the Glen Massan and Kilmun turn-offs, you come eventually after a few miles to the small unmarked township of Inverchapel. There remains nowadays only one inhabited dwelling, the old farmhouse, whose few acres straddle the Inverchapel burn just short of the southern end of Loch Eck. This peaceful, narrow loch – although prone to wild winter storms – is one of Scotland's least celebrated and yet most beautiful, running in a secluded blue streak for some six miles up to its head near Strachur. On both sides its calm waters are guarded by steep, craggy hills with peaks of heathered rock, and closely-forested lower slopes of spruce and larch. Almost bereft of human habitation, and trackless for much of its western shore, it is the haunt of sheep and deer and its higher cliff-faces the lonely nesting-grounds for hawks and eagles.

Just beyond Inverchapel farmhouse, over the old stone bridge, lies a dense coniferous wood, extending for an acre or so, skirting the road. Once a tended plantation, it has now run wild, and the damaging effects of gales, storms and unchecked growth are all too plain. Even if you stop the car in the lay-by and climb the drooping fence to enter the wood, you would do well to identify amongst the jumbled mesh of branches, bushes and toppled trunks the remains of a once well-kept grove bordered by cypress trees. These trees have long since been uprooted and have collapsed inward like a tent across the green clearing.

For all its neglect, it is a place of uncanny stillness; only the hush of the wind as it feathers the tree-tops high above and the occasional croaking of rooks break the heavy silences.

It would take the most tenacious, however, to detect below this thick interlacing of fallen, mossed trunks, a grouping of four flat tombstones: three set together in a row, and one, on its own, behind. If you lie flat and stretch out as far as possible you may just be able to reach to clear away the mud and layers of pine-needles from the surface of this tomb; gradually, a green plate is revealed, bearing a flowery coat of arms, and, below, the impressive legend: "Archibald John Kerr Clark Kerr, PC GCMG, First Baron Inverchapel of Loch Eck".

It is the burial place of one of the most intriguing and influential British diplomatists of the twentieth century; one who walked with emperors, kings and queens; who laboured in wartime with Churchill, Roosevelt and Stalin; but who remains now, like his final resting-place, largely forgotten and unacknowledged.

The grave of Archibald Clark Kerr, Lord Inverchapel, lies, in fact, in his ancestral homelands, and less than a mile away on the shores of Loch Eck stands Inverchapel Lodge, the house he built in the early 1920s, where he spent his precious vacations and the few short years of his retirement.

Despite the apparent appropriateness of the setting for his tomb, Lord Inverchapel's birth, upbringing and working life were spent far removed from this quiet corner of Argyllshire. Although Inverchapel always remained his 'spiritual' home, he could hardly have had a more varied and cosmopolitan life: born in Australia, brought up in England, educated there and in France and Germany, married to a Chilean, he also served in some fifteen different countries around the globe in his 40 years as a British diplomat.

The obscurity of his grave matches rather well the apparent confusion which surrounds his life and origins: most modern works which do refer to him do so in highly inaccurate terms. Whether resulting from carelessness, malice or just wild imaginings, not much truth has been written about Sir Archibald Clark Kerr, Lord Inverchapel. It is long past time that some effort was made to discover and assess the facts of his life and career, and lay bare to scrutiny some of the more extravagant claims made about him.

> Remember the former things of old... declaring the end from the beginning... calling the man that executeth my counsel from a far country.
>
> Isaiah 46

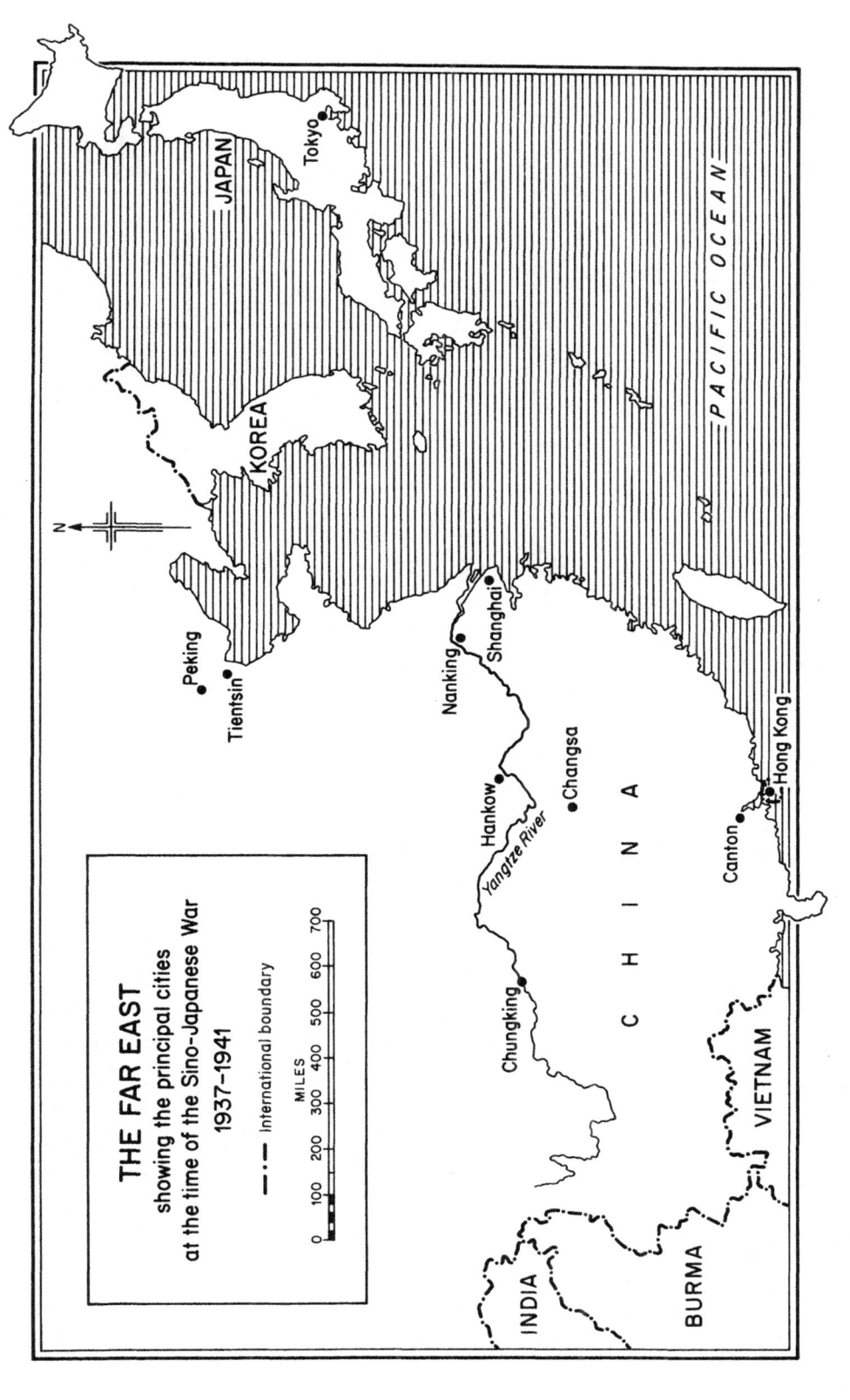

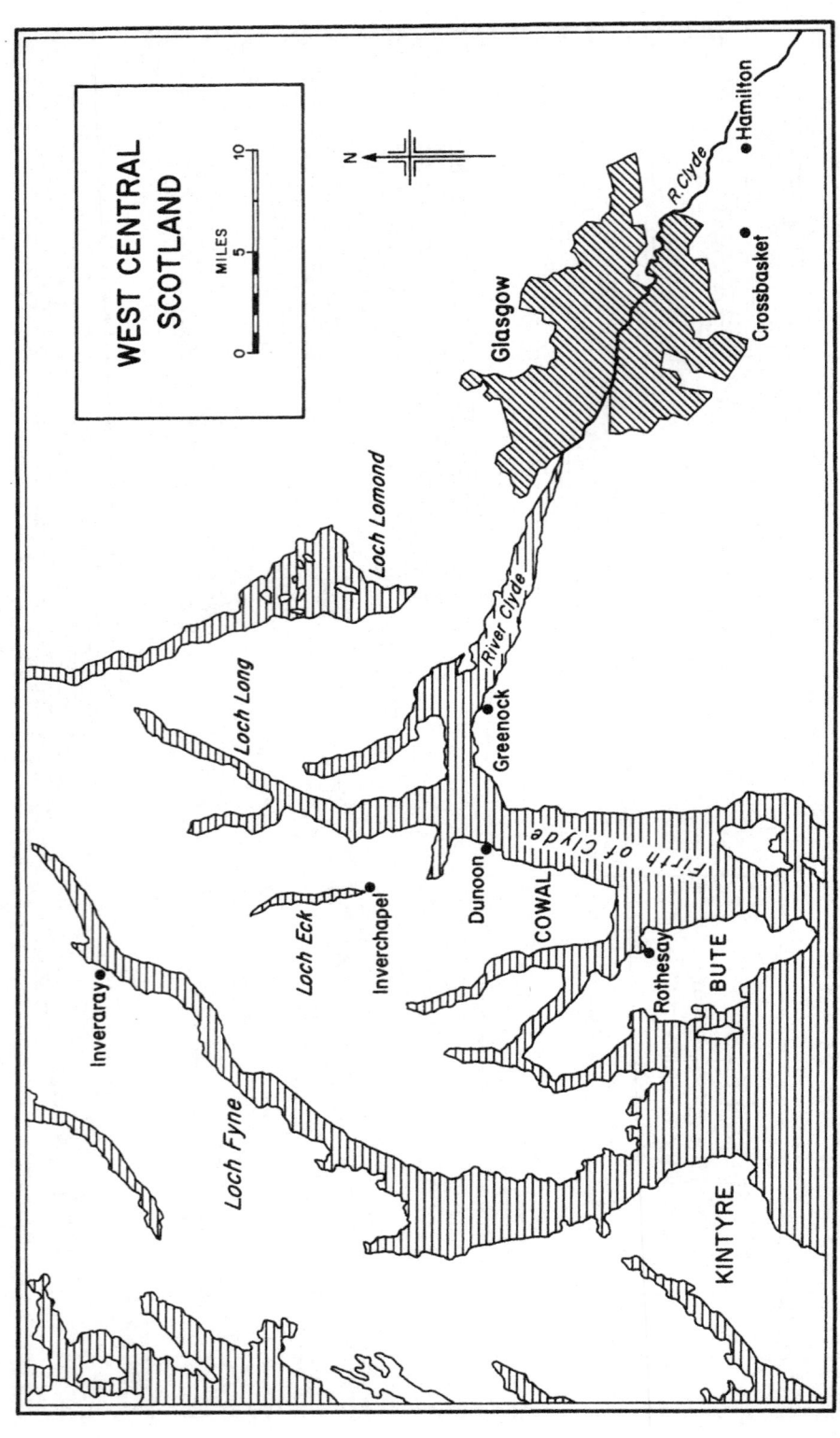

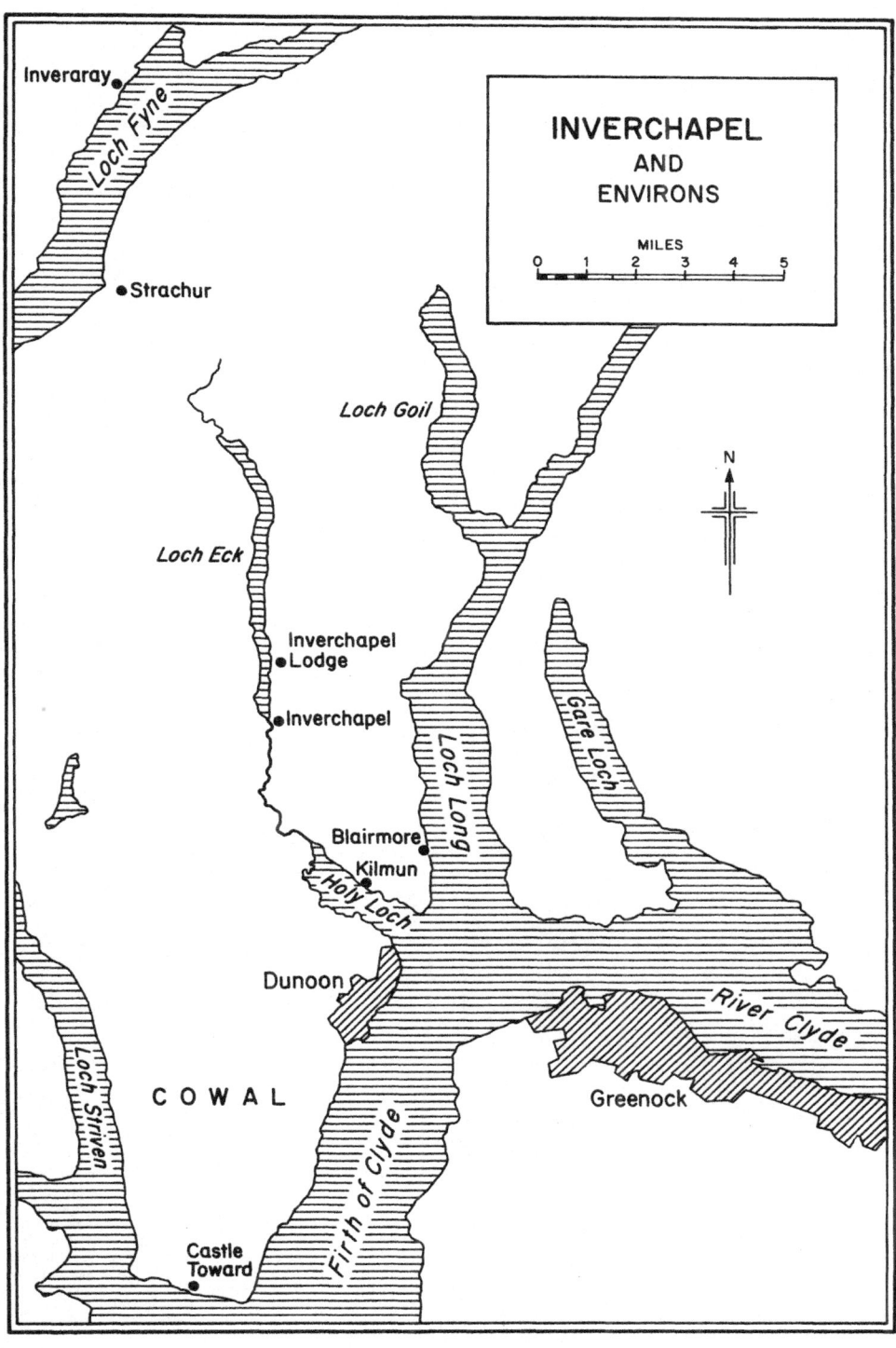

Family Tree of Sir Archibald Clark Kerr 1st Baron Inverchapel

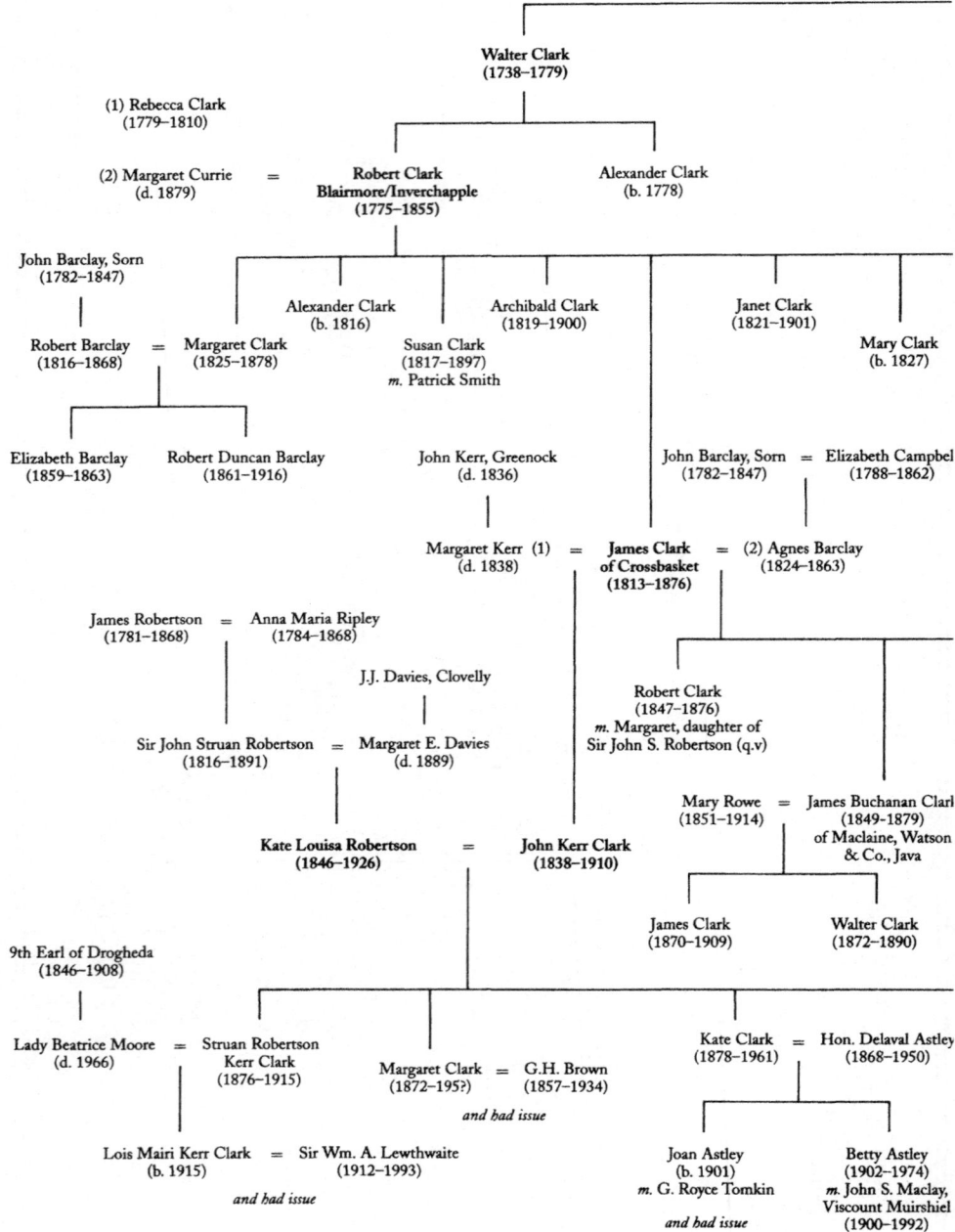

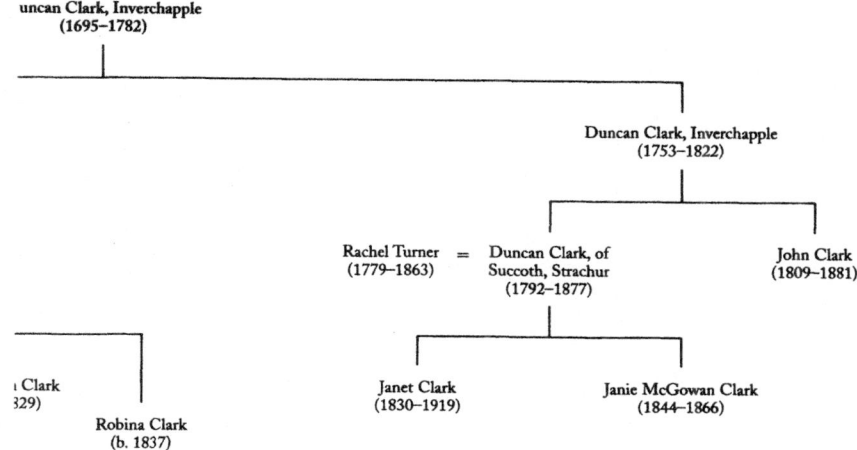
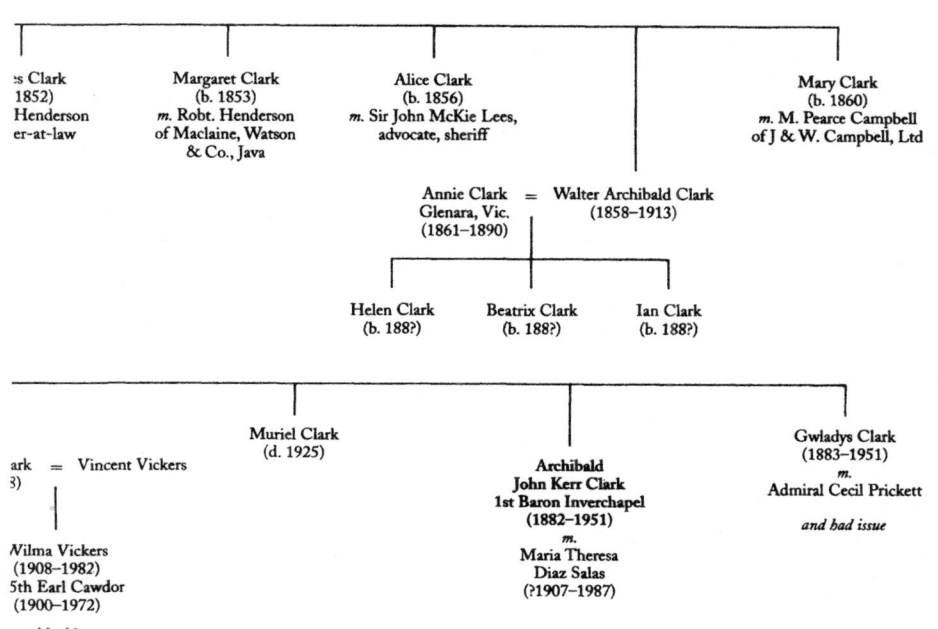

CHAPTER 1

Shore 1882–1900

Archibald John Kerr Clark was born on 17 March 1882 at his grandparents' home, 'Clovelly', in Watson's Bay, a suburb of Sydney, New South Wales. He was the tenth of 11 children born to John Kerr Clark (1838–1910) and Kate Louisa Robertson (1846–1926). Known then, and later in the highest political circles, simply as Archie, his surname by contrast evolved through a whole series of different forms – Clark, Kerr Clark, Kerr Clark Kerr, Clark Kerr, Kerr, before the final titled form of Inverchapel. For the sake of consistency, and ease of understanding, he will be referred to in this biography as Clark Kerr, the style he himself formally adopted in 1911.

Despite the Australian birthplace, there were strong Scottish connections on both sides of the family. Archie was named after his father's uncle, Archibald Clark (1819–1900) who was then farming at Inverchapel back home in Argyll. The Clark family had been in Inverchapel for generations – since at least the early 1500s – and had become successful farmers.

Clark Kerr was remarkable in having two extraordinary grandfathers, very different in character, but who both achieved striking success from similarly modest origins. Archie's paternal grandfather was James Clark (1813–1876), born at Blairmore not far from Inverchapel. Inverchapple, as the place was styled until the turn of the century, is a Gaelic name meaning 'river-mouth of the mare' and is in keeping with a number of placenames in the area which have an equine connection: Loch Eck itself derives from the Gaelic 'each', a horse. The later anglicised styling, Inverchapel, is therefore slightly misleading with its apparently religious link. Although James Clark was the eldest son, he did not take over the farm at Inverchapel when he came of age. Family circumstances now meant that he could have access to a good education and the opportunities which would thereby arise for a young Victorian. James Clark received a solid education locally before moving on to the University of Glasgow and later Edinburgh University, where he trained as a surgeon.[1] He never actually practised his profession however, apparently finding the constant experience of physical pain and disease too much for his gentle disposition. Instead he was destined for a career in commerce. Some time after quitting Edinburgh University, he returned to his home area and took up a position with a firm of Greenock merchants, Kerrs & McBride. At some point during his short spell with the firm, James Clark married Margaret Kerr, the daughter of John Kerr, the principal partner, and worked for a while in Newfoundland where the company had business dealings.[2] It was after his return, however, in October 1838, that his brief marriage came to a tragic end: in giving birth to their only child, Margaret died. Grief-stricken, James Clark returned to Inverchapel with the young child, whom he named John Kerr Clark.

A period of inactivity followed before he was given an introduction to the Glasgow businessman and politician Kirkman Finlay (1773–1842), whose vast country house, Castle Toward, lay a few miles to the south at the tip of the Cowal peninsula. James Clark travelled to the estate for an interview; Finlay was immediately impressed and, as part of his examination, asked James Clark to draft an imaginary business letter. Clark declined Finlay's offer of a steel-nibbed pen, requested a quill instead, and proceeded to compose an exemplary epistle in fine copperplate handwriting. Finlay, not given to lavish praise, was clearly very satisfied: 'You'll do,' he told him.

It was the beginning of an extraordinary business career. James Finlay & Company, of which Kirkman Finlay was still the head, had been a highly successful cotton manufacturing concern since its establishment in 1760. By 1839, when James Clark was recruited, it was something of an ailing giant. The principal partners were all of advanced years and the nepotistic system of renewal had failed to produce staff equal to the business challenge. In James Clark, however, they found their saviour: well-educated and with his Newfoundland experience behind him, James Clark swept through the machinery of the company, organising a complete restructuring and modernisation.

By 1851 he was the largest shareholder in James Finlay and Company and profits were such that he could afford to buy the sizable Crossbasket estate near High Blantyre on the southern outskirts of Glasgow. Apart from continuing business interests on the Continent, in India and in the East, James Clark also achieved considerable success as a landowner and cattle breeder and generally settled into the life of a prosperous member of the lowland landed gentry.

After education in Scotland, the young son John Kerr Clark enjoyed a period of travel and study on the Continent. His father's success and contacts can be gauged by the fact that in 1856–7 John Kerr Clark was moving in the most aristocratic social circles and was even a guest of the Grand Duke of Saxe-Weimar.

By this time James Clark had already three sons and numerous daughters by his second marriage – to Agnes Barclay, sister of a business partner – and perhaps the child of the first marriage was a little out of place at Crossbasket. Whatever the actual impetus may have been, John Kerr Clark was encouraged to seek his fortune abroad. With his uncle, Duncan Clark (b 1829), and the financial backing of his father, he left Scotland in 1860 for Australia.

At Ghoolendaadi, near Boggabri, some 250 miles north west of Sydney, they purchased property to serve as a sheep station. Gradually, they acquired neighbouring properties so that by 1868 the Ghoolendaadi station amounted to 232,000 acres – nearly 400 square miles – mostly given over to grazing for some 40,000 sheep. Despite its remoteness, John Kerr Clark was evidently still able to find some agreeable company, for in 1870 he married Kate Louisa, the daughter of a neighbouring landowner John Robertson, later Sir.

James Clark died in 1876, leaving a considerable fortune. Almost inevitably feuding broke out: between the family of the second wife and their close connections in Scotland, and the only son of the first marriage, John Kerr Clark, conveniently 12,000 miles away in New South Wales. The disputes consequent to this ran on for decades and the young Clark Kerr quickly became conscious of the rift between the 'Kerr' Clarks of the first marriage, and the 'Barclay' Clarks of the second. To make the issue more distinct, the Clarks of the first family adopted the name Kerr as part of the family surname so that the Kerr Clarks would not be associated with the 'Barclay' Clarks any more than was necessary.

The material welfare of Clark Kerr's family appears also to have riled the 'Barclay' Clarks, and so both branches of the family continued a form of petty rivalry, often acted out in an unseemly jockeying for social pre-eminence in later Victorian and Edwardian society. The desire to 'put one over', the Barclay Clarks was one which remained with Clark Kerr himself well into manhood.

On Clark Kerr's mother's side, the Scottish ancestry had been diluted somewhat but was no less definite. Kate Louisa Robertson was one of nine children born to Sir John Struan Robertson (1816–91), Premier of New South Wales on no less than five occasions. He was a rough and ready politician with strong liberal instincts and although he died when Clark Kerr was only nine years old, such an important and colourful a character was bound to have made a lasting impression on the young child. Clark Kerr's mother became very much the genteel Victorian matron, keen to see her family brought up to behave in a way appropriate to their lofty social status, and she tried very hard to expunge from her household all traces of the coarser aspects of her father's social ways. He was quite an extraordinary figure and his life deserves some further consideration.

John Robertson was born in Bow, Essex, in 1816, the son of a Scot who then emigrated to Australia in 1822 to take up sheep farming. He first squatted on property on the Hunter River and, later, further north on the Liverpool Plains. John Robertson married the daughter of a Welsh settler, Margaret E. Davies, in 1838, and not long after this took his first steps into politics, becoming involved in representing squatters in various disputes in the Namoi region. It was to this area that John Kerr Clark came in the 1860s, and through a mutual interest in matters pastoral the two men became acquainted.

John Robertson soon became known as a prominent and rather rough political agitator. His social coarseness apparently rendered him

> ... not acceptable to polite society. By 1850, his peculiar voice [he had a cleft palate] gave authority to a comprehensive repertoire of profanity and he had an enviable capacity to take and hold his liquor; his bushman's clothes were crumpled by constant riding; but he was handsome, with reddish brown hair and beard...[3]

In 1856 he was elected to the Lower House of the New South Wales Legislature, where he gained a reputation as a radical member with strong liberal views. In the House it was said that his voice was 'the loudest, his language the most violent, and his attitudes the most distorted'.[4]

In debates, for example, it was quite common for him to invite opponents to 'sniff my arse', and this belligerently anal aspect of his rhetoric remained with him throughout his political career, even when Premier. On one occasion, on a visit to a provincial town, he became exasperated by the political demands of an importunate local mayor. Eventually, Sir John, as he had by then become, rounded on him: 'See here, master bloody Mayor: if you think I'm a bloody spider to go and spin spider's webs out of my bloody arse you're bloody well mistaken'.[5]

John Robertson became Minister for Lands in 1858 and was Prime Minister in 1860 when he piloted Robertson's Land Act which introduced the system of selection to the ownership of land and so opened up much of New South Wales. Unfortunately the law was abused in later years but Sir John was too stubborn to change it and so admit error. His laws, in fact, reduced considerably Ghoolendaadi's acreage, so that by 1890 it was down to around 50,000 acres, less than a fifth of what it had been at its peak. Despite bankruptcy in 1870, Sir John was able to return to politics and was knighted in 1877. His fifth and last administration was a brief one in 1886 when he was in the Upper House and nearly 70 years of age.

Following their marriage, John Kerr Clark and Kate made their home on the Ghoolendaadi station. It was an isolated and primitive place and it took many years to create a home worthy of such an important landowning family. Kate found it hard to adapt to the barrenness of the area after the social life she had been used to in her Sydney girlhood, and the arid heat also affected her health. It was a rough and desolate place, populated by hard-working and hard-drinking ranchers. The homestead itself remained underdeveloped, and many locals believed that most of the profits were sent back to the family in Scotland, rather than being spent on improving the living conditions of Mrs Kerr Clark. Nonetheless, there was soon a growing family to look after, although the climate and conditions again took a grim toll, with four children – three boys and a girl – dying in infancy. Thereafter she tended to move to Sydney or even Tasmania to give birth in a better climate and be closer to the rest of her family. Of the surviving children, the first was Margaret, born in 1872; then came Kate, then Struan Robertson, known as Robin; then Mairi, Muriel, Archie in 1882, and finally Gwladys.

In 1879 a new overseer, G.H. Brown, came out from Hamilton to manage the station. This allowed John, Kate and their children to spend more time in Sydney at the Robertsons' home, Clovelly, which Kate greatly preferred. With the coming of the railway to Boggabri in 1882, Ghoolendaadi came within easier reach of Sydney but by this stage Kate had largely set her face against the place. Archie Clark Kerr therefore grew up in some comfort at Clovelly, attended by a nurse and governess and further enjoyed the attentions of an elder brother and four sisters as well as mother and grandparents.

The house at Clovelly was a sprawling verandahed dwelling set in extensive grounds, and it was there, under a Moreton Bay figtree which stands to this day, that young Archie was baptised. His Robertson grandfather had mellowed a little with age but made little allowance for the sensitivities of Victorian society. In the evenings he would set off on his white mare for the local Edmont's Hotel to sink a few beers. Whenever the horse ambled back to the house alone, it was a sign that Sir John had been 'delayed' and a buggy would be despatched from Clovelly to bring him home.

Sir John Robertson finally died in 1891, having been predeceased by his wife and two of his nine children. Two years before his death, Clark Kerr's mother and father decided to return to England, chiefly to see the children properly educated. Clovelly was abandoned, fell into disrepair, and after a brief career as the local haunted house, was demolished in 1903. On arrival in England, a house was purchased in Bath but Clark Kerr's father did not remain long in England and returned soon after to Ghoolendaadi, certainly before 1898. Whatever the reason for the estrangement, the marriage remained forever afterwards merely one of mutual support from a distance.

Residence in England had several benefits, not least of which for Archie was the chance to holiday from time to time at Inverchapel. He immediately developed a deep love of the area, even if family feuds meant that visits there were often difficult and the atmosphere invariably frosty. Apart from his Uncle Archie, there were also several maiden aunts in residence at Inverchapel, but they seem to have uniformly sided with the 'Barclay' Clarks, or the 'Philistines', as Clark Kerr's family dubbed them. However, in the absence of a father, and as an 'immigrant' only lately arrived from the colonies, Clark Kerr grew to treasure Inverchapel as a place which gave him the roots and security he needed. In the midst of change, Inverchapel was the one constant, where his family had always been and where he could feel he belonged.

The family fitted remarkably smoothly into the late Victorian social scene. Obviously they had enjoyed considerable status even when in Australia: Clark Kerr's father, for example, received an invitation to Queen Victoria's Jubilee thanksgiving service at Westminster Abbey in 1887. They had the all-important social 'connections', not only through colonial politics and Sir John, but also through the various landowners whom Clark Kerr's father had met in the line of business, and others through grandfather James Clark. Most English aristocratic families had some holding in Australia and it was natural that John Kerr Clark should be acquainted with some of them.

Archie Clark Kerr started school in England by following his brother as a pupil at Bath College in May 1892. He seems to have been a bright, intelligent, lively child. Bath College had been founded in 1878 and so was quite a young public school, but had a growing reputation, particularly in classics. One of its unique features was the public performance of a Latin play each Christmas. It was a small school – on average there was usually a roll of only 135 – and it struggled both to prosper and gain a place among the ranks of the great English public schools. After a long struggle against the odds the school finally closed in 1909, its buildings being turned into the Spa Hotel.

Not much is recorded of Clark Kerr's schooldays, and because of his reticence about them in later life, one might be led to assume they were fairly undistinguished from an academic point of view. In fact his reports show him always to have been at or near the top of his form, and to have been a sporting and social success also. Clark Kerr never credited Bath College with having been his school, preferring the phrase 'Educated privately'. The reason for this is not clear, but as a young man he does seem to have felt some snobbish embarrassment about the fact that Bath College was so little esteemed, and acute embarrassment when it finally folded.

His school record is peppered with glowing reports: in 1899 he was first in both the school's classical and final exams. On the sporting front there is a record of him playing hooker for the school rugby team during his last two years at school, 1899 and 1900; he is also listed as stroke in one of the school's rowing fours, and is also mentioned as playing in school cricket matches. The only other credit to his name in the school records is a small, but well-received, role in the Latin play of 1899. The play that year was the *Rudens of Plautus*, a romantic comedy. Archie had the part of a young maiden, Ampelisca, and although the school magazine described his performance as a 'highly finished rendering' it did have a word of rebuke:

> It was a great pity that his sense of humour got the better of him in the scene where the girls seek protection at the altar; this marred what was otherwise the best individual performance in the play.[6]

It was around this time in Archie Clark Kerr's school career that he began to have serious thoughts about his future. He had evidently been interested initially in pursuing a medical career but now decided, oddly similarly to his grandfather, that he did not have the right temperament to deal with blood and disease on a daily basis. Instead, he finally decided during the summer of 1899, following a suggestion of his mother, that he would like to aim for a career in the Diplomatic Service. He wrote to her in reply:

> Of course the exams are a bit stiff, but with hard work at my languages and also shorthand I think I could pass. I could, during my 3 years at Oxford, in the long

Summer vacs go abroad and learn the different languages. By then I ought to be able to take care of myself. (And then there would be a much greater possibility of my statue figuring on the spare pedestal in Trafalgar Square!)... I promise to work very hard and struggle to the utmost to get through. I hope the idea is pleasing to you and I know that the idea of my being a doctor did not altogether please you, though you never said so.

A facility with languages, and perhaps his experience of travel and life in foreign parts, were undoubtedly factors which led him towards diplomacy as a career. He had also the example of his brother Robin to consider: he had returned to Ghoolendaadi after leaving school in 1896. He was commissioned in the 1st Australian Horse and served as ADC to Earl Beauchamp, Governor General of New South Wales. This experience of government may well have been an influence on Clark Kerr's decision. However, the Diplomatic Service's reputation as the preserve of the aristocracy was the key attraction for the family and Clark Kerr was given every encouragement in pursuing his ambition.

CHAPTER 2

Upland 1900–15

Archibald Clark Kerr left Bath College in the summer of 1900. With the Diplomatic Service his chosen goal, the first steps now were to begin preparing for the entrance examinations which, amongst other requirements, demanded proficiency in four foreign languages. In fact it would take him nearly six long years to gain admission. First, there was a year spent in France, then a year spent at Scoon's, a private cramming college in London, whither the family moved to support his chosen career, followed by a further two years of study including time spent in Germany, Italy and again in France.

Letters written by Clark Kerr from France to both father and mother display all the attitudes to be expected of a young English public schoolboy with his background: devotion to Queen Victoria, support for the Tory party, disdain for Liberal politics and politicians, a horror of socialism, Irish rebels and Boers, and an interest in hunting, shooting, fishing and travel.

His summer vacations gave him the opportunity to indulge these pastimes on various Scottish country estates to which social contacts and friendships made amongst other Foreign Office hopefuls gave him entrance. Inverchapel was always a favourite summer destination even if family tensions with the resident 'Barclay' Clarks made the visits less than relaxing. Indeed one visit in 1901 was so unpleasant that the family, and particularly Clark Kerr, began to make efforts to acquire Inverchapel itself, partly for its own sake, but more to deprive these family enemies from getting their hands on it. It was at this point also that they seriously discussed adding Kerr to their name. Archie saw in this three advantages: it would distinguish them from the other Clarks, 'make our relatives more jealous than they are already... and then it would give a bit of

Scotch which would be nice, as it is hard – I find – to convince people we are Scotch!'

Photographs, together with pieces of heather plucked from the hills round the old family home, he faithfully sent out to his father in the wilds of Ghoolendaadi. At the same time he outlined his dreams for a house and sporting estate at Inverchapel. With tongue in cheek, but ambition in mind, he also wrote:

> I am also thinking seriously of getting made a peer a little later on. I should first have to get Inverchapel and would call myself Lord Inverchapel. 'Inverchapel' would be a nice signature. Then I should be promoted to Viscount Inverchapel and finally Earl Kilmun and my eldest son would be Inverchapel.

He was only twenty but he knew the future he wanted and it was one from which he did not waver over the next four decades.

At long last Clark Kerr decided he was ready to compete for a place in the Diplomatic Service. On 3 February 1905 he was offered a nomination to compete in the April exam when four places would be on offer. On this occasion, however, he failed to make the top four and distressingly had to make plans to try again the following year. The opportunity arose in January 1906 and Clark Kerr was one of 13 hopefuls competing for four places. On 7 March the long blue envelope from the Foreign Office arrived at Lower Sloane Street: Clark Kerr had scraped in, fourth. The celebrations and rejoicings were without measure; Archie Clark Kerr had entered the ranks of the Foreign Service of imperial Great Britain, the years of hard work and family sacrifice vindicated at last.

Clark Kerr reported to the Foreign Office at the end of March 1906 to begin his six month period of duty before his first overseas posting. The Foreign Office had been reformed substantially in 1905 but still belonged firmly to the *ancien* Victorian regime. Junior clerks such as Clark Kerr received no clerical assistance until 1908 when the first typists were employed, but in fact their duties were so simple that any assistance would have left them with nothing to do. Their duties largely consisted of opening envelopes, looking out previous papers relevant to the letters, and laying them out on the desks of their immediate bosses. Even so, any letters of a confidential nature arrived in special green jackets and had to be submitted untouched, the clerks being only responsible for registering their arrival. The greater part of their time was spent in minor tasks such as indexing and deciphering telegrams or despatching to Cabinet Ministers the pouches of Foreign Office papers. There was also the perpetual copying of documents and the monotony of filing. Even amongst other Whitehall departments, the Foreign Office was viewed as being particularly slow to delegate responsibility to its junior clerks, it being rumoured that one had to be over 30 before being trusted to write a letter.

With so little of interest to occupy themselves, it is little wonder that the clerks are said to have resorted to games of cricket in the august corridors, with a coal shovel for a bat and a roll of official papers serving as a ball, or to have been entertained by older colleagues who displayed daring feats of swordsmanship for the young diplomats.

Not long after joining, Clark Kerr was assigned to the China Department where, apart from his ability and wit, he soon gained a reputation as a flamboyant dresser. Unlike the Foreign Office clerks, who earned £200 a year, diplomats such as Clark Kerr began with no salary at all and received none until they became Third Secretaries. There was also what was known as the 'Property Qualification' which required each candidate for the Diplomatic Service to guarantee £400 per annum from his own resources – a considerable sum.

Clark Kerr enjoyed the social life amongst the young diplomats and their friends: apart from those he had known at Scoon's such as Rex Hoare, Nevile Henderson and Gerry Villiers, there were new friends such as Gerald 'Newt' Tyrrwhitt, Gerry Wellesley, Reggie Bridgeman, Greg Robartes and Henry Lygon.[1]

His six months elapsed, and in September 1906 Clark Kerr got word of his first overseas posting. He had been hoping for Italy but was told he was to be sent to Berlin. While he would have preferred somewhere more exotic, there was no doubting the fact that the Embassy at Berlin was the most important politically at that time. Although there were many points of contact between Britain and Germany, including close royal connections, the two countries were locked in a growing and increasingly hostile rivalry: one the satisfied and triumphant naval and imperial power, the other dissatisfied, the pretender to colonial ascendancy.

Clark Kerr arrived in Berlin at the end of November 1906 none too pleased with his lot: 'the thought of 16 months of this place fills me with the blackest despair'. His duties at the embassy were far from being arduous or stimulating: the Chancery hours were only from 11.00 until 1.00, and again in the evening from 5.00 until 6.00 or 7.00. There was no secretarial assistance, so the duties which fell to Clark Kerr were the dreaded familiar ones of deciphering and registering telegrams, typing and filing. There was plenty of time left for golf, riding and, whenever possible, shooting. Much time and importance was given to social pursuits with the German aristocracy and government officials. Sir Frank Lascelles, the Ambassador, viewed it as extremely valuable for his young staff to disport themselves creditably at as many social gatherings as possible. It was judged that it would reflect honour on Britain if her junior diplomats were sociable, handsome, charming and impeccably well-mannered. Clark Kerr, although still somewhat shy and diffident, and particularly self-conscious about what he termed his 'Inverchapel' nose, already had many German social connections and was able to move easily at the numerous functions he had to attend. Often wearing the kilt, he was naturally a subject for attention and comment and so gained the ear of many an influential personage, picking up important snippets of political and social gossip for the Embassy files.

For much of his time, however, he seems to have been unhappy, intellectually idle, and lonely. On leave in England in 1907, however, he was able to strike up a friendship, which ran on somewhat distantly for years, with Louvima Knollys, the rather flighty daughter of the highly-strung Lady Knollys, Lady of the Queen's Bedchamber. Louvima was a close friend of his sister Muriel, who perhaps as a result was herself invited to Balmoral as a guest of the Royal family.

In 1908 he received the news that he was to be promoted to Third Secretary, drawing a salary at last. Clark Kerr kept a diary for part of his time in Berlin, and the entries for 1908 demonstrate that he was not simply socialising and chasing sport but also closely involved in monitoring all the political and court manoeuvring that was Imperial Germany. It was a time of some tension between Britain and Germany and relations were further stretched by the resignation of von Bulow, the German Chancellor, the adventurism of the Kaiser, and the arrival of a new British Ambassador, Edward Goschen. Clark Kerr was in a specially favoured position to study the German political scene. For some time he had been acquainted with Princess Sophie, a sister of the Kaiser, who was married to Constantine, Crown Prince and later King of Greece. She was twelve years older than Clark Kerr but enjoyed his company immensely and in many a long conversation poured out her soul and intimate details of the court and royal family to the young British diplomat. By all accounts she was unhappy in Greece and, through her mother – the widow of Kaiser Frederick III but a daughter of Queen Victoria herself – was more favourably inclined towards Britain than the new Germany her brother was seeking to forge. In August 1908 Clark Kerr was invited, as a personal guest of Princess Sophie, to the German Royal family's summer retreat at Friedrichsdof in the Taunus mountains. In September he and Princess Sophie visited Oberammergau and at the end of the month, after much pleading from Princess Sophie who was due to return to Athens shortly, Clark Kerr was able to take yet more leave to visit Friedrichsdof again. Their relationship had been a mutually rewarding close friendship up until this point, if professionally very important and prestigious for Clark Kerr. By the last night of his stay, however, 26 September, it seems clear that both parties were experiencing something beyond friendship. For Clark Kerr it was not a little delicate: he was a foreign diplomat in a foreign country – worse, an 'Englander' in Imperial Germany – and his partner was a sister of the Kaiser himself, the wife of the heir to the Greek throne, and a mother of five. But for all that, he could not resist her charm and stimulating company, and as their last night together wore on, emotions were shaken and stirred:

> After dinner we danced... I blush to say that I danced almost the whole time with Sophie... and again I blush to say I derived a strange pleasure from holding her in my arms, and what is more was almost persuaded to think that the pleasure was shared by her – so completely did she resign herself to my grasp.

Decorum had to be reasserted: 'It is high time I went away' wrote Clark Kerr unconvincingly. But the night was not over: Sophie came to Clark Kerr as the ball was beginning to thin and invited him up to her suite once the other guests – mostly German officers and aristocrats – had retired. As Clark Kerr confided to his diary, he was thrilled and excited and yet could not dispel from his mind feelings of guilt. He knew, in his heart of hearts, that the situation was ridiculous: but he was human, it was late, she would soon be gone, perhaps for ever, and so in the midnight darkness of the royal palace he crept his nervous way through deserted salons and shadowy staircases up to her private apartment. It was with an odd mixture of understandable anticlimactic disappointment and relief, therefore, that when he reached the trysting-place, he was to discover that Princess Sophie was not alone but with her sister, who remained with them throughout. Next morning they had a private pre-breakfast date in a rain-soaked garden, where they parted 'genuine friends', Sophie to Athens, Clark Kerr to London. There, in a retrospective diary entry, Clark Kerr was able to review more calmly the emotional upheaval of the previous days:

> If you had asked on the evening of the 27th when I was waiting for my train whether I was in love I probably would have said that you were right! My heart was very full and very sorrowful and all the way in the train my brain was buzzing and I was thinking of Sophie. But now my heart has ceased to flutter and I have come to see the uselessness of it but still I continue persistently to think of Sophie.

On his return to Berlin, Clark Kerr was low in spirits: 'Berlin crushes all the virility out of one and makes one a sort of sexless jellyfish'. The Embassy was, however, a place of flurried activity with the resignation of von Bulow and the arrival of the new Ambassador and so there was little opportunity for reflection of any sort. He was now quite a senior figure in the embassy in terms of service in Berlin and this was a boost to his professional confidence and self-esteem as his reintroduction, with the new Ambassador, to the Kaiser in November demonstrated.

'How young these secretaries are,' commented the Emperor, receiving the staff of the British Embassy at a formal audience. Then to Clark Kerr himself he continued, 'You have too much hair. In my young days diplomats were all bald.'

'I could show Your Majesty some thin places,' returned Clark Kerr, quick as a flash.

'Whereat,' wrote Clark Kerr in his journal later, 'everyone looked surprised but when His Majesty was pleased to guffaw with laughter everyone else laughed'. It was an early indication of Clark Kerr's preference for fun and honesty over stuffy convention, an approach which brought, therefore, ease to his movements in even the most exalted circles. If one did not put on an act, if one was open and sincere, there was nothing to fear, no 'guard' to be embarrassingly dropped. Even at this stage of his career, Clark Kerr was especially scornful and critical of the type of fawning and dissembling adopted by many diplomats and courtiers who simply abandoned personality and natural instincts, and so were at a loss how to react until they first checked what was politic.

On the whole, things simply deteriorated, however. 'I am devoured with unspeakable hatred for Berlin,' he wrote in his diary. All Clark Kerr's hopes were now centred on getting to Rome, but even these were tinged with a bitter pessimism. He feared that it would never happen:

> ... deep down in my heart I know it won't. Such good fortune as this could never come the way of one of the sons of Inverchapel. Fortune has never smiled on us, why should she now?

However, there were always diversions to draw his mind away from the tedium of the work. One evening he noticed a new arrival in the embassy, a young handsome diplomat en route from St Petersburg. Seeing the young man's nervousness in new surroundings, he introduced himself and invited the man to dinner: the young man proved to be Harold Nicolson, and that night was the beginning of a firm friendship. All his life, Nicolson never forgot that occasion, and years later when he was serving in Berlin himself he wrote to Clark Kerr, then in Chile:

> I seldom cross the hall here without thinking of how you came up to me there and invited me to dinner – that was twenty years ago Archie, Good Lord! It is quite one of the three best memories of my life.

At Easter 1910, Clark Kerr at last bade farewell to Berlin. Reviewing his career a decade later, Clark Kerr looked back on those years with some regret: he felt, however accurately, that he had not paid enough attention to high affairs of state, that he had expended too much energy and devoted too much time to social intercourse and having a good time generally, and that his career had not been advanced as it could have been had he been more seriously exercised during these four long years. It is probably, however, a universal phenomenon, to look back on the early part of any career as having been full of missed opportunities and heedless ways. The fact remains that there is no indication of the Foreign Office having felt anything similar, and it is clear from his diaries and letters that he was a most conscientious and hardworking diplomat during his Berlin years.

Personally, at this stage Clark Kerr seems to have been an odd mixture: early diffidence was now matched by a penchant for the outrageous, possibly an unconscious compensation for this shyness. A favoured focus for this outrageousness was sex, and he never lost an amused interest in the topic and an undoubtedly morbid curiosity about its diverse manifestations, as demonstrated in the various corners of the globe in which he laboured. Acquaintances from this time did remark, albeit playfully, that he was a strange hybrid of the 'prurient and prudish', while another complained of the 'coarseness of expression' which had taken root in him. If anything, over the years this coarseness seemed to develop as his professional confidence grew, but it was allied to an ability to apply diplomatic charm which was the envy of friend and foe alike. The sentimentality of which Harold Nicolson complained never affected his professional life, although it certainly guided much of his personal life, particularly regarding his Scottish ancestry. Nevertheless, it is true that emotional sensitivity was present in his professional approach, often allowing him an enviable empathy and understanding of alternative viewpoints and feelings but at the same time rendering even more difficult the putting of policy into practice when so deeply aware of the potentially damaging effects on others.

His new posting was to Buenos Aires, but although in later years he was to view his very brief spell in Argentina as a period of great happiness and satisfaction, it was indeed brief. While on a tour to Paraguay, staying at a lonely lakeside camp opposite the resort of San Bernardino Clark Kerr was awoken abruptly in the blue chill of a late September dawn by a rider with an urgent telegram. From his sister Margie in Sydney came the short, brutal message: 'Father died peacefully twenty-second. Please go home break news mother. Funeral Ghoolendaadi twenty seventh.' Although his father had been ill for some time, it was still a bitter blow: the father he had not seen for a decade and more, the father with whom a rendezvous had been a lively hope for all too many years, he would never now see; his father who had shared the strains and triumphs of his entry into the Diplomatic Corps was now forever beyond reach in the dusty outback of distant Australia; and all Clark Kerr now had before him was a heart-breaking voyage home and the unpleasant prospect of having to be the messenger of death to his frail and sickly mother.

Leave of absence was efficiently arranged and sympathetically extended so that Clark Kerr was able to remain officially away from work up until 31 March 1911. In London, Clark Kerr's relationship with Louvima Knollys continued its uneven course, but at least the family had managed to recover from the death of their father. With his sister Muriel permanently at home, Clark Kerr could be reasonably confident that his mother was in safe hands and that he could return to employment. That is not to say that he was not a wholly devoted son: he was that and more. Over the years he wrote to his mother, at times as often as four or five times a week, constantly fretted over her, and sought to do all within his financial power to see that she was comfortable and happy. The letters demonstrate a love that is almost painful to read, and it was a love patently obvious to all who knew him.

In March 1911, Clark Kerr prepared to depart for his next overseas posting. This time it was to Washington, but he greeted it with a mixture of disdain and ennui. Before embarking for New York, Archie posted in the press notice of his intention to assume the surname Kerr in addition to that of Clark. He already had the name Kerr as a middle name and his family had been styled Kerr Clark for some time, indicating descent from his grandmother Margaret Kerr and distinguishing them from the descendants of Agnes Barclay, his grandfather James Clark's second wife. In his case it also had the advantage of emphasising more clearly his Scottish identity, of which he was very proud. From 22 March 1911 he became Archibald John Kerr Clark Kerr, although no other member of his family followed his example. Years before, he had expressed concern that the English mispronounced Kerr 'Carr' but throughout his life from now on that was exactly how his name was pronounced and he simply accepted it.

Archie Clark Kerr, therefore, arrived as Third Secretary at the British Embassy in Washington in April 1911. At that time the Embassy was very small, there being only nine diplomats; the Ambassador was the distinguished former Liberal politician James Bryce, who had been appointed in 1907, although 69 years old even then. He was to prove in his six years in Washington to be arguably Britain's most popular, industrious and successful Ambassador to the USA. Clark Kerr quickly came to admire him and envy his role, and to the ambitious young diplomat the top job in Washington immediately became a long-term goal and pipe-dream of his own. In a sense, Bryce became a hero to Clark Kerr who came to adopt more liberal views as aired by Bryce; and he much admired his intellect and eccentricity, particularly his habit of spending much of his mornings reading *Webster's Dictionary*.

Clark Kerr's fellow Third Secretary was Lord Eustace Percy, and the two struck up a friendship which was to last for many years. Eustace was a son of the seventh Duke of Northumberland, head of one of England's most noble landowning families.[2] Clark Kerr had a deep respect for Eustace's intellect, and although in later years he was put off by Eustace's reactionary political views, he was always somewhat in awe of his abilities. Indeed when Clark Kerr arrived in Washington in 1946 as Ambassador himself, his first words concerning his posting to a mutual friend, the US jurist Felix Frankfurter, were: 'It ought to have been Eustace'.[3] Percy, for his part, a prisoner of increasingly right-wing views, evidently grew unhappy later with Clark Kerr's unconventional manner and attitudes, for in 1936 when Percy's nephew, Gavin Maxwell, was offered the post of Private Secretary to Clark Kerr, then Ambassador to Iraq, he advised him against taking it for that very reason. His advice, which Maxwell was to regret having heeded, prevented Maxwell travelling at a young age to the diplomatic heights with Clark Kerr.[4]

Not long after his arrival in the US, Clark Kerr was dealt a hurtful emotional blow when on 17 June his sister Muriel reported to him the surprise engagement of Louvima Knollys to another. Clark Kerr was distraught: although she had rejected him in March he still harboured hopes. He had honestly felt himself to have been in love and to his diary he poured out his frustration:

> Did she not herself tell me that she loved me when I was in South America and would have married me if I had asked her that day in December? And did she not tell me when I offered myself in March that she had changed her mind... and yet didn't she give me tangible ground for hope that if I waited she would yield? And did she not tell Muriel that she nearly yielded that day in March? Oh God! that this should have happened.

In February 1912, however, came a very attractive proposition, this time from Walter Townley, who had been Ambassador when Archie was in Argentina. Townley was heading for Teheran now and wondered if Clark Kerr was interested in joining him. Clark Kerr jumped at the chance but a month later Townley had to withdraw the offer because of Foreign Office opposition. 'There would appear to be an impression in the Private Secretary's department that you are somewhat prone to change your posts too rapidly.' Clark Kerr was justifiably infuriated at this. He had only had three posts in six years' service and had only moved from Argentina because of circumstances quite beyond his control and for wholly understandable reasons. Someone in Whitehall had merely conducted a cursory check on his record without inquiring into the detail. In this off-hand way the Foreign Office blocked the move to Persia and slighted Clark Kerr's commitment. There was nothing he could do but remain, sulk and suffer.

In October 1913 Clark Kerr heard from Sir William Tyrrell that he was to be transferred to Rome. The Italian capital had been his original hope in 1906 but now he did not appear so keen. Indeed, apart from the changes in his personal life which did little to quicken his spirits, his continued status as Third Secretary at the age of 31 was something of a depressant. To his mother he complained:

> There remains the ambitious Tyrrell and the Townleys to satisfy. What a bore they all are! Why don't some of them die? There are still two people between me and the Second Secretaryship in spite of the fact that there are twenty seven miserable men below me.

Rome therefore held little charm without promotion, but at last it did come in February 1914, when he became officially a Second Secretary.

The last summer of European peace Clark Kerr spent on an idyllic cruise of the Mediterranean, meeting up again in Athens with his old German royal acquaintance Sophie whose husband had now succeeded to the Greek throne. He also enjoyed seeing her children again: George, then 24, was courting Princess Elisabeth of Rumania; there were also Alexander, and Helena, then only 18, but who would later marry the infamous King Carol of Rumania and whom Clark Kerr would not meet again until Bucharest after the Second World War when she was Queen Mother and the dark shadows of Stalinism were stretched across the land. With Queen Sophie Clark Kerr remained on good terms, corresponding frankly with her until her early death in 1932.

The return to the Chancery in Rome was very much a return to stark reality. In the wake of the murder of the Archduke Franz Ferdinand in late June, the simmering turmoil in the Balkans was in the process of developing into the bloody conflagration of world war. By August, when Britain became more fully involved, Clark Kerr was already considering enlisting. As the weeks passed, he became more and more convinced that he ought to join up, and began enquiring about obtaining leave from the Foreign Office to do so. His brother Robin had rejoined the army when war broke out and became a Captain with the 7th Battalion Seaforth Highlanders. This convinced Clark Kerr that he too should go to the Front. By November, Clark Kerr had redoubled his efforts, hoping his linguistic skills would see him taken on as an interpreter in the army. The military attaché in Rome was roped in on his behalf, writing to the War Office recommending Clark Kerr, but the problem was that there seemed to have been no clear Foreign Office guidelines on who could be released for war service and who could not. Much of it seemed to depend on local circumstances: if an Ambassador could spare one of his staff, then there was a very good chance of that person being allowed to enlist. Clark Kerr, therefore, began to lobby his Ambassador Sir James Rennell Rodd, of whom he had a low professional opinion, to inform Whitehall that he could be spared.[5] Unfortunately, Rodd found himself and the embassy greatly understaffed but Clark Kerr's importunity eventually wore him down and in December 1914 he informed Sir William Tyrrell, in charge of staffing at the Foreign Office, that Clark Kerr could now be released. Clark Kerr lost no time contacting a friend in the Grenadier Guards and secured from him the promise of a commission as an officer-interpreter as soon as the Foreigh Office released him.

Whether by design or not, the Foreign Office response was a cruel blow. Tyrrell accepted Rodd's suggestion that Clark Kerr could be allowed to go from Rome. He did not, however, accept the corollary that Clark Kerr was therefore free to enlist: instead he intended posting Clark Kerr to another embassy where help was required. Clark Kerr was, naturally, beside himself with anger and frustration. After all the months of persistent pleading to be released, he had been successful only to have the door slammed once more in his face. With justification he felt cheated. Tyrrell had taken advantage of him and used him cruelly, knowing full well his desperate desire to enlist. Apart from Clark Kerr's own wish to join up, his feelings of obligation, and his sense of envy at Robin's fortunes, there was also a point of honour, the awkward feeling that others would judge him to be avoiding war by remaining in the Foreign Service. These were powerful psychological forces, but were treated disdainfully by Tyrrell. Rodd also felt that unfair advantage had been taken of his altruistic gesture in letting Clark Kerr go. Rodd was, however, prepared to accept the Foreign Office line that the service could not afford to lose all its young men to the forces.

Almost despairing, Clark Kerr considered the ultimate measure. He resolved to resign his post, return to Britain, and join the Guards anyway. This he happily reported to the Foreign Office. The Foreign Office were not to be so easily defeated, however. Quite why they fought so tenaciously and crudely is not obvious, but that they did so is certain. Clark Kerr was informed in simple and chilling terms that if he did resign, then the Foreign Office would see to it that he would not be allowed to join up. They would ensure that the military would refuse him. Sir William Tyrrell had already seen to it that his commission in the Guards was cancelled and other necessary steps would be taken, if need be, to prevent his being accepted by the military authorities. For Clark Kerr it was a hopeless cul-de-sac: there was no route to the Front. Sir William, meanwhile, was pleased to offer him a post at the embassy in

Teheran. With no room now to manoeuvre, Clark Kerr reluctantly bowed to the inevitable. On 6 December, leaving for London to prepare for his Persian expedition, he wired his mother bitterly: 'Appointed Teheran. Accepted under pressure.'

This double-dealing by the Foreign Office hurt Clark Kerr deeply. His sense of grievance would remain with him always. He felt cheated, betrayed and, just as strongly, he felt he had been duped. Certainly as long as Tyrrell remained at the Foreign Office, Clark Kerr struggled to conceal this chip on his shoulder. It was almost as if he felt under personal attack from the officials and, during any subsequent dispute with Whitehall, Clark Kerr had difficulty dismissing from his mind the idea that there was malice involved. He had been embroiled in disputes before, but this matter concerned no political or diplomatic issue. It was his own personal career and wishes that were at stake, and with these he felt the Foreign Office had behaved abominably. They had retained his services, but they had played most foully for them. In this black mood he returned to London, still hoping to find a way out. He was fortunate that his literary friend and colleague Edward Marsh was Private Secretary to the First Lord of the Admiralty, Winston Churchill. They lunched together and Churchill vowed to do what he could. Even Churchill, having promised so much, could do nothing and served only to depress Clark Kerr further by his failure. There was no chance now of enlisting: to Teheran he must go.

Some years later, when the war was over, he tried to explain to his young friend Bob Boothby his feelings at that time. Boothby was then, January 1919, considering a career in diplomacy and Clark Kerr recounted his own experiences to him by way of warning, a warning in particular that government service involved strict and immutable limits to personal freedom. He wrote:

> Going into a Government service is a submission of self – a submission of self which I did not appreciate, nor accepted, nor felt the meaning of until August 1914 came.
>
> I hated to hear of my friends being killed and to have to stay on in Rome and do everyday things while everybody else was doing big things that I could only read about – to miss the biggest thing that had ever happened or rather to miss the sounds and shells and physical part of it – the purification of it - was a humiliation. I revolted against it – wrongly they tell me, but I know I should revolt again... I came to regard the machine of which I was but a small cogwheel as a sort of monster.

Clark Kerr – understandably, given the intensity of his feelings – took a long time to come to terms with this part of his life, and even in that letter – written five years after the events – viewed himself as still not reconciled with the Foreign Office for, after all his advice, he counselled Boothby against accepting it too readily: 'Never be guided,' he warned, 'by a man who has a grievance'.[6]

On 5 February 1915 he set sail from Newcastle for Bergen to begin the long journey to Persia by way of Sweden and Russia. In personnel terms it was something of a pyrrhic victory for Tyrrell. Clark Kerr was in no condition to expend himself for a Foreign Office capable of such duplicity, and even if he had accepted their decision more equably, his heart and thoughts were at the Western Front and certainly not in the sands of Persia. The Foreign Office had him in its grasp, but he could only offer the unwilling labour of the reluctant conscript, and in the wild expanses of the Persian interior there would be ample opportunity to mope, scheme and nurse his wrath.

CHAPTER 3

Foothills 1915–22

For Richard Hannay, the Great War in Persia was a period of dramatic excitement, of intrepid activity behind enemy lines, of much derring-do trying to outwit the dastardly Hun, as he fought his gallant way along the path he had chosen: '...the roughest road, but it leads straight to the hilltops'.[1] For Archie Clark Kerr, the two years of his career in Persia followed a much straighter path, rising ever so gently to the mere foothills: a limited role in a divided legation, whose very surroundings he found oppressive.

The situation in Persia when Clark Kerr arrived was one of considerable tension and confusion. The country's geopolitical position had rendered it subject to foreign interference for centuries, the chief culprits being Turkey, Russia and Great Britain. By 1915 Turkey had entered the war on the side of the Central Powers and Turco-German agents were widely dispersed throughout Persia trying to stir up local tribes, and the central Government itself, to join the Axis, and enter the war against Russia. Preaching a 'jihad' amongst the Muslim Afghan tribespeople, they also hoped to foment a rising on the Indian border, and so bog down the British, diverting their attentions from the European theatre. Feelings against Russia ran deep in Persia because of continual incursions by the Tsars into the north of the country, and British diplomacy in the early months of 1915 was mostly directed towards effecting a reconciliation between their allies, the Russians, and the Persian Government. If this could be achieved, there was less chance of Persia falling in with Turkey and Germany. At the same time, Britain did not particularly want to manipulate affairs to the extent that Persia entered the war on her side. The attractiveness of that possibility was merely superficial: Britain was in no position to lend adequate military support to Persia's weakened government and forces; Persia, as an ally in her current state, would be a colossal white elephant. The ideal situation would be that of benevolent neutrality, by which Persia would permit continued use of her territory for telegraphic communications from India, while at the same time restricting and obstructing the movements of Turco-German agents bent on stirring up anti-Christian feeling.[2]

The difficult position of the small British mission in Teheran was made more acute by the decision to replace Walter Townley with Charles Marling in April. Clark Kerr became very unhappy at the performance of British officials during the various political crises which marked his time in Persia: he was dismissive of Marling's efforts, holding his professional abilities in low esteem and disliking him socially. Marling and George Churchill, the oriental adviser, effectively sidelined Clark Kerr who, despite being Second Secretary, was given little to do and was never party to any important decision-making. Clark Kerr considered Churchill to be far too 'dangerous' in his political and diplomatic operations to be entrusted with the exalted role Marling created for him. Townley, who had by now reached England, concurred with Clark Kerr's judgement, labelling Churchill 'a false, time-serving beast of a most dangerous description'.

In a small, claustrophobic legation such poor personal relations made a difficult enough situation almost unbearable. In particular Clark Kerr took offence at Marling's ill-founded criticisms of everything Townley had striven to do during his period in Persia. This was even more galling given Clark Kerr's view of Marling's performance: he found it totally self-destructive and short-sighted. Marling bullied and abused Persian officials as a matter of course, which lost the British position all the respect and standing which Townley had built up, and left him absolutely no ammunition whenever such a belligerent approach may have been justified. Clark Kerr viewed this approach as both ignorant and foolish in the extreme.

Clark Kerr's relations with Marling deteriorated as the summer grew on, and he gradually withdrew himself from the scene to avoid confrontation. He concentrated on learning the language, at which he made his customary rapid progress, and became something of a recluse. This, at least, had one positive consequence, as he reported to his mother, to whom he was now writing three or four times a week: 'I manage to see very little of Marling... so the risk of my smacking him in the face has diminished'.

The problem with removing himself from the legation work and its interests was that it threw him back into self-reflection, with the danger of his depression and frustration reviving. To be fair, Clark Kerr had not so much withdrawn as been excluded from the real diplomatic activity in Tehran. 'Marling has succeeded in killing all the interest I had in the work here by very deliberately, but tacitly, preventing me from participating in it at all.' However, even if he had been more involved, he found the conduct of Marling and Churchill so distasteful that the position could never have lasted amicably:

> Marling and Churchill lie to each other and about each other. They lie to us, the consuls, to India, to the Foreign Office, so much indeed that it is impossible to keep up with the lies.

Feeling so disenchanted with his current employment, Clark Kerr was thus even more unhappy about his having been refused the opportunity to leave the service and join the forces. In June came news that his brother Robin had left for the Front, too: it filled him with envy; guilt, about his own absence from what he felt was his right and proper place at Robin's side; and bitterness at the Foreign Office which had so cruelly thwarted him.

As he grew ever more distant from the Legation officials, he gave his position a physical manifestation by shaving his head and adopting local dress, which he found immensely cooling, but which naturally shocked and scandalised the local British community. 'Going native' was next to treason in the list of heinous crimes Britons abroad could commit.

From the burnishing heat of the Persian desert he poured out his heart to his mother, bemoaning his lot and the cruel vicissitudes which had led to this wilderness outpost, far from family, friends and the Western Front for which his heart and soul yearned. For all that, in this letter of 12 August 1915, Clark Kerr was in no mood to despair: the struggle itself was part of the reward. To have achieved what he had in the severely stratified social structure of Edwardian England was victory enough. Without prestigious schooling, great wealth or influence on his side, he and his relations had secured for him a place amongst the Empire's political élite. Just because things had momentarily turned sour was no reason to quail. He had always viewed his progress in David and Goliath terms, and now he felt he still had youth and natural ability on his side, and a few pebbles in his sling.

His own account more poignantly reveals the wonder, pride and stunned delight which he and his relations must have felt about his early success in the Diplomatic Service, and, read in the context of a wartime letter from an exiled son to a widowed mother, there is added a heart-rending pathos which the passage of time cannot diminish.

With thick black ink, skilfully applied with his great quill pen, he wrote to his mother on his customary stiff cardpaper:

You must never reproach yourself darling for having put me into diplomacy. When we made it our goal it seemed a very big thing and it was a big thing, for, as you say, our weapons were poor and it stood up before us 'six cubits and a span' to be killed with a small smooth stone.

I so well remember the day you suggested it. You were in that great bed of yours – or at least it seemed great then (I couldn't have been more than 16) and I sitting at the foot of it and we gasped at our ambition and so did the Philistines.

And I remember the rather pompous approval of the scheme by Mrs Yorke Faussett [the headmaster's wife] – and your visit to the Balfours and your triumphant return – and my visit to Eric Barrington with a beating heart, new patent leather boots and Margie waiting in a hansom in the big courtyard at the Foreign Office. And all those years of work together – You, Doonie, Duttie [his sisters] and I – and when we killed our Goliath with a smooth stone it was a cause for rejoicing. And we did hug each other that night in March 1906 when the long, blue envelope came from the Civil Service Commission... that I hate it now with all my heart is natural because it has come between me and going to the war.

Robin, whom Archie considered 'a lucky devil', had been at the Front for several months now with his regiment, the Seaforth Highlanders. On 26 September he was involved in the disastrous advance at the Battle of Loos. Leading the line, Robin had hardly made any progress when he was hit, and killed instantly. Less than a fortnight later, on 5 October 1915, his wife gave birth to their daughter, Lois Mairi. It was a desperately tragic sequence of events, and yet one more grievous loss which Clark Kerr had to bear, helpless and alone, so far from home and family. Quite understandably it greatly strengthened his desire to enlist; it was as if he now had a personal score to settle with the Kaiser and his armies. Yet, as 1916 approached, with conscription to commence at home, there was still no opportunity for him to join up.

All that could be done was to remain in his post and try to immerse himself in work. In fact he had now come to a *modus vivendi* with Marling and took more pleasure and interest in the work of the Legation. Clark Kerr had been following the military campaigns avidly, but he had become more involved in commercial activities, having been appointed Commercial Secretary in May, which had brought another welcome pay rise.

In autumn, he at last got a taste of action from a surprising source. The Russian Minister, Etter, felt sorry for Clark Kerr's inability to enlist and fully sympathised with him. It was he who suggested to Clark Kerr that there might be an opportunity of joining a Cossack force in north-west Persia, as an observer. He jumped at the chance, was given a Cossack uniform, and spent the best part of three months travelling with the Cossacks as they tackled pro-Axis tribes on the Mesopotamian border.[3]

Of more importance to his career was the experience of being so closely involved in the diplomatic intrigues and political dealing which so marked this unhappy period in Persian history. It gave him unmatched experience in political strategy and tactics, experience of seeking to advance British interests in an environment where democratic niceties were not the guiding principles of political activity. These were circumstances admirably suited to Clark Kerr's strengths: shrewdness, political acumen and immense personal charm.

In November 1916, just as British prospects in Persia began to improve, Clark Kerr was struck down once more with a particularly acute attack of an eye trouble which had first surfaced in Berlin. So severe was the attack that, given the unsympathetic climate and conditions, it was deemed necessary for him to be sent home. After a difficult journey, Clark Kerr eventually arrived back in London at the turn of the year. After an emotional reunion with his mother who, in her seventy years, had now lost a husband, four sons and two daughters, Clark Kerr headed north hoping for some recuperation at Inverchapel. Apart from visiting the few remaining relatives in the area, he was also able to further his enquiries about purchasing the estate. Things at last began to look more promising in this regard and gave him just the boost his physical condition required. The eye trouble wore off as mysteriously as it had appeared and by March 1917 he was back in the Foreign Office at a desk in the Commercial Department.

Throughout 1917, Clark Kerr worked away in the depths of the Commercial Department, work which he gradually grew to enjoy. Nevertheless, in the midst of all this, the desire to enlist in the army remained as powerful as ever and he eagerly sought out any opportunity which might make it possible for him to join up. There had been the vague offer before he had to leave Persia of a post as an intelligence officer in Mesopotamia, but Clark Kerr wanted action.[4] Particularly upsetting and frustrating was being the butt of an unfair whispering campaign through upper-class society being conducted against those suspected of having evaded military service. In Clark Kerr's case it was wildly insensitive considering the sometimes desperate lengths he had resorted to in his efforts to be mobilised. By November he could stand the malicious gossip no longer and he approached Lord Hardinge, the Permanent Under-Secretary at the Foreign Office, to get some form of official testimonial which would bear witness to the truth of his war 'record' and confirm that it was the Foreign Office who had defeated his efforts to enlist, and would explain that the fact that he was not a combatant was evidence of neither shirking nor cowardice. Hardinge was more than generous in his official reply, going into all the minor details of Clark Kerr's case and vouching absolutely that it was the Foreign Office who had prevented him from going to the Front, and that it had also threatened to thwart him even if he resigned his diplomatic post.

It is indicative of the sort of social pressures Clark Kerr was under that he had to resort to such an extreme measure to get any respite from his accusers. Now he could socialise with much more confidence, Hardinge's embossed Foreign Office missive lodged comfortably in his breast pocket. However, Clark Kerr's position was undermined almost immediately by the decision of the Foreign Office to waive the rule against enlistment to allow Lord Drogheda and Lord Colum Stuart, then employees of the Foreign Office, to join up. Clark Kerr was incensed, not to mention gravely embarrassed since Lord Drogheda was a brother of Robin's widow, Lady Beatrice Kerr Clark. He could hardly now have any defence against the innuendo that anyone who really wanted to could join up. He appealed this time to Lord Robert Cecil, Under-Secretary at the Foreign Office, an action which precipitated another, fruitless, meeting with Hardinge. On 19 January 1918, he got official confirmation from the Foreign Secretary himself, Arthur Balfour, that his appeal had been turned down. There was no alternative: he must simply continue in Whitehall and try as best he could to negotiate the dangerous social waters of the time.

His latest bout of eye trouble proved to be more protracted than ever, and eventually a nasal operation was required to relieve pressure on the eyes. This he went through in March, and was able to take a few weeks' convalescent leave. Inverchapel was an immediate destination and he spent about ten days there planting trees and setting out plans for his new house by Loch Eck.

In April 1918 he returned to London with a new scheme freshly hatched. His new plan – which was to prove successful – was to obtain a medical note saying that the close reading demanded by the work of the Commercial Department was unsuitable for his eyesight and that there was therefore no useful reason to deny him leave to join the forces. His mother was not keen, however, particularly on financial grounds, at a time when he was on the verge of taking over several thousand acres of hill-farm at Inverchapel and commencing building there.

Success meant that on 7 June 1918 Archie Clark Kerr joined the Scots Guards as a private soldier at the ripe old age of thirty-six. Despite his social status, he did not join the officer corps immediately because Tyrrell's blanket embargo on his being commissioned was still in force. In the long run it worked out well for Clark Kerr, for in later years when serving under Labour Governments it was a fact that stood him in good stead. To be able to say that he had served in the Great War as a mere private certainly aided him in dealings with anyone inclined to be disdainful of the elitism of the diplomatic corps.

This was mere opportunism on Clark Kerr's behalf, of course, for within a few days of enlisting, he was posted to the Household Brigade's Bushey training camp for officer cadets, where he underwent the Guards' rigorous physical induction course. It was here that he first met Bob Boothby, a dashing eighteen-year-old fresh from Eton, and established a lasting friendship. Other officers with whom he became friendly were Lord Colum Stuart, of the family of the Marquis of Bute, Ian Campbell, heir to the Duke of Argyll, and Hugh Kindersley. To the young officers this unconventional pipe-smoking thirty-six-year-old was prize company: with his cosmopolitan background, influential social connections, professional experience, travellers' tales, wit and wartime Persian adventures he was a larger-than-life eccentric of magnetic attraction. A wealth of *risqué* stories and expert knowledge of classical and modern erotica were further intriguing features which made Clark Kerr something of a star in the barrack room.

After the years of struggle and heartache to enter the services, it was more than a little ironic that the war ended almost as soon as his training was complete and he therefore had no opportunity to serve overseas.[5] A mere four months after joining up he had been released and was back at a desk in the Foreign Office by January 1919. And so came what he termed 'the end of an inglorious episode', but at least he had created for himself the opportunity to serve his country, however short and inactive that service may have been, and he also had the satisfaction of being able, albeit privately, but still joyously, to thumb his nose at Sir William Tyrrell.

At Christmas 1918 he was a guest at a house party at Blenheim Palace with Balfour and Winston Churchill amongst others. Clearly the problems over enlistment were sensitive still, but Churchill was able to joke with Clark Kerr about it all. 'But for me you would be dead,' declared Churchill, recalling his own failure to help Clark Kerr enlist. 'Aren't you grateful? If I had been firm with Willie Tyrrell about you in 1914 you'd be dead now. A corpse. Do you hear me? A corpse I say, and you don't even say thank you. I never met anyone who was as sorry to be alive before.'

During 1919, Clark Kerr served under Lord Curzon in the Eastern Department of the Foreign Office. Here he became much involved with the nascent Zionist movement, and in particular forged a good relationship with the Zionist leader Dr Chaim Weizmann. So supportive was Clark Kerr of the cause that in 1920 the Zionist Organisation in London enquired if he would be interested in taking up an administrative appointment with them in Palestine.

Despite another disappointing attack of eye trouble, he was at last promoted to First Secretary in early September, and later in the month received news of his foreign posting to Tangier. The two years in Tangier were to prove highly productive and advantageous as far as his career was concerned. As First Secretary, he was second in command at the agency, as it was in Tangier, and so during any absence of his superior he had the opportunity to gain valuable experience as the head of a diplomatic mission. It was, admittedly, a small mission: other than the Consul General and Clark Kerr, the First Secretary, there were only two interpreters, two vice-consuls and their assistant.

Archie brought his mother with him, and not long after they had settled in, Sir Herbert White, the Consul General, went on a long period of absence and Clark Kerr was thus promoted to be acting agent and Consul General from March 1920 until the end of the year. The post should have been of no great political import but since the war's end it had assumed some significance because of the growing rivalry between France and Spain regarding the future of Tangier. The role of the British representative in the area thus became a highly sensitive one, demanding tact, political sensitivity and patience.

Tangier was one of those parts of the world whose strategic importance rendered it prone to imperial interference, squabbling and occasional military adventures. On the southern shore of the Straits of Gibraltar, Tangier became of increased relevance whenever various powers sought to gain naval supremacy in the Mediterranean or whenever the imperial powers took a notion to seek pastures, or deserts, new in North Africa. Over the years as a centre of diplomacy and the main artery for Morocco's foreign trade, Tangier also became a pandora's box of political and other intrigue. It gained some notoriety from the late nineteenth century as a haven for spies, foreign agents, smugglers, gunrunners and all kinds of unsavoury adventurers.[6]

When Clark Kerr arrived in late 1919 Morocco was divided into two zones – French and Spanish – with the area around Tangier a separate 'International Zone of Morocco' which was administered in a highly unsatisfactory way by a series of loosely organised international committees which served merely as the battleground on which conflicting French and Spanish interests clashed. Various half-hearted efforts to convene the international conference promised for years had so far failed: in the wake of the Great War there were other more pressing international matters to be resolved. In addition, although Britain was keen to see Tangier's internationalisation honoured, the French were reluctant to do so, judging that in the wake of the war they owed Spain nothing and that it was unreasonable of Britain to demand so heavy a duty of an ally.[7]

This was the tricky diplomatic position in which Clark Kerr found himself in 1920 as he assumed the role of chief British diplomat in the region. There was a treacherous line to be followed between the French and Spanish positions. Although Britain was more naturally inclined towards France as an ally of some standing, and also because the French administered their protectorate patently more efficiently and competently than the Spanish did their zone, the fact was that until an international treaty settled the issue there was nothing to be gained from taking sides too forcibly. On a purely practical level, Tangier lay in the centre of the Spanish zone and so an easy life for British residents and a fair opportunity for British commercial interests depended on maintaining a calm relationship with the Spanish authorities.

It was a situation tailor-made for Clark Kerr's diplomatic skills: fluent in both French and Spanish, he was quickly able to gain the confidence of both parties. Having gained their trust he was more than capable of keeping both sides happy: promising nothing tangible to either, but always hinting in the most tacit of ways that each could expect his favour.

However, as he gained more knowledge of the situation in Tangier he very rapidly lost much of his equanimity. The plight of the natives was, in many instances, pathetic, and Clark Kerr felt that both French and Spanish motives in Morocco were purely rapacious and that both countries were wholly indifferent to the resultant misery of the local Moroccan populace.

The influential and rogueish *Times* correspondent in Tangier, Walter Harris, had on several occasions used the press to highlight the sorry condition of the natives in the International Zone. Harris was, however, an outspoken supporter of the French case and argued continually that they should be given sole control of Tangier. Harris's view was that the idea of internationalisation was necessarily flawed and that the current situation was a direct result of that hopeless policy.

While Clark Kerr, as the senior British diplomat, necessarily had to court Harris and seek to establish a good relationship with him, he came to have a very low opinion of him and disagreed strongly over the causes of the misery of the local population. Clark Kerr felt that the current maladministration and political situation, far from being a result of a policy of internationalisation, was the direct consequence of internationalisation not being fully implemented. The war years had allowed matters to drift and the *ad hoc* committees established following the French intervention in 1912 were only remotely 'international'. Clark Kerr's case was firmly that a properly implemented international constitution was the way forward for Tangier. Giving the French a free hand would perpetuate the exploitation and wretchedness of the Moroccan people. The, admittedly hopeless, administrative system, where French and Spanish rivalries served to block any initiative, Clark Kerr saw as evidence that internationalisation, far from being abandoned, should be placed on an organised footing. Privately he denounced Harris as a 'charlatan, a mountebank, and a dangerous liar'. However, Harris was in a powerful position and used his numerous dispatches in *The Times* both to push quietly the

French line and to highlight the absurdity of international control as currently practised. Problems were also caused since Harris's open support of the French claims led to unfair suggestions that Clark Kerr must also favour the French, which was a most unpleasant aspersion at a sensitive time when efforts to set up an international conference on the Tangier problem were gathering pace.

Clark Kerr made strenuous efforts to make sure that other British newsmen would be more even-handed in their approach, and he was successful in persuading both Lord Northcliffe and St John Strachey of *The Spectator* of the wisdom of this strategy during their tours of the region. Naturally, he also fought hard to persuade the Foreign Office that a preponderately French Tangier was not the answer and, he argued, it was his judgement that the French themselves were prepared to accept some form of internationalisation.

During leave in May 1921, Harris had occasion to call at the Foreign Office to see Ian Campbell, son of the Duke of Argyll, an acquaintance of Clark Kerr's. Harris subsequently reported to Clark Kerr on the easeful sloth which permeated the building. The bloody horrors of a European war and the tribulations of a Paris Peace Conference had evidently done little to alter the pleasant ethos of the unhurried gentlemen's club. Harris's alarming testimony makes 'Carlton-Browne of the FO' appear positively Stakhanovite. Harris arrived at the Foreign Office at 10.30am.

> There was a policeman at the door... I asked for Campbell... but the messenger replied, 'No one comes here, sir, before eleven'. I replied that I would come back at that hour but he said 'I shouldn't come, sir, if I was you before 11.30. It generally takes the gentlemen half an hour or so to settle comfortably down to their work.

Thus selflessly strove the Foreign Office for British interests abroad.

As efforts to organise an international Tangier conference showed hopes of success, Clark Kerr was able to take some leave in the summer of 1921. Apart from a few meetings with British-Moroccan groups, there was much opportunity to catch up with friends. In London he met up again with Harold Nicolson, who supported his election as a member of Buck's Club. In August he was the guest of Lord Colum Stuart at Kames Castle on Bute; in the same month he was at Strachur Park with Ian Campbell, now a near neighbour; and he was also a weekend guest of Lord Eustace Percy at Alnwick. In September he joined a shooting party at Glamis Castle, as a friend of the young daughter of the home, Lady Elizabeth Bowes-Lyon.

Politically, he was also active, working with the British Merchants Morocco Association to influence public opinion and government policy. One step they had to take was to seek to reduce the influence of Harris, whose pro-French line continued unaltered. Clark Kerr arranged for a letter to be drawn up reflecting his own, and the association's, views, to be sent to *The Times* for publication, having been 'fathered' by Sir Basil Scott. These activities were almost certainly prohibited by the Foreign Office code of conduct, but are testimony both to the seriousness with which Clark Kerr took his post in Tangier and to his genuine concern to see that not only British interests, but those of the Moorish people, would be served by the outcome of international negotiations. However, he had barely returned to Tangier when he was informed that he was to be transferred to Cairo as First Secretary in the New Year.

Although there was much appeal in this move, there was some disappointment that he would not see the Tangier discussions through to a conclusion, but such was always the nature of diplomatic life. Clark Kerr could later take considerable satisfaction from the fact that the 1923 Conference on Tangier formally established the zone as an international free port, a situation which remained until Tangier was included in an independent Morocco in the 1950s.

A move from Tangier to Cairo might geographically be from one corner of North Africa to another, but in political and diplomatic terms it was a major journey for Clark Kerr from the outer margins to the very centre of British imperial policy.

CHAPTER 4

Outcrop 1922–25

Archie Clark Kerr bade farewell to Tangier on 17 February 1922. As is often the case in a diplomatic career, it was a parting attended by mixed emotions. Clark Kerr once said of the diplomat's life,

> ...the very nature of the work imposes on him the role of the inconsistent lover, who moves from love to love taking on the new almost before the embraces of the old one are cold.

There were the quite genuine feelings of regret from the British community, who were considerably upset at the thought of losing such a hard-working, fair and successful local representative. The local press also feted him and there was a particularly glowing tribute in the journal *Morocco*. It would therefore have been quite understandable if Clark Kerr had felt some pangs at leaving a place where he had done so well and where his efforts were so universally acclaimed and admired. Nevertheless, he had known since October of the intention to transfer him to Egypt and he was eager, having learnt of this, to have the transfer effected as quickly as possible.

There was no actual promotion in the move – his rank remained that of First Secretary – but Egypt was a posting of considerable status, both in its own right and because of its crucial importance to the British imperial policy of the time. To anyone with the ambition of Clark Kerr, the transfer to Cairo was an appealing one. As guardian of the Suez Canal, Egypt was the vital link between Britain and India: it was essential for the stability of the British Empire that she had free and untrammelled access to the canal.

Approaching his fortieth birthday, Clark Kerr was keenly aware that his performance in Egypt would determine absolutely the ultimate course of his career. From the relative shadows of Tangier he was moving into the spotlight of Cairo where his every move would be certain of close analysis and monitoring in Whitehall; it would expose his abilities to full and continued appraisal and so constitute a unique opportunity to make a name for himself in the Foreign Office. As events were to unfold, his three years in Egypt did prove to be the pivotal ones of his career.

To Egypt he brought considerable experience in his personal diplomatic bag: at the most basic level, he had now added to his perfect French fluency in Arabic, the two languages vital to a proper understanding of Egyptian affairs – one the language of government, the other of the people. His service in the Eastern Department of the Foreign Office in 1918–19 had also given him useful background knowledge, but most important of all, he soon realised, were his years in Persia during the Great War, where amidst all the bitterness and frustration, he had picked up invaluable experience of the machinations and intrigue common to middle eastern internal politics and, just as crucially, the meanderings of British foreign policy and its erratic execution on the ground. In particular, he found that the painful lessons learnt from the ham-fisted efforts of Marling and Churchill to influence, shape and control Persian affairs, though immensely dispiriting and often sickening to him at the time, had in fact constituted a matchless political education when he found himself, as he so rapidly did, attempting to steer British policy through the muddy and treacherous waters of Egyptian domestic politics. In Persia he had witnessed such a wide variety of political gaffes and diplomatic blunderings, and suffered their inevitable consequences, that, for one as sharp and ambitious as Clark Kerr, there was never the likelihood of repeating anything of the sort again. In such circumstances, Clark Kerr had learnt, diplomacy was a strict matter of strategic logic: of setting desirable and attainable targets, of identifying effectual means, of massaging people so that their actions would conform with the chosen strategy, and so bring the target within reach. Most important of all was the ability to discern between what was indispensable and what was not: the secret of successful diplomacy was to identify and cling to what was vital to one's interests, but always to be prepared to relinquish the chaff. Clark Kerr was disdainful of philosophising, of theories, of absolutes; diplomacy was a strictly practical affair and yet it is obvious that reaching this clear-sighted vision of his work had involved a great deal of analysis and critical thinking, as well as raw experience, over the years.

The situation in Egypt in March 1922 had taken on a new configuration. In a sense that was entirely fitting, as in the years to follow Clark Kerr was to find that calm, permanence and stability were states of affairs alien to Egyptian politics.

Although the position of Egypt and its internal affairs was confused and intricate, it is necessary to give some indication of their nature as a prelude to a consideration of Clark Kerr's tour of duty. When the Great War broke out, Egypt was still under the suzerainty of Turkey, although since the suppression of the Orabi ('Mahdi') revolt in 1882, Great Britain had enjoyed a special position in Egypt, one which had been formally recognised by the Great Powers in 1904. Further, as a result of Kitchener's campaign of 1898, Great Britain shared with Egypt the control of the Sudan. Following the outbreak of war with Turkey in 1914, martial law was declared and on 18 December 1914, Great Britain declared Egypt a protectorate, abolished Turkish rule, deposed the Khedive and appointed a Sultan in his place. On his death, Fuad, his brother, became Sultan in 1917.[1]

As was so often the case in British imperial affairs these actions proved somewhat insensitive. While Egypt was actually reasonably prepared for, and acquiescent in, these measures, the use of the word 'Sultan' was unfortunately reminiscent of the Turkish rule against which Egypt had for so long struggled. Even worse, the word protectorate in Arabic was exactly the same word, 'Himaya', as that used to describe the position of protected foreign subjects in Egypt. It was therefore closely associated with the long history of foreign injustice and tyranny in Egypt.[2]

Throughout the course of the war incipient nationalism grew in strength, fuelled by increasing dissatisfaction with the manner, if not always the course, of British control. Egyptians felt like second-class citizens in their own country. Efforts had been made through, for example, the short-lived Legislative Assembly of 1913 to take account of this, but by the end of the war various other factors contributed to make full self-determination seem a legitimate and achievable goal. Matters deteriorated through the British Government's refusal to allow an Egyptian delegation, or 'Wafd', to attend the Paris Peace Conference. This clumsy discrimination, when so many other countries and peoples were receiving better treatment, and in the face of President Wilson's Fourteen Points and pious Allied pronouncements on the principle of self-determination, led quite naturally to an outbreak of civil disorder throughout Egypt. Not content with such blundering, further fuel was lavished on the situation by deporting Zaghlul Pasha, leader of the nationalist movement, and three of his colleagues to Malta. A widespread and bloody revolt followed, and it was into this situation that the war hero Lord Allenby arrived as High Commissioner in March 1919.[3]

Faced with such a serious and sweeping insurrection, Allenby considered that only a removal of the principal cause would serve to restore order and relative normality to Egypt. On 31 March he recommended to the Foreign Office that the deportees be released and allowed to proceed to Paris. This was reluctantly agreed to, it being privately judged that Allenby was not only being too liberal, but also capitulating in the face of violence.[4] Calm did return to Egypt and, needless to say, Zaghlul's team achieved nothing in Paris other than a *volte face*, from Woodrow Wilson, who actually recognised the British Protectorate of Egypt. The British Government did, however, set up the Milner Mission, which arrived in Egypt in December 1919. Its terms of reference seemed so restrictive that the Egyptian nationalists immediately boycotted it and refused to be party to any of its deliberations.

Nevertheless, some informal contacts were made, and Milner surprisingly found in favour of the abolition of the protectorate and the contracting of a bilateral treaty approved by a 'genuinely representative Egyptian Assembly'. Great Britain still hoped to have certain rights in Egypt, particularly regarding the defence of the Suez canal, given its paramount role in imperial communications. Zaghlul and his supporters, sensing movement towards them in London and a massive mandate at home, declared the plan to be little different in essence from a protectorate and held out for a limiting of British troops to the immediate area of the Suez Canal, and for joint sovereignty over the Sudan.[5] Milner could not agree to these. In 1921 a further effort by the Liberal politician Adly Pasha similarly broke down over the issue of the Sudan. Being the source of Egypt's sole water supply, the Sudan was a sensitive matter for Egyptian nationalists.

As further disturbances continued, Zaghlul and five colleagues were again deported, this time to the Seychelles via Aden in late 1921, before finally being exiled in Gibraltar.

Allenby had by this stage realised that current British policy merely resulted in a vicious circle of riot, then repression. In February 1922, just prior to Clark Kerr's arrival in Cairo, Allenby travelled to London to argue for a change of policy. Basically, his position, and that of his principal colleagues on the ground, was that instead of demanding agreement on the controversial issues prior to independence being granted, Britain should abolish the protectorate, declare Egypt independent, and then seek to hammer out the relatively few, though thorny, unresolved matters such as Suez and the Sudan. Allenby had a tough time in London, but by dogged determination, and the threat of resignation, he got his way. He was not known as 'The Bull' for nothing. Yet, as befitting a man more versed in military force than diplomatic niceties, he failed to carry the Foreign Office with him in spirit, thus creating many hidden enemies and sowing the seeds for further trouble. In addition, his outlook made it impossible for him to indulge in either dirty politics or open opinion-forming, so that many wrong impressions of, and cruel attacks on, him were left unchallenged and uncorrected. It was not his style to respond or explain. From both sides he took flak, some of it deserved, but much of it ill-considered and prejudiced.

To old-fashioned Tories he had 'sold the pass' on Egypt, while to new-fashioned socialists he was a high-handed imperialist crushing Egyptian liberties. In the former camp were such as Winston Churchill and Lord Curzon,[6] but once Lloyd George had approved Allenby's plan, somewhat unwillingly, they were left isolated as a small Cabinet minority. Nevertheless, Allenby was further subjected to misrepresentation and smear when, in a grossly misleading allegation to the House of Commons, Austen Chamberlain, possibly acting on false information he had been deliberately fed, presented the case as if it were Allenby who had given way and the Government and the Foreign Office who had been the ones championing the final agreed plan.[7] Again, nothing was done by Allenby to challenge this fabrication.

The plan, agreed on 28 February 1922, was a draft declaration of independence, whose main clauses were as follows:

1. The British protectorate over Egypt is terminated, and Egypt is declared to be an independent sovereign state.
2. So soon as the Government of His Highness shall pass an Act of Indemnity with application to all citizens of Egypt, martial law as proclaimed on 2 November 1914, shall be withdrawn.
3. The following matters are absolutely reserved to the discretion of His Majesty's Government until such time as it may be possible by free discussions and friendly accommodation on both sides to conclude agreements in regard thereto between His Majesty's Government and the Government of Egypt:
    (a) the security of the communications of the British Empire in Egypt
    (b) the defence of Egypt against all foreign aggression or interference, direct or indirect
    (c) the protection of foreign interests in Egypt and the protection of minorities
    (d) the Sudan[8]

Unfortunately, this general policy approach of relinquishing control with selfish strings attached, which Britain came to adopt in many arenas across the world, was flawed. No matter how generous Britain might appear in relaxing her colonial grip and allowing fledgling states to take flight, her continued interference 'to protect vital British interests' seemed, as viewed by developing nations, by contrast to be even more imperialistic, and served eventually to create long-term damage for the sake of short-term begrudged gains. The policy in Egypt would end ignominiously in Suez in 1956; in Persia, where Clark Kerr had served, it would worsen with the unacceptable championing of the Shah, ending eventually in the coup of 1979 and diplomatic oblivion; in Iraq, where Clark Kerr served in the 1930s, similar interference and factional support would end in the 1958 coup, with worse consequences; and in China, where he was Ambassador between 1938 and 1942, it would end in the Maoist revolution and generations of difficulties. In all cases, Britain suffered major damage when the backlash came – however long in the coming. One wonders if Britain's long-term interests and future foreign relations would have been better served by a total abdication of power and involvement, trusting that this good grace would reap its own reward, rather than seeking to meddle and manipulate. Perhaps such idealism would, in effect, have been pragmatic after all.

On 1 March, Egypt was declared independent, the Sultan, Fuad, declared King, a monarchy proclaimed, and Sarwat Pasha, deputy to the liberal Adly Pasha, agreed to become Prime Minister and form a cabinet. On 3 April a Special Committee was set up to draft a constitution.

Apart from anything else, what particularly pleased Allenby and his advisers was that all this had been achieved without the involvement of Zaghlul. They hoped to convince the Egyptians that 'extremist' claims for total independence were impractical and would lead nowhere, whereas progress could be made, as had so clearly been demonstrated, when more 'reasonable' men such as Adly and Sarwat were in power. In one way, this was a plausible policy, but it was undermined by the fact of Zaghlul's deportation. Had it been achieved otherwise, with Zaghlul at large and left exposed as impotent in Egypt, it would doubtless have been more successful. With Zaghlul, however, out of the country, Egyptians began to wonder just what could have been achieved had he been allowed access to the political 'system' of his own land. Instead of being sidelined, Zaghlul became the focus for continued agitation and anti-British activity which again resulted in repressive British action, merely strengthening the resolve and widening the base of Egyptian nationalism.'

At this point in proceedings Clark Kerr arrived in Cairo for a short, initial tour of duty. As First Secretary he was subordinate only to Scott, the Counsellor to the Residency, and of course to Allenby, the High Commissioner. Without doubt he had, as he had hoped for so long, been thrust into an important and sensitive post where all his charm and political skill would be called into play. He was already firmly behind Allenby. At the time of the Commons debate on Egyptian policy, he had written to his mother, 'Tonight the House of Commons is to decide the future of Egypt and the fate of the Allenby policy. May God give them guts and liberal views.'

From the outset, Clark Kerr was favourably impressed by his chief. Writing to Bob Boothby on 6 March 1922, Clark Kerr declared:

> Then there is Lord Allenby – a splendid giant. Big head, big nose, big body, big voice and big mind. Not the heart of an intellectual of course. None of that intangible thing called 'brains' of which we have been idiotic to make such a fetish, but immense honesty, immense power and immense human sympathy... I feel sure that I shall love him.

In addition to the staff of the British Residency, there were also many British officials in the Egyptian Government and civil service. Of these the most important and powerful were Sir Reginald Patterson, the Financial Adviser, and Sir Sheldon Amos, the Judicial Adviser. With Amos, Clark Kerr cultivated an effective working relationship which was to lead to a lifelong friendship. A further important character with whom Clark Kerr became familiar was Gerald Delaney, Reuters correspondent in Egypt, who was a shrewd and deeply knowledgeable observer of the local scene. He and Clark Kerr came to share a vision of post-Protectorate Egypt and often worked in tandem, exchanging and sharing information and, more crucially, discussing and analysing the political situation as it developed, and setting in motion both short, and optimistically long, term political strategies. At late-night meetings in smoke-filled rooms, he and Clark Kerr, with other occasional guests, mapped out British strategy and constructed their plans and plots to influence affairs. It was a role and status, which for all its dangers and difficulties, Clark Kerr came to relish. Delaney may not, strictly speaking, have been a 'spy' but he certainly was an agent of the British Residency, bringing information to Clark Kerr in particular, and being used often to sound out the potential of certain British political options, or to prepare the way for the smooth introduction of British initiatives. As such, he was not simply a reporter of events, but a key actor.

Initially Clark Kerr spent only a few months getting to know Egypt and the situation. Even at this stage he was a significant figure, occasionally having audiences with King Fuad as Allenby's representative. At this point there was a growing awareness that the King was secretly plotting to undermine Sarwat's government and influence affairs so that the constitution would result in the arrogation of autocratic powers to Fuad himself.[10]

At the end of June, Clark Kerr left Egypt for some home leave, sailing from Alexandria to Venice and thence to England by train. He had a number of pressing matters to attend to, not least to oversee the beginning of building work at Inverchapel where, at last, his dreams of more than two decades were beginning to take shape.

There were also affairs of the heart which he was keen to settle. With the passage of time, he had become not a little pessimistic about his love life and the prospects of marriage. While sailing to Egypt in February, for example, he had reported to Boothby on the various romantic possibilities which the other passengers might offer if only fate would be kind. Underneath it all was a certain wistful resignation:

> At three tables distant there is an attractive flapper with a decidedly glad eye. But why three tables between us? Alas! throughout life there have always been three tables between me and everything good.

As he had feared, however, Clark Kerr returned to the turmoil of Egypt at the end of September decidedly still a bachelor.

Although Clark Kerr adopted a liberal attitude towards the Egyptian question, it was by no means pro-Egyptian. Indeed, when a young Egyptian politician returned from London predicting to a local newspaper that the Sarwat ministry would soon fall and Zaghlul would be released from exile, Clark Kerr asked him to call for a chat too. He told the young man, Amine Yousseff Bey, that nothing of the sort would happen; that Sarwat would remain in power; and that Zaghlul would never be released. Amine called his bluff and offered to bet £100 on the issue; at this Clark Kerr winced, before finally agreeing the stake to be that they would hold a dinner for each other's friends, the host to be the loser of the bet. Amine realised that Clark Kerr's reluctance to wager much on the issue indicated a lack of confidence in the views he was expressing, and so the initiative was something of a failure.[11] Even so, it does show that Clark Kerr was keen to foster the impression at all times that Zaghlul and extreme nationalism were simply not in the picture. He, and the British, wanted to continue to deal with the moderates, reward them with concessions, and so wean the ordinary Egyptian away from the outright independence demanded by the deportees.

In late 1922 King Fuad's scheming eventually cost Clark Kerr the price of a meal, for Fuad brought down Sarwat's Government, and replaced it with one led by Tewfik Nessim, largely composed of palace placemen. The danger was that they would work to manipulate a constitution confirming an omnipotent monarchy. The fall of Sarwat also scuppered Clark Kerr and Delaney's plan to bring forward the removal of martial law which Clark Kerr considered 'a very vicious thing'. Their plan had been that to end martial law would remove one of the key planks of the Zaghlulists' campaign and at the same time reward the Sarwat regime with this rich success. In fact, Clark Kerr and Delaney planned to release documents purporting to show Sarwat as being fully responsible for that success. However, the fall of Sarwat put paid to that plan and necessitated a much more defensive plan to prevent the King's autocratic designs coming to fruition.

Clark Kerr's general outlook at the time was that realism dictated that Britain would have to come to terms with Egyptian aspirations and that the favoured goal should be an independent Egypt, favourably inclined towards Britain, recognising the strategic importance of the Suez Canal to Britain and acting sympathetically thereto. The continued colonial status of Egypt was neither morally justifiable nor politically sustainable. The main threats to this policy outline were extreme nationalists in Egypt who refused to recognise any place for Britain or her interests in Egypt and the canal, and extreme imperialists in Britain who refused to recognise either the strength or legitimacy of Egyptian desires. Other threats were the total resistance to change of many in the British community in Egypt who resented any threat to their privileged existence, and gangs of Egyptian terrorists whose outrages merely served to stiffen the resolve of those disinclined to compromise on the constitutional issue. Finally, the behaviour of the King threatened to undermine all efforts if his anti-democratic scheming went unchecked.

Clark Kerr's outlook and related policy for Egypt depended for its strength and continued life on the support of a Foreign Office with a liberal outlook. Clark Kerr was therefore delighted by the growth in support for Labour at the October general election, much to the outrage of his mother, to whom he wrote, 'Reuter says that Scotland is going very Labour. It is always 50 years ahead of Great Britain in political thought.' The defeat of Winston Churchill also thrilled him. 'Winston out of the Government was a blessing, but Winston out of the House of Commons is almost too good to be true.' With the chances of a more liberal outlook at home increasing, Clark Kerr was able to turn to the Egyptian question with more optimism. However, things were seriously set back by the murder in December of Dr Newby Robson, an English lecturer in Cairo, who was shot and killed by Egyptian extremists. Many British civil servants and others in the British community in Egypt saw it as evidence of Allenby's lack of firmness on the constitutional issue, and as the result of being too soft with nationalist agitation. Clark Kerr agreed with Allenby's decision to sack the Director of Public Security in the wake of the outrage but refused to accept that the liberal policy was the cause.

> The unhappy officials are the victims, not of the Allenby policy, but of years of mistaken British policy, when Egypt was considered to be a place where commonplace Englishmen could earn large salaries for working six days a week from 9 to 1.30.

Nevertheless, it fell to Clark Kerr to lodge a formal complaint with the Egyptian authorities about the murder of Robson. His verbal bullying of the Prime Minister, Tewfik Nessim, reduced the poor man to tears as Clark Kerr rather guiltily reported

> ... tears so rolled down his cheeks that I had to pat and soothe him after the bullying was over ... Of course, he yielded to all our demands.

There was always a velvet fist in Clark Kerr's iron glove.

Although Clark Kerr very much admired Allenby, he did appreciate that Allenby was not the political animal the complex situation required. However, what he did like in Allenby was that he was open to persuasion, and that was Clark Kerr's forte. One unfortunate factor which served to aggravate the matter was Allenby's heavy drinking. On occasions this led to diplomatic difficulties at functions when Allenby got on to political topics while 'boyishly roaring tight'. Clark Kerr arranged for a physician to see Allenby, who was pronounced 'dangerously alcoholic' and ordered to cut down on his gin consumption by 50%. This alcoholism clearly was a factor in Allenby's notoriously volatile temperament, and one wonders to what extent gin, as opposed to personality, was responsible for Allenby's reckless behaviour in response to the Sirdar's assassination later in 1924. The chief diplomatic official, Scott, was meanwhile too detached and interested in golf to be of much assistance. In these circumstances, it was left to Clark Kerr and Amos, the Judicial Adviser, to set about devising policy, and in this they were ably assisted by Robin Furness, a junior residency diplomat. The main plan at this stage – which Clark Kerr struggled to persuade Allenby to support – was to get rid of the King's puppets in the cabinet, and seek to bring in the Act of Indemnity and end martial law, but only as a concession to friendly elements in the Government. Allenby still retained a rather naive respect for King Fuad, and was concerned at the potential implications of the removal of martial law. In this he was being unduly influenced by a hawkish Keown-Boyd, the new and understandably nervous Director of Public Security.

Meanwhile Clark Kerr was the new target of the King's intrigues, as Fuad rightly judged that it was Clark Kerr's perceptiveness and counteractivity which were hindering the King's autocratic plans. All of this Clark Kerr found difficult and uncomfortable, but at the same time he confessed to his mother that he was enjoying it as a 'tremendous education'. The King was now actively promoting the idea that the new constitution should include two preambulary articles, one naming him as King of Sudan, the other stating that the Sudan was an integral part of Egypt. Both were diametrically opposed to British policy. As such Clark Kerr and Fuad were on a collision course. Clark Kerr was clear that for his goals to be reached, the King's schemes would have to be defeated. In that, Clark Kerr recognised some danger: '... the most difficult thing will be to down him without making him a popular hero'. If the King were seen to be brought down by the 'imperialist English', it could make him an instant Egyptian hero. What Clark Kerr desired, therefore, was to set about creating a wedge between the King and the people, so that the Residency action when it did come could be seen to be on the side of the people and democracy, which it partly was, and against autocracy and potential tyranny.

The fight was engaged in early February but Clark Kerr's victory was ensured when he won over Allenby, and the King was forced to back down, resulting in the resignation of Tewfik Nessim over his failure to get the Sudan issue into the constitution. There was widespread praise for Clark Kerr's actions, which had resulted in so successful an outcome for British policy: the curtailing of Fuad's powers; the maintenance of control over Sudan; and the end of Tewfik's pro-autocratic administration. In addition, after a five-week inter-regnum, the sympathetic Ibrahim Yehia took over as Prime Minister.

Now Clark Kerr's principal plan could go into action: the rewarding of a gradualist government with important British concessions. The constitution was agreed in April, a leather-bound copy being presented to Clark Kerr as token of the Egyptian Government's appreciation. Even at the last moment the King was up to his tricks, trying to pretend that Allenby had agreed to certain terms when he patently had not. Clark Kerr took great delight in being instructed by Allenby to 'tell the King that if he does things like that I shall go and give him a root up the backside', although he was disappointed to find that the French translation he was required to deliver lost much of the flavour of the message in its weakened 'coup de pied par derriere'. Eventually, only when Allenby and Clark Kerr threatened to whittle the King's powers to nil did he give up and agree to the constitution. It was a triumphant occasion, and only the expected disapproval of the Zaghlulists served to cloud the achievement.

At about the same time news arrived from England of the engagement of the Duke of York – later to succeed to the throne on the abdication of his brother King Edward VIII – to Lady Elizabeth Bowes-Lyon, which came as a great personal disappointment to Clark Kerr. He has left a record that the moment he saw her at Lady Islington's dance on the night of his return from Egypt in the summer of 1922, and still more when they were introduced two days later, he thought her 'wonderful, beautiful, and so, so gentle – of the stuff of dreams, the voice and the spirit of the thing I had been hoping and waiting for for years'. They had met further at London and Scottish parties and dances and had much in common with their love of Scotland, their love of fun, and their resolve to play their parts worthily in their country's affairs.

In August 1922 when he was forty and she just twenty-two and he was staying at Invermark Lodge in Angus, she had written inviting him to lunch at Glamis, following it very shortly after with a letter to Inverchapel, dated 28 August 1922, confirming an invitation for him to go to Glamis the following Thursday when he would be met 'at Forfar at 4.20 by a large but rather uncertain motor car which was once green' and warning him that he would find nobody there at all except two cousins who always spoke in a whisper. This was confirmed by him in letters to his mother, saying how much he was enjoying being alone with the family and building a dam with the boys. He expected to be back the following Friday. He was disappointed not to receive a further invitation before he returned to Egypt from leave, but they had exchanged newsy letters for Christmas, she telling of glittering parties with quails, champagne and Cadogans, and encouragement for him to get 'his own back on the King of Egypt somehow'.

When he heard the news of her engagement he had evidently written confessing his sadness, as she wrote begging him not to feel sad, 'as surely we can remain friends as before', and so they did. The Yorks' marriage had taken place on 26 April 1923 and there are letters during his 1923 leave, and one dated 25 February 1924 asking what had been going on in Egypt. Then in December 1924, when the Yorks had to cancel a proposed visit to Egypt, she wrote to invite him to meet them in Khartoum on or about 8 April 1925, which he did, and it was followed by a visit to Glamis at the end of September.

There were further letters over the years, including one following the birth of the Princess Elizabeth on 21 April 1926 and one following the death of Mrs Kerr Clark the same year. Then in June 1929, on his returning to England on leave from Chile with his bride, there was an immediate invitation to lunch at 145 Piccadilly, followed by a number of meetings over the years, including a supper party on the night of the Duke of Kent's wedding in November 1934 and a visit to Windsor while on a visit from Russia in 1943.[12]

Following the news of the engagement in 1923, several of Clark Kerr's friends wrote to try to cheer him up and lift his inevitable depression. From a letter to his mother, quilled on 29 January 1923, it seems clear that he had managed to recover a little.

> Frankly there never was a moment since my visit to Glamis when I had any real hope of success, but nevertheless I had clung to it and tried to tell myself that all things were possible. And now that it has become impossible I feel tired and battered and dismal and whenever I think of it, and I think of it even in moments of greatest crisis, my head buzzes...' But he continued, '... don't you worry about it. I have got over those things before and will just have to do it again.

It was fortunate in a sense that life in Cairo was so hectic, because he could throw himself into his work as an escape. The success of his labours, however, could only dull the pain, not clear the memory.

The work was not just a useful distraction from heartache: far from it. It was an intriguing and stimulating business which, for all its time-consuming nature, Clark Kerr enjoyed immensely. It was certainly stretching him, but it was also high-profile, and this appealed to his vanity. Not that Clark Kerr was unduly vain, but he did possess a fair conceit of himself. He considered himself, rightly, to be a skilful and accomplished diplomat, and he was more than grateful of the opportunity to exercise his craft in a public way. If he did at times appear arrogant to some, it was because he often over-compensated in this way for his natural diffidence. There were, of course, certain drawbacks to the publicity, as he confessed to his mother: 'In Egypt, one lives in a house of glass – a deterrent to private debauch and a distinct stimulant to histrionic talent'. The other danger was that his high profile would make him a target for nationalist assassination, but he was confident that he was, in fact, too important a figure to be murdered, as the repercussions would be so severe, in terms of British reaction, as to be counterproductive to the nationalist cause. As Clark Kerr would have privately conceded, however, would-be assassins tend not to analyse political consequences in such coldly precise ways.

Having eventually got a constitution agreed, the next priority for the British in Egypt was clear: to see an Egyptian Government elected with whom they could negotiate an acceptable solution to the outstanding 'reserved' points in the 1922 Declaration. In addition, there were other lesser matters such as the compensation for the foreign officials whose posts would disappear in the new Egypt. Finally, there would be the need for an Act of Indemnity to end martial law.

Clark Kerr at this point moved into a substantial new house, commensurate with his national standing, in the Zamalek suburb of Cairo. It was a secluded villa, extending over three floors, and boasting seven bedrooms. By this stage, his reputation in Egypt as a meddler in Egyptian internal affairs was quite widespread and it was being rumoured, much to Allenby's dismay, that Clark Kerr had threatened the King with a cruiser at Alexandria if he did not agree to the constitution.

Clark Kerr now felt that it was necessary to have the Zaghlulist exiles released, as an Egypt without them was never going to be a peaceful or realistic proposition. Although Allenby was somewhat reluctant, Clark Kerr managed to persuade him of the wisdom of this, and in late March 1923 the Gibraltar internees were released. They could not, of course, return to Egypt until martial law was lifted. Not until mid-June did the Foreign Office agree to the necessary terms for this. Their worry was that, fuelled by the anger of many of the British community in Egypt, some 250 people condemned for rioting over the past years would have to be released under the Indemnity Act. Clark Kerr, who had made several informal contacts within the Zaghlulist camp, argued strongly for release of such people: 'any man who was a patriot would riot for his country's independence...' After much nerve-racking delay, the issue was finally resolved on 5 July when martial law was ended. The way was now open for the return of the exiled Zaghlul to Egypt, much to the anxiety of the British officials. Clark Kerr was not too concerned at this point, as in Zaghlul's absence his supporters had fallen into some disarray, and as the various parties geared up for the forthcoming elections there was hope that a less militant government might be elected. In the usual fashion, the British had seen to it that the moderate Prime Minister Yehia Ibrahim was not only credited with getting the new constitution in place, but also with the release of Zaghlul himself and the ending of martial law. Just in case this message did not get across, Clark Kerr was now acting as a middleman between the Government and certain newspapers, using bribery to see that the case was favourably presented. It was an activity which shocked Allenby, but Clark Kerr felt that it was not out of place in Egyptian politics where moral standards were not high. Clark Kerr argued that someone had to do it, and that being so, it might as well be someone from the British Residency. He had, of course, seen similar sordid activities in Persia during the war, and so it was hardly new to him. Nevertheless, it was a sign that Clark Kerr, so keen to see a just and successful future for Egypt, felt it necessary and justifiable to indulge in active politics, tantamount to meddling in Egyptian internal affairs. It was quite improper behaviour for a diplomat, but Clark Kerr had now become so personally involved in the drama that he viewed it as his duty to do everything possible to secure a settled future for the country. He was only acting professionally to the extent that his motives were to some degree guided by a desire to see British interests protected and maintained in Egypt, but he had also adopted clear, personal views on the status of Egypt which differed quite significantly from the official Foreign Office line.

It is hard to indicate very definitely Clark Kerr's political position at this point. He could be said to be fairly liberal at least on the grounds that he disliked the ill-considered imperialism and rigid attitudes of many in the Foreign Office and British political life. He was sympathetic to the aspirations of the Egyptian people, but at the same time unhappy at the thought of an anti-British Zaghlulist regime in power, seeking to end any British role in Egypt. He was therefore quite some way from a number of Labour politicians who actively encouraged and supported the Zaghlulists, but neither was he one of those who considered negotiations or dealings with Zaghlul the equivalent of supping with the devil. His liberal views were also coloured with pragmatism: the current British position in Egypt was untenable, and he sought a solution which did justice to the legitimate desires of the Egyptian people, while respecting British interests. To Clark Kerr, it was always fundamentally a question of realism.

His support for the Labour Party, which would remain with him, was also coloured by a corresponding distaste for Tory imperialism which had been created in him by a combination of his personal vendetta with Foreign Office mandarins over his army service, his awareness of serious flaws in imperial policy in Persia, and a stark realisation of the hopelessness of the future of imperialism when judged by the way of life in such places as Tangier and Egypt. His egalitarian instincts and natural human sympathy led him inexorably to a firm anti-imperial stance which would forever distance him from prevailing Tory opinion.

With the major constitutional issues and legal matters settled, there was a period of some relaxation as the Egyptian political parties prepared for the coming elections. As a result both Allenby and Clark Kerr were able to take some leave.

Clark Kerr returned to Britain on 21 August 1923 and was able to visit Inverchapel and see the lodge completed at last. There was, however, much else to occupy him: there were numerous meetings at the Foreign Office for briefings and informal chats with politicians on the developing situation in Egypt. Of particular importance was a meeting with Ben Spoor, the Labour

Chief Whip, who had taken a great interest in Egyptian affairs. The importance of this meeting was that Clark Kerr was able genuinely to impress a Labour politician not only with his knowledge of the Egyptian situation but also with his fair and reasonable attitudes towards Egyptian demands. Spoor was able to recognise that in Clark Kerr, at least, Britain had an able and modern-thinking official on the ground.

As usual Clark Kerr had a hectic social programme during the short weeks of his furlough. There were various weekend parties and shoots, at which his aristocratic and diplomatic friends could brief him on the latest social gossip. In the midst of all this came the news of his promotion to the post of Counsellor (Acting) which he was to take up as soon as Scott, who had fallen badly foul of the Foreign Office, had been removed from Cairo. Clark Kerr would now be second only to Allenby, and effectively the highest-ranking diplomat in Egypt, Counsellor to the Residency. Although ensconced in various country retreats for weeks, Clark Kerr was kept well-informed of the Egyptian scene by Tweedy and Wiggin at the Residency, who wrote regularly, but more helpfully by Delaney of Reuters, who wrote full and intelligent reports, not only of greater depth but which also gave impressions of the Residency performance. The most important happening of the period was the triumphant return of Zaghlul Pasha to Egypt on 10 September 10. In the event, it passed off peacefully considering that some 500,000 turned out to witness it. More optimistically for Britain, Zaghlul began with a number of conciliatory-sounding pronouncements on the political situation.

Clark Kerr did not return to Egypt until early November. Before his return he lunched with the editor of *The Times*, an important contact given the growing clamour from such papers as the *Daily Express* for an end to current British policy, which it deemed too soft, and a 'sell-out'. *The Times* generally supported the Allenby line, and this was vital.

Archie Clark Kerr officially took over as Acting Counsellor on 12 November. With the imminence of the elections it was an anxious time, not least because King Fuad was once again exploiting the situation for his own benefit, to the extent that in late December Clark Kerr was actually contemplating manufacturing a *coup d'état* to bring him down. In the end he decided to postpone such drastic action, but yet again this demonstrates in its gravity just how deeply committed to the situation Clark Kerr had become and how personally involved he felt.

Political upheaval in Egypt was matched by similar turmoil at home in the fall of Baldwin's ministry and the emergence of a minority Labour Government under Ramsay MacDonald (although not formed until January 1924). Clark Kerr showed his political shrewdness in his immediate recognition that this development marked a lasting and significant change in the face of British politics. On 8 December 1923, he wrote to his mother:

> ... when people begin to realise that Labour is here to stay,... if they are to save themselves, all 'moderates' must get to one side whether they call themselves

Conservatives or Liberals... there is no room for more than two large parties. There can only be a left and a right – a middle is impossible. But we shall probably have to have a taste of a Labour government before this comes about.

Despite his sanguine attitude, Clark Kerr was worried about the effect a Labour administration might have on Egyptian affairs. Apart from any change in policy, there was the fact that some Labour politicians had been actually campaigning in the Egyptian elections for the Zaghlulist party.[13] Even more seriously, during Ramsay MacDonald's brief visit to Egypt in early 1922, he had been widely quoted as sympathetic to the nationalist cause.[14] His emergence as Prime Minister and as Foreign Secretary could quite naturally be seen as lending succour to the fundamentalists in the nationalist camp.

During the elections in Egypt in January 1924, Allenby thought it judicious to absent himself, and went on a tour of the Sudan, although even in that there was the none-too-cryptic message that Sudan was still very much a British holding. During his leave, Clark Kerr became Acting High Commissioner. It was a pleasant moment for his aged mother to arrive on holiday and see her 'boy', the modern Joseph of Egypt. She remained with him until Allenby's return in May.

In early December it had become clear that Zaghlul's return had galvanised his 'Wafd' party to such an extent that they were more than likely to emerge as electoral victors. Gerald Delaney, who had been to see Zaghlul, was able to raise the matter of a meeting, and Zaghlul expressed a desire to meet Clark Kerr to discuss affairs informally. Unfortunately Allenby, always rather slow to appreciate the tidal patterns in Egyptian politics and to work out expedient reactions, refused to give Clark Kerr leave to meet Zaghlul. Nevertheless, in Allenby's absence, Clark Kerr went ahead with two secret and highly advantageous meetings with Zaghlul, at which he was able to convince Zaghlul of his own and Allenby's genuine desire for Egypt's good, and demonstrate their not inconsiderable role in winning the Declaration of 1922, in securing the liberal constitution of 1923, and in limiting the King's powers.[15] At the very least these meetings cleared the air and some mutual suspicions and prejudices were swept away.

On 12 January 1924, Egyptians went to the polls for the first time in a General Election. The result, while not unexpected, was surprising in the overwhelming extent of the Zaghlulist victory. In a chamber of 214 members, Zaghlul's supporters won 190 seats, and on 27 January this *bête noire* of British Egyptian policy and former exile became the first Prime Minister of Egypt under the new constitution. His position could hardly have been stronger: a massive parliamentary majority, the clear mandate of the Egyptian people, his political foes marginalised, and the King unable to counteract in any way. In addition, political events had so unfolded in Britain that the Labour Party was forming its first government, its MPs mostly sympathetic to the Egyptian cause, and its Prime Minister and Foreign Secretary, Ramsay MacDonald, personally known to Zaghlul and having often expressed support for Egyptian independence.

As far as the British Residency was concerned, the situation was somewhat sticky. Although Egypt had been guided very quickly and successfully to democratic government, the problem was that, despite their best efforts, they now found in power a body of people who had never deviated from a policy of demanding full independence, control over the Sudan and Suez, and an end to all British involvement in Egypt. The four 'reserved points' of the 1922 constitution, whose legitimacy Zaghlul rejected anyway, had been laid to one side to await negotiation until an Egyptian administration had been formed; but the administration now formed was of an uncompromising fundamentalist-nationalist nature and the prospects of any meaningful negotiation seemed remote. Not surprisingly, Zaghlul's election gave renewed hope and vigour to those calling for the absorption of the Sudan and the full realisation of the Zaghlulist programme.

In the circumstances, it seemed clear to Clark Kerr and accepted by Allenby that it was now necessary to be fully accommodating to the democratically-elected Egyptian Government, except concerning those issues vital to British interests. There was no point in haggling over lesser matters which would only arouse public disorder and to defend which, in any case, Britain had neither the moral weapons nor the justification for the use of military ones. The difficulty was going to be in defining those 'vital' interests: fortunately, Clark Kerr's views and those of the incoming Labour Government were largely congruent. Both accepted the inevitable but, having ceded so much, expected sympathetic responses from Egypt to the very real requirements of British imperial communication as far as Suez was concerned. Clark Kerr felt there was no justification for any British troops to remain on Egyptian soil, but that a defensive British force could remain on the eastern bank of the canal. On this matter he had the full support of Allenby, who judged that Suez, and Egypt for that matter, could be most effectively defended by Britain's Mediterranean naval superiority, and that land-based forces were superfluous except in the event of a military clash. As far as Sudan was concerned, both Allenby and Clark Kerr felt that the time was not right, nor Egypt advanced enough politically, for the absorption of the Sudan. These views, and any sympathy for the nationalist case, it ought to be recognised, were utterly abhorrent to most of the British community in Egypt: old imperialist and racist attitudes were not only rife but judged to be respectable. There was widespread unease over this 'soft' approach to what were dismissively regarded as the mindless riotings of backward natives ungrateful for the blessings rained on them by a motherly Empire. Socialists in Downing Street and coloured people in power in Egypt were shattering phenomena for a community used to ease, privilege and stability.

There were, in fact, interesting parallels to be drawn between the positions of MacDonald and Zaghlul. MacDonald, a member of a radical party, had been tempted into forming what was a minority government and was thus gravely weakened in his ability to put any of his policies into action. As far as is known, Zaghlul never came to terms with this crucial brake on MacDonald's freedom of action. The MacDonald who had befriended

Zaghlul and made encouraging noises on the quayside at Alexandria the year before was a very different creature, as far as freedom of action was concerned, from the MacDonald of the sober suit on the threshold of Number 10, the leader of a minority government. Furthermore, as a Foreign Office mandarin opined to Clark Kerr MacDonald felt that he could best establish proof of Labour's ability to govern in the field of foreign affairs.[16] The sceptical establishment was to be won over by the expertise and resolve Labour would show in its handling of the Russian, Egyptian and Ruhr questions. It was partly because of this that MacDonald himself took on the Foreign Office job in addition to that of Premier: there were to be no mistakes in this field. The establishment would learn, although Zaghlul never did until too late, that a Labour Government was 'fully as jealous of, and fully as capable of upholding, British vital interests abroad as any Conservative or Liberal Government'.[17]

Zaghlul had none of the anxieties of being in a minority. He did, however, still have certain important curbs on his freedom. The 'Wafd' had been divided on the whole issue of fighting an election under the banner of the 1922 constitution, whose very terms they had rejected. They had decided finally to fight the election but had then been divided over the issue of forming an administration thereafter.[18] Because they did, they virtually legitimised all that had occurred since 1922, and put themselves in the position of having to negotiate the four reserved points, on none of which their principles allowed them to give way. They had campaigned and agitated all along for full, unshackled independence: they had the overwhelming support of the Egyptian people on that demand, and had now stirred up great expectations on the issues of Suez and the Sudan. Anything short of that, any compromise or negotiated settlement, would involve loss of face: they would be seen to have failed. Zaghlul had come to power thanks to his populist image and message; but, as he knew only too well, those who live by the fickle mob, can also die by that mob. In retrospect, therefore, his decision to assume office can now be seen to have been a misjudgement. He was hardly the man best qualified to begin a process of give-and-take with the British Government. In January 1924, however, things had gone the nationalist way for so long, and so complete was his victory, that it is understandable if in the circumstances, made all the more favourable with the prospect of a Labour Government at Westminster, that Zaghul and his advisers judged that a total British climbdown was imminent.[19]

On 8 February 1924 Clark Kerr visited the new Prime Minister to discuss the question which Zaghlul had raised of an amnesty for prisoners. Estimating that this was not a vital British interest, though certainly a sensitive one for the embattled British community in Egypt, Clark Kerr judged it politic to make a conciliatory move to the new regime, and exceeded even the Wafd's hopes on this matter, offering to release all but those accused of attempted murder the previous summer. This went down very well with both Government and people in its magnanimity, and on 11 February Clark Kerr was able to report to Allenby that he was 'fairly happy about the way things are going'. The unfortunate consequence, unforeseen by Clark Kerr, was that his sincere effort at conciliation was misinterpreted by Zaghlul as yet another sign of weakness and the inevitability of capitulation.

All this, and Clark Kerr's memo on the course of the elections met with MacDonald's entire approval,[20] and Sir Sheldon Amos, home on leave, was able to report that in the Foreign Office Clark Kerr's stock was now very high indeed. Despite this, the Foreign Office was unwilling to hurry negotiations with the Zaghlulist regime, recognising that there was little hope of an amicable settlement on the outstanding issues until the Egyptian Government showed some signs of a willingness to compromise. There was no real problem for Clark Kerr in the Foreign Office's position, for he felt that they shared his own general view of things, and MacDonald's Private Secretary at the Foreign Office was Walford Selby, who had served in Egypt himself and knew the situation well.

In early March, even before the Egyptian Parliament officially opened, Zaghlul showed that he, at least, had no intention of delaying matters, and publicly expressed a wish to go to London to open discussions.[21] The Foreign Office was worried in case there would be a breakdown in talks which would have damaging consequences in Egypt. MacDonald himself was not greatly enamoured of the idea of a visit either, preferring that the main business be conducted in Egypt and that only a final settlement be agreed in London. Although this demonstrated faith in Clark Kerr's abilities and judgement, it did not commend itself to Clark Kerr, who felt that Cairo was hardly the calm arena in which negotiations could be satisfactorily conducted and that there was more chance of a shift in Zaghlul's position in London, where he would be far from extremist proddings, press propaganda and the madding crowd. Allenby considered that there was no point in unnecessarily offending Zaghlul, who had shown a willingness to travel to London, and suggested that Clark Kerr should go to London with Zaghlul since he had 'established close personal contact with him'.

MacDonald, however, managed to delay matters, which in the circumstances was just as well, for it soon became clear that senior figures in the Foreign Office did not share the realistic attitude which Clark Kerr and Allenby had come to adopt on the Egyptian question. On the question of the presence of British troops and the protection of Suez, Clark Kerr and Allenby had a strong case, politically and militarily. There was no justification on either grounds to maintain forces except in the immediate, preferably eastern, environs of the canal. On the Sudan question, Clark Kerr had come to recognise the fact, which Delaney of Reuters had long sought to impress, that since Sudan was the source of the Egyptian water supply, it was a highly sensitive matter and that it must be appreciated that the presence of British troops in the Sudan had an, albeit unconscious, intimidating effect on an Egypt where water was such an emotive and perilous concern. The Foreign Office had not come to accept either of these points. On 10 April, Clark Kerr forwarded a Foreign Office paper to Allenby with some concern:

> I had been under the impression that HMG appreciated that withdrawal to the canal was an almost essential condition of securing an agreement with Egypt. Mr Murray [a senior Foreign Office figure] now casts doubt on their willingness to withdraw even from Cairo and its suburbs.

While Allenby agreed with Clark Kerr, he only wanted withdrawal to the canal after an agreement had been reached, and not for that to be conceded during the negotiations with the Egyptian Government. On 21 April Clark Kerr had visited Zaghlul to deliver MacDonald's belated invitation to come to London in the summer for such talks.

The dated imperialist instincts still prevalent in the Foreign Office surfaced a month later when a shocked Delaney reported to Clark Kerr, then en route for Britain too, on a meeting he had just had with Murray and Selby. Delaney was appalled by Murray's reaction to the points he made about the Sudan. Murray had exploded at the thought of any compromise or *modus vivendi*, fulminating in apocalyptic terms. 'Mahdiism! – growing and growing Mahdiism! Not only in and around Khartoum – but everywhere from the Red Sea to the Atlantic!' As far as the Foreign Office was concerned, a just settlement in Egypt would mean giving succour to independence movements in other parts of the Empire, and that was a price too high. Delaney, not surprisingly, had a more encouraging meeting with Ben Spoor, and was hopeful that by the time Zaghlul came to London in June that Ramsay MacDonald would have been persuaded of the wisdom of having no troops west of Suez.

Clark Kerr was due in London on 21 May for two months' leave. He had already arranged to meet with Spoor and Delaney at the Commons on the twenty-seventh to discuss the Egyptian situation and also hoped to meet Ramsay MacDonald himself. Amongst interested parties, Clark Kerr's arrival was eagerly awaited: he was, after all, the senior career diplomat in the British Residency, and best able to present to political and diplomatic figures the true nature of the situation and his, and Allenby's, feelings on how British policy should now be shaped.

Clark Kerr had several meetings with Delaney in clubland to discuss tactics, and he followed those with meetings with Lord Curzon, former head of the Foreign Office, John Jacob Astor, the MP and *Times* newspaperman, and with Walford Selby, MacDonald's private secretary.

He was able to escape from London in mid-June and take 10 days' proper holiday at Inverchapel, where there was the chance to unwind, do a little walking and fishing, and attend to the affairs of the estate generally. Events in Egypt were not neglected. He could hardly avoid, even if he had wanted to, the continuing press coverage of the growing agitation in Egypt, both within and outside parliament. He received regular reports from his colleague Robin Furness in Cairo where, despite the hostile atmosphere, there were hopes that Zaghlul would come to London, possibly via France, for talks. Even at the opening of the Egyptian parliament in March there had been a demonstration against British rule in the Sudan and the agitation continued unabated thereafter. In April an RAF corporal was murdered by two students, the first such attack for nearly a year. Within the Egyptian Parliament the position of Sir Lee Stack as Sirdar, or Commander-in-Chief, of the Egyptian Army and Governor-General of the Sudan was attacked. The parliament also refused to vote the annual contribution made by Egypt to the army of occupation, and the amount of money demanded by Britain for the compensation of departing foreign officials was denounced as unacceptable.[22]

Within the Wafd Party, however, there were problems, and Zaghlul was finding it increasingly difficult to appease the more extremist elements who were becoming unhappy at the lack of progress. The administration had made no impact on the economy and social fabric of Egypt, and indeed it was doubted if it had any programme at all. On the national question, no tangible progress had been made either. Indeed Zaghlul was so concerned about possible reaction to having entered, or contemplated, negotiations with Britain that he had to seek binding assurances from Britain that the talks would not be termed as such.[23]

The Wafd position was relieved on 24 June when Lord Parmoor delivered an uncompromising speech to the House of Lords declaring that Great Britain was 'not going to abandon the Sudan in any sense whatsoever'.[24] Immediately the British became the main target of unrest once more, and there were massive demonstrations of protest throughout Egypt. Despite the fallout, MacDonald was able to arrange a meeting with Zaghlul in London for the end of September. On 12 July there was a major scare when Zaghlul was shot at and wounded in Alexandria, where he was preparing to embark on a visit to France. Clark Kerr immediately telegraphed a note of sympathy from London, but the injury was not serious. It is uncertain who was responsible for the attack, or who stood to gain by it. There were many possible motives for the attack, but the most likely culprits would be a group loyal to the ex-Khedive and Turkish interests, and strongly believed to be behind much of the terrorist activities.

Clark Kerr left London in late July to relieve Allenby, who was required in London for talks and to be present at the impending discussions with Zaghlul. This was to be the most momentous period in Clark Kerr's career so far: from 30 July until 24 October 1924 he was to be His Majesty's Charge d'Affaires in Egypt, in effect the acting High Commissioner. It was a very exalted position for one only forty-two years old, but what made it even more seductive for Clark Kerr was the high public profile, the constant press attention, the dazzle and interest his every move attracted. Here he was where he longed to be: the centre of attention in a key post, fully aware of all its intricate details, certain of his policy objectives, and fully confident in his own abilities to see these attained.

Hardly had Clark Kerr taken charge when serious trouble broke out in the Sudan. Influenced by developments in Egypt, unrest had sprouted amongst detachments of the Egyptian armed services stationed in the Sudan. Rumblings had continued for some time, but Clark Kerr was inclined to lay more of the blame at the door of the British military, which he distrusted for its jingoistic attitudes and political ineptitude. He was particularly critical of the public-school types in the colonial and military service in the Sudan, whom he considered not only second-rate but dangerously so. What was especially galling was the thought that all his hard work in Egypt, which was now about to culminate in the undreamt-of spectacle of the nationalist demagogue of old, Zaghlul, entering into open talks in London in a reasonable frame of mind, would be undermined by the bunglings of overgrown schoolboys in the Sudan whose qualifications Clark Kerr contemptuously labelled 'more athletic than academic'.

Trouble in the Sudan worsened, commencing with an armed demonstration by military cadets which was quelled without casualty. This was followed by a far more serious insurrection by the Egyptian Railway Battalion at Atbara. In response, some Sudanese soldiers, at the order of an Egyptian officer, fired on the rioters and inflicted some casualties. Because of earlier fears of a coup attempt by the ex-Khedive, Clark Kerr had already asked for a battleship at Malta to be put on standby, and in the wake of the massive public outcry at the Sudan shootings, he now requested that the HMS Marlborough be despatched to Alexandria as a precaution. Clark Kerr vainly tried to persuade the Egyptian public and press that the shootings had not been perpetrated by British soldiers at all, but by Sudanese at the command of an Egyptian! In London, Allenby and Sir Lee Stack, the Sirdar, had met with Ramsay MacDonald on 13 August to discuss the situation. Allenby felt that the situation demanded a military response, although he doubted how much the disturbances could be laid at the door of the Egyptian administration itself. Nevertheless, it was agreed that only a military threat might dissuade the Egyptian authorities from continuing to foment unrest on the Sudan question. It was agreed to send a warning note to the acting Egyptian Premier, Mohammed Said, over his government's responsibility for the present developments.

Before this could happen, however, Clark Kerr was at the centre of a serious diplomatic incident. On 13 August, Clark Kerr had a long talk with Mohammed Said, deputising in Zaghlul's absence, over the Atbara incident, where he tried to impress on him the truth of the circumstances. Despite that, Mohammed did nothing to correct the impression he had already helped to publicise – that it was the British who had fired at Atbara. An Egyptian note of protest delivered to the Residency stood by this misrepresentation of the facts. Clark Kerr returned with a strong Foreign Office rebuke in which it was clearly intimated 'that Great Britain considers itself, through the Governor-General, responsible for the maintenance of order in the Sudan'.[25] At the same time, Clark Kerr took the opportunity of delivering a strongly-worded protest at the misleading character of a press communiqué which the Egyptian Government had issued on the Atbara incident. This protest he delivered on his own initiative, judging that immediate action might prove salutary for the acting Prime Minister. It was decisive action which brought praise from Allenby and MacDonald, who had now come to the position that the Sudan was not an issue over which the Government was prepared to give way. He informed Sir Lee Stack 'that whatever he found it necessary to do in the Sudan, His Majesty's Government would support him'.

At this point in the proceedings, MacDonald wrote to Zaghlul in unfortunately accusatory terms which Clark Kerr considered a 'bad mistake', as he questioned Egyptian good faith, and seemed to have penned the letter in anger. The fact that MacDonald was now adopting a more reactionary stance than that of British representatives on the ground, such as Clark Kerr, gives some indication of how only a few months of minority government had shifted MacDonald's politics. As Harold Nicolson wrote to Clark Kerr on 3 September:

> where you are lucky is that you have caught the Government in a British Empire Exhibitionist mood and that when they relapse into a Trades Union mood it will be Allenby and not you who'll be running the show.

The result of MacDonald's letter was depressingly predictable: Zaghlul took offence at its tone, called off the planned talks in London, and announced that he would return to Egypt. Yet beneath the public posturing there was more common ground than either could admit: MacDonald could not for fear of offending his increasingly shrill Tory opponents, still the largest party in parliament; Zaghlul could not for fear of offending the more extremist elements in his Wafd Party. On 2 September, Zaghlul's emissary, Castro, made an informal visit to Clark Kerr during which he explained that Zaghlul was not really feeling very aggrieved but had felt impelled by circumstances to take the action he did. Castro also admitted that Zaghlul felt that Mohammed Said had bungled the whole situation and was mostly to blame. The problem did not disappear. Less than two days later a report, allegedly from Reuters, appeared in the *Daily Express* in which Ramsay MacDonald was quoted as saying, 'I firmly believe that recent disturbances were engineered by members of the Egyptian government and Zaghlul Pasha has pandered to the extremists'. Clark Kerr was astounded, and frantically wired the Foreign Office for confirmation, intending to resign if it were true, considering that in the circumstances consequent to such a statement 'it would be useless to attempt to continue the struggle here'. By 6 September, however, the press report had been repudiated firmly by Ramsay MacDonald and all was sweetness and light with Mohammed Said, who effected a reconciliation. Two days later relief was complete when Clark Kerr learnt that MacDonald and Zaghlul had also been reconciled and that the Egyptian leader had been reinvited to London. It was thought that the talks would commence on 25 September. Following a private dinner at home for Mohammed Said, Clark Kerr even sniffed the possibility of the nationalists dropping the question of the Sudan for the forthcoming talks. In this atmosphere, he grew more hopeful of even being able to encourage Zaghlul to go beyond mere conversations, and to enter into full negotiations. Castro, Zaghlul's press agent for the London visit, claimed that the Egyptian side would not be averse to this. Clark Kerr's main fear now was that the 'extreme Sudan party' in London – those who were opposed to any concession to Egyptian aspirations and some of whom were calling for British annexation of the Sudan – would prevent Ramsay MacDonald being able to compromise on the Sudan at all. In Egypt itself, the military commander General Haking and the Financial Adviser, Sir Reginald Patterson, were both of this obstinate viewpoint, and Clark Kerr despaired of this extremist attitude, which had even been adopted by the Sirdar. There seemed to be a general resentment of any form of Egyptian autonomy or any move to improve the status of the Egyptian in his native land.

The irony was that the mood within Egyptian circles as the London talks approached was favourable and hopeful. In an attempt to give support to MacDonald's more accommodating instincts, Clark Kerr wired him just prior to the opening of the talks, and tried also to impress on Lord Thomson, MacDonald's Air Minister, who was visiting Cairo, the need to drop any extreme imperialist dogma from the talks.

As Clark Kerr awaited anxiously in Egypt, the long-delayed talks finally commenced in London at 10am on 25 September. Zaghlul was in no mood for compromise over the days of talks, demanding a total British withdrawal from both Egypt and the Sudan, neither of which MacDonald could countenance. The final meeting on 3 October drew matters to an inconclusive close as both leaders agreed simply to disagree on almost every position.[26]

Clark Kerr was naturally disappointed at the failure of the talks, attributing blame mostly to Zaghlul's obstinacy and his failure to appreciate political realities in Britain. In particular, his insistence on a British military withdrawal to Palestine, never mind the east bank of the canal, was viewed by Clark Kerr as a position that was simply unnecessarily extreme, and to which Ramsay MacDonald could never have agreed and hoped to survive. Clark Kerr did, however, recognise some problems on the British side and sensed that the impending election in Britain really prevented MacDonald from pursuing a settlement with any zest. He did take heart, though, from MacDonald's use of the word 'sites' when addressing the troops issue and hoped that this might mean that British troops would not be stationed forever in Cairo and Alexandria.

Clark Kerr's reaction was quite sanguine, and in Egypt the reaction was also one of calm with everyone awaiting the verdict of Zaghlul on his return on 20 October. The Foreign Office was very concerned that the breakdown might precipitate another rebellion in the Sudan, particularly as there was a growing lack of confidence in Sir Lee Stack's abilities as Governor-General and Sirdar. Not only was there concern on that front, but also over the fall of the Labour Government on 8 October. Both Allenby and Clark Kerr had been favourably impressed by MacDonald, and had hoped that he would not leave office. Clark Kerr held MacDonald in high regard for his intelligent, fair-minded and even-handed management of Egyptian affairs. It was quite unique for someone of Clark Kerr's social background and professional status to view a Labour Government with such favour, but it was also typical of his open outlook on life, an outlook which led some to view him as perversely unconventional. This was not so: certainly he did not slavishly follow any belief, party, policy or leader; but his adoption of unconventional postures was not done for mere show or to shock. He thought deeply about matters, came to a considered judgement on the merits of the case alone, and argued for his position rationally. In that sense, he was an ideal diplomat, able to look dispassionately on the situations he found in the many posts and countries in which he served and, having considered the realities of these situations, able to advise and lobby his masters with unmatched insight and understanding. It was this openness and inherent impartiality which endeared him to so many, not only in Egypt but wherever he served his country. People recognised that here was not a superior British aristocrat sneering at the idiosyncrasies and 'lower' ways of the natives: here was a man who was open to reasoned persuasion and to whom fairness and justice were the chief principles of action. Of course it was inevitable that such an attitude would be held in disfavour by some in the British Foreign Service who considered their duty to be a blind faith in the aged certainties of Britain and the Empire, twinned with an unyielding prejudice against any deviation from the Anglo-Saxon norm. Archie Clark Kerr, for his part, never strayed from his goal of seeking to do what was right, even if it involved hard words and tough arguments with Foreign Office heads.

It was therefore perfectly natural for Clark Kerr to view the Labour Government's Egyptian policy and record in an equitable way and, having done so, be prepared to voice his commendatory opinions even when they shocked his more mulish colleagues and his Victorian mother. To her he declared Ramsay MacDonald

> ... far the best Prime Minister we have had for a very long time, and he has enormously increased our prestige abroad and has almost succeeded in re-establishing our reputation for honest dealing that was shattered by Lloyd George.

It is important to notice again that his approval was based on the fact that MacDonald had sought to do what was right, fair and honest. There is little evidence that Clark Kerr shared any of the Labour Party's other political principles at this point in his career, and indeed he had joked that he might lose his lands at Inverchapel if these 'Bolsheviks' came to power. However, this makes his complimentary comments all the more laudable: he was prepared to give credit where he deemed it due, and ignore the more ludicrous of the establishment's scaremongering – scaremongering which fuelled the Zinoviev scandal and helped defeat the Labour Party at the polls. Meanwhile, of Churchill's defection from the Liberal to the Tory Party he wrote: '... politically he must remain in the long run a danger to the country. Please God we shall not see him in office again.'

As Egypt waited for Zaghlul's return, there was much political manoeuvring on all sides. Delaney and Clark Kerr began, along with the Egyptian Liberals, to prepare for the prospect of Zaghlul's downfall in the wake of his failure in London. As far as Clark Kerr was concerned, the aim was to arrange affairs so that a more amenable cabinet could be installed, willing to do a deal with Britain. What it amounted to was to plot the defeat of Zaghlul, as Clark Kerr acknowledged in response to a long letter from Delaney on 12 October which analysed the options open. Delaney argued that if Zaghlul returned and flouted the status quo then, as even Egyptian liberals such as Mahmoud and Afifi agreed,

> Britain must act in an uncompromising manner. That would surely mean the downfall of the ministry and they share your view that the Residency should not attempt to manoeuvre any particular body of men into power, but that a strong cabinet should be allowed to emerge...

The plan was clear: Britain would react to any move of Zaghlul with the toughness necessary to bring down his Government. The only issues to be settled were what was to trigger this reaction, and of what the reaction would consist. Delaney felt that seizure of the customs, a source of vital revenue from tobacco, would amount to economic strangulation and would do the trick:

> If you find yourself obliged to seize the customs in due time, I feel it will create such an atmosphere of alarm that the wise elements will find a safe haven for action. I feel it will wean men like Nessim, Ziwar, Mohammed Said and Mazloum from Zaghlul...

The strategy was simply a variation of the old tactic: Zaghlul's 'obstinacy' and 'extremist' position would be met by robust British action, his policies and viewpoint discredited, and his Government brought down to make way for one more acceptable to, and receptive to, the British position. It was a dangerous game to play: Zaghlul was an immensely popular political figure, the very embodiment of the Egyptian nationalist ideal, and to tackle him was to risk the wrath and reaction of the mass of the Egyptian people. A wrong move by the British officials could, instead of isolating Zaghlul, merely serve to unite the people behind him and fatally discredit Britain. The plan was going to require shrewd judgement and a steady nerve if it was to be implemented effectively.

The Wafd and Zaghlul's supporters were only too well aware of the problems failure in London might create.[27] It could well be argued that even with a friendly government in London, Zaghlul had failed to make any progress and, in fact, that more had been achieved when he was out of office, if not out of the country. As a result, there were various cabinet changes so that, at least, some progress in social and economic terms might be made bringing some credit to Zaghlul's Government, even if there was stalemate on the national question.

However, there were some changes forced on Zaghlul which were not to his benefit. To appease the more extreme elements in his party he had to offer them political office even though many had little experience and merely brought incompetence and corruption. To maintain public support, he had to appeal to the extremist elements also, and in so doing he made ever more impossible the settlement with Britain which could resolve the situation. As these two problems snowballed, the position grew ever more dangerous. Clark Kerr and Allenby, who returned in late October, were aware that a crisis was coming and could not be avoided.[28]

The problem was now judging when the time was right to act against Zaghlul. At this point – 4 November 1924 – the Conservatives won a landslide victory in the British General Election, increasing their number of seats from 258 to 412, while Labour lost 40, leaving only 151. The main losers were the Liberals who lost over 100 seats, effectively ending their major role in parliamentary politics. Baldwin became Prime Minister and Austen Chamberlain took over as Foreign Secretary. It was quickly recognised that the effect of the landslide as far His Majesty's Government's Egyptian policy was concerned would be that the hands-off policy would be abandoned and, as Murray of the Foreign Office put it to Clark Kerr, 'take the initiative and adopt an offensive policy'. Zaghlul was well aware also of what the departure of the MacDonald administration would mean and, despite his increasingly uncompromising position, began to cast about for means to reach an understanding of some sort with the British Government. Zaghlul was looking to Clark Kerr as the kind of reasonable and progressive character through whose offices a *modus vivendi* could be reached. Clark Kerr had no intention at this stage of lending any assistance to the Zaghlul regime, and took no steps to help Zaghlul out of his predicament. Clark Kerr was maintaining his clear policy objective of seeking the downfall of the whole Zaghlulist regime. There was to be no compromise and certainly no olive branch at this juncture. The position of the Egyptian Government was considered so hopeless that Clark Kerr and Delaney deemed intervention on their part to be unnecessary: it was looking quite likely that without their machinations, Zaghlul's Government would self-destruct through its incompetence, corruption, increasing tyranny and unfulfilled promises. It was judged that there was no need for any British action, and indeed they feared that would prove counterproductive.

All this – all of the schemes, hopes and plans, all the careful diplomacy, the designs and manoeuvrings of the last two years – was to be rendered utterly useless by the catastrophic events of Wednesday 19 November 1924.

On that day, Lord Allenby had arranged a small luncheon party at the British residency in Cairo for the former British Prime Minister Herbert Asquith. Among the few guests invited was Sir Lee Stack. Clark Kerr was not to be present, and was preparing to leave the residency for lunch at home when, just a little after 1.30pm, he was aroused by a commotion in the residency hallway. On rushing out, he found Campbell, the Sirdar's ADC, with a bullet-wound in his chest, and at the door a car with the Sirdar himself lying slumped on his side, having also been shot. He had been hit by three bullets – in the hand, leg and abdomen. In the confusion, the facts of the case emerged uncertainly. It transpired that Stack, his ADC and his chauffeur were on their way to the residency by car when they were ambushed by a group of Egyptian students who had thrown a bomb at the car. When that failed to explode, they sprayed the car with about 25 shots, before fleeing by taxi. The Sirdar's chauffeur, despite having been hit himself, had the presence of mind to drive straight to the residency.

Clark Kerr quickly saw to it that the Sirdar was brought into the residency and made comfortable on a sofa in the drawing-room. In the meanwhile, Lord Allenby and the other VIPs were summoned from luncheon. Unfortunately, in this moment of crisis, they were of little assistance. According to Clark Kerr's account, Lord Allenby was 'emphatically under the influence of gin', Sir Sheldon Amos, the Judicial Adviser, was 'still more alcoholic' and Sir Reginald Patterson, the Financial Adviser, was 'grumpy drunk'. Clark Kerr himself, therefore, had to see to affairs, including informing Zaghlul, who arrived with his entourage in a state of shock at 2.30pm. Allenby buttonholed him immediately, and pointing at the injured ADC and chauffeur, intoned: 'This is your doing'. He was on the verge of hauling Zaghlul off to face the stricken Sirdar himself before Clark Kerr managed to dissuade him. Lady Stack had just arrived too and a confrontation of that sort might not have been politic. Zaghlul left immediately.

There was no doubting the grave political implications of the murder attempt. Clark Kerr realised that the moment had now come for stern action:

> ... we can hold our hand no longer. We shall be obliged to take vigorous action against Zaghlul, for morally he and his government are responsible and they cannot be allowed to escape responsibility.

This was the line also adopted by *The Times* the following day. While absolving the Egyptian Government of direct complicity, The Times still contended:

> in another sense neither the Egyptian government, nor the Egyptian Chamber, nor Zaghlul himself can be acquitted of moral responsibility. They have deliberately and systematically created the frame of mind of which violence and murder are the natural results. Very likely they did not desire the end, but they desired the steps from which the end inevitably follows.[29]

Once the immediate situation had been dealt with, and Stack removed to hospital, Clark Kerr and Allenby began urgent discussions on what the British response should be. In a series of telegrams to the Foreign Office that day,[30] they suggested six immediate measures to be taken against the Egyptian Government, calling on them to make apology, apprehend speedily and punish severely those responsible, pay an indemnity of £500,000 damages, accept that the office of the Sirdar be undivided, agree to the previously disputed issue of the amount of pensions to be awarded to departing foreign officials in Egyptian employ, and agree to keep on the two posts of Financial and Judicial Adviser. Following further discussion, Allenby and Clark Kerr considered that some demand be made which would create a much more powerful impression on the minds of the Egyptian people, emphasising the gravity with which the

British Government viewed the matter. The measure would also have to convey to the Egyptian populace the massive potential power at the disposal of the British Government. On Thursday 20 November, they asked the Foreign Office to consider a further clause relating to the irrigation of the Gezira region of the Sudan. The point of this was that the Egyptian water supplies were dependent solely on Sudanese goodwill. Allenby proposed that the further clause should read: '... that the Egyptian government shall consent to increase as need may arise the area of land to be irrigated under the Gezira scheme'.[31] The implicit threat here was that it was quite in Britain's power to reduce the Egyptian water supply at will, and redirect it to Gezira.

That evening, when there was still no reply forthcoming from London, Allenby sought to convince the Foreign Office of the need for haste.[32] The fear was that Zaghlul would resign before Allenby had a chance to serve on him the British demands. It was part of the usual British ploy, as Clark Kerr knew well, to seek to hammer Zaghlul with these demands, force his resignation, and then, when a more amenable government came to power, seek to reward their reasonableness by withdrawing certain of the demands, and generally act more leniently. If Zaghlul resigned first, then tabling these demands to a new government would be pointless and run counter to British long-term goals.

The situation became even more hazardous when, shortly before midnight that very evening, Stack died in hospital of his wounds. When the Foreign Office reply did come, Allenby and Clark Kerr were deeply disappointed to find that it did not endorse the force of Allenby's proposals.

> In their reply the Foreign Office referred to the fine as seeming to them the least part of the reparation to be expected. They whittled down the irrigation clause so much that it would have made no kind of impression in Egypt, and they cut out a clause that granted to all British and foreign officials the right to leave Egypt if they wished to...

Both Allenby and Clark Kerr were very unhappy at the Foreign Office line. For their part, the Foreign Office regarded the demand of a £500,000 fine as vindictive, not in the tradition of British diplomacy, and open to international disapproval. They also, perhaps rightly, questioned the propriety of seeking to relate the issue of Egyptian civil servants' pay and conditions to the matter of the assassination of Stack.[33] Clark Kerr had understandably tried to take advantage of the situation to settle as many outstanding problems as possible, but the Foreign Office were quite justified in questioning the fairness of this. On the other hand, the Foreign Office clearly had no idea of the implications of the clause concerning the Gezira scheme. Their proposed rewording of the clause – '... agree to extend the area of irrigation in Gezira without detriment to Egypt by a technical commission to which Egypt will be invited to appoint a member'[34] – rendered the measure valueless and utterly ineffectual.

Clark Kerr and Allenby replied immediately to this initial Foreign Office instruction:

We represented very strongly to the Foreign Office that a communication in the terms they suggested would be inadequate and would fall flat here. The situation was one that demanded immediate and vigorous action and it was immensely important to give Zaghlul and his part of Egypt a really good jolt.

Allenby tried to explain to the Foreign Office the intention behind the Gezira irrigation clause which the Foreign Office had considered unacceptably harsh:

I hold to my suggestion regarding Gezira irrigation. That will also strike the mind of the whole country. It does not of course affect our eventual guarantee of Egypt's water supply as we have promised but this is no time to mention anything advantageous to Egypt.[35]

Time was ebbing away. The Egyptian parliament was due to meet on Saturday 22 November at 5pm. It was widely rumoured that Zaghlul would tender his resignation at this session. Indeed, it was believed that King Fuad had received a draft letter of resignation from Zaghlul already.[36] Allenby and Clark Kerr desperately wanted to hand him the official British note before that time. The whole thrust of their arguments rested on delivering the British demands to Zaghlul and no one else. They pressed London for a speedy reply.

The British Cabinet met in emergency session at 10am on Saturday morning. They approved the text which Austen Chamberlain had already proposed to Allenby, but there still seemed to be no realisation of the necessity for speed. As late as 2pm, Allenby was still pressing for a response.[37]

In Cairo, meanwhile, the funeral service for Stack was taking place. It was an immensely solemn and tense ceremony, not least because Allenby had insisted on the presence of Zaghlul and his Cabinet, very much to the displeasure of the the British community present. Allenby felt, however, that having to face the funeral in person would impress on the Cabinet members the full horror and gravity of what had occurred. After the service, the funeral procession wound its way along hushed and crowded streets to the graveyard, the cortege taking over an hour to pass any one point. In Cairo, the event passed off peacefully, but in Alexandria a memorial service became the target for an anti-British demonstration.[38]

The funeral over, Allenby and Clark Kerr waited impatiently for the long-delayed Foreign Office reply. As the minutes ticked by, the concern now grew that the 5pm deadline might pass before the Foreign Office telegram came through. Zaghlul might resign before anything had been done. At 4.15pm Allenby decided that he and Clark Kerr, accompanied by a detachment of cavalry to make a dramatic show, should deliver the list of British demands to Zaghlul immediately. Clark Kerr was wholly in agreement that the note they should present should be their own original version and not the one suggested by the Foreign Office. They had put their case they felt and, in the absence of a reply, felt justified in going ahead. They were still well aware that the text they were going to present had earlier been questioned by the Foreign Office. As they were about to depart, news was brought that the Foreign Office message was coming through. Clark Kerr rushed back inside the residency. The message would have to be deciphered, of course, and there was little chance of that being completed prior to 5pm. However, from its length it was patently clear that it constituted no simple acquiescence to Allenby's proposed text.

Allenby and Clark Kerr now made a fateful decision. They decided to proceed as they had proposed, regardless of the content of the Foreign Office telegram. Their excuse would be that they had to act before 5pm and that deciphering would have prevented this.[39] The real position was that they knew only too well that they were acting contrary to Foreign Office instructions and, indeed, acting in direct defiance of a decision of the British Cabinet. Unaware of the background realities, *The Times* wrongly reported that the Cabinet had approved the text of the Allenby note; in fact the text the Cabinet approved fell considerably short of its range and vigour.[40]

Having decided to ignore the Foreign Office telegram, Allenby and Clark Kerr set off at once for the Prime Minister's office, just opposite the parliament where the deputies were arriving for the 5pm sitting. With a flourish of trumpets from the accompanying lancers to herald his arrival, Allenby in a grey lounge suit strode into Zaghlul's residence, read an English text of his demands, left a French translation, and turned on his heel, giving Zaghlul a deadline of 8pm on Sunday to comply. His dramatic arrival had brought the startled deputies out onto the balconies, some fearing that parliament was about to be summarily dissolved, or that they would all be arrested.

On returning to the residency, Allenby and Clark Kerr fearfully read over the text which the Foreign Office and the Cabinet had approved. It was significantly different in tone from the demands just presented by Allenby: there was no demand for a fine, the Gezira issue was much less stringent, and another clause much less extensive. It was not a text which found much favour with Allenby and Clark Kerr, and so they remained unrepentant about their actions. In any case, they had a well-prepared excuse regarding the lateness of the Foreign Office message.

It seems clear that Clark Kerr was quite at one with Allenby in this matter and, indeed, may well have been the driving force. In London, at the Foreign Office, it was the common opinion that 'Bull' Allenby had suffered another bout of temper and that he, alone, was responsible for going beyond his brief. In a sense Clark Kerr was glad that the occasion had arisen, however tragic the circumstances, through which Zaghlul could be forced from office. He had no doubt that Zaghlul would have to resign and the beauty of it all was that it had all come to pass without any direct involvement from Clark Kerr.

This is to assume that the gravity and strength of the British response was both justifiable and apposite. As the London reaction suggests, there was no real consensus even in British circles regarding the correct policy to be adopted against Zaghlul's Government. However, if *The Times* viewpoint was in any way indicative of official opinion, it seems obvious that there was nonetheless a general feeling that Zaghlul and his supporters were, through their relentless agitation and declamatory rhetoric, in some way morally responsible for the murder of Stack. Within Egypt this was vigorously disputed: not only was Zaghlul a peaceable character, firmly opposed to political violence, but this very assassination served to do him immense harm and, far from serving his cause, dealt him a shattering blow. His supporters could not believe that he could be held responsible in any way, and were immediately suspicious that the crime had been deliberately planned to discredit his government.[41] They suspected that most of the political violence in Egypt was being orchestrated largely by external forces sympathetic to the former Khedive, Abbas Hilmi. This was a view which had been supported in the past by Clark Kerr and Delaney.

Why Clark Kerr took such a different view on this occasion can be explained by various factors. Firstly, and crucially, Clark Kerr had been awaiting for some time an opportunity to act against Zaghlul. Although circumstances were not perfect, the chance was too great to pass up. While only a week before he had been prepared to leave things be and watch the cabinet self-destruct, the assassination had changed things utterly. The situation demanded strong action and also created the political climate in which other thorny matters, such as foreign officials' pensions, could be pushed through to a settlement. Secondly, there had been a very hostile and vengeful response from the British community in Egypt to the murder and, coupled with the long-standing criticisms of Allenby's 'pussy-footing', that amounted to very heavy pressure on the Residency to take stiff action. Lastly, the very fact that the Governor-General of the Sudan had been killed naturally associated the crime very closely with Zaghlul's agitation and demands regarding that territory. It did indeed appear that hotheads, inspired and sustained by the Zaghlulist vision, had taken the law into their own hands and disposed of the British figurehead in the Sudan in a brutal and bloody manner.

The combination of all these factors makes Clark Kerr's action seem more understandable. What is less easy to grasp is the reasoning which led him so confidently and strongly to oppose and exceed clear Foreign Office guidelines. And this behaviour was by no means over. On Sunday afternoon, 23 November, the Egyptian Government replied to Allenby's demands, through the Minister of Foreign Affairs, Wassef Bey Ghali. While expressing horror and regret at the crime, and agreeing to pay the indemnity, Zaghlul refused to accept responsibility and rejected the other demands tabled the previous day.

Allenby's reply was immediate and fierce. It ought to be remembered at this point that the Foreign Office, while prepared to support Allenby's note to Zaghlul which had been delivered in terms somewhat removed from what they had intended, had now made clear the general parameters of action within which Allenby could act. Clearly, the irrigation matter could not be pursued, nor issues regarding the employment and severance pay for foreign officials. The Foreign Office considered both to be of no relevance to the Sirdar's death, and thought it unfair to tie them in with the main issue.

Yet within an hour and a half of Zaghlul's reply, Allenby told Zaghlul that as a result of his failure to comply fully with British demands, instructions were being sent to the Sudan to effect the removal of all Egyptian officers and army units from that country, and that the Sudan Government was now at liberty to increase the area to be irrigated in the Gezira scheme to 'an unlimited figure'.[42] This last move was utterly at variance with the instructions of the Foreign Secretary, Austen Chamberlain, and was tantamount to threatening to cut off the Egyptian water supply. This was certainly how it was viewed both in Egypt and Britain.[43] As if such a threat were not draconian enough, Allenby even proposed taking nationalist prisoners from the jails and using them as hostages, shooting them at intervals if any further attacks on British or foreign nationals occurred.[44] Fortunately, Allenby heeded Chamberlain's absolute refusal to sanction such drastic action.

As Allenby's senior adviser, Clark Kerr was both acquiescent in, and responsible for, all of the Residency's actions. Apart from these moves, Allenby ordered marines from naval vessels, which had been moved to Alexandria, to seize the tobacco customs at Alexandria as guarantee for the fulfilment of the other conditions.[19] (Significantly, this was the very move hypothetically discussed by Delaney and Clark Kerr only a few weeks before.) This was carried out on Monday 24 November without waiting for Chamberlain's approval. Chamberlain had questioned the wisdom of the customs seizure, and now had to order Allenby explicitly not to proceed to declare Martial Law without Cabinet permission.[46]

There was no chance of Zaghlul agreeing to these British conditions, but nor could he afford to bring any more of Allenby's wrath down on his countrymen. In this hopeless position, but at least with some dignity and his integrity intact, Zaghlul had no option other than to go to King Fuad in the Abdin Palace and tender his resignation, although he did announce that Egypt would appeal to the League of Nations over Britain's threats. Later that evening, the former President of the Senate, Ziwar Pasha, accepted the premiership and, with his reputation of being friendly to Britain, there came hope of a relaxation and settlement.

At the Foreign Office in London there was growing unease. Chamberlain now feared, with considerable justification, that Allenby was embarked on a private campaign of revenge, paying less and less heed to official instructions. It also appeared manifest that the Counsellor to the Residency, the senior career diplomat on the ground, Archibald Clark Kerr, was either acting in complicity with Allenby, or powerless to control Allenby's behaviour and unable to persuade him of the rightness and force of the Foreign Office line. The situation was indeed serious, compounded by an alleged paucity of communication from Allenby, about which Chamberlain complained.[47] Not only had the original ultimatum been deliberately presented in a form unsanctioned by Chamberlain, but now the Alexandria customs had been seized in the heat of the moment without official permission.[48] Further, the continuation of the threats regarding the Egyptian water supply was completely out of line. In defence, Allenby later claimed, as did Clark Kerr, that the execution of that threat was not one they seriously contemplated but one merely delivered to effect Zaghlul's resignation, and open the way for the emergence of a more amenable administration, with whom compromise could be reached.[49] Chamberlain rejected this justification, pointing out that such a threat, so obviously empty, was valueless. Even Allenby, claimed Chamberlain, admitted that the threat was 'evidently to an informed and intelligent examiner an unreal one'.[50] Allenby, with these new orders regarding the increase of the irrigation to an 'unlimited degree', had, however, gone no small way to turning that 'unreal' threat into dangerous reality. That Clark Kerr was in full agreement with all of Allenby's actions is difficult to believe, and yet it is not only a fact, but one of which he was proud. Even his former 'soul-mate' Ramsay MacDonald, now in the Opposition, sought to distance himself. In the course of that hectic weekend he criticised the tenor of Allenby's original ultimatum, naturally unaware that it had also been the target of Foreign Office criticism, and objected strongly to the threat to the water supply. Speaking at Port Talbot, MacDonald said that 'the great mistake was that we mixed a just and proper indignation against murder with certain political matters that could only be settled by agreement' and he 'regretted that in the ultimatum Egypt had been threatened with a reduction of her water supply'.[51] However, another ex-Prime Minister, Herbert Asquith, still in Cairo, fully supported the Allenby line and wrote to Chamberlain in those terms.[52]

Chamberlain, following Allenby's unilateral action on customs seizure, was now facing the real danger that Allenby, flirting with insubordination, would run wild altogether. Chamberlain felt that he had to act quickly to rein him in, but in such a discreet way as not to lessen his perceived authority in Egypt and his standing in Egyptian eyes. What he chose to do was not in itself injudicious but it was handled in an insensitive and ill-considered manner. Just as Zaghlul was resigning, and thereby lessening tension and putting an end to any further sorties from Allenby, Chamberlain, unaware, decided to send out to Cairo a Foreign Office representative ostensibly to brief Allenby, but in reality to render assistance to Clark Kerr in controlling Allenby and preventing further temperamental over-reaction. Accordingly, Austen Chamberlain arranged for Nevile Henderson, a diplomatic acquaintance of Clark Kerr's from their days at Scoon's together, to be sent out to Cairo to apprise Allenby more fully of the views of His Majesty's Government. This decision was reported to Allenby on the morning of Tuesday 25 November. There had been no prior consultation about Henderson's role, nor the nature of his mission, but Chamberlain claimed in the wire to Allenby that he had 'explained to him [Henderson] verbally with a completeness which is not possible in telegraphic communication the objects at which HMG are arriving and the difficulties which they wish to avoid'.[53] As it turned out, this was some way different from the truth: Henderson had been recalled hurriedly from holiday, had no prior knowledge or experience of Egypt, and had only had a mere half-hour briefing from Austen Chamberlain before being packed off to Egypt. His real function was clearly no more than to act as a warning to Allenby. By not laying any groundwork to prepare either Allenby or Egypt for the announcement of Henderson's appointment, Chamberlain failed to anticipate and scotch the inevitable rumours which would, and did, begin to circulate in Egypt. It was seen as marking a change in British policy and interpreted as supercession, at least in part, of Allenby's authority.[54] Clark Kerr informed his mother:

> The FO have been yelping at us... and have finally ended in biting us and in ruining Lord Allenby's position by appointing Nevile Henderson to Cairo and thus publicly giving the impression of want of confidence or change of policy.

Even more careless was Chamberlain's failure to appreciate the dire consequences of appointing Henderson, as he did, to the rank of Minister. He failed to see that this would effectively demote Clark Kerr and badly affect morale.

Clark Kerr was furious when he heard of Henderson's title as Minister, a move which would demote Clark Kerr to number three in the Residency ranking order. He complained bitterly to Allenby to try to get the appointment stopped or at least to have his own position clarified. At first Allenby seems not to have been fully aware of the implications of Henderson's appointment: only through Clark Kerr's explanations did he come to see the effect on his own position also. Allenby first wired Chamberlain seeking an assurance that Henderson was not going to supersede the Counsellor 'in whom... I have complete confidence'.[55] Chamberlain replied in a cursory, insensitive way that there was no reflection on the Counsellor but that, as Minister, Henderson would naturally rank next to Allenby, and that this was no time to quibble on minor staffing issues.[56] Little wonder that Clark Kerr dubbed it 'a bloody telegram'. Allenby was incensed and on 27 November told Chamberlain, 'You have missed my point... Henderson's appointment is ruinous to the position of HM High Commissioner... It has already had a lamentably bad effect.' He therefore stated that in the circumstances, unless Henderson's appointment was made temporary – say for a week – it would be clear that Allenby no longer enjoyed the confidence of Chamberlain, and he would wish to resign his office as soon as it could be arranged.[57]

There followed a flurry of telegrams with Chamberlain trying to explain that Henderson's role was one of support and not supercession, and that in any case the posting was not a matter for debate. Even Chamberlain's cabinet colleagues, none of whom supported Allenby, recognised the hash Chamberlain was now making. Churchill, the Chancellor of the Exchequer, complained to Lord Birkenhead: 'Austen... has sent exactly the wrong answer and as usual is making the heaviest weather over the personal point'.[58] Chamberlain tried to make Allenby change his mind on the resignation matter, but Allenby was adamant that unless the remit of Henderson's mission was altered he had no other option:

> I have long experience here and I know that if you neglect my advice you are running into great peril'[59]

'I can see no way out of the difficulty unless you can arrange and announce that Mr Henderson only comes on a specific mission and for a very brief period.'[60]

Chamberlain was in no mood to compromise, although it would have been possible to do so had he not foolishly appointed Henderson to the rank of Minister, an appointment which could not be justified for a brief diplomatic mission. He refused to alter the terms of Henderson's posting, to which Allenby responded:

> Either you have confidence in me or you have not. Since you have made a striking appointment to my staff in the midst of a crisis without consulting me and published it without giving me the opportunity of expressing my opinion, I presume you have not.[61]

It was therefore his duty to resign and Chamberlain reluctantly agreed, on the twenty-ninth, to pass on Allenby's letter of resignation.

The British press were naturally quite unaware of these diplomatic fisticuffs, or indeed the sensation Henderson's appointment caused. *The Times* blithely commented that the Residency had been 'opportunely strengthened by the dispatch of Mr Nevile Henderson'.[62]

Unfortunately for both Allenby and Clark Kerr, their recent indiscretions put them in a poor position to challenge Chamberlain's judgement. He was able, at every turn, to point out their recent insubordination and tactical errors in a tetchy correspondence which ran on well into late December, by which time, almost unnoticed, Ziwar Pasha's Government had come to an agreement with Britain, parliament had been dissolved, dates for new elections set, and a short-lived mutiny amongst departing Egyptian officers in Khartoum put down.

Much to Chamberlain's chagrin, Henderson, feeling intensely awkward, wholeheartedly adopted the Allenby line once in Cairo. He argued in favour of his appointment being only brief, took the Residency line on the Gezira threat, gave evidence that his appointment was being viewed as signalling a change in British policy, and rounded it all off by baldly stating:

> There is no blinking the fact that my appointment has done a considerable amount of harm out here and rendered Lord Allenby's task more difficult than it was.[63]

Even with excisions, it was a most damning document for Chamberlain to lay before the Cabinet sub-committee dealing with Egypt. However, Chamberlain did have the odd support of the King, who had expressed grave concern to the Foreign Office after reading a report in *The Times* in which it was stated, in passing, that Allenby had been wearing a grey suit while on official business. This was a serious departure, apparently. The only other issue in the crisis to worry the King, apparently, was that he understood with concern some Egyptian flags were allowed to be flown, albeit below the Union Jack, on official buildings in the Sudan.[64] Even Chamberlain, glad of any support, did have to advise that Allenby may well have had good reasons for dressing the way he did.

For Clark Kerr, the whole situation was something akin to a tragedy. Barely a month after he had been at the dizzy heights in his role as acting High Commissioner, he was now merely number three, had offended the Foreign Office by being party to Allenby's bout of indiscipline, and was now embroiled in a nasty dispute between Allenby and the Foreign Secretary. It was a dispute in which there could only be one winner, and Clark Kerr was tainted at every stage by being seen as Allenby's ally. Worse still, some at the Foreign Office suspected his direct involvement in the issue of Allenby tendering his resignation.

In a letter to his mother, who was by now en route to Cairo with Muriel for a few months' visit, Clark Kerr recognised what it would all mean. However, he had no regrets: he felt he had done the right thing, and that was what he valued even more than diplomatic prestige and careerist advancement. He was ambitious, keenly so, but he did have principles which he would not abandon. He also respected Lord Allenby, admired his style, and fully supported his action. Despite the great differences in age, background and temperament, they had become firm friends. There was, of course, a heavy price to pay for all of this. Yet it was not so much noble principles which brought Clark Kerr down. If anything could be blamed it was that he had become too personally involved in Egyptian politics, become too eager to influence and shape Egypt's internal affairs, and too reluctant to let Egyptians run their own government when he saw it leading to trouble. In a sense, all the strategic planning and scheming with Delaney had momentarily distorted his vision: he had sought to fit reality to his long-term plans instead of *vice versa*. Clark Kerr could not bear to see all his hard work go to waste; he wanted to see a speedy and just outcome to all he had done regarding the constitution, the controlling of the King, and the creation of youthful democracy. He cared deeply for the future good of the Egyptian people. Unfortunately he cared not wisely but too much.

As the inevitable consequences of his actions fell into place, he was initially calmly untroubled:

> We have incurred the severe censure of the Foreign Office for what we did and how we did it... It was we who were responsible for (1) the fine (2) the extension of the area for irrigation in the Sudan (3) the right of officials to leave Egypt (4) the stopping of demonstrations. I do not wish in any way to escape full responsibility for any of those things. They may not improbably mean the disappearance of Lord Allenby from Egypt and for me a long twilight at some post where thinking and acting and taking risks will be superfluous. If it had all to be done again I should do it again in just the same way... if we have been weighed in the balances and found wanting all I can say is that the balance is not a true one.

Clark Kerr was fortunate in that Allenby, as the senior figure, attracted most of the Foreign Office obloquy. Clark Kerr, while taking some flak for suspected collusion with Allenby's recklessness, was generally spared the full brunt of the mandarins' wrath. Nevertheless, the fact that he had failed to control Allenby, and possibly pushed Allenby into resignation over his own effective demotion, stood against him. As Clark Kerr fully recognised, punishment would be forthcoming, most likely in the form of a posting to some diplomatic *cul-de-sac* far from the public eye. On top of this, there was some displeasure in the Foreign Office at the cool reception Henderson had received in Cairo. In the circumstances it was hardly surprising, but it is clear from his memoirs that although Henderson himself was most apologetic for the problems his arrival created, and not the sort of person to force himself on the Residency, he did hold Clark Kerr responsible for orchestrating the frosty welcome he had experienced and the icy treatment which followed.[65]

There was, indeed, to be no doubt about Foreign Office thinking on Clark Kerr's behaviour during the debacle. In January 1925, Nigel Ronald, an acquaintance of Clark Kerr's, reported to him in a private letter on the Whitehall reaction to the Egyptian crisis:

> I hope you have survived the opprobrium poured on you over recent troubles. In case you do not know it – you should realise that oceans of mud were thrown at you and Sir Eyre Crowe [the Permanent Under Secretary] was very cross with you.

Meanwhile, the political *imbroglio* within Egypt became even more confusing. Following the dissolution of parliament in late December pending elections planned for March, the King set about taking advantage of the hiatus by seeking to increase his own powers and to undermine the whole parliamentary process. He set up an unashamedly pro-royalist party under Yehia Ibrahim which could be manipulated for his own autocratic purposes. Zaghlul, meanwhile, was fighting the election on the question of Ziwar Pasha's unconstitutional role in the dissolution of parliament in the first place. However, the very real danger posed by the King's intrigues brought even Zaghlul to indicate that he was looking to Great Britain to protect the Egyptian people from the King's tyrannical bent. It was indeed a bizarre change of circumstances where Zaghlul Pasha, the uncompromising nationalist, was actually proposing that Great Britain remain in Egypt for a time to preserve the constitution. At long last, political affairs appeared to be moving in Britain's favour.

In the event, the elections of 12 March represented a check to Zaghlul, whose supporters lost over 100 seats, including those of four cabinet ministers. When parliament met on 23 March the existing non-Zaghlulist Government of Ziwar Pasha and Sidky Pasha was able to continue with a majority of four. However, when a vote for Prime Minister was taken in the chamber, there was an overwhelming vote for Zaghlul Pasha! This was clearly unacceptable to Britain, and King Fuad refused to accept it, dissolving parliament once more instead.[66]

Clark Kerr became more hopeful of a settlement, and reacted angrily when Sir Sheldon Amos, now retired, wrote from London to say that Clark Kerr would be as well moving to a new post since there was no more reputation to be made in Egypt. Infuriated, Clark Kerr scrawled across the letter: 'My God! When will they realise that it isn't a question of reputation-making? I am interested in the business and believe a solution to be possible.' Clearly, he was still taking a personal, as well as professional, interest in Egyptian affairs. It was, in fact, quite unrealistic for Clark Kerr to suppose that with a new High Commissioner and Henderson still in place, there could be any role for him in Egypt. Indeed, in early March he had been assured by Selby from London that Austen Chamberlain had 'carefully borne your claims in mind and has reserved a good Counsellorship to offer you when the time comes'. Clark Kerr had requested on private grounds that the post would not be too remote, mentioning Constantinople as his fancy, but fearing a tropical backwater instead. His mother and sister Muriel were still with him; the private reasons for wanting a handy posting were simply that he did not wish to be sent to some far-distant legation where he would have his mother, now in her frail seventies, to support.

At this time of considerable personal anxiety came yet another family tragedy. His sister Muriel, barely forty years old, and who had only lately returned to England from Cairo, took ill and died quite suddenly. She had been the sister closest to Clark Kerr, and he took the shock badly. As the two unmarried members of the family, they had naturally been more in each other's company, but she had been a true friend and genuine support for him over many years. Quite apart from that, she had been his mother's helpmeet for a long time, and Clark Kerr now would have to cope on his own.

CHAPTER 5

Corrie 1925–37

Towards the end of May, Clark Kerr got word of his new post: Counsellor in the Tokyo Embassy. Japan was hardly the 'not too remote' posting he had requested and, given that his mother would now be dependent on him, personally quite inconvenient. It also represented no promotion, but merely a sideways move. In the absence of any alternative, Clark Kerr accepted it and returned home for a few months' leave before departure. It was yet another painful parting in so many ways. Besides his own mixed feelings, tinged with so much disappointment and personal sadness, there were the genuinely touching expressions of regret from many Egyptians, even those with whom he had wrangled for so long, who could not fail to recognise that Clark Kerr had a real and profound interest in the good of Egypt.

As he embarked at Alexandria in mid-June, Clark Kerr could reflect on three torrid years, the peaks and the troughs. Undoubtedly he was leaving under a cloud, the result of his indiscretions in November. Yet there was much of merit that he had achieved, not the least of which, in retrospect, was his establishing of a solid reputation in Labour Party ranks where he was credited, as Harold Nicolson had rightly anticipated, with having been the liberal realist and pragmatist to Allenby's wild imperialism. It was, of course, somewhat adrift from reality, but it was a perception which would do Clark Kerr much good in the future. His astute friend Gerald Delaney wrote to him:

> It is considered that a Labour Ministry may well assume power in a couple of years and then you will get your opportunity. You must remember that you are well known now. You have made excellent friends everywhere, particularly among the

Press and this is going to help you a very great deal. It is the FO that has failed and not you, and most people know it.

The thought of London brought not only grieving family images to mind but also concerns about the Foreign Office. While there was no flinching in his belief that he had acted correctly all along, he knew full well that he had not followed orders and that exile to Japan was due punishment for such sin. He now viewed the Foreign Office with an unholy mixture of distaste, contempt, trepidation and embarrassment. He had felt distaste for their treatment of his career over many years, even prior to the refusal to let him enlist in the early years of the Great War; contempt for such figures as Austen Chamberlain, Walford Selby, Jack Murray and the treacherous William Tyrrell. Yet he was also a little embarrassed at his own excesses and a little in fear of how he might be treated on arrival in Whitehall.

Once in London, Clark Kerr gave the Foreign Office a wide berth, although he did see to it, as he put it, that Tyrrell and Selby got to know 'that I thought they had behaved like complete shits'. He did have a chance to speak to John Buchan, something of an eminence grise, whom he found cordial enough but very guarded and mysterious about the FO's future plans for Clark Kerr. Buchan said that the Japan posting would not be for very long, only a year or so, and that only as a sop to the traditions of the service as it was felt that he had been in the limelight too long and that a short spell in the shade was requisite. Clark Kerr was thereby given some hope that his stock at the Foreign Office would not be low indefinitely, but it was all rather uncertain and vague for a forty-three year old diplomat with 20 years' service.

Arriving at Inverchapel in mid-July, Clark Kerr spent some time considering his future. Reflecting on the totality of his position, he came to the conclusion that he simply ought to leave the service and look for some more promising commercial opening. He made several none-too-discreet inquiries, having in mind some role as a company representative in Egypt, or at least in some foreign posting where his experience, contacts and linguistic skills could be put to good use. In actual fact, although he represented otherwise, there does not seem to have been much progress made. The only definite position offered carried a mere £500 salary which would not do. It was perhaps a natural pride which prevented Clark Kerr confessing to the failure of his attempts to procure a commercial post for himself, but around this time, too, Clark Kerr became involved in another much more public, and somewhat silly, misrepresentation of the truth.

In 1925, he had for the first time been listed in *Who's Who*. When his entry in the following years was fleshed out, it proved to be misleading in part, and plainly false in another. For a start, he gave his date of birth as 'March 17th, 1887', making himself out to be five years younger than he really was. This false information Clark Kerr continued to supply for several years until, as was surely inevitable for one in public life, the truth was discovered, after which he simply omitted to enter any date of birth at all. It was a rather stupid thing to have done, especially for one so mature, and merely exposed him to social gossip and ridicule, and provided needless ammunition for those who were either jealous of his success, mistrusted him, or disliked his politics.[1]

Quite why Clark Kerr supplied this false information cannot now be explained incontrovertibly, but there are two likely reasons. On the one hand, there is the possibility that as an extremely ambitious and thrusting diplomat he was keen to be seen to have been successful at at even younger age than was the fact. From a very early stage in his career he had set his sights high, and consequently took very keenly any setback or delay in what he considered to be rightful promotion. It is therefore quite possible that he wished to show himself in a favourable light in this regard. The one flaw in this analysis is that misrepresenting his age in *Who's Who* was hardly likely to further his career, since it would not feature in the deliberations at the Foreign Office where, in any event, his true age was well known and recorded.

The more credible option is that it merely sprang from vanity and a worrying consciousness of encroaching middle age. Clark Kerr had always been very conscious of his physical appearance, his flaws and, as something of a fitness freak, tried to keep himself in peak, youthful, condition. He even resorted to dyeing his hair. More than anything he was troubled by his continuing bachelor status and that the chances of marriage were slipping by as he moved into his middle forties. It seems most likely that he merely altered his age to suit his physical appearance and make himself slightly more eligible a bachelor.

As to the other details he supplied to *Who's Who*, they are mostly accurate, although there is evidence of both coyness and minor misrepresentation. The coyness surrounded his educational background, which he entered as 'Educated privately', a phrase he was to continue to employ for the rest of his days. He had been uneasy about Bath College for many years in a slightly snobbish way: he felt that it was an unfashionable and underrated establishment. During his early years in the service he had been upset that the school was so little recognised and he constantly fretted that it would prosper, expand and acquire a good reputation on the public school circuit. Ever since the school's collapse, he had been careful not to mention, or at least publicise, his association with this failed enterprise. In later years, he made much instead of 'travelling the continent with a tutor' to cover these years, and also overplayed his brief attendance at Bonn University.[2] Many who knew Clark Kerr discount the idea that there was any snobbery in his make-up: what does seem to be the case is that he was very sensitive to the snobbish attitudes of others, and tried to cover up anything which might expose himself to sneering comment from these quarters.

Clark Kerr was also similarly reticent about his birthplace: there was no mention of Australia whatsoever. Instead, there was considerable play made of his connections with Scotland, although he had not been born there, had not been educated there, and had never lived there other than for short vacational breaks. The connection was boldly established in his *Who's Who* entry by styling his father 'John Kerr Clark of Crossbasket, Hamilton'. This was slightly misleading, not least in the sense that his father had not lived there since very early manhood, and the property had been out of Clark family hands for 40 years. It also led people to believe that he, too, must have been born at Crossbasket. Later he even named it as 'Crossbasket Castle' in his *Burke's Peerage* entry. It is fair to say that by parentage Clark Kerr was about as Scottish as it is possible to be, but this does not disguise the obvious insecurity he felt about his Australian roots. At every turn Clark Kerr sought to emphasise his Scottish background: the very assumption of the surname 'Kerr' had itself been motivated by a desire to forge a more definite Scottish identity.

One result of this was that in later times, when his Australian background did emerge, it was laid to his charge that he had deliberately covered up the matter and attempted to mislead people.[3] In addition, the rather grand references to Crossbasket led people to believe that his own property in Scotland amounted to a massive country seat nestling amidst countless acres of woodland, hills and heather. Again, when the true proportions of his home at Inverchapel were discovered, people felt, justifiably, that he had sought to exaggerate and mislead. Certainly the snobbery of others is evident in the way that the Inverchapel property was snootily referred to as a 'roadside bungalow'. It was something rather more than that, yet, given the modesty of its proportions, it does seem rather silly of Clark Kerr to have spoken of it as being some baronial splendour, which he evidently did.[5] To be fair to Clark Kerr, it ought to be remembered that Inverchapel Lodge was only designed as the estate manager's residence, and that the main dwelling-house – a mansion of major proportions – was planned for a plot just above the mouth of the Inverchapel burn.

In September 1925 career events took an unexpected turn for the better. Out of the blue, Selby wrote from Geneva offering Clark Kerr promotion to Minister at the Guatemala Legation, instead of going to Japan. Clark Kerr had little hesitation in accepting this welcome surprise, even although it was a move to a far-flung outpost of little importance. A few days later he got official notification of his promotion to the rank of Counsellor – he had only been acting in Egypt – and fuller details of his post. Not until December would he be officially promoted to the rank of Minister, becoming one of the youngest diplomats at that time to hold such a rank. The Legation in Guatemala was very small, there being only a clerk besides the Minister, but he was also informed that he was to be accredited to the republics of Nicaragua, Honduras and Salvador.

Clark Kerr returned to Scotland for part of October, before finally travelling to London, via Edinburgh, at the beginning of November. This was the occasion of a most fortuitous meeting which was to give him an unrivalled opportunity to square things with his Foreign Office masters. At Waverley Station, as he waited for the London train he was unexpectedly, and loudly, hailed – 'There goes Egypt!' – by an ebullient Winston Churchill, then Chancellor of the Exchequer, who was also travelling south. Churchill and he dined together, with the former waxing lyrical on the previous year's events in Egypt. To Clark Kerr's considerable surprise, Churchill began thumping the table to emphasise his points about the Foreign Office's behaviour: 'From the start I told them you were right. They were after you like a pack of wolves. You! But I backed you up... I didn't put up the same defence for that poop Allenby... do you know what they wanted you to do? To go and ask for your ultimatum back and to give Zaghlul theirs instead!' So he continued, obviously convinced that Clark Kerr was wholly at one with Churchill's own rather reactionary imperial outlook. Nevertheless, having Churchill as an ally was to give Clark Kerr considerable influence. Churchill had heard that Clark Kerr was to be transferred and promised to do all he could to help him. He thundered on, 'And now I hear they are kicking you out to China [sic]. That won't do. I've had one talk with Austen about you and I'll see him again when I get to London.' Chamberlain had told Churchill that their impression was that Clark Kerr had put Allenby up to resign. 'I ought to tell you,' confided Churchill, 'that there was a moment last year when we thought that you in Cairo were not playing the game.'

Churchill was as good as his word, however, and following his new chat with Chamberlain reported to Clark Kerr that the black mark had now been removed. This was confirmed when Clark Kerr met Chamberlain at the Foreign Office for a talk, albeit a frosty one, on 19 November. Churchill went even further and arranged a dinner date with Lloyd George, and later invited Clark Kerr to lunch at 11 Downing Street where Sir William Tyrrell, Clark Kerr's hate-figure, was also a guest. At the close of the meal, Churchill got Clark Kerr and Tyrrell together. Putting his arm round Sir William, Churchill was at his most disarmingly chummy: 'Beaver, I want this young man to feel that he can go away happy. I want him to feel he has friends here on whom he can count. He knows he has got a friend at the Treasury. I want him to know he has one at the Foreign Office.' Whatever his inner thoughts may have been, Tyrrell had no option but to assure Clark Kerr and Churchill that all was well and bygones were truly bygones.

It was ironic that Winston Churchill of all people should prove to be Clark Kerr's guardian. Clark Kerr had been nothing if not consistent in his distaste for Churchill and his views over the years. Still, Clark Kerr now found himself in an excellent position: not only had his troubles with the Foreign Office been smoothed over, but he was now held in high regard by no less a person than the Chancellor of the Exchequer, on whom he could clearly now depend for full support. In addition, he had numerous admirers within the ranks of the Labour Party, chief of whom was Ramsay MacDonald himself. Almost by accident, Clark Kerr now found himself well respected in both political parties, for bizarrely contradictory reasons. Furthermore, there were several other MPs on whom he could rely for both information and support: Bob Boothby and Lord Colum Stuart, his former Scots Guards colleagues; Lord Eustace Percy, MP for Hastings and President of the Board of Education; David Balneil; and the Astors, J.J. and Nancy. There were also numerous characters on the fringes of Westminster with whom he was on excellent terms and who had influence in Whitehall, such as John Buchan, and R.B. Cunninghame Graham, a founder of the Scottish Labour Party, who was now involved in the infant National Party of Scotland.

Departure for Guatemala was finally organised for 25 November. His mother and the servants would travel too; with Muriel no longer there, Mrs Kerr Clark's future was now inextricably linked to Archie's. In fact it was decided that the family home in Great Cumberland Place should now be disposed of, and that she simply make her home with Clark Kerr wherever in the world it might be.

And so he took leave of Britain once more. Although still a little tender over the Egyptian debacle, he was reasonably settled in his mind and looking forward to this new part of the world with some relish. There were unlikely to be any grave political matters to keep him active and, indeed, the most pressing matters seemed to be those of keeping Winston Churchill well supplied with butterflies for his collection and the Royal Botanic Gardens with orchids and other exotic Latin American flora. The long voyage gave him another chance to reflect on his position: it was considerably better than a sideways move to Japan would have been, and he had the tentative promise of a better post after a brief period in his Central American purgatory.

Once settled into the residency in Guatemala, Clark Kerr lost no time in undertaking a lengthy tour of duty, which was in fact essential as he had to present his credentials in Honduras, Nicaragua and Salvador. The main foreign influence in these parts was the USA and much of Clark Kerr's reports during his period in the region concerned the political situations of each state and the American efforts, often heavy-handed, to interfere. It was not something which Clark Kerr found very appealing, and quite often his reports were very critical of the American undermining of the various regimes. In fact, when he had arrived in the area he was viewed by the State Department as being 'violently anti-American'. This opinion appeared to have originated in Cairo, having as its source an American there who bore a grudge. In any event, Clark Kerr was able to arrange things so that the State Department became convinced that the report must have been false. It was indeed fortunate that Clark Kerr got to know of the State Department view, through the alert British consul in Tegucigalpa, as such a report could have done him great damage in the long run.

After the cauldron of Egypt, it was little surprise that Clark Kerr very quickly found the post rather boring. While there was political ferment in Honduras and a simmering revolution in Nicaragua to keep his eye on, it was quite unlike Egypt in that he had no role whatsoever except that of local observer. It was a situation he found frustrating.

The general loneliness which Clark Kerr was experiencing in his new post was rendered meaningless by yet another tragic blow in the summer of 1926. On the night of 6 July, after a mild illness, his mother passed away peacefully in her room at the legation. Clark Kerr decided immediately that she ought to be taken home to Inverchapel for burial beside his father and Muriel. Accordingly he set sail with her remains on 16 July, and the burial took place at Inverchapel on 6 August. Returning alone to Central America was naturally a sad occasion for Clark Kerr, but it was also tinged by the added feeling that the whole family line was beginning to disappear. He had always been extremely interested in the Clark family history and, alone on the ancestral land at Loch Eck, he could not help but be keenly aware that he was now the last male Kerr Clark. His father, brother, mother and two sisters were now dead. There was no young Kerr Clark male left; alone at Inverchapel with his grief, Archie was in effect the last of the line. Indeed, were it not for his own sterling efforts, even the foothold the family now had at Inverchapel would have long since gone. Certainly there were still three sisters alive, but with husbands and children of their own they were naturally less clearly identified now with the Clark family.

Clark Kerr refused to let his exile depress him overmuch, and remained ostensibly optimistic during his Latin American penance. To Bob Boothby – significantly now Churchill's Private Secretary – he wrote of his activities:

> I am determined not to grumble, and so I write boyish despatches about local politics and I dig in my garden and of course I sulk... I feel sure that you are a coming man... and so am I still.

Boothby was a valuable friend and contact at this time. Clark Kerr took an avuncular interest in his career, but there is no doubt that he also valued and shared many of Boothby's political opinions. In particular, they felt the same about the General Strike: both had hoped for a society with much closer links between capital and labour, and saw the circumstances which led to the strike as disastrous. Both blamed Tory 'diehards' for political folly and myopia.

Yet as 1927 progressed, Clark Kerr's restlessness grew, and he became more and more anxious about his next posting. As the Foreign Office silence continued, the nagging obsession that they still bore a grudge against him surfaced once more. A less equable note about his situation and his future with the Foreign Office begins to creep into his notes to Boothby: '... they rather expect me to grumble and I like to be able to say sucks', he was writing in May 1927, but had to confess, 'I have not enough to occupy me and it isn't much fun'. The letter ends with a rather despairing plea to be remembered to Churchill. Another correspondent, Eustace Percy, still a cabinet minister, sought to reassure him that there was no such grudge and that his chances of promotion were not being prejudiced. Yet, so far from the centre of things, Clark Kerr was naturally unable fully to shrug off his suspicions. Eventually, in December, the Foreign Office offered him the post of Minister to Chile, not a promotion, but certainly a more prestigious post. He was not to take any leave between posts but was to proceed straight to Chile, where he arrived in late March, complete with his entourage of servants, and his big Alsatian dog, Hodge.

Chile proved to be an enjoyable posting. It was not simply that it was a bigger and more important legation, but also that Britain was held in some regard in Chile. Thus, the post of British Minister was both eminent and influential. It was exactly the kind of role in which Clark Kerr flourished. While he would doubtless have preferred to have been posted to one of the great European capitals, in Santiago there was at least, for once, a very pro-British atmosphere in which to operate, which made the job all the more rewarding and pleasurable. He soon became a popular figure, not just among the sizable British population but also in government and diplomatic circles.

The work itself was not very taxing, although there were always numerous social tasks which the British Minister was called upon to fulfil. There were gatherings to attend, events to open, speeches to be made. Clark Kerr had never relished public speaking but familiarity with it bred a form of stoic endurance.

One such speech he had to make was to the St Andrew's Society of Valparaiso on 30 November 1928. Clark Kerr's written notes – in copperplate quill with the long Germanic 's' twisting throughout – still survive, and are interesting for the insight they give into his sense of Scottishness. Certainly the speech was tailored to suit the expectations of the emigré audience but there is no doubting the underlying sincerity. There is more than a mere hint of the 'kailyard' in several sections, but then again two things have to be remembered in this regard. First of all, Scottish national feeling was still very much adolescent at this point, groping its way out of Victorian 'North Britain', and it would indeed have been remarkable if Clark Kerr's awareness of Scottish identity had not been tainted with the prevalent Harry Lauderism. Secondly, Clark Kerr's own experience of Scotland was largely that of the country house weekend and the grouse moor: a latifundian retreat flowing with trout and whisky. He had only lately purchased any property in Scotland and had no personal contact with ordinary Scots and their real lives. Not surprisingly much of his knowledge of Scotland and the Scots came merely from literature, and the popular Scottish literature of his early days had been that of the 'kailyard' school, novels and stories of rustic sentimentality somewhat detached even from the reality of their own time.

It was essentially a humorous and light-hearted speech, fitted to the occasion, which went down very well. He spent some time initially mentioning all the good things and great people which Scotland had given to England – the Duchess of York was one he listed – but he climaxed with the gift of the Red Clydesiders to the English 'for their purification in the House of Commons'. Much of the speech was in similar vein. However, he did touch on what it meant to him, and others, to be Scottish.

> Wherever he lives and however deep the roots he sticks into the ground here and there, the heart of the Scot is always in Scotland. I speak not only of him who was born and brought up in that bonnie land, but also of the Scot who has never had the happiness of either of these things. For him, nevertheless, Scotland is always home, though maybe he has never even been there. For him the pull is just as

strong. It is clearly something in the blood, something that has been given by his father or his mother. For the fortunate ones it is the memory of many things they have seen with their eyes and felt with their hearts. For some it is the castle and the tall streets of Auld Reekie washed in sunlight; for others it is the mists and smoke and those amber sunsets of Glasgow, the majesty of her Clyde... For some again it is the granite, the cloisters, and the draughts – or shall I call it the song of the winds? – at St Andrew's.

For others it is the silver sweep of the Tweed as she passes Melrose or Dryburgh. For some it is the window in Thrums and for others it is the whisky. Whatever it be, it catches our hearts and makes us sad and happy at the same time. For me it is the calling of the curlew – the crying of sheep at the time of the gathering – the sound of a hundred burns – the sight of some Highland Mary calling the cattle home – or 'shooing the coos' – whichever you like – the turn of the road whence you catch the first glimpse of the long and lonely loch – a small and ever lessening group of people who still call me 'Master Airchie' – that large flyblown bottle of black or striped balls in the window of the village shop. Scones and honey for tea. For all of us these are things which make Scotland for us quite unlike any other place in the world – slight and simple things and yet so strong and so compelling that, as I said, we feel obliged to hug ourselves, as it were, over them, even at the risk of appearing ridiculous and sentimental and even perhaps offensive to the English.

If there was mawkishness, it can perhaps be understood not only in the terms mentioned above regarding Clark Kerr's experience, but also in the fact that he had not been home for nearly four years, except for the brief, upsetting trip to bury his mother at Inverchapel. Again, his acute and recurring awareness of his family's diminishing numbers comes through in the reference to the 'ever lessening group' who knew him intimately. Scotland was for him gradually becoming a place more associated with family loss and death. Inverchapel was not just his country retreat and a place to shoot and fish. It was also the last resting-place of his family, a family which was fast dying out, as far as Clark Kerr could see.

The momentous event of Clark Kerr's time in Chile was one which came as a surprise in every way. While on holiday at an exclusive beach resort, Clark Kerr fell in love with a beautiful young Chilean girl. According to the story which went the rounds, it was Hodge who first took an interest in her, and as Clark Kerr went to call his dog away he too became attracted by the shape of her neck as she sunbathed a little way from him on the sand. They were introduced, and soon began courting. She was Maria Theresa Diaz Salas, the daughter of a millionaire from a distinguished Chilean family. At eighteen, she was 29 years younger than Clark Kerr, and at 5 foot 1 inch in height, some ten inches shorter than he was. She was reputed to be the most beautiful girl in Santiago, a rare blonde, educated in France, refined, cultured and stylish. At ten, she had suffered a mild attack of polio and it took two years of patient work with her uncle, a surgeon, before she was able to walk freely again.[5]

At forty-seven, Clark Kerr had no time to lose, and now perhaps equally as important no mother to consider or placate: romance blossomed, and much to the surprise and delight of all who knew him, he and Maria Theresa announced their engagement, and were married, a little over a month later on 24 April.

Immediately after their marriage, Clark Kerr and Tita, as she was known, set sail for England, where they arrived in mid-summer. They were something of a sensation on the social circuit of that summer: Clark Kerr, bronzed, barrel-chested, but undeniably thinning on top; on his arm, Tita, the tiny, blonde, stunningly attractive Chilean teenager. She was presented at court in late June, simply the start of a bewildering cycle of social engagements which filled their diaries until their return to Chile in October.

There were some hopes that his wilderness years of post-Egyptian exile might be over, but nothing tangible transpired. Indeed Harold Nicolson, who had just resigned from the service, was incensed when Clark Kerr was passed over for the post of Ambassador to Greece, which was then vacant. Like Clark Kerr, Harold had expected that the return of a Labour Government, albeit a minority one, after the election in June, and the welcome departure of the monocled Austen Chamberlain from the Foreign Office might signal a change in Clark Kerr's fortunes. Harold Nicolson voiced his dissatisfaction to the old Etonian Labour MP, Hugh Dalton, now Parliamentary Under-Secretary at the Foreign Office. Harold described the decision to overlook Clark Kerr as 'grotesque' and vowed to use his new role as a journalist on the *Evening Standard* to good effect.

By early 1930, however, Clark Kerr had been informed that he would be moving at last, although there was no definite destination for Clark Kerr as yet. He and Tita took final leave of Chile in August. It must have been quite a wrench for a young Chilean girl leaving her home and parents with little prospect of ever returning. There was still no word of where Clark Kerr was to be posted, but with a Labour Government in power and Ramsay MacDonald at the helm, he had every right to expect an upturn in his fortunes. The real lift to Clark Kerr's spirits, however, came with the confirmation that Tita was expecting a child. The prospect of becoming a father for the first time at forty-eight, and that an heir to Inverchapel was soon to be born, was a tremendous boost to him. For one who valued tradition and family so highly it was more than a joy to know that the Clark line was to continue and be restored to the hills and shores of Loch Eck.

What actually occurred on that voyage home to Britain cannot now be discovered in any detail. The tragic outcome is all that remains: a complication developed with the pregnancy, Tita fell gravely ill, and the child, a boy, did not survive. As Tita slowly recuperated, the couple's darkest fears were confirmed. Such was the nature of the problem that Tita would never be able to bear a child again. One can only guess at, but never fathom fully, the sorrow and pain which Clark Kerr and his young bride must have suffered. Yet tragedy always has seeds of consolation, however small. The death of the baby and the knowledge that their marriage would forever be childless, drew Clark Kerr and Tita even closer together, their shared loss uniting them in that love which surpasses understanding. It also created in Clark Kerr a great love for and interest in the young, a real regard for their needs, views and welfare, and these were virtues recognised and treasured by young people wherever he went in his later career.

When Clark Kerr did arrive back in London there was still no word of his next move. It was becoming not only unsettling but also most inconvenient as Inverchapel had been let on a long lease, just at a time when security and a period of peace were most needed. By November, when his leave was concluded, Clark Kerr was put on half-pay and was effectively unemployed. He did get the chance to have a long talk with Hugh Dalton, who was much impressed, and promised to exert what influence he could.

At the start of 1931, Clark Kerr and Tita went alone on a skiing holiday to Switzerland, and it was while they were there that Selby at last wired to confirm that Clark Kerr was to be the new Minister to Sweden. Although he expressed his delight and gratefulness, privately he was rather disappointed to have been despatched to such a relatively minor and unfashionable post.[6] It was not even an embassy, but a legation, and other than himself there would only be a First Secretary, an attaché and several military officials. It was quite definitely a minor role, but at least it brought him back to Europe.

Clark Kerr and Tita arrived in Stockholm in April 1931, where she became quite a sensation with Swedish society and the subject of regular features in magazines and journals. To others, Clark Kerr and Tita appeared a couple very much in love, although to outsiders Clark Kerr often seemed to treat her as a child. Life in Stockholm was not ideal, however: Clark Kerr found the Swedes a little too formal for his liking and viewed his social life as rather boring; Tita, for her part, although feted by the press as 'a rose in an icy climate', and by others as 'the pocket Venus', also struggled to settle. As she remarked to a friend, 'The three things I hate most in life are darkness, smoked fish, and bridge. That's what you get here.'[7] In this she was at one with Clark Kerr, who dubbed bridge 'the world's worst way of wasting time'.

As she grew more depressed, Clark Kerr and Tita agreed mutually that she should return to London for a break. Even Clark Kerr was finding Stockholm something of a struggle, and took to inviting a number of friends from England to stay and to attend various functions. By a regular flow of these visits, a fortuitous dual purpose was served: British influence in Sweden began to achieve some growth and Clark Kerr was spared boredom.

Although they had planned leave in June, Clark Kerr and Tita were also able to take a trip to Athens in the spring of 1932. Quite by chance a fellow-traveller on the ferry from Venice was the writer Virginia Woolf. She evidently had no idea who Clark Kerr was, which does certainly indicate that his vaunted status in literary and artistic London before the war must in reality have been quite insignificant.[8] Writing to her friend Vita Sackville-West, whose own husband Harold Nicolson had lately left the Diplomatic Service, Virginia Woolf paints a rather unflattering, but clearly objective, portrait of Archie Clark Kerr.

By the way, who is a sandy middle-aged red-faced ex-diplomat, married to an Italian wife, who was minister in Norway and talks at the top of his voice about Austen, Bill Bentinck, Lascelles, Billy Tyrrell and so on? He almost got on to you, but caught me listening and drew his horns in... Lord, how wearisome diplomatic talk is – d'you know Bill Bentinck, etc, etc. – you are well out of it.'

Virginia Woolf had clearly not been listening too closely, judging by the numerous factual errors regarding Clark Kerr and Tita, but as a first impression it must be accepted as a fair one. Given Clark Kerr's views on Austen Chamberlain and Sir William Tyrrell one can imagine that the air on the ferry must have been particularly blue.

Despite the excitement and success of an official visit to Sweden by the Prince of Wales, Clark Kerr grew more and more dissatisfied with his lot. Indeed, the Prince's visit had been something of a strain. A notoriously low tolerance of boredom meant an exhausting array of entertainments had to be served up for the Prince who, significantly, particularly wished to see any modern movies 'especially new German ones'. Hangovers which detained the Prince, pyjamaed, until noon were therefore a welcome relief for Clark Kerr, although he was left with having to stall the Swedish Crown Prince, who had naively paid an early morning visit. As Clark Kerr had christened him the 'most boring man in Europe' this awkward situation proved doubly trying.

But Clark Kerr was restless. At 51 he was a relatively successful diplomat, but Sweden was a dull post, failed to stretch him intellectually, gave his flamboyant nature no outlet, and had served to bore his wife so much that she spent more and more time in London. Of the Swedes, Clark Kerr had declared: 'They are only interesting when stark naked; dressed they are the worst of bores'. Clark Kerr was an expert, of course, having taken up sketching nudes in his spare time. Even though a teacher was always present to prevent scandalous gossip spreading, it was a pastime which even Harold Nicolson thought ill-judged. Nicolson was also taken aback by the lifestyle the Clark Kerrs had adopted to cope with local circumstances: Archie often never rose until 11.00 and attended to the little morning business in dressing-gown; Tita remained in bed reading detective novels until 1.00. Not surprisingly, Clark Kerr was restless for a move, and once more contemplated resignation. Harold Nicolson, who visited Stockholm to lecture in May 1934, sought to dissuade him. Nicolson was sure that an upturn in his fortunes was imminent:

> It would be madness to break out of prison only a few months before your legitimate, inevitable, and honourable (three adjectives) release.
> You have a good chance of Madrid. Tita would blossom there... You would be a Privy Councillor and have ribbons across your breast. You would, if you then resigned, have a pension and peace with honour. If you chuck now there won't be much peace and no honour at all.

The job offer, however, was not Madrid but Mexico City. Clark Kerr felt that Mexico, not even an embassy, was beneath him, and proof that the Foreign

Office thought little of him. He argued his case to Bob Boothby, citing the *Times* Correspondent in Sweden who had quoted his editor, Geoffrey Dawson, as saying, 'I can't understand why the Foreign Office have a down on that fellow in Sweden'. Boothby did not swallow Clark Kerr's predictable conspiracy theory, but he did suggest that Clark Kerr's marriage was viewed as 'unfortunate' and a professional liability. Boothby, a Conservative MP, was very likely accurate in this assessment of Whitehall opinion, but Clark Kerr rejected the implications. 'Tita is much the most important thing to me,' he declared, and outlawed totally any suggestion of changing to suit 'a group of stuffy old men at the FO'.

However, Boothby was able to pass on more welcome news. According to him, there was the suggestion that if he did well in Mexico there was a hint that he might be offered Moscow in 1937. There must have been some truth in this rumour, for in August Harold Nicolson also wrote to say that he would be offered Moscow 'within a year or so', depending on his success in Mexico.

Clark Kerr was much taken with the hint of Moscow. 'That is very tempting,' he replied to Boothby, '... I share your view that it is one of the few worthwhile posts and that it will soon be by far the most important embassy in the world'. Clark Kerr also surmised that what was needed in dealing with the Russians was diplomatic 'cock-teasing', and he supposed that to be his own foremost professional skill: the ability to charm, lead on those with whom he dealt, hinting at a promise of success and rich reward, without ever having to produce the goods. There is no doubt that Clark Kerr was a supreme diplomatic cock-teaser: many testified that he often seemed to get 'something for nothing', drawing on the other side without giving anything away in return.

In any event the promise of Moscow was sufficient bait for Clark Kerr to accept Mexico before leaving for London in July 1934. However, only six weeks later, the Foreign Office changed its mind and offered him instead the post of Ambassador to Iraq in the new year. This was something more prestigious and appealing and Clark Kerr gladly accepted, although Harold Nicolson did warn that Tita would hate Baghdad and that it was 'one of the most horrible places I have ever seen'. Clark Kerr, however, was much taken with the prospect, and began again rushing around organising his 'circus' for another golden journey. In addition to his normal retinue, he also wished to arrange for the transfer of his bagpiper from Stockholm to Baghdad.

In December came the not unsurprising but still very thrilling news that he was to be created a KCMG in the New Year Honours List: Sir Archibald Clark Kerr, KCMG, he would be at last, and Tita, at a mere 23, Lady Clark Kerr. Although pleased with his promotion and impending knighthood, Clark Kerr was unhappy still that four precious years had largely been wasted during his 'stagnation' in Sweden. Nevertheless, he had done well in the post as a *'Times'* retrospective acknowledged, referring to the new feeling of rapport between Britain and Sweden, mentioning how Clark Kerr had been 'extremely successful in penetrating below the placid surface of official Sweden'.[10]

Clark Kerr and Tita left Sweden on 12 January 1935 and returned to London, where they had obtained a new flat in Grosvenor Street, Mayfair. At the end of the month they had an audience of the Prince of Wales, and then on 9 February Clark Kerr was received by the King to be knighted. In March they began the long journey to Baghdad, going by way of Cairo, where Clark Kerr got his customary hero's welcome.

At fifty-three, Clark Kerr was now an ambassador for the first time. To be sure of achieving his real ambition of one of the more prestigious embassy postings, much would depend on his performance in Baghdad. Although he could count on the friendship and admiration of both Anthony Eden, back in the cabinet but not Foreign Secretary until the following year, and Hugh Dalton, who in any future Labour administration could well find himself as Foreign Secretary, without obvious success in Iraq he would be condemned to completing his career in a series of unfashionable, commonplace capital cities. It is clear that Clark Kerr approached his new post with a great measure of enthusiasm and a firm belief that his career was on the move at last. To Gavin Maxwell, whom he had offered the post of private secretary in Baghdad, he said, 'I'm going to the top and I could take you with me... Washington. Ambassador to the USA is the summit of my profession, and I'm going to reach the summit.'[11]

The Iraqi situation in 1935 was one which uniquely suited Clark Kerr's diplomatic abilities. Although it would have offended Clark Kerr's egalitarian instincts to have admitted it, there is little doubt that he flourished in circumstances where a form of paternalistic British diplomacy was still required. Until the Sirdar debacle, Clark Kerr had blossomed in Egypt – like Iraq, a colonial power feeling its way to independence and parliamentary democracy. Clark Kerr was able to combine a sincere desire to see the country reach a settled form of self-government, with a rather avuncular approach which seemed to endear him to Egyptian politicians but which still reserved for him a status of some elevation from which he could promote effectively British interests. In a sense, Clark Kerr expertly presented old-fashioned British imperialism trimmed to fit modern times and the aspirations of national liberation movements. It was his liberal opinions, this avuncular approach, and his informal and unconventional style which gave him a respected place amongst local politicians and produced the necessary leverage for British political and economic interests to an important place on the agenda. Few other British diplomats, if any, were flexible enough or conscious enough of modern sensibilities to be able to represent Britain abroad effectively in the emerging states of that time.

As far as Britain was concerned, Iraq, like Egypt, was chiefly desirable as a means of communication with India. Since the discovery of oil in 1927, however, and the subsequent involvement of British Petroleum, the country was also of significant economic interest. For that reason, Britain was keen to see Iraq remain favourably inclined towards her. Britain wished to maintain bases in Iraq, particularly airforce bases, as stopover points from Egypt to India.

By a Treaty of 1930 Iraq gained a form of independence from its post-war position under a British mandate, and in 1932 was admitted to the League of Nations. Britain had manoeuvred the Amir Faisal into position as king following the Great War, and supported his role by bloody RAF repression in the early years. The introduction of parliamentary democracy in Iraq developed along farcical lines. Elections were rarely contested but by government-sponsored candidates, there were no real political parties, cabinets rose and fell as the various strong personalities involved compromised or clashed. There was no free press, editors being bought off with free seats in parliament. Even amongst the able politicians corruption was rife and pockets lined. Few politicians followed any programme save that of personal advantage, largely achieved by toeing the line of whichever cabinet leader happened to have his hands on the public purse-strings. In a sense, it was Faisal alone who managed, at least as a figurehead, to keep the country united and functioning. The natural reservations which had arisen at the time of his enthronement had not been borne out by events. He had managed to steer a careful course and, against a background of constant cabinet changes and political infighting, served as a valuable symbol of stability. In 1933, however, while on holiday in Switzerland he died quite suddenly in mysterious circumstances. His young son, Ghazi, became king in his place.

In 1935, just as Clark Kerr arrived in Baghdad, a new government came to power. In his two years in Iraq Clark Kerr had to deal closely with a succession of ephemeral administrations, and did so very successfully. So valued was his political mind that at one time he boasted to Boothby that he was effectively Finance Minister, Education Minister and Health Minister for one particular government. Clark Kerr loved intrigue and the various machinations of local politics, and these he reported colourfully to his superiors in London.

King Ghazi himself was viewed by an anxious Foreign Office as hopelessly ill-equipped to control Iraqi affairs. In fact during his audience at Sandringham in February, Clark Kerr had been asked by King George V to try to bring pressure on Ghazi to act in a more regal way and temper his behaviour somewhat. If Clark Kerr was intrigued by this, he soon discovered the facts on his arrival in Baghdad at the end of March 1935: the King's weakness was compounded by a general public distaste for his scandalous personal ways. Although Clark Kerr quite liked the young King, he had to report to the Foreign Office that his outrageous court behaviour was wholly undermining his constitutional position. The King, who had been educated in England, retained a childish love of pillow-fights, and as often as possible indulged in bouts with the male courtiers. King Ghazi had modified the rules of his hobby to suit his adult tastes, with the inevitable result that during one such bout with a favourite footman he managed to contract syphilis. This he passed on to the queen, much to her understandable distress, since she had so far escaped unscathed from her own diversions, which had also all but exhausted the male coterie in the royal household.[12]

These events became the natural subject of social gossip, and did nothing for the monarchy's waning status. Clark Kerr, of course, took his customary delight in uncovering the facts and reporting them graphically to London.

After an initial tour of only five months, Clark Kerr and Tita were able to take leave in England, remaining at home until mid-October. It was a time of growing tension with the Italian attack on Abyssinia, Nazi Germany's expansionist stirrings, and the descent to civil war in Spain. However much Clark Kerr was enjoying his new status in Baghdad, he could not help but feel that he was still rather isolated from the real centre of things in Europe. He had been keen to get the Madrid post, and as a strong supporter of the Republicans would have had a more than interesting period there. In addition, after the boredom of Sweden, he was concerned that Baghdad would again prove to be a burden for his young wife.

Back in Iraq, Clark Kerr was confronted with scandal resulting from King Ghazi's egregious frolics. One of the King's pleasures was watching aircraft stunting; another was watching his footmen vomit. He decided to try to combine these two pleasures on one occasion by encouraging the pilot son of Nuri es-Said, the Foreign Minister, to perform some daring feats with a young courtier as a passenger. The sole purpose of these aerial acrobatics was so that the King could have a chance to see his palace favourite in the cockpit being sick with fright as the plane skimmed the runway upside down. The not unpredictable outcome of this indulgent recklessness was that the plane crashed and Nuri's son was seriously injured.[13] This had further ramifications as the great amount of money taken from state funds to pay for expensive treatment and rehabilitation in Europe for the Foreign Minister's son bred public resentment and strengthened the opposition.

Further damage was also done to the King's prestige when his sister, one of the royal princesses, eloped with a Greek waiter and further shocked Moslem Iraq by embracing Christianity. This scandal served further to distance the King from his government and, in addition, the British Government could not but indicate to Ghazi that his credibility with them was also greatly undermined.

It was possibly a combination of these factors which led Ghazi to seek to curry favour amongst opposition groups instead. Because of parliamentary vote-rigging and corruption, there was little scope for effective opposition within the system. Instead, disaffected elements were left to scheme outside the existing political structure. By mid-1936, opposition to the government had grown considerably, largely because of its openly corrupt nature, the fear of it developing into dictatorship, and the burgeoning wealth of its senior members. Quite apart from these political opponents, jealous malcontents, and a sulking King, there were Iraq's perennial dissatisfied groupings – Kurds, Shi'ites and rebel sheikhs.

In mid-1936 there was, in fact, a successful coup in which Clark Kerr had no doubt that King Ghazi was implicated, although the evidence remains inconclusive.[14] With the new regime Clark Kerr was able to establish good relations, but these events unfortunately served to set a pattern for Iraqi politics of that period with a succession of military coups and political murders. Britain itself was suspected of involvement, not only in the death of General Bakr Sidqi, the leader of the 1936 coup, but more than likely in that of King Ghazi, who met his untimely end in an unexplained car crash the following year.

As Clark Kerr was attempting to come to terms with the new regime and analyse the effect on British interests, word came from Anthony Eden the Foreign Secretary that he was to be offered a new post. He was to go immediately to China to take over there as Ambassador. Clark Kerr was absolutely delighted: it was an important post in itself, and with the Japanese military assault on China having commenced in July, it would be a post which would demand a great deal from him, putting him very much in the public spotlight. It is also clear that Baghdad had been another unsatisfactory period for Tita. Looking to the future in early 1937, he had written to Boothby: 'Lay off Moscow. I want some place where there will be some social and physical amenities for Tita. She has had enough of queer places.'

For Tita, a China under attack from Japanese forces was likely to be very 'queer' indeed, but for Clark Kerr it was irresistible. To Anthony Eden, whose stand against appeasement he fully supported, he wrote on 19 December 1937, accepting the offer of China with pleasure:

> You have made me feel proud and flattered. To have been chosen at this moment for China is as good a compliment as I ever want and all the more so because it comes from you. It seems to suggest that you do it because you believe in me. And I like that, because I believe in you too – like hell! At the same time I must confess that I know nothing about China... but I shall learn and I need not say that you may count upon me to put my heart into it.

The long exile was over: at last he was climbing back out into public view, ready to prove himself once more.

CHAPTER 6

Ridge 1938–42

Clark Kerr travelled alone to London in early 1938 in a mood of some exhilaration: at last he felt that his abilities were being fully recognised, his talents appreciated, and that the opportunity had finally arisen for him to fulfil his own perceived potential. Every human harbours a vision, however ill-defined, of some ideal set of future circumstances in which they believe their true self will flourish. Whatever image of such a future Clark Kerr had previously cherished, there is no doubt that in the transfer to China he felt that events were at least beginning to approximate those of which he had once but dreamed.

What China held out was that desirable combination of a demanding role, an exalted status and the glare of public attention. Like all in public life, Clark Kerr had a craving for appreciation, and he responded predictably to praise and reward; and, as he had pointed out to Eden in his letter of acceptance, the very fact of Eden's confidence was fillip enough.

For all that, the approval of the Chamberlain government, albeit in the more charming and acceptable form of Anthony Eden, was something of a dubious blessing. For some time Clark Kerr had made known his unease at the accommodating tendencies of the Chamberlain cabinet towards the European dictators. He had been unhappy at the failure of the British Government to render support to the Spanish republicans against Franco's fascists. Clark Kerr's general feeling of disquiet was not just shared by those on the left but by many in the Conservative ranks, of whom the maverick Churchill was the most outspoken. However, Clark Kerr was delighted to accept the China post despite his serious misgivings about the drift of Chamberlain's foreign policy.

The situation in China was highly dangerous and unstable. Indeed the circumstances which directly led to Clark Kerr's hurried appointment had brought Britain to the very edge of military involvement.

Since the early 1930s, Japan had been pursuing a steady policy of expansionism in North East Asia. Manchuria (Manchukuo) had been effectively annexed in the early stages, a development which resulted in Japan's walking out of the League of Nations after that body had criticised Japanese action. However, the League had also exposed itself, as it would again over Italy in Abyssinia, as ultimately impotent. Japan had taken advantage not only of the League's inability to act but also of China's internal divisions. Rival warlords had been the perennial obstacle to Chinese unity, a cohesion already undermined by the presence of large, powerful European communities within China who exercised economic control in their own interests. While the efforts of Sun Yat-sen had revived a national movement which almost succeeded in fully uniting the country in the early 1920s, following his death in 1925, rivalry and mistrust flared between Mao Tse-tung's communists and Chiang Kai-shek's Kuomintang nationalists. By the mid-1930s, in the wake of Chiang's sudden and bloody attack on the communists, the country existed in a state of uneasy tension. While Chiang presided over a national government at Nanking, Mao and the remnant of the communists who had escaped the purge and survived the celebrated Long March, were holed up in a semi-autonomous retreat in Yenan, deep in the interior.

Paradoxically, it was Japan's advance which served as the impulse to a reconciliatory pact between the nationalists and the communists. Japan, in whose interests lay continued Chinese division, helped by her aggression to heal that very wound. Following a bizarre kidnapping in late 1936, in which Chiang was captured by mutinous army officers and disappeared for some days, a united front against the Japanese incursion was agreed between both sides.

The phoney war with Japan stumbled into something more serious following a clumsy clash outside Peking between Chinese and Japanese forces on 7 July 1937. Initial diplomatic efforts, probably insincere on Japan's behalf anyway, gave way soon to armed conflict. The Chinese, poorly equipped for full-scale war, were quickly forced to abandon Peking and Tientsin which, apart from the foreign concessions, became Japanese-controlled. By August the Japanese had launched a massive assault on Shanghai, which fell after a stout three-month defence and 60,000 Japanese casualties. By mid-December Nanking itself had also been captured. Chiang and his government were forced to flee the city: the Foreign Ministry was established at Hankow, while the seat of government was settled at Chungking, several thousand miles up the Yangtze.

Within Britain there was a genuine feeling of sympathy for the plight of the Chinese. Japan was the aggressor, China the offended underdog. But more than that, the atrocities perpetrated by the Japanese at Nanking and their indiscriminate use of air raids against civilians outraged the public. Great Britain had considerable economic interests in China, largely centred in the quaint extra-territorial concessions which existed in the main Chinese cities. These were effectively colonial pockets wholly under the control of officials, and subject to the laws, of the country in whose name they were held. There was genuine concern that Japanese advance would threaten the continued existence of these concessions and future British access to the potentially vast Chinese market. This became all the more serious when a Japanese puppet government was installed in Peking in December. For all that, the British were also concerned that a complete Chinese victory, and the national self-confidence that would create, might also sound the death knell for British economic involvement.[1]

The British ambassador in China since 1935 had been Sir Hughe Knatchbull-Hugessen. In late August 1937, Hugessen had been on one of his periodic visits to the seat of nationalist government, then still hanging on under attack at Nanking. Following the completion of his mission, he drove from Nanking to Shanghai to visit the embattled British business community there. Although his official car was clearly marked with a huge Union Jack on the roof, it was attacked by Japanese fighter aircraft on the afternoon of 26 August. The ambassador was hit and seriously wounded in the stomach. He was rushed to Shanghai, where a bullet was removed from close to his spine. After a short period of hospitalisation, he was shipped home to England, where he made a remarkable recovery.[2] Apart from the doubts about the Japanese excuses of mistaken identity, the failure of the Japanese to apologise in an adequately contrite manner raised British hackles. Nonetheless, British consciousness of impotence in the Far East and an understandable preoccupation with European crises, resulted merely in a tentative protest to the Japanese which was so muted that even the Chinese expressed surprise.[3]

The appointment of a new British ambassador was therefore a matter of some urgency and sensitivity. The fact that he was called upon in an hour of national need was naturally a great boost to Clark Kerr and contributed significantly to the feeling of delight with which he took up his post. Like many on the British left, Clark Kerr viewed as crucial the maintenance of the Chinese defence and resistance to the Japanese advance. Japan, politically close to the fascist ideas of Hitler and Mussolini, was viewed with utter distaste, and her expansion in Asia seen as just one more example of the worldwide march of tyranny. It is most likely that Clark Kerr's views were known in Whitehall and it can thus be judged that his appointment indicates the general pro-Chinese drift in Foreign Office circles at this time.[4] Such a line was not, however, popular in Cabinet. Since July the Chinese had appealed for British efforts to galvanise international disapproval and push for economic sanctions against Japan. In addition, China hoped that Britain would lead an attempt to broker peace. Chamberlain was reluctant to be seen to do either with any alacrity: he also padded away Chinese requests for military and financial aid. Although Eden favoured assistance to China, even he feared what the Japanese response might be to any open tangible British support.[5]

Britain had four distinct options: a firm line against Japan and open support of China; a policy of benevolent neutrality as far as China was concerned; a wholly impartial stance; or appeasement of Japan. Military weakness, European preoccupations and an inability to rouse the American lion from his den ruled out the adoption of any firm stance. As far as the Foreign Office was concerned, although Sir Robert Craigie, the Ambassador in Tokyo, pushed for a more accommodating approach to Japan, the almost unanimous feeling was one of antipathy towards Japan and a feeling that some sort of showdown with her over the Far East was inevitable. Some advisers even wanted this sooner rather than later.[6]

In those circumstances, British policy was unclear for some time as the various options were considered and balanced against Britain's parlous military position in the Orient. In a sense, Chamberlain was quite happy for inactivity to remain as the unwritten policy guideline for as long as possible. The inconclusive Brussels Conference on the issue in November seemed to sum up the prevailing attitude.

As far as Clark Kerr could tell from his audience with Chamberlain the essence of his role in China was to try to keep the Chinese happy 'with little more than smiles and fair words'.[7] As a temporising policy it was sustainable; however, as it continued month after month it placed a severe strain on Clark Kerr as he sought to maintain good relations with China while his government did next to nothing to stop Japan or support the resistance.

After his audience with Chamberlain on 10 January 1938 and various talks with Foreign Office advisers, Clark Kerr consulted as many other knowledgeable parties on China as he could, including his MP friends Harold Nicolson and Bob Boothby, both firm anti-appeasers, and others, particularly on the left, who viewed China as a vital buttress against dictatorship. Oddly enough, the left's promotion of China as the acid test of democratic commitment in the West coalesced with that of business and old imperial interests in Britain, which also viewed the retention of China's 'independence' as crucial for British economic interests and as a check to any Japanese moves against British colonial Asia.

Clark Kerr's support for China was certainly influenced by the growth of his leftward views at this time, but the fact that they matched the views of others at the opposite end of the political spectrum gave him added strength in his new role. Both his experience of the Depression and an awareness since his period in Egypt that the days of the British Empire were numbered had served to distance Clark Kerr decisively from the Conservative Party and its attitudes, and in China he was further to complete his political education.

One of the most influential meetings Clark Kerr had in London was with the business-orientated China Association Committee on Friday 14 January. Many have assumed that British business interests were keen for a settlement with Japan in order to restore stability and conditions favourable to economic growth. While it is certainly true that some in the British concessions in Japanese-held Chinese cities looked for some deal with Tokyo as a solution, the China Association Committee took a very strong anti-appeasement line. They argued that they 'could work the Chinese, however nationalist their government may be' but that there was no hope of such accommodation with the Japanese.[8] Indeed, far from looking for a settlement of the dispute on any terms, the China Association Committee argued:

> If we have to choose between a Pax Japonica and general disorder due to continuance of sporadic Chinese resistance, we prefer the latter... as we can trade under these conditions, whereas Manchukuo shows us that it is increasingly difficult under the former.

They were determined that Britain's favourable economic position and rights in China should remain and, fearful that a Japanese China would drive out foreign capital, were prepared to see China riven to preserve them.[9]

Whatever Clark Kerr may have thought of the rationale for that position, he was greatly bolstered by the association's stout defence of China. He was more than ever determined that, whatever the pusillanimous Chamberlain might not do, he would give as full and as powerful support to the Chinese will to resist as he could.

After a hectic ten days in London, Clark Kerr and Tita left for the East, arriving in Hong Kong on 17 February 1938. That evening he was guest at a large dinner where he had the opportunity of meeting many influential locals, including the key figure T.V. Soong, financier and politician, one of whose sisters was Madame Chiang Kai-shek and another Sun Yat-sen's widow. Clark Kerr had intended delaying in Hong Kong to discuss matters with the authorities there and the military, but Bob Howe, who had been charge d'affaires since Knatchbull-Hugessen's departure, urged him by wire to reach the embassy in Shanghai as soon as possible. Howe explained that the situation in Shanghai, occupied by the Japanese military and controlled with an 'aggressive, intolerant disregard of the ordinary rules of international intercourse', was very tricky and that morale in the large British community had sunk to an unprecedented low. Howe argued that Clark Kerr was urgently needed to give the community a lift and give a strong lead in the resistance to Japanese attempts to crush British prestige and influence in that part of China.[10]

Since the turn of the year, the British Embassy had sought to embolden the Shanghai Municipal Council against Japanese pressure and attempts to interfere in concession affairs. Whatever difficulties Britain had in coming to China's aid at the international level, there was a feeling that no Japanese interference in legitimate local British business and administrative affairs would be tolerated. Since December, there had been increasing Japanese threats to British freedom of action in China. On 5 December 1937, during a Japanese raid on Wuhu, three British merchant ships had been damaged and the HMS Ladybird hit by splinters. The Ladybird again came under attack a week later, as did the HMS Bee; during the same attack the USS Panay was bombed and sunk with loss of life. Japan claimed it to be accidental, but most observers felt that it was an attempt by some sections of the Japanese military to provoke outright war with Great Britain and the United States.[11]

Despite the circumstances, the United States had not been forced into any marked retaliation, and Britain, without American backing, had also felt restricted in response. Nonetheless, the Foreign Office instructed the Embassy not to let the international difficulties allow the Japanese to take liberties with British interests on the ground.

On 4 January 1938, following a terrorist bomb attack against a Japanese march-past in Shanghai, the Japanese authorities began to demand a controlling interest in all the municipal organs of Shanghai. This the Embassy strove to resist.[12]

In fact, the importance of Shanghai to the British created something of a diplomatic difficulty for Britain. It was felt by the Foreign Office that the presence of the Ambassador was needed in Shanghai to give strength to the sizeable expatriate community. In addition, attention had also to be given to Britons in the other concession cities. However, the Chinese Government was many miles away in Chungking and the Foreign Ministry in Hankow. To the Chinese it was something of an affront that the British should so concentrate their diplomatic efforts around their own community, showing an apparently lesser degree of interest in the legitimate Chinese Government and its headquarters. At a time when China was growing restive at the lack of British support, it was another grievance which grated. Although Clark Kerr had arrived on Chinese soil in February, it was not until 12 April that he presented his credentials as Ambassador to the Chinese Government in Chungking. It would certainly have been understandable if the Chinese had viewed the tardiness with chagrin.

However, Clark Kerr had immediately demonstrated a clear sympathy for the Chinese cause, and his well-publicised tours of bombed-out areas and genuine expressions of concern created a favourable impression which did much to counterbalance the baleful effects of British political inactivity.

The difficulties of the post were made even more acute by the resignation of Anthony Eden as Foreign Secretary on 20 February. Although there was no immediate change of policy, the departure of Eden and the appointment of Halifax did suggest that a mood of appeasement would now be the prevailing one in cabinet. However, as far as Clark Kerr and the China desk at the Foreign Office were concerned the situation remained unaltered.

After a month in Shanghai becoming acquainted with the country and the situation, Clark Kerr and Tita set off on their arduous journey to Chungking. After a few days conferring with the naval authorities in Hong Kong they travelled by gunboat to Canton. From there they went by special train on the 500 mile trip to Hankow. Then the last leg of the journey was completed by plane and they arrived in Chungking on 9 April 1938. Sir Archibald and Lady Clark Kerr were then conveyed in some style by sedan chairs from the airstrip up the steep cliffs to the temporary capital. On 12 April the official ceremony of accreditation was performed in top hats and tails.[13]

After a very brief sojourn, Clark Kerr and Tita left Chungking by river steamer through the treacherous Yangtze Gorges to Ichang, whence they flew to Hankow. There Clark Kerr met with the Soviet and US Ambassadors, and on Sunday 24th April finally met with Chiang Kai-shek over dinner. Although they had to converse through the medium of Madame Chiang, who spoke excellent English, having been educated in America, they got on well and Clark Kerr was instantly impressed by the Chinese leader. He appeared an assured, confident and intelligent statesman, and Clark Kerr left Hankow more convinced that the Chinese could withstand a further Japanese onslaught. Chiang pressed Clark Kerr hard about the lack of British aid, and also requested that he spend more time in Hankow at least to dissuade the Japanese from launching more air raids. Chiang felt that, following the Hugessen incident, the Japanese would not risk injury to another British Ambassador and therefore that Clark Kerr would act as some kind of insurance policy for the city. Clark Kerr was unable to commit himself on either score without further consultation with London. That first meeting was, however, sufficient to convince Clark Kerr of Chiang's integrity and ability, and he remained a firm backer of Chiang throughout his time in China.

On 1 May, following an absence of five weeks, Clark Kerr and Tita finally returned to the relative comfort of the Shanghai embassy. Tita was quite drained by the experience and resolved that any further jaunts would be limited and undertaken strictly on her terms. For his part, Clark Kerr, under this pressure from Chiang to make Hankow his base, decided to have a more roving role, visiting frequently the various centres of power and areas of British influence.[14] If Britain could offer only token financial and military aid to China, at least the Ambassador could be seen to circulate amongst the Chinese people, seeking in his own unorthodox way to boost morale. His tours also served to stiffen the resolve of local British consular officials whose posture under Japanese pressure would otherwise have been invertebrate.

In a sense, Shanghai was a good vantage-point from which to survey the nature of Chinese society under Kuomintang rule. A city of over three million people, 'where East and West met on the worst possible terms',[15] it exhibited all the economic and social extremes of Chinese life. Despite the surrounding warfare and carnage, Shanghai continued to glitter by night, at least within the international settlement. While others, including Tita, enjoyed the epicurean delights, Clark Kerr rarely ventured out at night, tending to work into the small hours. Beyond the bounds of the international settlement, however, the rest of Shanghai and, indeed, China, simply festered. The Kuomintang Government had neither the political will, nor perhaps the opportunity, to address the appalling poverty, unspeakable housing conditions and wholly inadequate public health facilities which the vast majority of her countless millions had to suffer. Chiang himself, primarily a military animal, had no great aspirations to being a political radical, and much of the government activity was riddled with corruption and indifference to the prevailing desperation.

In those circumstances, it is little wonder that the tales which had begun to filter from the communist areas so fired the imagination of western journalists. Apart from the agrarian developments and the evident egalitarian ideals which permeated the Communist organisation of their own areas, it was the sheer contrast with the horrors of everyday China which was the major attraction.

The Kuomintang itself was hampered by jealousy and internal strife. The more democratic and sympathetic views of T.V. Soong were particularly disliked by his brother-in-law H.H. Kung, the Finance Minister, who it was believed ran the economy of China mostly for his personal aggrandisement. Soong was aware that the appeal of the communists could only be countered if Chiang could demonstrate a similar impetus towards economic and social reform, but Chiang seemed merely concerned with establishing effective military control. Although the communist-nationalist tension would not resurface in any marked way for several years, it is instructive to note that as early as May 1938 Sir Arthur Blackburn, the distinguished oriental specialist, was counselling Clark Kerr:

> It is important, I think, that we should not link our fortunes too closely with the Kuomintang if, as now seems most likely, that regime is doomed to eclipse. It will not only mean material loss, but it will make the establishment of relations with any supervening regime more difficult.[16]

Blackburn was Clark Kerr's most senior local adviser, and they worked well enough together, if of contrasting personalities.

The occasion of Blackburn's memo was the continuing British debate over financial aid to China. Chiang had claimed this was the least Britain could provide since China was, in effect, fighting for British interests in the Far East.[17] Halifax actually supported the loan initially in the face of strong opposition from Sir John Simon and the Treasury, which feared the consequences for relations with Japan.[18] Clark Kerr argued that China's stout defence and guerilla successes would be all the more marked if Britain gave her the financial aid required to intensify the struggle. He repeated to London Chiang's argument that the Chinese struggle was the British struggle, and further argued that British support was even more valuable from a self-interested viewpoint since it 'would put the Chinese under an obligation to us which would stand us in good stead when the time comes for reconstruction in which we... ought to play a prominent part.'[19]

As the pedetentous debate in the Cabinet and Treasury drifted towards an indecisive stalling,[20] Clark Kerr felt moved to offer more practical support to the Chinese resistance himself. One of the journalists Clark Kerr first invited to the residence after his return to Shanghai was the American Edgar Snow. An experienced China hand, Snow had recently published his *tour de force*, *Red Star Over China*, which had dramatically caught the public imagination in the West. Snow's sympathetic study of the Chinese communists captured the mood of the moment as so many Americans warmed to the resistance of the Chinese against the bully-boy Jap. Clark Kerr had been greatly impressed by the book and was keen to elicit from Snow some information about the nature of the communist organisation and military potential. The British Embassy was largely ignorant about Mao and his followers and relied, at their peril, on Kuomintang information about what had been, until Snow's book, dismissed as a 'bandit remnant'. It was clear now that the communists were a far more potent and honourable force.

Snow, for his part, was impressed by Clark Kerr's manner and intelligence, and his leftish sympathies also took Snow quite by surprise. Snow reported favourably to other journalists and westerners on the new unconventional British Ambassador who appeared to set traditional imperialist diplomacy on its head. This good news came at an opportune time for a small group of Sinophiles who had been knocking around ideas aimed at helping the Chinese war effort. The main participants were Edgar Snow himself, his wife Nym Wales, fellow journalists J.B. Powell and Rewi Alley, and John Alexander, a consul in the British service in China. They had in mind a scheme to help the Chinese economy cope with the demands and needs of the military in the face of the Japanese attack on industry and the economic structure generally, and in the light of the failure to secure adequate foreign aid. Their plan was to set up a system of decentralized industrial co-operatives throughout unoccupied China which would be responsive to local needs, keep the economy vibrant, and engender a spirit of national solidarity.[21]

The problem was to convince the Kuomintang Government sufficiently to enable finance to be released to fund the establishment of the chain of industrial units. Given the record of Chiang and the Finance Minister H.H. Kung, there was only a very slim hope of success. The key hope now was that Sir Archibald Clark Kerr could be persuaded of the merits of the scheme and that he, in turn, would bring the decisive pressure to bear on the Kuomintang Government.

Accordingly, on 27 May Snow and Alley returned to the Ambassador to present their scheme for approval. Rewi Alley was something of an eccentric hero in China amongst the media and westerners. Born in New Zealand in 1897, Alley had arrived in China in 1927 and lived there ever since. Possessed of inchoate radical ideas, Alley was sickened by the Chiang purge of the communists during the early years of his stay, and became involved with a number of communist sympathisers such as Agnes Smedley, the American journalist.[22]

The talks at the embassy went well, Snow and Alley being able to provide convincing answers to the Ambassador's hard-nosed questioning. Clark Kerr agreed to lend his support to the scheme and to lobby the Chinese Government. Although the plan itself was a form of basic socialism, Clark Kerr felt that it was just the sort of development necessary to help prevent the spread of communism.[23] If the Kuomintang could make a success of it, the appeal of communism would fade amongst the Chinese peasantry. Clark Kerr was, however, afraid that the Chinese communists would see his involvement in the plan as proof of its roots in British imperialism. Snow therefore suggested that they approach Mme Sun Yat-sen for backing, as the communists revered her and would never dream of subjecting to attack one who shared many of their ideals.

To this Clark Kerr agreed, and accordingly he and Alley left within the month for Hong Kong to secure Mme Sun Yat-sen's approval.[24] Clark Kerr then travelled to Hankow for talks with Mme Chiang and Mme Kung on behalf of Alley's plan, now known as Indusco. Their support was won and so Gung Ho – 'Work Together', as Indusco was known in Chinese – was launched.

Rewi Alley was appointed overseer of the scheme, and the all-out effort and runaway enthusiasm which characterized the early years of the scheme actually led to the term 'gung ho' being introduced into the English language to denote any kind of energetic, selfless activity. By the end of the first year over 1200 industrial cooperatives had been established, and by 1940 the figure had reached 3000, employing some 300,000 Chinese workers all bent on supporting the military resistance.[25]

While the Kuomintang were appreciative of the material aid to the armed forces, there were lingering anxieties about the nature of the enterprises: help was fine but the notion of workers' co-operatives and employee control was another issue altogether. Nevertheless, the Kuomintang took every opportunity to publicise Indusco in the USA where the obvious merits of the scheme attracted the all-important dollar donations to the Chinese cause.[26] Unfortunately, back in China it was H.H. Kung, the anti-democratic crook, who held the purse-strings. He refused to release all but the minimum of funding for the scheme, which he thoroughly disliked and distrusted, and it was only the repeated proddings of Clark Kerr which drew even these funds from central control.[27] Soon Kung's private secretary was demanding a $50,000 bribe to have funds released, and this system of operating quickly became the norm, effectively preventing Indusco achieving all it could. By 1942, official hostility led to the sacking of Alley and the virtual collapse of the scheme.

For Clark Kerr, the Indusco episode was very important. Firstly, it convinced both influential Chinese politicians and sympathizers of his full commitment to the Chinese cause; further, it established him as a 'good sort' in the eyes of the western media, particularly Americans who were depressed and frustrated at the hands-off approach of their Ambassador, Nelson Johnson[28]; and, at a time when Britain was swithering over aid to China, it represented at last tangible British support on the ground, which boosted Britain's diminished prestige in China. At a personal level, the co-operative scheme impressed Clark Kerr as a practically successful measure in an economy where free-market capitalism had created such a miserable, polarized economic structure. At the same time, as he had acknowledged to Edgar Snow, it seemed to represent a middle way between the two extremes of capitalism and communism. Clark Kerr saw it as the sort of economic and political answer to the appeal of communism, and the whole experience firmed up certain socialist ideas with which he had lately been toying. For all that, Clark Kerr never really embraced much of socialist philosophy other than a basic feeling that society should be more egalitarian and less stratified. His views were unreservedly Fabian and mild, although still unusual in one of his standing.

In Hankow Clark Kerr had met the distinguished American 'Red', Agnes Smedley, then a journalist and the intermediary between the press and the Chinese Communist party.[29] A controversial figure, she has lately been portrayed as the leading Comintern agent in China during these years.[30] Naturally somewhat dismissive of the politics of the stereotypical British Ambassador, Smedley was nonplussed by Clark Kerr, finally coming to the conclusion that his professions of leftist sympathy were genuine: 'a good Scotsman fallen among diplomats' was her analysis.[31] It was hardly surprising that Smedley was puzzled, as Clark Kerr would often preface any remarks he made with 'We socialists...'[32] Amongst the stuffed shirts, monocles, and cocktail glasses it was, indeed, odd. More than anything, this was a pose, designed to shock and surprise – which it did invariably. Most of his colleagues considered his professions of socialism mere affectation, and simply an example of Peter Pan politics – attempting to identify himself with the current fashions amongst Britain's educated youth.[33]

Apart from Clark Kerr's own sterling efforts to embolden the Chinese resistance, the British Government still equivocated over any support, particularly financial, to the embattled regime. By July 1938 the matter came to a head, being the subject of several cabinet meetings. Chamberlain was of the mind that Britain's non-intervention in Spain should be the example to follow to avoid difficulties. Halifax at this point was still pressing the Foreign Office line, which was in favour of aid. By 11 July, Sir Alec Cadogan, the Permanent Under-Secretary, had, however, decided that China should not be aided after all for fear of involving Britain in a Far Eastern conflict while the European scene remained in the balance.[34] Oliver Harvey, Halifax's private secretary, who had witnessed the Cabinet's deliberations, found the mood 'defeatist and timorous in the extreme', judging that the Japanese were now bogged down in China and in no position to threaten British interests seriously.[35] This had been Chiang's line, and was one which Clark Kerr had impressed on the Foreign Office. He agreed that much of the Japanese policy was based on bluff and would collapse under pressure.[36] Despite his arguments, on 13 July 1938 the loan to China was finally refused by the Cabinet. He and the Chinese both suspected that Sir John Simon had been the major snag.

Clark Kerr was greatly disappointed by the decision, particularly because of the added difficulties it presented for him in an already troublesome posting, and he bluntly told the Foreign Office: 'I confess to a feeling of some embarrassment when asked to define our policy'.[37] The Chinese were very upset by the British refusal and even hinted that they might have to turn to Soviet Russia if no other aid could be found.[38] Although Hong Kong was still a conduit for material into China, fear of the sincerity of these Chinese suggestions, and an awareness that the Hong Kong coast and that whole maritime region of China might fall into Japanese hands, persuaded the British to accelerate their efforts to clear a road from Burma into southern China. Despite this, the road would not be completed until December 1938.[39]

For all its awkwardness, the meeting with Chiang in Hankow on 15 July was quite a boost for Clark Kerr. After dinner he was ushered into an anteroom where Chiang and he had a private chat. It was clear that Chiang valued his advice greatly. 'You are the only foreign ambassador I have ever asked advice of,' he told him bluntly. 'In fact, you are the only one I have ever trusted... I feel very warmly towards you. You are not a diplomatist. You are a statesman. I respect you. I like you. I trust you.'

Not surprisingly such a tribute almost floored Clark Kerr, and he reported it to Tita verbatim with no small amount of pride. However private the meeting had been, the Japanese must have had ears nearby, for within a short while it soon became common gossip in Japanese circles that Sir Archibald Clark Kerr was basically a senior adviser to the Generalissimo. Given the nature of their recent talks, this gossip was not far from the truth. In fact, however, the Japanese needed no subterfuge to discover Clark Kerr's views: their officials visited him as often as twice a week and were given no reason to suspect that the British Ambassador felt anything but revulsion for their 'cause'.

Meanwhile the summer of 1938 saw the sticky relations between British authorities in Shanghai and the occupying Japanese forces reach breaking-point. Since the terrorist bombing in January, the Japanese had been steadily exerting more and more pressure against the city administration. Both Clark Kerr and the Foreign Office counselled against bowing to the occupiers' demands. However, as the year progressed and the prevailing Cabinet view of not offending the Japanese gained ascendancy, a more conciliatory approach was recommended.

Sir Robert Craigie, who firmly believed at all times that a happy alliance with the Japanese was just around the corner, had long been critical of the failure of the British authorities to meet the interests of the Japanese half-way. In May 1938, Craigie's adviser Maj. Gen. Piggott had been sent from Tokyo with Chamberlain's full approval to try to improve relations in Shanghai. Piggott, a romantic pro-Japanese military man, had good links with some of the older and peripheral Japanese staff officers, and actually did manage to thrash out a temporary deal during his trip to Shanghai.[40] Unfortunately, this only bolstered the case which he and Craigie promoted about the favourable chances of a deal with Japan at the highest level. By most other British officials in the East, Piggott was viewed with distaste. He was judged to be wholly out of touch with the political realities of modern Japan and in far too exalted and influential a position in the Tokyo Embassy. Peter Fleming, in Shanghai during this tense period, wrote to Clark Kerr, then in Hankow, warning that Piggott was 'a preposterous and fatal man who ought to be removed at once'. Craigie, Fleming thought, was 'a poor sap' who, though well-intentioned, lacked the slightest idea about the true situation in China. Fleming urged Clark Kerr to invite Craigie to visit so that he could be put in the picture. Clark Kerr acted quickly on this suggestion and invited Craigie over for talks in September.

By August, some in the Chinese Government now let it be known to Clark Kerr that they favoured a peaceful solution, particularly if Hankow fell. Halifax, however, pointed out that any terms which the Japanese offered would be unlikely to be acceptable to the Chinese. Over the course of the next few days the plans fell through.[41]

The failure of the British Government to take any part in the attempt by the Chinese to sue for peace greatly disturbed Clark Kerr. The Chinese had wanted a joint US-UK-French initiative of offering their good offices to bring about peace, and had intimated this to Clark Kerr on 26 July.[42] Halifax had initially stalled, claiming that there was no hope of a just peace. Craigie then demurred, arguing that a joint approach would not be acceptable to the Japanese: parallel action would be more judicious. As Clark Kerr kept up the pressure, Halifax then reported that nothing could be done as the US had told their ambassador in Tokyo to have nothing to do with any such demarche.[43] In the circumstances, the Chinese would have to drop, or modify, their scheme. Clark Kerr was not very keen on the task of informing the Chinese Government of this development. Having refused to help fund the war effort, Britain was now refusing to join in the peace effort. Clark Kerr wanted to tell the Chinese that Britain had been willing but that it was the refusal of the US to play which had scuppered the scheme. At least this might have retained some standing for Britain in Chinese eyes. Halifax, understandably, ruled out any such move for fear of the American reaction if it should become known.[44]

Despite Britain's aloofness, there were constantly confusing signals being given which, in a sense, did truly reflect the contradictory views within the Government in the weeks up to Munich. In late August, for example, Halifax was approaching Clark Kerr for ideas on how to increase pressure on the Japanese in China as a response to the recent indiscriminate bombings of Chinese urban areas.[45] Craigie, for his part, was complaining that he had been let down by the Foreign Office and left in Tokyo 'to make bricks without straw'.[46]

The failure of the British Government to agree to any clear Far Eastern policy line had resulted in a situation where neither Japan nor China was satisfied and few of the British aims had been met. On the other hand, it seems clear that, at bottom, Britain simply wished to keep out of the conflict, and this had certainly been achieved. In the meanwhile, a largely pro-Japanese embassy in Tokyo and a largely pro-Chinese embassy in Shanghai slogged away trying to keep their respective hosts happy. For Clark Kerr it was a trying and unrewarding struggle as the course of British policy veered steadily away from his own viewpoint until it slammed into the ignominious buffers of the Munich Agreement on 30 September 1938.

With an imminent meeting with Chiang scheduled in Hankow, Clark Kerr pleaded with the Foreign Office for something favourable with which to keep Chiang sweet. A year of defending the indefensible and being unwillingly cast in the role of salesman without stock, had taken a severe toll on him, as he informed Whitehall: 'I confess that I am feeling parched and barren'.

Munich and Craigie's predictable glee at the prospects it might afford for better UK-Japanese relations greatly increased Clark Kerr's depression. From Shanghai on 14 October he reported:

> The effect of the Munich accord on foreign opinion as seen from here is that perfidious Albion has been true to form and let down her friends again. The Chinese reaction... is that we are entirely self-seeking and have merely been keeping them in play with fair words, throwing them a bone now and again, hoping they would go on fighting long enough to exhaust Japan and so remove a potential danger to ourselves. The Japanese reaction... is that we are prepared to put up with almost any indignity rather than fight. The result is that, all in all, our prestige is at a low ebb in the East...[47]

Halifax replied with the stock answer: Britain was in no position to challenge Japan in the Far East at the moment.

With little prospect of having anything pleasant to tell Chiang, Clark Kerr set off from Shanghai on 18 October, not returning until 24 November. These numerous trips, the tension of living under the threat of war and the unhealthy climate tended to roughen the natural frictions of married life and served to make Clark Kerr's relations with Tita rather strained at this time. The fact that they could not have children had been a sad burden to bear down the years, and at times it did affect them deeply. At fifty-six, Clark Kerr was becoming increasingly conscious of his mortality and the fact that, without an heir, Inverchapel would, after his own passing, be lost to the Clark family and revert simply to being just another dull and empty corner among high and distant hills.

From Shanghai Clark Kerr went, via Hong Kong, on an extensive tour before arriving in Changsa for his meeting with Chiang on 4 November. During his peregrinations, matters took a dramatic turn: 30,000 Japanese troops landed at Bias Bay, just north of Hong Kong, on 12 October. Canton was quickly captured; the rail-line to Kowloon was cut off, and Hong Kong effectively isolated from mainland China. On 25 October, Japanese forces climaxed their Yangtze campaign by capturing Hankow itself.

At about the same time, following the Munich agreement, Japanese authorities in Tientsin applied more and more pressure on the British concession. It culminated in their demand that one Ssu Ching-wu, a Chinese guerilla leader who had been arrested in Tientsin, be handed over to them.[48] The British at first resisted. E.D. Jamieson, the Consul-General, argued that anti-Japanese activities could not be a crime under British laws. Craigie, from cosy Tokyo, argued that Ssu should be handed over. Into this situation, Clark Kerr weighed: 'This man's only crime is that he has been fighting for his country and I should not like to have to face the Chinese were he handed over...' Clark Kerr argued for internment, but did agree that Chiang should be warned about his men using the concessions as a base for terrorist activities.[49]

However, under threat from the Japanese military, Jamieson began to backtrack. His idea was to release Ssu where he could easily be recaptured by the

Japanese. Clark Kerr dubbed such a deceitful ploy as 'grisly' and one upon which 'none of us could ever reflect without shame'.[50] Despite Jamieson's protestations and Japanese pressure, the Foreign Office stuck to Clark Kerr's viewpoint. In the wake of Munich it was a timely, if minor, example of resolution.

Before Clark Kerr's meeting with Chiang in Changsa on 4 November, events took another dramatic turn. On 2 November, the Japanese Government published its plan for a 'New Order' in Asia. This amounted to a call for the removal of all Western interference in East Asia and seductive talk of strong links between Japan, Manchuria and China. With the war going so badly, it was clear that many Chinese would be attracted by such talk of 'Asia for the Asiatics'. Britain was already in a considerable quandary: temporising inaction had led to the alienation of both China and Japan, while at the same time British trade with China – the 'bottom line' – had suffered severe setbacks. Trade had slumped from £4.1m in the first half of 1937 to a mere £1.8m in the second half of 1938.[51] Now the Japanese New Order proposals raised the spectre of total exclusion from Asia.

Chiang pressed Clark Kerr hard during their talks. He claimed that the fall of Canton and subsequent encirclement of Hong Kong was a blow from which China could still recover. For Britain, however, Chiang forecast that it marked the 'life and death turning-point in British Far Eastern Policy'. With no more aid to China possible through Hong Kong, Chiang wanted to know just what Britain planned to do in this precarious situation. Chiang claimed that if Japan won, Britain was finished in the Far East. Clark Kerr could do little but promise to forward Chiang's views, with which he largely sympathised anyway, to Whitehall.

This he certainly did. To Halifax he reported:

> As I see it our whole position in this country is fast slipping from under us, partly on account of inaction forced on us by the situation in Europe, but more because of general indecision of our policy which, as seen here, is governed by fear of Japan.

He appealed again for a loan to China and claimed that Chiang was right to say, '... we are at the parting of the ways'. Clark Kerr argued that 'the time has come to decide once and for all whether we are going to do something for the Chinese side.'[52]

Aid was essential to maintain Chiang's goodwill, particularly as a few in the Kuomintang were now favouring peace terms with Japan. Such peace terms would be bound to involve the exclusion of Britain from China. Later Clark Kerr was able to show that pressure was being exerted on the Chinese along the lines of 'Asia for the Asiatics', and that the New Order initiative proved beyond doubt that Japan was clearly on a collision course with British interests in China.[53]

Clark Kerr had great respect for Chiang, possibly misplaced, and laid great store on his pronouncements. While Chiang had clear leadership qualities, invaluable in this wartime struggle, Clark Kerr and British diplomats generally underestimated China's capacity for disunity and Mao's dissembling ability to embrace nationalist principles as his own during the communist forces' highly successful guerilla resistance campaign.[54] Mao's unstinting anti-Japanese stance greatly enhanced the communists' stature in inland China.

Nevertheless, the talk of a New Order and the Japanese success in capturing Canton and Hankow did push the Western powers into action. Even the United States, fresh from a formal protest against Japanese excesses in China, initiated parallel representations with Britain and France against the closure of the Yangtze River and the consequent restriction on trade.[55]

Although Halifax was unwilling to forward a loan to help the Indusco scheme, which Clark Kerr strongly supported,[56] on 10 December 1938 he informed him that export guarantees for up to £10m for China would be put in a parliamentary bill. In practice this was only to amount to £500,000 for lorries. The key factor in this shift was that the USA had lately announced a credit to China of $25m. However, just as crucial for China, and to relieve the strain on Clark Kerr, came the opening of the road from British Burma into southern China in mid-December.

Despite this clear indication of support for China, little more was done to develop this policy. Even Craigie pointed out that the net effect of such piecemeal, inconstant action was to alienate Japan without coming anywhere near satisfying China.[57] The promised loan was a long time coming. In addition, British heel-dragging had the effect of raising Chinese suspicions that Britain was only interested in protecting her own position in China, even up to the point of doing a clandestine deal with Japan. Certainly, Craigie's lengthy, if intermittent, talks in Tokyo gave substance to such a view. Clark Kerr pressed Halifax not only on the loan,[58] but also on voicing a clear statement of support for an emancipated China and an agreement to negotiate on the whole future of the extra-territorial question with the new Chinese government, once rid of Japanese occupation.[59] Halifax firmly rejected giving any such hostage to fortune, dismissing Clark Kerr's desired endorsement of democratic values as 'pious statements'. Clark Kerr's anti-imperialist sentiments and his commitment to self-determination for 'subject' nations were simply too advanced for the prevailing Foreign Office attitude.[60]

At the end of 1938, Wang Ching-wei, a senior figure in the Kuomintang Government, defected to the Japanese side, emerging shortly afterwards as the leader of the pro-Japanese puppet government. Although a blow, it did not represent any greater shift in the mood of Chiang's government. Negotiations with Japan were ruled out and Clark Kerr prophetically described Wang's move as 'political suicide'.

The end of the year, therefore, brought simply renewed vacillation over the British policy in China. One of the toughest years in Clark Kerr's career had ended much as it had begun: vainly trying to argue China's case and persuade the Government to come in fully on her side. For all that, things did seem brighter in that, however slowly and reluctantly, the Government did appear to be coming round to China's side. Clark Kerr's performance in his impossible role greatly impressed most observers. Even the Chinese, rightly disgruntled at Britain's cold-shoulder treatment, warmly respected his efforts in their behalf. There was no doubting his sincerity, concern, and personal bravery, and the energy with which he went about his tasks. For many Western journalists, Clark Kerr's steadfast support of China, his unorthodox style – he insisted all called him 'Archie' – and evident glee in annoying and impeding the Japanese occupiers, and his helpful 'off the record' briefings, raised him to hero status. No journalist in China at the time failed to pay tribute to Sir Archibald Clark Kerr's skilful manipulation of the near hopeless task which had fallen to his lot.

The opening months of 1939 brought a gradual change in the nature of the conflict in China. Despite considerable military success, the Japanese were soon discovering that the Kuomintang policy of retreating into the huge expanse of the Chinese interior, coupled with occasional skirmishing successes of their own, created a situation in which outright victory became a distant prospect. As many observers had foreseen, the Japanese offensive was becoming bogged down. Without slackening on the military front, the Japanese did, however, begin to direct more attention now to the economic war. From their stronghold in occupied China, centred in Peking, the Japanese now launched an economic pincer movement: to seek to disrupt Chinese trade, and to undermine the Chinese currency. Significantly enough, it was these attacks and their consequent disruption of the foreign trading position which would ultimately draw from both the British and the American Governments the reaction which the suffering of the Chinese people had failed to provoke.

The foreign concessions, therefore, became far more of a target for Japanese pressure because of their vital role in the economic life of China. If Japan could undermine the stability which foreign business and economic administration gave the Chinese economy, then there would be a good chance of starving the Chinese to the negotiating table.

For the first part of 1939, Britain continued to wriggle with the issue of financial aid to China, but also had the problem of supporting the Chinese currency with which to wrestle. Although Britain did agree in February 1939 to contribute to a fund to stabilise the Chinese dollar, this hint of a more favourable British attitude to China was immediately undermined by the Chinese decision to suspend servicing foreign loans which were secured on the Chinese customs.[61] Britain had come to an agreement with Japan over the control of Customs in occupied China, but it was an agreement with which China had refused to concur. Britain, much to Clark Kerr's annoyance,[62] wanted to make the currency loan dependent on Chinese acceptance of the customs agreement.[63]

While very sympathetic to the Chinese position, Clark Kerr felt that the timing of Chiang's announcement of the suspension of loan payments would have 'disastrous consequences' in Britain as far as any future aid was concerned.[64] Generally, however, Clark Kerr found all talk of economics, currency, loans and matters fiscal both puzzling and tedious, and contented himself with repeated basic lobbying for aid to China, regardless of the minutiae of Chinese macroeconomic affairs.

In fact, the stabilisation fund was crucial to British interests in China, and marked the first decisive entry into the conflict. If Japan gained economic mastery in the occupied territories and induced the demise of the Chinese currency, her colonization of China would be complete and British involvement finished forever.[65] By bolstering the Chinese dollar, Britain effectively halted Japan's economic offensive.

In February 1939, Clark Kerr made his first visit to the British concession of Tientsin, which had been feeling the full force of Japanese pressure for some time. The very fact that the British and French colonies in that city still survived intact was a source of annoyance to the Japanese, and their independent economic activity a major hindrance to their efforts to force their own currency into the economic structures of northern China. By March 1939, the Japanese had declared Chinese dollars no longer legal tender, but they continued to circulate freely in the concessions, as did nationalist guerilas, much to Japanese disgust. Life in the concessions was made difficult, barricades were erected, and Europeans harassed. Into this situation Clark Kerr arrived in February 1939, although by then there had been some relaxation in the Japanese grip on the British concession. Nevertheless, many of the British community who lived life comfortably removed from the desperate standards of the Chinese peasantry saw no great strength in the Chinese case and wanted to settle with Japan and return to cocooned normality. Clark Kerr's robust opposition to the Japanese invader did not go down well among them, though among others his refusal to bow to Japanese pressure met with enthusiastic approval. It was, however, difficult for Clark Kerr to counsel others, facing hardships he did not, to stand firm against Japanese attack.

Britain's perceived weakness in China and her palpable failure to support the resistance simply encouraged the Japanese to continue to clamour for more control over activity in the concession, and to practise humiliations against the British community. In particular, Clark Kerr's success in holding out against the demands of the Japanese authorities, reluctantly backed by the local British officials, for the handing over of the suspected guerila leader Ssu Ching-wu, rankled. Clark Kerr knew it well, and took almost boyish delight in openly annoying and obstructing the Japanese authorities. As tension increased, they took to searching citizens in the British concession and other excesses. In an effort to reach some sort of local agreement to make life more tolerable, Craigie suggested once more the despatch of Maj. Gen. Piggott to Tientsin.[66]

Piggott was, of course, a much despised figure amongst Clark Kerr's circle, and even in the Foreign Office he excited scorn. Sir John Brenan, a key adviser to the Far Eastern Department, bemoaned Piggott's continued influential status. Brenan, to his credit a stout anti-appeaser, deplored Piggott's 'fulsome attitude towards the Japanese military authorities and the self-complacent tone of his reports'. He also complained that it was 'unfortunate that we have to go on employing an agent who is so fanatical and indiscriminating in his attachment to the people who are practically our open enemies'.[67]

While Piggott was on his way to Tientsin, Craigie sailed to Shanghai, arriving in late March for talks with Clark Kerr. For several reasons they did not go terribly well: at the most basic level there was simply little hope of compromise between Clark Kerr's pro-Chinese convictions and Craigie, who still believed even at this point that Japan and Britain were natural allies. In addition, Clark Kerr's studied informality sat rather uneasily with Sir Robert Craigie's humourless stiffness. The two men had little in common and failed to reach any agreement. Clark Kerr, with some justification, felt that Craigie was essentially the Chamberlain of the East, a well-meaning but foolish appeaser. Clark Kerr was, in fact, so unhappy with Craigie's outlook that he regarded any in his staff who took up Craigie's reciprocal offer to visit the Tokyo Embassy as guilty of 'consorting with the enemy'.[68]

It was clear, however, that Clark Kerr, and not Craigie, had the crucial support of the Foreign Office. His fine performance in difficult circumstances had attracted the attention of the highest figures, and he was now even being mentioned for the crucial, if unenviable, Berlin post in place of the hapless Nevile Henderson whose appeasing approach had brought no results.[69] Whatever the views in the Foreign Office may have been, it does seem incredible that Chamberlain would have considered anyone with Clark Kerr's trenchant views to conduct negotiations with Hitler and the Reich. Nevertheless it is possible that a growing disenchantment on Chamberlain's part and an appreciation of Clark Kerr's abilities *in extremis* may have have contributed to Clark Kerr's being at least considered at this point. In the end, no change was made and Nevile Henderson was sent back to Berlin.

Following his fruitless conversations with Craigie, Clark Kerr left for Chungking, where he arrived on 19 April. He was by this time alone, the tense situation and constant threat of air-raids having persuaded Tita to return home to Chile for a break. Chungking itself was a foul place at the best of times, but wartime conditions had worsened things considerably; partly because of this the British Embassy delayed removing there until October. Set high on cliffs above the Yangtze river, the city was shrouded in fog and rainy mists for six months of the year, a climate which left its buildings and narrow, terraced alleys coated in a noxious slime. In summer the temperatures hovered around the 100° mark with intense humidity. The normal population of 200,000 had risen to the million mark by mid-1939 with a huge influx of refugees.

While Clark Kerr was en route for Chungking, Piggott had been set loose in Tientsin. To give him his due, he did succeed in organising a liaison system so that the Japanese and British officials could co-exist without too much friction. After Piggott's grimly optimistic tour, which had consisted largely in uneasy attempts to bring together wholly unmatched British and Japanese officials on a social level, there was a certain degree of black humour in the event which marked, and effectively prevented, Piggott's departure on 9 April.

On that day a Mr Cheng Lien-shih, the manager of the Japanese puppet bank in China and newly appointed superintendent of Customs, was assassinated.

A prominent symbol of Japanese control in northern China, he was shot and killed as he left a cinema in the British concession in Tientsin. At first, criminal investigations seemed to go quite well, and joint operations with the Japanese military to track down the killers were carried out. It now seems clear that the arrangements which the consul at Tientsin, E.G. Jamieson, no doubt harried by Piggott, informally agreed to with the Japanese far out-distanced what he himself conveyed to Clark Kerr, then en route for Chungking, as being the case. On 19 April, Clark Kerr had, in fact, objected to Jamieson's proposed plan of co-operation with the Japanese, arguing that only terrorist acts should be the offences against which joint action could be taken, and that political activities, albeit anti-Japanese agitation, ought to be sanctioned within the concession. The Japanese had wanted to curtail any anti-Japanese activity, including restrictions on freedom of speech.[70]

It is certain that Jamieson did make personal promises to the Japanese which both Clark Kerr and the Foreign Office were not prepared to honour. Clark Kerr was naturally sympathetic to the Chinese resistance, but he was also now resident in Chungking, had met Chiang on the twenty-second and even been for a picnic the following week with the Generalissimo and Madame Chiang. In those circumstances, he was more than ever determined to show himself impervious to Japanese pressure. On 30 April the Tientsin incident was raised by Chiang: Clark Kerr told him bluntly that terrorist acts could not be permitted to pass unchecked in the concessions and that Britain 'could not afford protection to people whose actions imperilled the safety of our Concession'.[71] However, he did agree with Chiang absolutely that the terms of Jamieson's proposed cooperation would 'make a deplorable impression'. Clark Kerr said that Jamieson ought to hand over any guilty of violent acts to the *de facto* Chinese authorities, but that for any other suspects 'internment followed by speedy removal to Hong Kong' was the fairest solution. He also counselled Halifax against being pushed by Japanese pressure 'into doing anything about which upon more leisurely reflection our consciences should trouble us'.[72]

Halifax, weighed down with European crises and cabinet equivocation on the Soviet approach for alliance, discounted internment at Hong Kong as being impracticable, but on 8 May, despite the pleadings of Jamieson and Craigie, agreed with the general thrust of Clark Kerr's plan, suggesting instead that those guilty of non-violent acts should be 'expelled in such a way as not to fall into the hands of Japanese authorities'.[73]

On 13 May, Jamieson explained that four suspects had been arrested and sought leave to hand them over to the Japanese. Two had confessed to the crime, although later claimed that these confessions had been extracted by water-torture. Perhaps fearing that Clark Kerr had gained Halifax's ear, Jamieson warned of dire consequences if the Japanese were thwarted in this instance.[74] Jamieson's assurances to the Japanese had still gone unreported[75]; as a result, even Halifax dragged his heels on the matter and Clark Kerr was determined to make a resolute stand on the issue. Sustained bombing raids on Chungking from the 6th of May had only stiffened his desire not to back down.

Clark Kerr argued that the suspects should merely be expelled from the concession and on 19 May he made a strong stand against Jamieson's pleas that they be handed over.

> This imposes upon me a decision from which I confess I flinch. The problem reduces itself to a repugnant simplicity to sacrifice the four or perhaps even more scapegoats in the hope that by this sacrifice the Japanese may be persuaded to hold their hand for a time... The truth is that we should be handing over these men to be killed, and that is a thing which I for myself cannot at present reconcile with my conscience and I would beg to be excused from the duty of giving the Consul-General [Jamieson] the authority for which he asks.[76]

Unaware of Jamieson's hidden assurances to the Japanese, Clark Kerr had pitched his camp firmly on moral high-ground where he was determined to remain. He left Chungking on 19 May, travelling to Hong Kong, where he hoped to sort out the practicalities of his proposed internment scheme. In Hong Kong he also had several meetings with Edgar Snow, Gunther Stein and others of the pro-Chinese left in the colony who strengthened his resolve on the issue.

From Hong Kong he advised Jamieson merely to expel the four suspects from the concession[77]: Jamieson stalled, claiming that it raised legal questions and was unsuitable in any case for two suspects who had been found in possession of bombs.[78] This added fact was news to everyone outside Jamieson's office and Halifax accordingly ordered that these two be handed over and the remaining two interned, pending further investigation.[79] The situation then reached farcical depths when Jamieson wired on 31 May that the two bombers he had referred to were not connected to the current four suspects but were others who had been detained since February. An exasperated Halifax now ordered that these two only be handed over, but not the main four, on the grounds that they had been tortured.[80]

For several days Jamieson continued to delay as Japanese pressure and press hostility reached fever pitch. Clark Kerr had reached Shanghai on 29 May, and it was from there a week later that he formally instructed Jamieson to follow Halifax's suggested course of action.[81] The long delay infuriated the Japanese who were now threatening reprisals against the British Concession and grave consequences for its inhabitants. Indeed on 25 May they had arrested the British military attaché to China for alleged spying and continued to hold him until September.[82]

On 10 June, the 'Tientsin Crisis' reached its peak as Japanese forces began to make arrangements for a full blockade of the British concession, setting up a barbed wire perimeter fence, stopping the movement of all goods, and searching all who entered or tried to leave. Two days later, Clark Kerr was reliably informed that there was an assassination plot being mounted against himself by pro-Japanese elements in Shanghai.[83] It was no mere rumour: he was now regarded by the Japanese regime as public enemy number one in China. Bullet-proof vests were now to be worn, bodyguards employed, and arrangements made for a bullet-proof car to be put at Clark Kerr's disposal.[84]

On 14 June, following a rejection of Clark Kerr's plan for an international tribunal to assess the guilt of the four suspects, the full-scale blockade began. The reaction in the British press was one of firm determination not to be intimidated, and Clark Kerr's policy was fully supported. The Cabinet were also reluctantly determined, particularly as the Japanese were now demanding not just the hand-over of the four men but a total abandonment by Britain of all support for China.[85]

Under fire from Sir Robert Craigie for his attitude, Clark Kerr fired off a salvo of his own on 15 June.

> Sir Robert Craigie considers we are risking our whole position in North China by our present attitude. My view is that we should lose it altogether not only in North China but throughout the country if we allowed the Japanese to threaten us into submission.[86]

Even Craigie accepted that to back down under the blockade could not be done without the gravest consequences, or Britain's international reputation,[87] but still regretted Clark Kerr's actions earlier. These were finally put in their proper context on 22 June when Jamieson, after over ten weeks of prevarication, finally revealed to Halifax what had gradually been emerging as the truth: 'There is no doubt whatever that the Japanese were given to understand that the men would be handed over'.[88] Why Jamieson took so long to reveal the facts is unclear: Clark Kerr certainly always viewed him as being too soft and accommodating towards the Japanese, and it may have been that Jamieson, aware that his undertakings, given in the heat of the moment, would not be supported by the Ambassador, simply tried to cover up for as long as possible.

The Tientsin Crisis which thus tormented the British Cabinet over the summer months was, therefore, one largely created by the refusal of Clark Kerr to comply with the demands of the Japanese military and honour a pledge of which he had not been made aware. That was certainly how Neville Chamberlain viewed matters, judging that Britain was neither morally justified nor militarily prepared for the consequences of refusing to hand over the four suspects. Chamberlain generally supported Craigie's outlook and viewed the Foreign Office as anti-Japanese.[89] The nub of the issue was best identified by P.B.H. Kent of the China Association in Tientsin. He sympathized fully with Clark Kerr's desire to uphold the rights of the Chinese people and his wish to, and the ultimate British need to, resist Japanese pressure in China. However, he correctly pointed out that the terrorist affair was an issue insufficiently clear-cut to bear the weight of moral indignation Clark Kerr had applied to it.[90] There is much accuracy in Kent's analysis. On the other hand, the nature of the Japanese demands now being made regarding British recognition of the New Order in Asia, and the information coming from espionage work behind the Japanese lines, made it abundantly clear that Clark Kerr was absolutely correct in his judgement that this was primarily a test of British strength and commitment in China, and much less a squabble about the custody of four Chinese citizens.[91]

The longer view which Clark Kerr was taking, and the effect that had on his assessment of current policy needs, was one which was shared by a growing number of Foreign Office advisers, parliamentarians and the public.[92] British interests and Japanese interests were incompatible, and unless a stand was made, all would be lost. In fact, the failure to make a firm stand from the beginning may well have been influential in Stalin's decision to move away from the mooted alliance with Britain in the summer of 1939.

In late June 1939, some heat was removed from the situation by the agreement that Craigie should begin talks in Tokyo to seek a settlement. Given Craigie's general outlook, Clark Kerr was very apprehensive about the potential for appeasement, and constantly lobbied Halifax about the danger of Craigie agreeing to any formula which might disappoint the Chinese. Craigie's initial draft did just that[93] and Clark Kerr argued unsuccessfully that the negotiations should be immediately called off rather than continued along such flawed lines. The nervous government and the Foreign Office hierarchy, who now felt that they had blundered their way into the crisis in the first place[94], were quite prepared to accept the conciliatory tone of an amended formula. Britain was keen not to be seen as having changed policy in China, although, by adhering to the revised formula published on 24 July, Japan was arguing that Britain had done just that. Whatever gloss may be put on it, the formula was undoubtedly craven in tone.[95] Clark Kerr was extremely unhappy, and concurred with those who viewed it as a 'Far Eastern Munich'. In Britain, apart from *The Times*, the reaction was generally unfavourable. The formula spoke of Britain recognising 'the actual situation in China', Japan's 'special requirements' there, and Britain's desire not to 'interfere' with Japan's need to take steps to suppress public disorder and 'remove any such acts or causes as will obstruct them or benefit their enemy'. Clark Kerr had rightly wanted Craigie to stick only to the Tientsin issue but instead, with Chamberlain's blessing, a wide-ranging mealy-mouthed formula was initialled which greatly upset the Chinese.[96] Rightly, Clark Kerr feared that such a broad agreement between Japan and Britain would drive the Soviet Union into alliance with Germany. This was indeed what happened in August 1939 when the Ribbentrop-Molotov Treaty caught the general public by surprise. For the East it marked a significant turning-point: shocked at the implications, the Japanese government fell, the talks with Craigie being fortunately abandoned. Almost as an irrelevance, following legal opinion, the four terrorist suspects were handed over to the District Court on 6 September and on 12 September Ssu Ching-wu was delivered to representatives of the Public Safety Bureau. This man, whose only real crime was, according to Clark Kerr, that 'he has been fighting for his country', was never heard of again. Clark Kerr viewed the whole affair with utter revulsion.

By now, however, all attention was focused on Europe. Poland had been invaded and Britain, from 3 September, had been at war with Germany. The great fear that Britain's ability to wage war in Europe would be compromised hopelessly if war broke out in the East had now become a reality. From now on, Britain strenuously avoided any situation which might strain further the tense relations with Japan. For Clark Kerr the natural sense of relief that the 'phoney' war was over was balanced by a recognition that his own role in China would now be more, rather than less, difficult. That is not to say he was not enjoying the post: he relished the intensity of the demands and the fact that, hard as it was, he alone was responsible for keeping British prestige afloat when the drift of British policy could well have scuttled everything.[97] At the same time, he did feel intensely that once more, as Britain went to war, he was exiled, excluded from the real centre of the action. To Bob Boothby he wrote:

> It is frankly bloody hell to be here in the middle of the hottest crisis in our history. Fancy being in Chungking when all that is happening at home!

Over the next few months he and Craigie resumed their lobbying for the ear of the Foreign Office. Talks on the thorny question of the Tientsin silver had resumed and Japan, eyeing Britain's difficulties in Europe with delight, began to exert pressure. Oddly enough, it was the USA which provided the best hope: since its remarkable rebuff to Japan on 26 July, following immediately on the infamous Craigie-Arita formula, in which Roosevelt suddenly announced his decision to end the 1911 Commercial Treaty with Japan, there was at last the real prospect that US power might be used to curtail Japan. The US was still greatly suspicious of Britain's imperial agenda in the Far East and steered clear of any joint action against the Japanese.

Both Clark Kerr and the distinguished Japanese historian Sir George Sansom continued to press the case that Japan's New Order in Asia could not be squared with British interests.[98] Clark Kerr had high hopes of the change in US attitude

> ... we now know it is the purpose of the Americans to use the power they possess to frustrate the New Order and it is clear their government has popular opinion behind it. It is obviously in our interests to see this frustration takes place...[99]

Sansom similarly argued that the New Order meant 'the ultimate displacement of Great Britain in the Far East'.[100]

Although Craigie stubbornly held to his view that Britain and Japan could find some common ground on which to reach agreement, particularly regarding anti-communisim, he was privately less clear-sighted. In May 1940, for example, he was quoted as still clinging to his absurd picture: 'England [sic] and Japan were ultimately striving for the same objective – namely lasting peace and the preservation of our institutions from extraneous and subversive influences'.[101] Then, only a few months later, he was quoted as saying that he was 'utterly weary of the policy of appeasing Japan'. As he was one of the main proponents of this policy, such self-loathing seems rather odd, but more loathing was reserved for the Japanese: he was 'nauseated with being polite to the little blighters' and had recurring dreams of being able 'to go all out in retaliation against the dirty little bastards'.[102] These may well have been his real views but two points are worth making: they were made following the demise of Chamberlain's premiership, and they were made to Western newsmen while he was on a trip to Shanghai.

In fact, Sir Robert Craigie's attitude in early 1940 was probably less contradictory than appears at first sight. A clue to the full nature of his views becomes evident in a communication sent to the Foreign Office on 4 July 1940. While urging compliance with yet another Japanese request, he explained that he only did so on the understanding that 'when we have defeated Germany we and the United States of America will be able to teach Japan a lesson which she will never forget'.[103] Craigie's line thus appears much more realistic: long-term co-operation with Japan was no longer possible, but war could not yet be contemplated and, until then, Britain would have to swallow her pride and accept Japan's *de facto* power in Asia.

If Craigie had mellowed in viewpoint, so too had Clark Kerr. Clearly concerned that the Kuomintang's ability to withstand Japanese pressure was not unlimited, Clark Kerr sought leave for some of his more minor consular colleagues to establish informal contact with the Japanese puppet administration in various districts. Although he never seriously doubted the Chinese capacity to continue the resistance struggle, he was sufficiently pragmatic not to dismiss all eventualities. Clark Kerr's ideas were not wholly accepted by the Foreign Office, particularly because of the fear about how the local consular officials would handle matters. The most astute response to Clark Kerr's suggestion came from Sir John Brenan who was of the opinion that a situation of rival governments – Chinese and puppet – could well develop into a civil war between the communists and the anti-communists.[104]

The coming of war in Europe had not eased Clark Kerr's position, and nor did the arrival of Churchill at Number 10. While Churchill's line was generally more in tune with Clark Kerr's, he fully recognised the military weakness of the British position in the Far East and the constraints this put on taking any firm stance on the Sino-Japanese conflict. The desperate days of the Battle of Britain gave the Japanese another opportunity to prosper while all British efforts were centred on Europe.

In mid-June, the Japanese Government informed the British Embassy in Tokyo that unless the Burma Road and the Hong Kong border were closed, war between Britain and Japan could not be avoided. The first British reaction to this chilling ultimatum was simply to refuse on the grounds that the war material for China imported by these routes was minimal.[105] After a Japanese rebuff, Craigie suggested a three-month closure of the road on the pretext of allowing breathing-space in which to seek a general peace settlement. In mid-July a three-month closure of the road was agreed with Japan.

This decision was quite disastrous for relations with China. Chiang felt, with justification, that he had been betrayed. Clark Kerr's position was bleak:

ever since the Molotov-Ribbentrop accord, many of the pro-Soviet communists and sympathizers in China had been strongly anti-British and their sniping campaign now seemed to have been justified. They were now joined by many Kuomintang supporters who also now viewed Britain with utter contempt.[106] Many within the British cabinet and the Foreign Office felt that the Japanese threats were a bluff.[107] Oddly enough, Churchill was the most powerful supporter of surrender on the issue. In fact, the closure coincided with the rainy season when little transport could travel anyway, but it was the principle of the matter which rankled.

With the decision to close the road agreed, however, all Clark Kerr could do was to fight his corner as best he could. With all the power at his disposal he sought to convince the Chinese that all was not lost; to the Foreign Office and to any other interested parties he energetically pushed the case for aid to China and for the reopening of the Burma Road. In the early part of 1940 he had successfully persuaded Sir Stafford Cripps, then on a tour of the Far East. Cripps strongly represented to the Cabinet on his return that British timidity and prevarication had led to her name being 'mud' in China.[108] The greatest influence on British policy was, however, the growing involvement of the United States, which was adopting a more resolute approach. In that atmosphere, the British Government felt Britain could take a tougher stance with Japan. In addition, the success of the Battle of Britain had eased pressure a little. Then when on 27 September 1940 Japan, Germany and Italy formally concluded their Tripartite Pact, all thought of improving relations with Japan disappeared. The decision to reopen the Burma Road in October, accordingly, became less difficult than might have seemed likely when the three month closure was begun. In fact, it is debatable if the closure achieved anything for Britain as the decision to reopen caused no Japanese backlash at all. A similar refusal to close in July might also have had the same lack of response. However, the parlous state of local defence in the Far East ruled out any risk-taking on that front.

The decision to reopen the Burma Road was a great relief for Clark Kerr, who had returned to Chungking on 4 September after an absence of two months in Shanghai and Hong Kong. In Chungking his regular talks with Chiang Kai-shek, occasionally interrupted by bombing raids from Japanese aircraft, coincided with, first, growing optimism and then the final welcome decision regarding the Burma Road. A good early warning system for the Japanese air-raids had been organised in Chungking, and the city's steep cliffs were brought into use as shelters, small caves being dug into the rockface. The Chungking population was gradually reduced to 250,000, the number who could safely be accommodated in these rock dug-outs. In late June, while Clark Kerr had been in Shanghai, the consulate in Chungking was almost completely destroyed and the adjoining diplomatic mission badly damaged. There were no injuries, however, and a few days later the consulate was removed to the safety zone south of the Yangtze. The use by the Japanese of incendiary bombs reduced much of central Chungking to charred ruins but generally, after heavy casualties in 1939, the shelter system prevented any great loss of life.

The bombed-out embassy building, however, continued to be used by Clark Kerr and his small staff. Keeping the Union Jack flying near to the Chinese Government buildings, when most of the other embassies had fled south of the Yangtze, was something of a coup for Clark Kerr. If constant retreat from Japanese threats had been the essence of British policy in China, at least in Clark Kerr's defiance some 'face' was saved. He made much of this 'macho' image: alone of the Chungking residents, he regularly swam in the treacherous waters of the Yangtze and, having met Ernest Hemingway at a function, dismissed him derisively: 'Tough ? Why, I'm tougher than he is!'[109]

Clark Kerr's private residence in Chungking was a handsome pavilion belonging to Chiang, set high on a hill above the Chialing river. There he could live life very much in the Chinese style – he had made great progress with the language – and could indulge his pursuits of watercolour painting and sunbathing. He entertained Chinese novelists and intellectuals regularly, and made something of a study of Confucian philosophy, although much of this activity was inspired by exhibitionism rather than profound interest. And, given his reputation for political wisdom and status as some sort of oracle, his home became a magnet for numerous Chinese officials. During more peaceful days, when the mists were down on the hills, he could almost imagine himself back in Argyllshire and, dressed in tweeds and with the ageing Hodge by his side, he could stroll along the cliffs for a ruminative pipe. It was here he would take Chiang during their talks, and there is no doubt that during these perambulatory conferences along Chungking's precipitous hillsides Clark Kerr was able to achieve much more than circumstances might otherwise have allowed.

After his earlier days in China, when some in the Foreign Office felt he had fallen too much under Chinese influence, Sir Archibald Clark Kerr had now established a sound reputation. Indeed, in early December, when the British Ambassador to the United States, the Marquess of Lothian, died very suddenly, Clark Kerr was one of the few career diplomats to be quoted for this, the Diplomatic Service's most prestigious post.[110] His chances of succeeding were always rather slim, and some stuffy Foreign Office prejudice about his wife's alien status certainly told against him. In fact, Churchill took the opportunity to fill the post by despatching to Washington the Earl of Halifax from the Foreign Office. In his place, Anthony Eden was reappointed Foreign Secretary. Talk of Clark Kerr succeeding to the Washington post provoked the establishment of a small group of Western journalists in China under the name of the 'Clark Kerr Must Come To Washington' committee, or CKMCTW for short. The driving forces behind this group of Clark Kerr's admirers were the US journalists William H. Lawrence, John Hersey and Richard Lauterbach. In actual fact it was mostly just a humorous game, but did stem from a genuine acknowledgement of both his professional abilities and his attractive social manner.

By the beginning of 1941, relations within Chungking itself were growing more and more strained. Although Clark Kerr admired Chou En-lai, Mao's urbane representative in the capital, relations with the communists were very difficult because of the adherence of the Chinese Communist Party newspaper to the spirit of the Nazi-Soviet pact. Often Clark Kerr was forced to deliver formal protests about the line of the communist press.[111] More importantly, relations between the Kuomintang and the communists themselves were deteriorating rapidly. Since 1939 no foreign journalists had been allowed to travel to the communist areas, the Kuomintang suppressed any news of successes of communist-led forces against the Japanese, and Hollington K. Tong, deputy Minister of Publicity, dubbed anyone attending communist news conferences as 'an enemy of China'.[112]

The main problem was that as the Japan's offensive in China had been spiked and her attentions turned to other more promising areas of Indochina, there was less of a need for the close Kuomintang-Communist alliance being maintained. It was now widely suspected that both sides were simply hoarding military supplies for an eventual internal clash.

In January 1941 came the notorious New Fourth Army incident in which, after repeated minor skirmishes, nationalists and communist forces were involved in a full-scale battle on the banks of the Yangtze. The Communist forces of the New Fourth Army were attacked and massacred; the Kuomintang arrested the Communist General; and the New Fourth army itself was later disbanded. The bitter recriminations which followed effectively led to the breakdown of the whole wartime communist-nationalist alliance.

At the end of February 1941, Clark Kerr left Chungking for a lengthy tour culminating in an important, and very worrying, Imperial Defence Conference in Singapore in mid-April. Increasing Japanese threats against the Dutch East Indies had set the alarm bells ringing for the British position in Singapore, Malaya and Burma. Whatever other personal problems Clark Kerr and Tita may have had, nearly five years without a holiday, the bleak security position and grim living conditions greatly added to the marital tension. Some-time during the three months of his absence, Tita made a final decision to leave him and head for the safety and more glamorous life of the United States. She was not yet thirty five years of age, and life with a preoccupied husband in war-ravaged China had steadily been reaching the point of being unbearable. Brief breaks away in previous years had only whetted her appetite, and in Clark Kerr's absence, Tita took the opportunity to slip away. The actual circumstances are not clear but in the incestuous diplomatic and foreign correspondents' circle it was the subject of the hottest of gossip: the most common tale – utterly groundless – was that Tita had run off with an American military attaché.[113]

Clark Kerr was shell-shocked at the news, and although privately he was almost broken, he did manage admirably to continue his professional duties without obvious hiccup. He bombarded Tita with letters – at least one a day – and continued to provide financial support when she finally did resurface in an apartment in a fashionable quarter of New York. Tita was, however, sufficiently exhausted with the marriage to acknowledge Clark Kerr's mail in a purely formal and cursory way. To one who set such store on correspondence, this treatment was a heavy blow to him.

He had returned to Chungking on 2 May 1941 where he discovered the devastating news of Tita's flight. This period was also a time of intensive Japanese bombing, and rumours were widespread that the conference at Singapore had agreed to a second closure of the Burma Road and a shift of policy away from favouring China. A few days later, with no little sense of the dramatic, Clark Kerr hosted a cocktail party for Chinese officials and foreign journalists on the lawn of the British Embassy, whose windows had only the day before been blown in by an air attack. In the middle of the festivities, Clark Kerr rose quietly and read out a short statement, ending with the steely proclamation: 'The Burma Road will remain open'. There was a short pause; the Chinese were the first to clap, and then thunderous applause rang out over the Yangtze cliffs.[114] Later in the summer when bombing raids injured the senior British diplomat Sir Arthur Blackburn, flattening his house and killing two Chinese staff, the British Government advised Clark Kerr to heed the Japanese warnings and remove to the safety zone south of the Yangtze. Standing in the bomb-scarred embassy building which had now become a symbol of British faith and Chinese determination, Clark Kerr announced to the gathered officials: 'The Foreign Office have ordered me to move the Embassy; they cannot order me to move my body!'[115] To the long-suffering Chinese, it was a display of genuine fellow-feeling and the much-vaunted bull-dog spirit, then a marked rarity in the Orient. Of all the diplomatic missions, only the British and the Soviet one faced out the war at the Chinese side. A press attaché at the time, by no means partial to Britain, has written:

> There can be few more striking examples in our time of the personal example and influence of an ambassador doing so much to redress the balance of an ill-conceived government policy as was achieved by Archie Clark Kerr in China over the years of British appeasement.[116]

Perhaps it was typical of Clark Kerr's career that, following Pearl Harbour and the uniting of Britain, China and the USA in war against Japan with all the happier prospects for full and friendly co-operation after years of unease, caution and evasion, Clark Kerr should almost immediately be offered a new post. In the New Year Honours list Clark Kerr was awarded the GCMG, Eden commenting that 'nobody has ever deserved an honour more'. There were many in Britain who had a degree of guilt that it was being left to Clark Kerr to do publicly, and take responsibility for, what they themselves thought privately ought to be done they feared to do, or even say, openly. Shortly after Eden's tribute came the offer of the Moscow post; although still stimulated by the work in China and feeling a little flushed with new-found success, Clark Kerr had little option but to accept. He was to leave China in March and proceed directly to Russia to take over the reins from Sir Stafford Cripps, who had not enjoyed the best of fortune in the Soviet capital.

Before leaving China, there were the customary farewell dinners and valedictory functions to attend. At all of these Clark Kerr was lauded, the Chinese press describing him as 'the most popular diplomatist Britain had ever sent to China'.[117] For himself, at a dinner given in his honour by Chiang Kai-shek, Clark Kerr declared that he was 'fully confident that Mr Churchill's promise to knock out and flatten Japan would be fulfilled'.[118] In a farewell message Clark Kerr gave a glowing tribute to the Chinese people and their struggle for survival:

> For four long years it has been my honour and my pride to live among the people of China and to watch every phase of their fight against Japanese aggression. This has been a thing which no man can ever forget, a matter for amazement and the highest admiration and, as such, an inspiration which has taken hold of me and gives me new strength which I had thought to be now beyond my reach.[119]

With the benefit of hindsight, following the Maoist victory of 1949, many have attempted to read into Clark Kerr's time in China a failure either to appreciate or to report the true character and potential of the Chinese communists. While the criticism of British diplomats has been less vocal, criticism of US policy led to an unpleasant and very bitter campaign against many able diplomats who served in China in the 1940s. In his despatches from China since 1938, Clark Kerr maintained the same line on the communist influence: even in his final communiqué he wrote of 'the mild radicalism that in China is called communism'.[120] The failure of Clark Kerr to report the revolutionary basis of Mao's party, and Clark Kerr's friendship with many leftist characters in wartime China have been added together, stirred vigorously, and presented as evidence of nothing less than conspiratorial negligence. Certainly Clark Kerr openly associated with such as Agnes Smedley, Rewi Alley and Gunther Stein, and also briefly employed as his press secretary James Bertram, a communist propagandist. However, on the other hand, Clark Kerr was so fully supportive of Chiang that Tom Driberg, leftist himself, took him to task for it in the press.[121] Clark Kerr was a great admirer of Chiang's abilities throughout his time in China: '... a tower of strength... who commands the unquestioning faith and affection of his people...' he wrote in his final report. He did also point out, in this same report, the anti-democratic stance of many of Chiang's closest associates and the corruption and ineptitude which riddled his government. In that sense, there is little surprise that Clark Kerr should have been more favourably inclined towards individuals whose democratic principles were more in keeping with his own. Even Joe Alsop, veteran US journalist and a confirmed anti-communist, who visited China and Clark Kerr in 1939 was appalled by the corruption and anti-democratic nature of the Chiang regime. His memoirs, and support for those able US diplomats later to be pilloried by McCarthyites as responsible for the 'loss' of China make illuminating reading.[122] If anyone 'lost' China it was Chiang and his coterie who, scared and dismissive of democracy, lost touch with their people and political reality.

The fact is, however, that no one during these years publicly suggested that the Chinese communists were either a dangerous threat or able to seize power.

A masterly review of the subject[123] indicates that Kuomintang controls prevented journalists seeing much of the communists from 1937, and the early idealistic picture of the communists as 'agrarian reformers' was actually encouraged by the Kuomintang to safeguard continued US financial support. Edgar Snow has also argued that Chiang was desperate to avoid reports of communist successes being released which might lead the US to question continuing to finance his struggle. Similarly, in order to prevent the Japanese from exploiting the propaganda potential, journalists were reluctant to reveal anything indicating the growing nationalist-communist rift.[124]

The picture of the communists as 'agrarian reformers' was one which Clark Kerr faithfully reported to the Foreign Office. No doubt the more informed sympathizers such as Agnes Smedley and James Bertram were keen to promote this rather 'bumpkin' image to make the Maoists more appealing to the West, and worthy of support.[125] However, it was further strengthened by other observers, such as Edgar Snow himself, who failed to appreciate the strength of the underlying ideology which had merely been veiled by the communists because of the necessity of the wartime alliance. Other figures who travelled extensively among the Communists, and so were infinitely more knowledgeable and experienced than Clark Kerr, also argued that the communists were merely 'liberal democrats', seeking 'equality of opportunity and honest government'.[126] This became the prevailing opinion throughout the foreign press corps. Chou En-lai, the Communists' affable representative in Chungking, was also assiduous in seeking to present this favourable, mild image.

However, the situation is less clear-cut than appears. First of all, in January 1940 Mao had argued forcefully in an interview with Edgar Snow that 'we are always social revolutionaries; we are never reformers'.[127] This rejection of the 'agrarian reformer' tag could not have been more explicit and seems to make evident, whatever his apologists thought, that Mao himself had no intention of presenting anything but his true colours. Given this revelation, it does seem perverse for Clark Kerr to be peddling the 'reformer' myth in a report to the Foreign Office two years later. In a way, the myth became so much the accepted view that no evidence to the contrary was properly evaluated. Nonetheless, Clark Kerr must have been aware that 'mild radicalism' was a far from comprehensive description of the communist programme. If one adds to this his excessively glowing depiction of Chiang himself, one is forced to the conclusion that Clark Kerr may have allowed his enthusiasm for the cause of Chinese survival to colour his reports to the Foreign Office. This caused him to present the situation as more favourable and stable, and so worthy of support – financial and military – than it ever was in reality. On the other hand, the very same picture of China was emanating from the US, French, Australian and other legations: all failed to recognise the strength of Mao and the weakness of Chiang. Yet, in a society with no democratic institutions, of 600 million people and three million square miles, it is simply impossible to gauge opinion and predict the political future. A much more reasonable conclusion about the whole affair was that Chiang went to great lengths to cover up his communist problem, the threat posed, and used the diplomatic corps as a means to present his false position to the world. Far from serving the communists, the diplomatic corps and Clark Kerr were bolstering Chiang's regime.

Perhaps more damning of Clark Kerr was the fact that to acquaintances in China – intellectuals and visiting journalists – he had been airing the opinion as early as the spring of 1940 that he fully expected that the communists would ultimately win in China. He expressed himself unruffled by the prospect, viewing it simply as an inevitable historical development.[128] If this is true of his impression of internal Chinese affairs, it was one he never gave Foreign Office. While he had acknowledged in 1941 that 'the differences between the Central government and the communists have not been settled' and that it was 'impossible to foretell what developments may occur', he never indicated that the communists had any chance of posing a great threat to Chiang's position. In any event, they represented nothing more than 'liberal' or 'mild' reform. Again, however, this can be read as simply an attempt not to undermine Chiang in the eyes of the West. An appeasement-minded British Government would have leapt at the chance to deny Chiang support on the grounds that he was liable to be superceded by a communist regime. Clark Kerr's suppressions, if such there were, served to strengthen rather than weaken Chiang's position, therefore.

More criticism of Clark Kerr's time in China has centred on his friendships: with Agnes Smedley and others, particularly Russian diplomats.[129] Complete appointment diaries for Clark Kerr as Ambassador in China still exist, fully documenting these meetings. While, obviously, some private meetings may have taken place, appointments with leftist sympathizers were kept quite openly and properly. There can be no suggestion of conspiracy. If anything can be said, it is possible that Clark Kerr was manipulated by some of these communist apologists, but this could only have been minimal. Clark Kerr was no political greenhorn, and never a dupe.

As far as meetings with Russian diplomats are concerned,[130] several points can be made: since Hitler's treacherous and bloody Barbarossa assault of June 1941, Britain and the Soviet Union had become allies and co-operation at a diplomatic level had become both natural and desirable. Furthermore, the Soviet Union had been a key supplier of the Chinese resistance since the early days, and so had been linked long-term with the very aims, if only tacitly admitted, of British policy in the Far East. For Clark Kerr to have attempted to establish contact on the ground was both sensible and practical. An additional motive was that the UK and Soviet Embassies were the only two which remained functioning in the government area of Chungking throughout the blitz of that city: all other legations were moved south of the river. It is therefore perfectly understandable that Clark Kerr and his colleagues became more fully acquainted with the Russians as a result of their common discomfort. Lastly, by the end of 1941 when Clark Kerr had discovered that he was to go to Moscow, he would have been inordinately foolish not to have taken the opportunity of briefing himself on the USSR more expertly from his Russian counterparts in Chungking.

Perhaps the most damaging claim has concerned the close relationship which Clark Kerr established with the journalist Gunther Stein, who had undoubted communist sympathies and connections. Of all the journalists operating in China, Stein is the one whose name most frequently crops up in the Embassy appointment diaries. Following the end of the war, Stein was implicated in the Richard Sorge spy-ring case, and has admitted to having run errands for Sorge himself.[131] Sorge was a Soviet agent operating in Tokyo who managed to gain access to the secrets of the German Embassy there and gain valuable information for his Soviet bosses. Unfortunately Stalin's neurotic distrust of his own agents meant that his valuable piece of filching – the date and nature of the Barbarossa attack – was disregarded. After the war Stein took British citizenship, thanks to Clark Kerr's sponsorship, and stoutly maintained that he was innocent of any spying charges, and that his involvement with Sorge was merely friendship with a fellow countryman and journalist of a similarly leftist outlook.[132]

Stein, a likeable German of part-Jewish origin, was born in 1900. He had been in China on and off since 1932 and had also spent a year in Moscow as a correspondent of the *Berliner Tageblatt*. He visited the communist areas in 1937 and from 1939 to 44 was the China correspondent of the *Christian Science Monitor* and also provided copy for the *Guardian* and the *News Chronicle*. In 1937 he had also been in Japan where his flat was used by Richard Sorge for transmitting messages, and later that year was asked to leave Japan, because of his leftist views. Thereafter he occasionally acted as a courier for Sorge, taking packages to Shanghai and bringing back other material. Although Stein may well have been simply acting out of friendship, a man of his political awareness and experience must have been fully cognizant of the nature of Sorge's activities.[133]

These facts are certainly important, but they still present a very poor case for detracting from Clark Kerr's success. Clark Kerr met countless journalistic and diplomatic people during his years in China but reading anything more into friendships would be reckless. After all, one of his most frequent callers was James McHugh, a US attaché, who has been described as an 'extreme anti-communist' but this was clearly no reflection of Clark Kerr's views.[134] While Stein might well have had influence with Clark Kerr and might have coloured his views regarding the 'harmless' nature of Mao's communists, little else of certainty can be asserted regarding their relationship. It should also be noted that Clark Kerr had also sponsored for British citizenship Tom Barman, a Norwegian journalist whom he had known in Sweden, and who thereafter rendered invaluable and sustained service for British Intelligence. Critics have, predictably, chosen to ignore such evidence.

The final verdict must be that Clark Kerr did misunderstand and underestimate the nature, if not the potential, of the communists in China. In this, he was by no means alone, but merely subscribing to the prevalent, and expert, opinion. The more heinous and culpable error must be his failure to record officially his own private view, which he held at least as early as 1940, that the communists would finally triumph. However, one cannot therefore deduce that he was intentionally misleading his superiors so that the communists could somehow sneak their way to power with his connivance. Mao, obviously, in his forthright maintenance of his revolutionary principles was following no such clandestine programme. Indeed, as Edgar Snow has pointed out, it was Chiang and the Kuomintang who stood to gain by, and vigorously pursued, a policy of publicly misrepresenting the power of the communists and of covering up their successes. Clark Kerr's reticence in voicing his own beliefs was actually to the benefit of the Kuomintang: as has already been argued, the Chamberlain Government would have leapt at the opportunity to withhold support from Chiang on the grounds that he could not hold China in the future. Clark Kerr's consistently flattering references to Chiang in his despatches suggest that he was indeed seeking to bolster the Kuomintang in the eyes of Whitehall so that China was presented as a united front against Japanese aggression. He was, however, honest enough to indicate the wretched nature of Chiang's court and its reactionary, undemocratic views, however upstanding Chiang himself might be. On the inadequate evidence available, nothing of any real substance can be laid to Clark Kerr's charge. A very important piece of evidence which confirms Clark Kerr's attitude to the internal conflict in China is a note to the Foreign Office sent later from Moscow in the summer of 1942.[135] An idea had been produced by SOE (Special Operations Executive) to bypass Chiang's regime and get aid through to the communist forces fighting so much more effectively against the Japanese. Clark Kerr, then in Moscow and with no reason to forward any opinion at all, utterly abhorred any such idea: 'I feel bound to place on record my strong dissent from any attempt to make use of the Communists without the knowledge of the Chinese government'. That surely proves where his true sympathies lay.

His four years in China were, if anything, the most valuable service he rendered to Britain: virtually abandoned and defenceless, he was still able through his charm, skill, courage and energy to keep British interests and prestige above water when everything had pointed to Britain's total disappearance from the oriental seascape.

Indeed the gravity of Britain's position was grimly exhibited while Clark Kerr was in India en route to Russia: the two British battleships sent east to threaten Japan were sunk within days and, later, on 15 February 1942 came the greatest and fatal blow to the British Empire in the East: the ignominious fall of Singapore itself.

From India Clark Kerr went on alone to Baghdad, and thence to Teheran before finally reaching the *dreich* wartime Soviet diplomatic centre of Kuibyshev, on the Volga, a few days before his sixtieth birthday. He could have been forgiven had he felt a degree of self-pity as he settled in once more to a disagreeable wartime billet: the four years of China had been marked by the crippling desertion of his beloved Tita; the death of the faithful Hodge, whose inquisitive charm had been the very instrument of his first encounter with Tita long ago in Chile; his flat in Grosvenor Street, London, had been flattened by a German bomb; many personal effects and belongings sent on from China had gone down in a ship sunk by Japanese torpedoes; and, for reasons of personal security, his manservant Arthur Maddox and his wife had decided to see out the war years in the safety of Sydney, Australia. Thus it was that Archie Clark Kerr arrived in the Soviet Union, as lonely and desolate as he had ever been, and once more entrusted with a trying and unrewarding diplomatic mission. He had lost everything but his extravagant abilities, his reputation and his unswerving ambition.

CHAPTER 7

Mountain Top 1942–46

From Chungking to Kuibyshev, a distance of several thousand miles, amounted in practical terms to the exchanging of one disagreeable billet in an ugly, overcrowded city for another in a less ugly, but possibly even more crowded, city.

For Clark Kerr, it was something of a culture shock. His Britannic Majesty's Ambassador was treated simply like any other foreign diplomat: with suspicion and at arm's length. From Chungking, where he could mingle at will with great and small, where his every word was eagerly awaited by a voracious press corps, and where every move of his bullet-proof Rolls was the subject of intense and extended gossip and conjecture, Clark Kerr now found himself largely ignored, with no access to any agreeable society, and little practical to do. For all its status as one of the top posts, the post of Ambassador to the Soviet Union was a considerable let-down for Clark Kerr in those first few weeks. Fresh from his triumph on the Chinese stage, he had hoped for rather more than a mere walk-on part in a provincial Russian backwater.

In fact, despite appearances on the ground, it was a time of much diplomatic activity as regards British-Soviet relations. Relations between the two countries had never been very easy, mostly because of the circumstances in which the Soviet Union came into being, a mere 25 years previously. Mutual suspicion had been the hallmark: as Clark Kerr knew, even in China when both states were aiding the Chinese resistance, there was little attempt to co-ordinate activities. Following Munich and the abortive talks in the summer of 1939, Stalin had turned to a pact with Hitler to give the Soviet Union their much-needed breathing-space. Relations with Britain remained sour until Hitler's invasion of the Soviet Union in June 1941. The very next day, in one of his most admirable moves, Churchill had pledged full and unqualified support to the Soviet resistance. Allied by circumstance, the two countries still remained uneasily distant during the massive German advances of late 1941.

In the wake of parliamentary and press lobbying, some attempt was made to build up aid for the Soviet armies. Initially, having watched the poor efforts of the Red Army in their Finnish skirmishes of 1939, the British military were pessimistic about the prospects of the Soviet Union withstanding the Nazi onslaught for long. In addition, many of the leading British generals were outspokenly anti-Bolshevist, and the choice of one of these, Gen. Mason-MacFarlane, to head a military mission to Moscow was not the greatest opening gambit Britain could have made.[1]

At the same time the Soviet Government began to press the British and American Governments for aid, mostly of an extravagant and unrealistic nature, and then proceeded to berate Churchill when the impossible duly failed to materialise. Churchill rightly pointed to the fact that until June 1941, during the months of the Battle of Britain and the fall of France, the Soviet Union had, as paper allies of Germany, been of no assistance to Britain. Stalin's complaint at British inactivity, lack of support, and the failure to open a 'second front' in Western Europe to relieve pressure on the Soviet armies in the east continued unabated. Yet his complaints did have force, whatever recriminations could be adduced from the past. Accordingly in September 1941, Churchill despatched Lord Beaverbrook, the Minister of Supply, along with Roosevelt's roving Ambassador, Averell Harriman, to Moscow to thrash out a deal to set aid to the Soviet Union on a firm and agreed footing. The conference was successful, and Beaverbrook returned in some triumph, well primed by Stalin on the urgent need for a second front.

Sir Stafford Cripps, meanwhile, ostensibly the foremost British diplomat in Moscow, as Ambassador, felt himself frozen out by Beaverbrook's very public performance. The choice of Cripps as Ambassador had seemed sensible at the time of his appointment in 1940: as a left-winger he might have seemed a sound selection, despite his lack of diplomatic experience. In fact, however, Stalin judged that because of his leftist principles Cripps could have no influence in capitalist Britain. He tended to ignore Cripps, whose austere teetotalism was also anathema to the carousing Georgian. Cripps was held in low esteem by the Foreign Office, and when he expressed an interest in returning to Britain, officials were more than pleased to smooth his passage. By this stage, Cripps had lost Churchill's confidence and, having no influence with Stalin, nor backing from the Foreign Office, was now something of a lame duck in Moscow. The British public opinion of Cripps remained high, however, as it would even on his return.

Although sympathy is due to Cripps, given the timing of his appointment, his most serious blunder was one which continued to haunt British-Soviet relations until the end of the war. It seems certain that, despite strong representations that no such approach be made, he did suggest to the Soviet authorities, in a clumsy attempt to force them into the war prior to Barbarossa, that if they did not enter, then Britain, following Hess's arrival, might be forced into making a separate peace with Germany.[2] This foolish move, coupled with an irresponsible delay in forwarding a warning about German plans for attack on the Soviet Union, served only to provide the Soviet Union with needless propaganda and to fuel Stalin's already well-nourished paranoia. Cripps was viewed by the Soviets as simply an *agent provocateur* to the extent that even his genuine information about the date of Barbarossa was discounted as mere trouble-making. In fact it probably did the Allied cause a service, for if Stalin had massed forces on his western borders to meet the Nazi invasion, they would have undoubtedly been utterly crushed and the Soviet Union defeated within days. Instead, by stretching the Nazi lines of communication, Stalin gained time to regroup and strengthen resistance.

Stalin's suspicions of British perfidy and possible secret peace deals with Hitler were further strengthened by the reluctance of some in the British establishment to pal up with the 'Bolshies', and by the outspoken comments of some in the military who hoped to see the Nazis and Communists kill each other off. The worst culprit was Col. Moore-Brabazon, Minister of Aircraft Production, who was quoted as saying he was glad that Britain's 'two greatest enemies' were now at each other's throats.[3]

By late 1941, with Cripps preparing to return home, and touted by some as a possible replacement for Churchill, there was genuine concern in government circles over relations with the Soviet Union. Against all the odds, she had survived the Nazi *blitzkrieg* and might well prove victorious. There was a worry over what she might gain from the war, and a need thus to reassess her position *vis-à-vis* Britain.

On 18 November 1941, a major conference was held in the Foreign Office on the problem.[4] Something had to be done to allay mutual suspicions and to interweave the two states' individual war aims. The need for a firm agreement between the two countries was decided on and the Foreign Secretary, Anthony Eden, was sent to Moscow in late December to lay the grounds for such a treaty.

From the beginning to the end of the war, British officials struggled vainly to understand Soviet motivation and interests, and to anticipate her diplomatic and political strategy. So many inveterate Foreign Office memo-mongers and assorted experts and mandarins chipped in that the result was an undecipherable mess. Occasionally, some wise words were penned, but these were soon lost or forgotten in the sea of words. Churchill, himself, had set the tone in his oft-quoted pronouncement of 1 October 1939 when he stated: 'I cannot forecast to you the action of Russia. It is a riddle wrapped in a mystery inside an enigma.' Churchill did, however, go on to offer a sensible suggestion, not often recorded: '... perhaps there is a key. That key is Russian national interest.' This was correct, but only in part; the Soviet Union also had ideological principles which came into play. British officials were more at home when they rightly, but too comprehensively, sought to interpret Stalin's aims in old-fashioned Tsarist terms. What they did not appreciate until too late was the influence on Soviet policy of the evangelical desire to spread the Marxist gospel. Just as in China, when Clark Kerr and other diplomats, before and after, failed to appreciate the strength and sweep of Maoist philosophy, so in Soviet terms not enough was understood of the Marxist seam which now ran through the age-old Tsarist expansionism and craving for security. Few Foreign Office employees had studied Marxism: those that had, as it only later transpired, seemed to have embraced it as their own.

As Britain struggled to judge Soviet aims and objectives in preparation for finalising a treaty, the most succinct expression of the British viewpoint came from Lacy Bagallay, who was then charge d'affaires in Kuibyshev, pending Clark Kerr's arrival.

In a memo of February 1942, he wrote:

> the Soviet Government are only interested in us as allies to the extent to which they think our activities will assist: a. their own victory in the war; b. their own security after the war.[5]

When the war had passed, this proved to be the simple truth, although even then Britain failed to realise fully the way in which the Soviets would seek to achieve that security: not by sealing up impregnable borders, or even by seeking to influence her neighbours, but by actually establishing puppet governments in all surrounding states. An early acceptance of the Soviet Union's purely expedient and coldly practical approach to alliance with Britain, and an avoidance of fond hopes for lasting unity, might well have served Britain better in the long run. It would have meant less comfortable and downright awkward relations, but it would certainly have prevented the deep sense of disappointment which the Cold War brought to many who had been involved closely with the Soviet Union at this time. Clark Kerr was perhaps chief of these, but with a common purpose and mutual benefits at stake, it would be an odd diplomat who did not seek to develop those into something much more friendly, open and permanent.

Throughout the early months of 1942, British and Soviet diplomats negotiated the terms of the proposed treaty. At this stage, the received wisdom in the Foriegn Office was that the Soviet post-war aim would be the securing of her national boundaries by dominating her eastern European neighbours. The Soviet Union made it clear in negotiations that their price for agreeing a treaty would be for Britain to recognise the Soviet acquisitions of 1939: the Baltic states and part of eastern Poland. This placed Britain in an awkward position: Britain had gone to war precisely to defend the integrity and independence of Poland; to agree now to the dismemberment of that country would be hypocritical in the extreme. Hypocrisy and diplomacy have been partners for generations, but it must always be a secret liaison. In addition, Stalin's deal over Poland and the Baltic states had been made with Hitler himself: Britain could hardly be expected to nod through such a squalid arrangement.

A further complication had arisen through Churchill's wooing of Roosevelt and their subsequent marriage contract of 1941 – the Atlantic Charter. This document, rather impressively drafted on the back of a menu by Sir Alexander Cadogan, laid great stress on there being no agreement on border changes without the consent of the peoples concerned. Despite that, and recognising that the Soviet Union had complete control of the areas in question and that official British recognition entailed no practical change, Eden, Cripps, Halifax and Clark Kerr himself were amongst those who pressed for acceding to the Soviet requests. Churchill, Attlee and others argued that it was impossible to recognise Stalin's illegal annexations, and the United States Government made it clear that they could sanction no such agreement. The most strident voice in favour of recognising Stalin's absorptions was Lord Beaverbrook, who was vociferously arguing also for a commitment to establish a second front at the earliest possible date. Irritated by Churchill's refusal to budge on the issue, and seduced by the idea of actually being a potential successor to the premiership itself, Beaverbrook resigned from the Government on 9 February 1942.

Clark Kerr's views were predictably pragmatic: there was no chance now of removing the Soviet Union from the Baltic and it was best simply to accept the fact. More than anything, however, he desired to have something tangible to offer the Soviets in talks in Moscow. He had suffered in China from a similar diet of political bread and water and had no wish to continue in that style.

However, in late May, following Molotov's visits to London and Washington, an agreement was reached without specific reference to the Baltic states or Poland. The main terms of the 'Anglo'- Soviet Treaty, as it became known, were a commitment to mutual help and assistance throughout the war and beyond, and an agreement not to enter any unilateral negotiations with Nazi Germany. Clark Kerr was delighted with the terms of the treaty, not least because its formal declaration of alliance made his position so much the more comfortable, as he reported to the Foreign Office: 'I have moved from something akin to despair to something like real hope'.[6]

Clark Kerr's initial despair was understandable. Kuibyshev was a crowded, unpleasant and dull base for his diplomatic style. Since the great panic of 15 October 1941 it had served as the provisional seat of government when the Foreign Ministry and others were hastily relocated from Moscow as the Nazi guns threatened. Stalin and Molotov remained, with an ostentatious display of bravado, holed up in the Kremlin, thereby acting as powerful symbols of Soviet determination. In Kuibyshev, the Foreign Ministry was placed under the control of the notorious Vice-Commissar, Andrei Vyshinski, the terrifying state prosecutor from the show trials of the 1930s.

The main problem in Kuibyshev, apart from the crowded accommodation and lack of lavatorial facilities, was simply that there was nothing to do. The only entertainment, excellent though it may have been, was the Bolshoi ballet; but there was no one with whom to socialise, and Clark Kerr was followed everywhere by four NKVD agents. He reacted badly to the enforced idleness. To Cripps he wrote: 'With Vyshinski I have established a happy enough relationship... but with Vyshinski nothing fundamental can be done', and was concerned that he was in danger of disappointing his superiors, who had only chosen him because of his record in China of working wonders in impossible situations.[7] British Ambassador to the Soviet Union, while now second only in importance to Halifax in Washington, was proving to be even more frustrating than China where, at least, Clark Kerr could openly fraternise with the local population.

Cut off in Kuibyshev, there was little option but to join the diplomatic circus, something he had never much enjoyed. He soon discovered, however, that the small clique of ambassadors which had orbited around Cripps was nothing but 'an anti-Soviet sewing bee' and so he quickly removed himself again. The US Ambassador, Admiral Standley, and the Czech Ambassador, Dr Fierlinger, albeit a 'declared Communist', he reported as being the only decent company.[8] His main hopes rested in building up a good relationship with Stalin and Molotov whenever he got the chance to travel to Moscow.

In late March, Clark Kerr was granted permission to make the 20-hour journey to the capital to present his credentials to President Kalinin and to meet Stalin and Molotov. The meeting with Stalin proved both odd and a resounding success. After being led along the interminable Kremlin passages, the air-raid sirens suddenly went off just before Clark Kerr was to be introduced to Stalin. 'My first surprise was the shape and size of him', Clark Kerr later recorded.

> I had expected something big and burly. But I saw, at the end of the long room, a little, slim, bent, grey man with a large head and immense white hands... When he shook my hand he looked, almost furtively, at my shoulder and not at my face.[9]

Asked if he would join Stalin in the air-raid dug-out, Clark Kerr at first courteously declined but, seeing that his presence there was expected, he 'had to change a clumsy no into a clumsier yes'. He and Molotov were seen into a lift by Stalin, but when they reached the dugout below Stalin was miraculously already waiting, having evidently sped down by a secret route.

As pipe-smokers, Clark Kerr and Stalin were soon exchanging and discussing tobacco. Despite this apparent camaraderie, Clark Kerr noticed that, whenever he could, Stalin would peer closely at him, sizing him up, but that whenever he turned to meet his gaze, Stalin would avert his eyes sheepishly. Clark Kerr reckoned that he was not unlike 'a possum you would get very fond of (against your better judgement), but would have to keep a sharp eye on, lest he nip you in the buttocks out of sheer mischief'.[10] Because of the air-raid, they were detained in wide-ranging, light-hearted chat for a considerable time. Inevitably, but very productively as it transpired, Clark Kerr steered the subject onto sex, and he and the Soviet dictator exchanged notes, and swapped tales, on this most urgent of topics. As far as marital relations were concerned – a tender subject for Clark Kerr – Stalin, rather predictably 'favoured the early use of the stick' to keep wives 'in line'! 'As time went on,' wrote Clark Kerr to the Foreign Office, 'he seemed to get restless, for he began to walk up and down'. Fearing that he was boring Stalin, Clark Kerr offered to go but Stalin brushed his suggestion aside, and soon was revealed the reason for restlessness:

> His belly, which is biggish, and rather schlap, was rumbling – not as yours or mine might, but stupendously. I mean really on the dictator level. He was a bit shy about it and he was trying to drown its booming voice with his own... But sometimes he had to pause and my translator was not man of the world enough... to raise his voice too. So as the rumbling went on echoing down the long room, Stalin was driven to banging his pipe loudly on a tinny ashtray.[11]

After Clark Kerr's unique audience, he was full of hope that he could, indeed, make a success of his mission. To Cripps he enthused:

> That boot-faced Molotov made me the most formal promise of close cooperation and with Stalin I like to think that I have clicked. We fraternised over pipes and were amused by each other's jokes. Indeed, I found him to be just my cup of tea. And now he has done something which the staff here declare to be without precedent. He has sent me a present of a large quantity of his own pipe tobacco.[12]

To Eden, Clark Kerr accounted for his instant rapport in a rather rosy-tinted way:

> ... probably no more than a juxtaposition of two old rogues, each one seeing the roguery in the other and finding comfort and harmony in it, and chuckling over it – chuckling all the more because of the governessy presence of that boot-faced Molotov.[13]

They may have been two old rogues, but one was surely more roguish than the other: only Stalin had the blood of more than 5 million fellow-countrymen on his hands. Clark Kerr was determined not to let such reputations interfere with his work. Vyshinski, for example, he knew had a 'black and bloody background' but Clark Kerr felt that 'if we let ourselves be disturbed by backgrounds in Russia today we shall get nowhere and I prefer to wipe them out...'[14]

This was, perhaps, too accommodating a stance for Clark Kerr to assume. A more pragmatic approach would have been not 'to wipe out' such reputations but merely to put them to one side for the present. Although there is no doubt that Stalin and Clark Kerr did genuinely hit it off from the start, Clark Kerr was misled into believing thereby that Stalin's chumminess would produce diplomatic benefits for Britain, and that this side of his character was in some way the norm, or excused his other excesses.

Nevertheless, it is only fair to point out that Clark Kerr himself was well aware that socialising happily with Stalin, on the odd occasion, did not amount to very much. He declared strongly:

> This does not satisfy me. I want to plunge into the mind of the Russians and that seem to be impossible... I came here to offer a hell of a lot – all I had. But there is no one to take it! What is a fellow to do?... A fellow like myself needs, I won't say an audience, but a sympathetic readership on the part of others to turn over and have a look at what he has to offer.[15]

Back in depression in Kuibyshev, he was warning Eden that Soviet secrecy, fear and repression were tremendous obstacles to his work. Nevertheless he was:

proud to have a shot at it. But it may well take a long time to show any results – indeed there may never be any results to show, unless there be a radical change of heart here and with it a general loosening up.[16]

Clark Kerr was anxious also for some leave and to Eden he pled passionately that it was now four years since 'the last time I smelt my native air, listened to the talk of my own people, and breathed the atmosphere about them...'[17] But with the Treaty talks so delicately poised, there was no hope of being granted his desire.

After the rather puritanical Cripps, Clark Kerr was a pleasant change for the Russians, and on 2 May Vyshinski gave a dinner party for the embassy staff in Kuibyshev. This, too, was without precedent. Clark Kerr reported on the event to his senior, Christopher Warner, head of the Northern Department at the Foreign Office. 'It was a tough party,' he admitted, 'for Vyshinski is a practised and stout brandy drinker, whereas I am but a puny drinker of wine. The occasion clearly demanded a departure from habit and I did my best.' Clark Kerr almost succumbed but he fought bravely, considering it to be a test of his manhood and British prestige. He was saved:

... fortunately, the dinner was followed by a long movie of which I can recall little or nothing, as I was concentrating on coming to. This I managed pretty successfully, so successfully indeed that I began to feel something not unlike contempt for brandy. No member of the embassy staff could tell me next day what the movie had been about.[18]

Clark Kerr dutifully praised the brandy, and a few days later Vyshinski sent him four bottles as a present. Clark Kerr then reluctantly had to part with, in return, four bottles from his own precious whisky supplies.

These tales of tobacco, booze and parties no doubt enlivened grey days at the Foreign Office but the fact was that, starved of anything else, this was all to which Clark Kerr could turn his famous quill. There was little else for him to report on; so he spent his days filling his customary heavy sheets of lined foolscap with his elegant handwriting, consulting Fowler at length, and lingering over them like a poet. He was always a stickler for grammatical exactitude, and these standards he applied even to these, chatty, gossipy notes to HQ.

In hindsight, however, it is the case that Clark Kerr's ability to establish a good working relationship with Stalin did prove crucial in smoothing out the many difficulties which arose during the war years. While their intimacy perhaps clouded Clark Kerr's ability to recognise in time the sinister moves being planned and enacted by Stalin in Eastern Europe, without Clark Kerr there is a good chance that the alliance with the Soviet Union would have foundered long before it actually did in the post-war fallout. It is, for example, hard to imagine any other British diplomat being able to settle down to a drinking session, punctuated with bawdy jokes and coarse tales, with the Politburo. The very thought of Lord Halifax, for example, in such a situation is laughable.

Languishing in Kuibyshev, lonely and depressed, that summer of 1942 he settled into a relaxed routine: every morning he began with an hour of exercises, a cold bath, and then would move bare-chested to the garden where he would conduct business clad only in black bathing shorts. He had managed to acquire a few geese and whenever one of his quills wore out, he would simply grab one from a protesting gander, cut a nib and resume his work. If it was not to Tita he was writing – and he wrote once a day – he would linger over his drafts to the Foreign Office, seeking out with pleasure any uncommon *mots justes*. Many of these were not in the cypher book and had to be spelled out laboriously letter by letter by the unfortunate operator. Clark Kerr cared not a whit: he wanted to imprint his personality on his messages.

Following the signing of the Anglo-Soviet Treaty on 26 May 1942, Clark Kerr was brought much more firmly into play. A problem had arisen because of a difference of opinion over the agreement reached during Molotov's visits to London and Washington. Despite his incredible stonewalling negotiating style, these talks had bred success. In Washington, Molotov had induced Roosevelt to agree to a communiqué which contained the words 'full understanding was reached with regard to the urgent tasks of creating a Second Front in Europe in 1942'. The British Government, disappointed by Roosevelt's laxity, was unhappy at delivering such an unnecessary hostage to fortune and sought to repair the damage by having Churchill deliver an *aide-memoire* to Molotov on June 10th which made it clear that a cross-channel invasion in the autumn of 1942 was a hope and not a promise.[19]

Despite that, back in Moscow Molotov made it clear to Clark Kerr, in an interview at the end of the month that he stood by the communiqué's 'firm commitment' to opening a second front in August or September.[20] Clark Kerr was instructed to correct Molotov, which he did on 4 July, but the Soviets, although acknowledging the existence and contents of the *aide-memoire*, made no attempt to dampen public expectations of a second front, which had been unfairly raised.[21] The likely explanation is that Molotov was scared to have to admit to Stalin that he had not, as he had been instructed to and had at first indicated, managed to secure a definite undertaking on the second front for 1942. Clark Kerr certainly suspected that Molotov was wriggling:

> Although Molotov professes to have passed on faithfully to the Soviet Government all that was said to him in London ... it now looks as if he had to some extent failed to interpret to Stalin the mind of the PM.[22]

As July wore on, Churchill firmed up his disinclination to risk a cross-channel invasion with a growing counter-enthusiasm, belatedly shared by Roosevelt, for an invasion of French North Africa. Clark Kerr began to experience uneasiness at these developments: first of all, Churchill had visited Roosevelt again in late June to woo the President away from any rash attempt to invade northern France; then, in early July, a regular convoy to deliver war material to the Soviet Union by the Arctic route was scattered and crippled by German U-boats. Of the 34 ships which had sailed, 23 were sunk. In view of this disaster, it was decided reluctantly to suspend further sailings until security could be tightened. Then, at the end of the month, American military chiefs travelled to London to discuss strategy. The increasing closeness between the USA and Britain, militarily and politically, to the effective exclusion of the Soviet allies, was bad enough. The suspension of the convoys and the growing silence on the matter of the second front was a heavy blow to Soviet resistance and morale. This was made all the more grave by the stunning German advances in south-east Russia, culminating on 27 July in the fall of Rostov and the crossing of the Don river.

Not surprisingly, Stalin, whose missives often simply reflected Soviet morale at the time of writing, responded fiercely and indignantly.[23] While the Soviet peoples and soldiers were being slaughtered in their thousands, the British were reducing rather than increasing their aid, and talk of postponing the second front until 1943 was further cause to despair. Clark Kerr wrote accurately on 25 July:

> What the USSR wants is some tangible evidence that we realise that the time will come when great and costly efforts will have to be made so far as land fighting on the continent of Europe is concerned. As I see it they are not yet convinced that we understand this, or that we are yet taking the war seriously. They set up their own enormous losses against our (by comparison) trifling losses in men and material since the close of 1939.[24]

Apart from the strategic limitations which restricted Churchill's capacity to wage war, and the influence of his own private memories of the disaster at Gallipoli, there was also the fact that Churchill was a democratic leader in a much more open society, and so liable to public criticism and parliamentary censure, as he had been following the jolt of the surrender at Tobruk on 21 June. Stalin had no such checks on his freedom of action: he also had no qualms about sacrificing countless numbers of his forces, of which there was little shortage. Churchill could ill afford another disaster after Singapore and Tobruk, and had no intention of flirting with it in an ill-conceived attack on northern France.

Clark Kerr felt, in these inauspicious circumstances, more than a little exposed. He felt things slipping, and decided that the interests of both countries could best be served and relations improved if Churchill were to meet Stalin face to face to iron out the problems. It would also let Clark Kerr off the hook a little. Accordingly on 28 July he suggested to Eden that Churchill be encouraged to come to Moscow to try to staunch the deterioration in relations.

Despite the likely unpleasantness of the task, Churchill jumped at the opportunity, intending to visit Cairo en route to conclude preparations for allied advances in North Africa. Of the nature of the job in Moscow he was fully conscious: to Roosevelt he described it as 'a somewhat raw job', requesting that Roosevelt's adviser Averell Harriman be released to travel with him to lend support.[25] In his own memoirs, Churchill described his mission as akin to 'carrying a large lump of ice to the North Pole'.[26]

Having visited Cairo, the British Prime Minister and his party, accommodated in three planes, left for Moscow via Teheran. Churchill arrived on the afternoon of Wednesday 12 August, but the plane carrying his chief diplomatic and military advisers was delayed in Teheran. Churchill, therefore, was even more exposed than he otherwise would have been on his arrival. The most colourful account of Churchill's visit, of the many published, is Clark Kerr's own. Indeed the Permanent Under-Secretary at the Foreign Office, Sir Alec Cadogan, was reluctant to use it as a formal record because of its personal and rather flippant tone. Clark Kerr was amongst a large crowd of Soviet, British and American dignitaries who gathered to greet Churchill on arrival. Clark Kerr described the scene in his own eccentric way:

> The first glimpse I had of the PM was a pair of stout legs dangling from the belly of the plane and feeling for terra firma. They found it, and then came the plump trunk and finally the round football head, and quite a normal hat. All this stooped under the machine, but it scrabbled successfully out and drew itself up. It was like a bull at the corrida when it first comes out of its dark pen and stands dazzled and bewildered and glares at the crowd. Like the bull's, the PM's eyes were bloodshot and defiant and like the bull he stood and swayed as if uncertain where to make the first charge. But the charge came from the crowd, headed by Molotov, and the bull was lost to sight in a wild scrum.[27]

After the usual platitudes for the media, Churchill was whisked off to the dacha on the outskirts of Moscow where he and his immediate party were to be based. Not such a good omen was the fact that Churchill's ubiquitous two-fingered victory signal was apparently misinterpreted by Russian onlookers as an indication that the second front was imminent. Once ensconced in the dacha, Churchill was briefed by Clark Kerr about his impression of Soviet expectations. They amounted to the opening of the second front, and as this was not now immediately possible, Clark Kerr suggested that Churchill get this bad news over quickly and bluntly, before elaborating on the North African alternative.

During the meal before their departure for the Kremlin that first evening, Clark Kerr, perhaps deliberately, allowed Churchill to overhear him chatting to Harriman about the chances of the much-coveted move to Washington. Churchill turned on him 'What are you talking about? Don't you realise that I have just appointed you to the most important job in the world? The most important job in the world!'

The fact that Clark Kerr thought it relevant to include this in his report for Eden tends to suggest that he was setting out his stall somewhat obviously. It is clear, however, he was quite certain that he would achieve the Washington goal, even without blatant lobbying. To Gavin Maxwell he wrote that, despite the blackness of the outlook from Moscow, he was as certain of winning the war as he remained of being the future Ambassador to the USA.[28]

On Churchill himself, Clark Kerr wrote:

> I envy most his mastery of the English language. That is rare... rarer still his ability to transform his face from the rosiest, happiest, the most laughing, dimpled and mischievous baby's bottom into the face of an angry, and outraged bullfrog!... I cannot get anywhere near it. Whatever my emotions, my face remains like a ram's.[29]

With the absence of his main advisers, it was a small party which accompanied Churchill to meet Stalin at 7pm. Churchill had evidently not briefed himself on local geography to any great extent. As they skirted the Kremlin, Clark Kerr pointed it out to Churchill, who replied excitedly 'Oh! Is this the Nevsky Prospect?' (the main thoroughfare of Leningrad). At the meeting in the Kremlin were present Churchill, Harriman, Clark Kerr and his interpreter Dunlop, ageing and, as it later transpired, dying. On the Soviet side were Stalin, Molotov, Voroshilov representing the military, and the interpreter Pavlov.

After a brief review of the current military situation, about which Stalin voiced severe pessimism, Churchill turned to the question of the second front. He explained in detail why it could not take place, promising instead that 'the British and American governments were preparing for a very great operation in 1943'.[30] Stalin was very unhappy at the news, although he brightened up at the news of extensive bombing of Germany. Although Clark Kerr thought Churchill's method of approach 'masterly', the meeting was riddled with tension as Clark Kerr minuted in the manner which Cadogan found so inappropriate.

> Each one was very restless. Stalin kept getting up and walking across the big room to a writing table into which he delved for cigarettes. These he tore to bits and stuffed into his absurd curly pipe. In his turn the PM when he had shot a bolt got up and had a walk, pulling from his heated buttocks the seat of his trousers which had clearly stuck to them. It was indeed a warm night. There was something about this dumpy figure, plucking at his backside, which suggested immense strength but little distinction.[31]

Despite the tension, the meeting ended at 10.40 on a positive note, with Churchill's powerful presentation of the plans for the invasion of French North Africa.

Back at the dacha, as they reviewed the night's work, Clark Kerr became rather annoyed at Harriman who, he felt, 'tended... to bumsuck the PM and clearly the PM liked it'.[32] Clark Kerr felt it his professional duty to advise as valuably and objectively as possible but Harriman, by no means alone in this failing, made no attempt to offer anything other than what Churchill wanted to hear.

Next morning, Churchill was in a foul mood, owing partly to a Russian hangover. He seemed to take it out on Clark Kerr, who had failed to match the obsequious flattery of the Americans in his dealings with Churchill: 'The little I said seemed to irritate him... and certainly the lot he said irritated me'.[33]

Clark Kerr's failure to fall in line with Churchill's tetchiness irked the PM. Clark Kerr noted:

> I fancy that he saw the battle in my eye and this made him peevish. It wasn't much fun and the sycophancy of the US Ambassador at luncheon and the sustained bum-sucking of Harriman made me feel and probably look like an angry ram.

While Churchill threw hostile glances Clark Kerr's way, he pawed theatrically at Harriman: 'I'm so glad, Averell, that you came with me. You are a tower of strength.'

After lunch, Clark Kerr was a little relieved by a brief talk in the garden with Sir Charles Wilson, Churchill's doctor, who told him that Churchill's 'black bile' was a 'frequent manifestation'. In the meantime Churchill had an unhappy meeting with Molotov while Clark Kerr had to return to the airport to meet the delayed advisers. Their attitude on arrival infuriated him: they fussed over their luggage and pointedly ignored the Russian dignitaries. Clark Kerr was angered by Wavell in particular, who was a Russian speaker but made no attempt to use his skill, and was not impressed either with Sir Alan Brooke, the Chief of the Imperial General Staff. 'He has a face like a rabbit,' he wrote in one of his customary animal comparisons, 'not the quick, white scutted little animal that dashes out of the bracken to be shot, but the hatch rabbit, the Belgian hare, that placidly nibbles lettuce leaves and then makes a hell of a stink because he can't help it'.[34]

Whether or not connected to that morning's petulance, Clark Kerr returned to the dacha to discover that he had been dropped from the team for that evening's meeting with Stalin. Clark Kerr had no doubt that it was childish spite on Churchill's behalf. Churchill's doctor had told Clark Kerr that the PM's chief weakness was that 'he was surrounded by yes men and he took pleasure in being so surrounded'. An exhausted and exasperated Clark Kerr evidently concurred: 'Well, well, boys will be boys! What a bloody day,' he wrote in his diary.[35] That same night he complained to Cadogan about life in Russia, and even questioned the point of his being transferred from China where he was doing well and thriving, to end up in a post where thankless monotony and boredom was the norm.

The next morning, 14 August, the atmosphere in the dacha had sunk further. The meeting with Stalin, who had been at his truculent worst, had been something of a disaster. The Prime Minister had been furious at Stalin's attitude; now Churchill paraded around in his flowered dressing-gown 'like a wounded lion'. He had mislaid some of his clothes into the bargain and staff were running round frantically. Clark Kerr was encouraged to assist in the hunt: 'The Clarks,' he declared, 'do not valet anybody. Not even the PM.'[36] Churchill was now saying he would be damned if he would attend the dinner Stalin had arranged for that evening. Clark Kerr was brave enough to counter him.

I advised very strongly that he should and I got it in the neck.

At lunch the PM was at his bloody worst. He seemed to concentrate his ill-humour upon me. It was difficult to sit through the meal with any semblance of patience and good manners. I fear I didn't make a success of that, for I felt like giving him a good root up the arse. My respect for him and faith in him have suffered sadly.[37]

Despite his sulks, Churchill was prevailed upon to attend the dinner in the Kremlin. It was a grand affair with much alcohol, but Churchill was in no mood to be placated. Stalin vainly attempted to lighten the atmosphere but Churchill who, Clark Kerr judged, was 'unduly brief and lacking in warmth' left grumpily at 1.30am, Stalin trotting after him trying to maintain a semblance of amity.

Back at the dacha, Churchill was at his most stubborn, refusing to agree to a communiqué and muttering about leaving Stalin to fight his own battles. Clark Kerr was fully aware of the crippling effect which a failure to agree to a joint up-beat communiqué would cause. He was very irritated by Churchill's performance. 'I don't like to see a man in whose hands lies the fate of whole peoples behave like a spoilt child.'

In the morning, 15 August, things had, if anything, deteriorated. Churchill was determined to leave without meeting Stalin again, and to forget about any communiqué. When Clark Kerr arrived, both Cadogan and Sir Charles Wilson, the doctor, independently urged him to try to talk the PM round. A failure to agree with Stalin would have the worst possible effect on allied morale and the whole war effort, and would simply embolden the Nazis. There could be no telling where the harm would end.

Sir Archibald Clark Kerr's resulting talk with Churchill was probably the most important diplomatic coup of his career. Without his efforts, the skill and calculated flattery of his approach to Churchill, it is possible that the whole course of the Second World War could have been fundamentally altered. It is, of course, possible that Churchill could have repented of his own will, but there does not appear to have been anyone else in the party sufficiently willing or able to tackle him as Clark Kerr did. It is, therefore, not inconceivable that Churchill's visit to Moscow could have perversely brought about the severing of relations with the Soviet Union were it not for Clark Kerr's vital intervention.

His own account of his private chat with Churchill in the grounds of the dacha is worth recounting in full. It demonstrates superbly his masterly grasp of human nature, the fears and the hopes, the weaknesses and the conceit. And it thus confirms him as a consummate diplomat of gentle manner but iron determination. It was Clark Kerr's finest hour.

> I asked Alec [Cadogan] to leave me alone with him [Churchill]. I found him lowering and sullen.
> 'I hear you want to see me.'
> 'Yes. Let us go for a little walk. I talk better if I walk and so, I have observed, do you.'

He didn't like my facetiousness.

'I haven't much time.'

'I shall not keep you long.'

He put a preposterous ten gallon hat on his head, and arming himself with a stick, he went out on to the terrace leaving me to follow him.

'May I be frank?'

He stopped and stared at me.

'Frank ? Why not ?'

'I may say something that is unpleasing to you.'

He snorted. 'I've been used to that all my life. I'm not afraid.'

And then began one of the most remarkable talks I have ever had. I wish that I could reproduce it intact. I can't. I didn't compel him to the fatigue of high argument, for I did all, or nearly all, the talking. But it must have been just as fatiguing for him to hold himself in as he did. It was like this: I talked and he stomped along in front of me among the fir trees. I addressed myself to a pink and swollen neck and a pair of hunched shoulders. This had to be, because the path I had chosen was too narrow to let me keep abreast of him. Perhaps he didn't want me to watch his face unless it was ready for me. Every now and then it was ready, for, as I shot each one of my bolts, he stopped short and turned to stare at me. On the whole I find it easier to talk to a face than to a neck and for myself I should not have chosen a dodging in and out fir trees as the best occasion in which to say something that mattered.

I began by saying that it seemed to me he was going about this whole business the wrong way. He stopped and stared at me. Well, perhaps that was a bad start and I began afresh. God had been particularly kind to him when he bestowed his gifts. I needn't mention them. He knew what they were, and when he cared to use them he could do so with devastating effect. It had been my own memories of these gifts and my belief in their power that had led me to suggest his coming, for deep down in me I had felt that from a meeting between him and Stalin immense good must flow. His pace slowed down. I had had great faith in him and he had disappointed me. This brought him to a halt and he stared again. By this time there was no withdrawing and my God! I didn't want to. If his mission to Moscow, on which we had all set such high hopes, were a failure, it was his own fault, as he was making no use of these matchless gifts of his. After the first day when I had watched him use his charm with admirable effect, he had put them all away. His approach to the Russians had become all wrong. What was wrong was that he was an aristocrat and a man of the world and he expected these people to be like him. They weren't. They were straight from the plough or the lathe. They were rough and inexperienced. They didn't discuss things as we discussed them. They thought aloud, and in thinking aloud, they said many harsh and offensive things. They had angered him and his pride was hurt. That didn't surprise me. They angered me too. But what did surprise me was to see him letting the hurting of his pride blur his judgement. He stopped and stared.

'That man has insulted me. From now on he will have to fight his battles alone.'

(The very words the doctor had quoted)

I let the second bit pass, saving it up for my next salvo and I took him up on the insult. I suggested that nothing had been said at the second meeting that had not been said in the early stages of the first. Why had he felt affronted at the second meeting when he hadn't at the first? It had probably been Stalin's disingenuous memorandum that had put him in bad humour. I confessed that it was an unhappy document, but he had been wrong to let it warp his judgement. Things were too important to let what he had overlooked when he thought he was going to get away with it influence him when he felt he was going to fail. For myself I didn't think he was going to fail. It was all too important. But he would fail if he went on as he was going now. He must sweep away all that had passed and make friends with Stalin. At the Kremlin dinner Stalin had made it clear that he wanted to make amends but the PM had coldshouldered him. He must meet Stalin halfway.

'But the man has insulted me. I represent a great country and I am not submissive by nature.' (This sulkily over his hunched shoulders).

Then I went on. He had said just now that Stalin would have to fight his own battles. Did he mean that seriously? I couldn't believe it. He stopped and stared and then dodged on amongst the fir trees, in which he seemed to find some protection. Had he reflected upon what it would mean to the issue of the war? If Russia went down for want of support, his support, which only he could give? How many young British and American lives would have to be sacrificed to make this good? Had he thought of that when he decided, as I understood he had decided, to break off his talks with Stalin and to go home? He stopped to stare again. And I went on. He couldn't leave Russia in the lurch whatever Stalin had said to hurt his pride. He would have to swallow his pride if only to save young lives.

'The man thinks he can upset my government and throw me out.' And here followed quite a long speech about his strength at home, his hold on the public mind, and on the House of Commons. He even enumerated the great chunks of votes he could count on in Parliament. 'If he thinks he can throw me out he is very much mistaken.'

I asked if I might go on. Yes, of course, today he had immense strength. I well knew that. But tomorrow if he abandoned Russia he would find his strength falling away. He would soon be alone. He would be the man who had thrown Russia to the Nazis. (A stop and a stare.) And all because he was offended. Offended by a peasant who didn't know any better. That seemed to me to be a pity. It seemed to me a pity to come all this way and to make a mess of things. That pulled him up short.

'A mess of things? You mean that you think it's all my fault?'

'Yes. I'm sorry but I do.'

'A mess of things?'

By this time we had got out of those blasted dodgy fir trees and were walking abreast. We had nearly reached the house. He stopped and glanced at the ground in front of him. After a longish pause he said:

'Well, and what do you want me to do?'

I told him quickly that I wanted him at once to send a message to Stalin to say that he wanted another talk. Just the two of them. I felt convinced that Stalin was ready for it. Witness all the trouble Stalin had taken at the Kremlin dinner and I enlarged upon what Stalin had done, making much of the unprecedented trot to the front door. I assured him that it was within his power to nobble Stalin, if he made good use of those gifts of his which I had spoken of. I was prepared to bet that he would be successful if he allowed himself to be himself. It was very important. He listened carefully and then he said:

'But I am not a submissive man.'

'I don't ask you to be submissive. I only ask you to be yourself.'

'Myself.'

We were now near to the dacha door and into it he suddenly strode, leaving me in the mild sunshine, to reflect upon what I had said. Somehow or other I didn't feel that any part of it had cost me special effort. It had all seemed to be quite easy and natural. Certainly no effort of courage. I was just about to look for the doctor and to speculate with him about the probable results when Alec called me into the PM's room. They were alone. The PM said he wanted to discuss plans. We sat down.

'Ally' he said. 'He' (pointing at me) 'says that it's all my fault.' (This with half a baby's bottom face.)

And suddenly he chuckled and Alec laughed and I knew that it was all right. In a twinkling Pavlov was sent for and told that the PM wanted to see Stalin and see him alone and to have a good man to man talk.'[38]

A meeting was arranged for 7pm, and Clark Kerr further sought to smooth things by replacing the sickly Dunlop with a younger interpreter, Arthur Birse, who had been attached to the military mission in Moscow.

While Churchill was conducting a highly successful final meeting with Stalin which ran on unexpectedly until 2.00 in the morning when a final communiqué was agreed, Cadogan and Clark Kerr were entertaining General Anders, the head of the Polish military-in-exile. With Churchill, surprisingly but happily delayed, Clark Kerr took the opportunity of a sleep on the sofa. From his reverie he was roused by an ecstatic Churchill who returned in triumph, regaling the party with his splendid evening with 'that great man'. While he fulminated he undressed for a bath, parading up and down in his underclothes, a huge cigar wedged in his mouth. Clark Kerr could not resist depicting the comic scene for his eager readers back at the Foreign Office. 'From under his skimpy vest penis and a pair of crinkled, creamy buttocks protruded.' To make things quite clear, Clark Kerr appended a splendid little pencil drawing of the great Prime Minister in this pose: fat cigar, truncated vest, and the merest glimpse of the nether parts.[39] It was certainly an amusingly human and very satisfying conclusion to what had been a trying and potentially disastrous occasion. All was once more sweetness and enthusiasm, and Clark Kerr was able to declare to what had previously been a rather sceptical press corps that the talks had been 'an epoch-making event'.[40] Clark Kerr was able to report to Eden of Churchill, with some sense of relief, that he 'forgave him all his bloodiness and all his folly' in the light of that final successful meeting.

Churchill's visit was more personally, rather than politically, successful. On the morning of his departure, for example, *Pravda* published a pointed cartoon depicting as cardboard the German defences in Northern France. The simultaneous military talks had yielded little in the way of organised future co-operation, the talks made little positive impact on the Soviet peoples, and Admiral Standley the American Ambassador, for one, felt they had not been very fruitful. The most important result was that Churchill and Stalin had managed to gel together socially and establish reasonably cordial relations. Most important of all, thanks to Clark Kerr's astute intervention, disaster had been averted.

Churchill, himself, was pleased at the progress made, and thanked Clark Kerr warmly: 'You were a constant help and wise adviser. I hope my visit will make it easier for you to carry on the arduous and difficult duties you are doing so well.'[41] Clark Kerr had also been assured by Molotov that Stalin had been impressed by Churchill's spirit and dynamic qualities.[42] Clark wrote to Cadogan:

> For myself, I feel that the visit has been immensely worthwhile and that the PM is much to be congratulated upon the way in which, by sheer force of his personality, he has beaten down the barrier which seemed so unshakeable and dispelled the longstanding and tenacious suspicions which have clouded the judgement of Stalin. I am left with high hopes that the way has now been cleared of much that cluttered it up and that we may now look forward to the future with some confidence.[43]

This was probably too fine a gloss, and as the Soviets began the grim defence of Stalingrad against German attack, the Politburo was in no mood to view Britain and her 'minor' efforts with very much approbation. Despite the apparent amity of the talks, there were still fears that the Soviet Union might be tempted into a separate peace with Hitler. Therefore, despite difficulties, convoys to Russia were resumed and in late September 27 ships out of 40 managed to reach Archangel unscathed.

A further problem in British foreign relations arose around the same time in Moscow. At the end of September 1942, Wendell Willkie, the defeated US Presidential candidate of 1940, arrived as part of his world tour. He made the customary favourable noises regarding the second front to please his hosts, but also divulged to Clark Kerr, who found 'something fundamentally decent' about Willkie, just how poor the image of Britain was in America.[44] Willkie said that Americans still felt Britain was clinging to the empire, into whose defence they were trying to inveigle the United States. The American people did not understand the concept of the Commonwealth, and similarly Churchill's talks in Cairo had made a bad impression in America.[45] Clark Kerr had these views confirmed in chats with US newsmen and passed on his findings to Cadogan. Although Cadogan fully appreciated these views, it was some time before the Foreign Office would actually take them to heart and seek to allay American suspicions.[46] This problem continued to dog US-UK relations until well into the days of the Cold War.

Willkie's visit was the occasion of the usual bibulous dinner given by Stalin. The Politburo in general seemed to take delight, in a rather boyish way, in trying to intoxicate any foreign guest to arrive in Moscow. Since his early experience in Kuibyshev, Clark Kerr had taken care to pace himself at these affairs. The dinner on Saturday 25 September was some affair: Willkie himself claimed to have drunk 53 straight vodka toasts but still walked unaided to his car. After the meal itself there was the inevitable Soviet propaganda film to be endured in the basement. After a few more drinks the atmosphere became quite relaxed. Clark Kerr was the butt that night of several jokes from the Soviet Marshals Voroshilov and Budyenny. Because of his sun-tan, misshapen nose and physical fitness, the British Ambassador was nicknamed 'the Partisan'. Accordingly, Voroshilov produced a tommy-gun, asking Clark Kerr if he knew how to use it as a partisan would. Clark Kerr accepted the challenge and, pretending to fire from the hip, raked the bellies of Stalin, Molotov and Willkie. Voroshilov instead fired from the shoulder, aiming at Clark Kerr. Stalin then declared that he would show them how to use it as a politician and he seized the weapon. Trilling his tongue, Stalin swept the gun round and fairly decimated his guests, which he seemed to enjoy immensely. As Clark Kerr reported: 'I could not help noticing that he picked off nearly all the members of his government'.[47] There was a rather nervous hiatus thereafter and, with much of the warmth gone, the party broke up soberly and quickly.

In fact Clark Kerr got on much better with Stalin than he did with Molotov. Stalin not only shared an interest in pipes and tobacco but also a bawdy sense of humour, whereas even with his best jokes Clark Kerr could only coax the merest smile out of Molotov. Stalin and Clark Kerr were much more earthy: at official functions Stalin would quite often communicate his blunt opinions to the British Ambassador, occasionally pointing across the room, for example, and saying 'Don't you think that fellow over there is bloody ugly'.[48]

Unfortunately, these occasional contacts with the Politburo were about the only contacts Clark Kerr was permitted with the Soviet people, and it was a constant disappointment to him. However, his relations with Stalin made up for it. On the last night of Willkie's visit, Stalin had made a few pointed remarks on the quality of war material being sent to him, and claimed that some 152 planes intended for Russia had been diverted to Britain. Willkie tried to calm the situation but Clark Kerr rose to respond. He praised Stalin for his bluntness and said that it called for bluntness in reply. Courageously, he launched into a clear rebuttal of Stalin's charges: the Soviet Union, Great Britain and the United States were united in a common cause. If any planes had been diverted from Russia, the aim was only to further the cause of all three countries. He was sure Stalin had known about it in advance and knew it was for the best. Stalin accepted Clark Kerr's bluntness in return. Stalin's remarks did prove the depth of suspicion and, in the press, hostility directed towards Britain. It was not until the landings in North Africa in November that Clark Kerr could report an improvement: 'The Kremlin is now sending out warm rays'.[49]

At the end of 1942, he was at last granted some leave, his first for over five years, and he arrived back in London on Friday 27 November. Before his departure, Clark Kerr penned a summative report of his perception of Soviet foreign policy, still the object of much debate in the Foreign Office, particularly regarding post-war aims. Clark Kerr opined that the Soviet Union's chief objective would be reconstruction of her own devastated areas, but did correctly identify territorial issues as being predominant in her main foreign aim of securing strategic frontiers in the west. In this regard, Clark Kerr felt that the Soviet Union would hope to retain the Baltic States, eastern Poland and Bessarabia. Further, he correctly forecast that 'she may claim a sort of undefined protectorate over the other Slav people of Europe, and a somewhat more tangible influence over... Bulgaria'.[50] Despite that, Clark Kerr did feel that the horrors of the war were such that in the immediate post-war years the Soviet Union would 'probably be prepared to take things quietly for a considerable period of time'.[51] Generally, the Foreign Office was very suspicious of Soviet aims in Eastern Europe, particularly as Stalin had been so lukewarm on the idea of national confederations in Eastern Europe. It seemed to some that Stalin had some hidden plan of his own which did not include the idea of Balkan unity or co-operation.

Clark Kerr was fully convinced that the only way to gain Stalin's confidence and create an acceptable relationship was by opening the second front, as promised. Back in England, he let everyone know just how unhappy he was in the job, and how distinctly he dreaded having to bear any more bad news about the second front back to Stalin. Stalin's refusal to leave Moscow, at the height of the battle for Stalingrad, to join Roosevelt and Churchill in Casablanca further highlighted the lack of cohesion and openness in the alliance. On 15 December Clark Kerr had the opportunity of addressing the Chiefs of Staff on the necessity to open the promised second front in 1943. The Chiefs of Staff were none too optimistic, offering instead merely talk of a limited attack on the Cherbourg peninsula. Clark Kerr dismissed this suggestion by Brooke, the Chief of the Imperial General Staff: Stalin had been promised 'a considerable operation involving a million men and with this promise he had been kept quiet'. Without such a front, even a separate Hitler-Stalin peace could not be discounted. Portal argued that there was probably no chance of an invasion unless the Russians defeated Hitler, and that efforts should be concentrated on North Africa and knocking out Italy. Clark Kerr could hardly contain himself at this glib suggestion: there was a total failure to recognise the strain under which the Russians were now carrying on; they even 'feared that we were building up a vast army which might one day turn round and compound with Germany against Russia'. Clark Kerr also commented that he 'regretted to say' that there was a body of opinion in British circles which indirectly supported this Russian belief. His pleas fell on deaf ears. He finished by saying that a report that there would be no second front in 1943 would be 'a bad shock for Stalin'. He 'could not say what the results would be, but they would be serious'.[52] Such was the lack of understanding at the meeting that many of the senior officers left with a prissy feeling that Archie Clark Kerr was improperly pro-Soviet, rather than with the more appropriate response that something had to be done to assist the Soviet resistance and smooth relations. In a sense time had already run out. The tide was turning against the Nazi advance in Russia and so the Soviet Union had less urgent need now of Western aid. This was suggested by the failure of Air Marshall Drummond's visit to Moscow in November when the Russians rejected his offer of RAF bases in the Caucasus. In fact the Chiefs of Staff were generally opposed to anything but the bare minimum in co-operation with the Soviet military, although to be fair, the Soviets also seemed reluctant to co-operate.[53]

The day following his unhappy talks with the military, Clark Kerr lunched with Churchill and Eden, and he continued high-level talks throughout the month. Generally speaking, Clark Kerr found his leave rather unhappy: England seemed foreign to him after five years, and he was upset by some of the anti-Soviet views he was subjected to, particularly in the City, but even in the Foreign Office. Many of the officials there, and many of the emissaries in key posts abroad, he thought hopelessly out of touch and still living in the 1880s. The likely postponement of the cross-channel invasion also meant that his return to Moscow would be even more disagreeable than circumstances already determined. He was so fearful of taking such news back that he was even campaigning for Beaverbrook to go in his place and take over as Ambassador. Brooke had already refused the suggestion that as CIGS he should break the news.[54]

During his three months' leave Clark Kerr met and talked with a broad range of individuals, pushing for a wider acceptance of the need to gain Stalin's trust by a commitment to the second front. He met many of the young left, such as Richard Crossman and Ritchie Calder, and sought to make links between young English writers and their Soviet counterparts. He thus became friends with the young writer John Lehmann, who was also trying to establish literary links.

In fact, these attempts to create some sort of literary alliance were unsuccessful generally. A dinner in Moscow which Clark Kerr hosted for some young Soviet writers was a bit of a disaster: both his flippant talk and outdated literary allusions completely baffled his guests. For a while, however, it did seem as if some good could be done by that route. Already the press attaché in the Moscow Embassy had been issuing a regular 50,000 copy run of the British Information Service newspaper to try to put over better the British perspective. Despite difficulties the publicity was useful, although Ralph Parker, the *Times* correspondent, often referred to it negatively. Clark Kerr, however, felt that Parker was 'vain, irresponsible, and a confirmed busybody,' declaring him *persona non grata* at the embassy because of his undermining criticisms.[55]

Before returning to Moscow on 18 February 1943, Clark Kerr did get the chance to broadcast, on BBC radio, a speech which was widely reported. His likely link here was Guy Burgess, who was involved at that time in commissioning politically acceptable material for the BBC's own propaganda effort. Clark Kerr spent a whole day rehearsing his 15-minute slot, before recording his talk that evening in English, French and German. His theme was that the British people should ignore the attempt being made to paint the Soviet Union as ideological enemies. He ascribed to German propaganda this attempt to drive a wedge in the alliance by 'rattling the so-called Bolshevist skeleton'. Despite his own misgivings about attitudes in officialdom, Clark Kerr delivered a vigorous public tribute to the strength of the alliance. 'We stand solidly together. We do not intend to be divided.' The alliance was not only a 'solemn bond', but there was now 'a human pact between two nations... We shall do all we can to see that it runs smoothly and we shall do it with heart and soul. In the Soviet Union, in its turn, I have found an equal desire to give this pact a full, enduring and ungrudging meaning.'[56]

Preparing to return to Moscow, however, Clark Kerr was still uncertain exactly of the line which Churchill and the Government wanted him to take with the Soviets. He lunched with Churchill on the eve of his return, but was little rewarded. At length when he was about to leave in despair, Churchill called him back: 'You want a directive?' he growled. 'All right. I don't mind kissing Stalin's bum, but I'm damned if I'll lick his arse!'

Clark Kerr didn't even blink. 'Thank you, Prime Minister,' he said. 'Now I quite understand.'[57]

Although Churchill was disinclined, both Eden and Sir Orme Sargent, Deputy Under-Secretary at the Foreign Office, were willing to approach the Soviets formally, through Clark Kerr on his return, about the whole question of post-war reconstruction in Europe.[58] Eden was particularly keen not to be seen to omit the Soviet Union from any discussions with the United States which might take place on this issue. Eden wanted an agreement on Germany primarily, in the light of comments made by Stalin in his November speech, in which he seemed to hint that a distinction should be drawn between the 'Hitlerite state' and Germany proper. Generally, however, the concern was over Soviet domination of liberated areas in eastern Europe. Eden was anxious to see this included in post-war policy at an international level.

Clark Kerr took up the matter immediately on his return, meeting Molotov on 20 February 1943. Molotov was uneasy when the issue was raised and Clark Kerr, therefore, decided to put it in writing so that Molotov could consult with Stalin fully. This formal approach was rather more than the Foreign Office wished, aroused Churchill's suspicions when it surfaced, and so caused the whole affair to be dropped rather ignominiously. Both Eden and Sargent felt that Clark Kerr had mishandled the issue and should only have raised it verbally with Stalin himself. Since he saw that no progress with Molotov was possible, Sargent felt he ought to have left it until an occasion with Stalin himself arose. On 1 March Eden formally instructed Clark Kerr to drop the issue, mostly because of Churchill's opposition to broaching postwar details with the Russians.[59] This merely compounded the problem: having set alarm bells ringing in the Kremlin, it would have been better to have seen the matter through to a conclusion. Instead, it meant that Stalin had the breathing-space to complete the formulation, and expedite the implementation, of his own post-war European policy. With the stunning German surrender at Stalingrad on 31 January, there was every possibility that the Soviet Union would soon have a free hand in Eastern Europe anyway. Consequently the Soviets began immediately to increase pressure on, firstly, the Polish government-in-exile to grant concessions to meet Soviet defence and foreign policy aims.

The return to Moscow unsettled Clark Kerr following what he termed 'the terrific stimulus of these weeks at home'. He berated Stalin, once he had delivered his presents of pipe and tobacco from London, about the failure to let him have freer access to the Soviet people.[60] To John Lehmann he declared that his leave had left him:

restless and even rebellious... As the years rattle by and I get nearer and nearer to the museum I find it harder and harder to feel grown up, and hardest of all to be tolerant of my own preposterous way of life...[61]

Despite his own misgivings, Clark Kerr's reputation was rising at home. One Foreign Office diplomat told him, 'You're still talked of with bated breath in London to the right and left alike. The general consensus is that we could do with 15 similar heads of mission.'[62]

Despite the announcement cancelling yet another Arctic convoy to Russia, Clark Kerr found Stalin in friendly mood in early April when he met him to introduce formally the new head of the military mission, General Martel: 'I have never seen Stalin in sunnier temper... God knows why.'[63] There was not a little tragic irony in that: on 13 April the Nazis announced the discovery of a mass grave at Katyn, near Smolensk, containing the bodies of nearly 10,000 Polish officers. These officers had disappeared in 1939 following the Nazi-Soviet Pact: the thumbprint of Stalinist massacre seemed all too obvious. At a time of strained relations with Poland, it was the last thing diplomacy needed. The Russians protested their innocence, and when the Poles, disregarding British disinclination, joined the Germans in a call for a Red Cross investigation, the Soviet Union broke off diplomatic relations with the Polish Government-in-exile on 25 April 1943. Like most British officials, Clark Kerr felt certain that the Russians were guilty but also that protecting wartime relations with Moscow effectively meant that finger-pointing was ruled out. On 21 April he reported:

> In a horrible way it seems to fit in with the Poles' story of the disappearance of 8300 officers. Then anger and unconvincing terms of Soviet denials suggests a sense of guilt.[64]

Yet he felt that probing further would be to court disaster, as the Poles quickly discovered. Churchill, already irked by the pestering style of Polish diplomacy, agreed fully with Clark Kerr, but still felt that the breach between the Poles and the USSR was of such gravity that silence on the issue had to be broken. In a rare swapping of roles, Clark Kerr rejected Churchill's first letter as being too apologetic towards the Soviet Union, but a revised letter merely brought out vociferous, if insincere, protests of innocence from Molotov and a tirade about the Poles' acquiescence in pro-Hitler propaganda.

The Soviet behaviour over Katyn was quite unforgiveable, but the perceived needs of wartime Europe and the reality of power politics meant that both the British and the Americans had to bite their tongues and shut their eyes to the full horror of Katyn Woods. Oliver Harvey's comments, written slightly earlier in the year, encapsulate the quandary in which the allies were placed.

> The Russians are very tiresome allies, importunate, graceless, ungrateful, secretive, suspicious, ever asking for more, but... They are winning the war for us.[65]

Not only had the Russians shot the Polish officers in cold blood, for no obvious reason – as gruesome a crime as one could imagine – but what even exacerbates the barbarism is that, having been discovered, they took their false and distasteful denials to the lengths of actually declaring themselves insulted and wronged by the natural and justified doubtings of the Polish Government. The Katyn massacre thus seems to descend from the level of atrocity into the very realm of evil itself. Not only was the break with the Polish government executed on a fallacious and contrived pretext, but was also foully used as an opportunity by Stalin to establish an alternative pro-Soviet Polish regime-in-exile which would lay the foundations for 40 years of repressive tyranny.

Despite the Katyn debacle, relations between Britain and the USSR did not founder. Indeed 1943 – the year of 'perelom', the 'turning-point' in the Great Patriotic War – developed a wildly mercurial pattern. At times relations were strained to breaking-point; at other times they were bizarrely and wonderfully bright. One step planned to aid relations was the Soviet disbandment of the Comintern, announced on 22 May. There was some design in the timing, coming as it did at the first anniversary of the Anglo-Soviet Treaty, which was marked by various events in Moscow. These were partially overshadowed by the arrival of Joe Davies, a former US Ambassador to Moscow, who had been sent on a private mission by Roosevelt to arrange a personal meeting with Stalin, and who was also using the occasion to publicise his film 'Mission to Moscow' which painted an absurdly rosy picture of the Soviet Union during the great purge. Clark Kerr was present at the premiere of the film at one of the traditional late-night Kremlin showings. Even members of the Politburo sniggered at the film's sentimental inaccuracy, but Davies was undaunted.

Davies was, in fact, unpopular with both the US Embassy and the press corps because of his self-publicity and unrealistic pro-Soviet stance. The US Ambassador at this time, Admiral Standley, was one of only two diplomats in the country whom Clark Kerr admired, the other being the Czech communist Fierlinger. Standley had bravely stood up to the continued taunts about the lack of a second front and of support for the Russian struggle against the Nazis. In March, Standley had bluntly complained, during a press conference, about Russian 'ingratitude' and the 'ungracious' Russian attitude towards both the private Aid-to-Russia and the US Government help generally.[66] Clark Kerr was full of admiration for Standley's candour and referred to him later as 'the best colleague I have ever had'.[67] Standley's remarks caused something of a stir, and by June Roosevelt was already offering his post to Averell Harriman.[68] Harriman's skills at 'bumsucking' Churchill were deemed suitable now for Soviet rears.

By June, Stalin had also been officially notified of the postponement of the second front again, this time to 1944. Stalin's response was to change his ambassadors in Washington and London. Maisky, the Soviet Ambassador to Britain, had been a popular diplomat, and his replacement by Gusev, held in low esteem, was met with concern in Whitehall. Clark Kerr argued that it was merely poverty of choice and nothing more sinister that had obliged the Soviet

Government to make the appointment. Clark Kerr felt that Stalin was head and shoulders above the rest of the Politburo and that in appointing Gusev the Soviets were probably doing the best they could.[69] His own experience of the little-known diplomat led him to describe him to the Foreign Office as 'like a sea-calf and apparently no more articulate'. Later examination forced him to refine his opinion: '... something sired by a sea-lion on a pumpkin'.[70]

The venom of Stalin's cables and the panic over the removal of Maisky, the awkwardness of the Russians over visas for British subjects, and the harsh treatment of British convoy personnel in Northern Russia all combined to make the Foreign Office rethink their whole attitude to the Soviet Union. Further unease arose from Polish-Soviet relations and Soviet courting of the Czechoslovak Government. This prompted Eden to raise again his idea of a European Advisory Commission to help thrash out problems in relations before they reached prime ministerial level.[71]

Suggestions of a further meeting with Stalin by Churchill were shelved in the short-term, but there was talk of Eden being sent to Moscow following the Quebec Conference.[72] The problem was only aggravated by the fact that Stalin would be neither present nor represented at Quebec. Churchill and his supporters were pleased to see this as there was less chance of Britain being forced into any action or agreements by a US-USSR combination. The whole attitude of the Foreign Office to the USSR was beginning to exasperate Clark Kerr and others. There was a general lack of frankness and a studied equivocation. On 31 July Clark Kerr complained, 'It is painful to me to have to go on telling my masters that half truths will not do and they must learn to be sincere and candid',[73] Geoffrey Wilson, a confidant of Clark Kerr's in the Northern Department, laid the blame squarely on Churchill:

> His statement... about consulting the Americans and informing the Russians was no slip of the tongue... now that he can see the end of the war in sight my impression is that he does not care two hoots about the Russians. If they come to tag along with us, well and good; if not, they can go and boil themselves.[74]

Clark Kerr picked up the idea and reported to the Foreign Office that the Russians were tired of being treated as 'country cousins' in the alliance.[75] A further irritation, Clark Kerr observed, lay not so much 'in our inability to open a second front but in our having let them believe we were going to'.[76] Before Churchill left for the Quebec Conference in mid-August 1943, Clark Kerr reported that 'in his heart' he felt that the Russian complaint of still being treated as inferiors was right. In a somewhat revealing choice of metaphor, he expatiated:

> We have not let them into the club. They are still scrutinized by the hall-porter, stared at by the members and made to feel that they do not really belong... We consult Washington and we inform Moscow... We shall have to learn not to be snobs and still more not to be fools.[77]

With Churchill in an anti-Soviet mood, Clark Kerr was particularly keen to see that Stalin would not be left ignorant of relevant developments at the Quebec conference. Not only were Churchill and Roosevelt ensconced together but, following the fall of Mussolini, events were also moving apace in Italy – again of interest to Stalin but beyond his direct control. There were far too many possibilities that Stalin's inferiority complex would be reinforced. Stalin did have some cause to be touchy: despite the cracking by British intelligence of the German secret codes, no attempt was made to convey their content to the Soviet military, even when the information was crucial to their defensive survival. For example, the German plans for the Battle of Kursk, the crucial clash of 1943, were known by the British but were not relayed to the Russians. This may have had some political justification but it served instead to be wholly counter-productive. Through John Cairncross, a Foreign Office employee sympathetic to Communism, the Russians did receive, illegally, the vital information which allowed them to anticipate the German advance and ultimately inflict the decisive set-piece defeat on the Nazi military machine. However, whether Cairncross's treachery may have been morally justifiable or not, the result of his actions was to reveal to Stalin that the British were demonstrably not being as co-operative as they could have been. With Churchill and Roosevelt in Quebec, the second front postponed, information restricted, and political manoeuvring in Italy, it is little wonder that Stalin felt rather isolated and not a little concerned that Britain and America were following a different agenda than the one presented publicly. The actions of Cairncross, whatever their military value, served politically to widen the gulf between the West and the Soviet Union. All the Communist spies of the era produced exactly that same result: far from averting schism and maintaining the alliance, their actions gave evidence to Stalin that collaboration was limited, and destroyed whatever spirit of goodwill there could have been.

Although Clark Kerr could not have known all the reasons for Stalin's anxiety, he was very conscious of it, and desperate to see it allayed. There had to be proper communiqués and reports from Quebec quickly and frankly conveyed to the Soviet leadership. Stalin, heartened by the successes of the Red Army, was more sociable by early August. On 11 August, Clark Kerr and Admiral Standley jointly visited Stalin to inform him of the secret talks on the Italian armistice.[78] While Stalin was cautious, he did suggest that with Italy removed there could be an earlier opening of the second front. Clark Kerr was more interested during the interview in the subtle changes in Soviet iconolatry which the 'patriotic' war had effected. He reported to the Foreign Office on the return of dusty Tsarist heroes from the political storeroom to prominent display on the Kremlin walls:

> The portraits of Suvorov and Kutuzov [military heroes of the Napoleonic era]... interesting as a further symbol of the throwback to the past which has been manifesting itself... Marx and Engels looked all out in the cold in the corner they had been pushed into.[79]

The change in fortunes on the battlefront not only cheered Stalin but also improved the atmosphere in Moscow. In the summer, as a tribute to the episode in the Kremlin basement during Willkie's visit, Clark Kerr was presented by Molotov with a gift of the two millionth tommy-gun produced by the Russians in wartime. It was handsomely packed in a case, and Clark Kerr took it as a genuine attempt at friendship on the part of the awkward Molotov. It was a warm summer, and Clark Kerr was able to conduct most of his paperwork bare-chested in the embassy garden. Although still deprived of any real society, the embassy staff worked well together and Clark Kerr was able to devote a lot of his energy to tending the allotment. It was still a very lonely business, made worse by the fact that Tita was no longer even acknowledging any of the countless letters he sent. The upturn in atmosphere also meant that the full diplomatic corps could now be recalled from exile in Kuibyshev, and although Clark Kerr should have welcomed it, he was in no mood to face the cocktail circuit again. He much preferred informal rigorous discussions with journalists, writers or intellectuals to the stuffy pleasantries of empty diplomatic soirees. To bolster his own team following the untimely death of Lacy Bagallay, he had chosen Tom Barman, an acquaintance from his Swedish days, now in PWE (Political Warfare Executive) but ostensibly a press attaché, and John Balfour also arrived as a direct replacement, and so number two in the Embassy. Of the return of the other foreign diplomats, Clark Kerr sighed:

> I confess that I don't look forward much to that girlish Swede waggling his buttocks about the place (nor the Belgian's stories about them), nor to the scented Afghan begging me to let him have Karachi, nor to the chatter of the Greek and the shouting of the Fighting Frenchman and the yelling of the Mexican, and, perhaps, least of all to the Cuban's 'Do you know the one about the girl in the train?'[80]

Apart from the Yugoslav and the Czech, the only other ambassador whom he actually looked forward to meeting was the Turk whose calling card had so intrigued him: Mustapha Kunt.

At the close of the Quebec Conference, Clark Kerr was delivered a resumé of the main decisions of the summit to pass to Stalin for comment in some cases, and straight information in others. Given the circumstances, he was anxious to lose no time. Unfortunately, the text arrived incomplete, and Clark Kerr was unable to deliver a full version to Stalin. It was a hopeless position: had he delayed, Stalin would have suspected conspiracy; having been presented with only a partial picture of the situation, especially re Italy, Stalin still sniffed intrigue.[81] Nevertheless, the discussion of a cross-channel invasion in the spring of 1944 was enough to placate the Georgian panophobe. The speed of developments also persuaded Stalin to agree to a foreign ministers conference to be held in Moscow in October and to a meeting of the Big Three subsequently. Stalin obstinately refused to travel from the Soviet Union on the grounds that he had to be on hand to control military affairs. In fact, an important factor was the desire not to be seen to chase after the West, but have them come courting to Moscow instead.[82] This ought to have alerted observers, such as Clark Kerr, that admission to the Western Club was not actually the top priority for Stalin and his government.

The conference of foreign ministers met for 12 days in Moscow from 19 to 30 October. The odd and contradictory nature of UK-USSR relations in 1943 can be gauged by the fact that the conference was conducted in a remarkably good spirit, while only days before a very rough correspondence between Stalin and Churchill on the issue of northern convoys had been ended dramatically when Churchill had refused to accept from Ambassador Gusev an unpleasant message from Stalin. The hapless Ambassador was led quietly to the door, the envelope pressed into his hand, and then he was pushed gently out before he could react. There was not much chance of a verbal reaction from poor Gusev anyway, whose only English appeared to consist of saying 'How are you?' in a voice of thunder.[83] Molotov, by contrast had a wider grasp of the language: 'Yes' (rarely used); 'No' (his favourite); and 'second front'.

British preparations for Moscow, although meticulous as usual, were hampered by the fact that both Eden and the Foreign Office were being thwarted stubbornly by Churchill, who refused to countenance their desire to discuss post-war frontiers at the conference. The Americans were also unwilling, for different reasons, wanting to leave all border questions to their proposed post-war 'international organisation'. The arguments within the British Cabinet were fierce with Eden threatening not to attend Moscow at all at one stage.[84] As far as Clark Kerr was concerned, his hopes for the conference were of a more general nature: 'not so much aim at reaching formulae on individual points as at making the talks a test of Russian attitude to collaboration in the future'.[85] He wanted tests devised to check on Russian goodwill, worrying that the Soviet Government seemed unable to operate a system of give-and-take. Always willing to think the best of people, Clark Kerr typically attributed Soviet diplomatic boorishness to a kind of political roughness and greenness born of the regime's youth and inexperience.[86] Despite Clark Kerr's tenacity in seeking to achieve full and equal status for the Soviet Union in the alliance, there is undoubtedly a patronising streak to much of his representations on this issue. As he had argued to Churchill at the time of their 'walk in the forest', he felt that the Russians were too uncivilized and uncouth to know better.

The American delegation led by Cordell Hull, the Secretary of State, and Harriman, the new Ambassador, were deeply suspicious of British motives on the frontier question. Churchill's declared position of defending the Empire in the post-war realignment offended their democratic principles, and they were wary of any attempts to redraw the map of the world in smoke-filled rooms. In any case, that whole method had been outlawed by the Atlantic Charter of 1941. The Americans were more interested in their ideal of international post-war co-operation, a policy more in keeping with Roosevelt's simple political instincts and Hull's woolliness. In fact, the 72 year old Hull had only been a late replacement for his Under-Secretary Sumner Welles, who had actually been closer to the President's ear and would have led the delegation had he not been forced out of office in late August after details of homosexual indiscretions had surfaced.[87] As a result, and given Standley's supercession, the US team were less experienced and knowledgeable in Soviet affairs that they otherwise could have been.

The senior British team comprised: Anthony Eden, the Foreign Secretary; Sir William Strang, representing the Foreign Office; Sir Archibald Clark Kerr himself; and General Ismay. Clark Kerr was thus the foremost career diplomat present, Lord Halifax left behind in Washington as he would be at all the wartime conferences. Given Churchill's wariness of Clark Kerr's liberal instincts, it is a tribute to his skill and professional abilities that he was still felt indispensable to the British team, and was really number two to Eden at the conference.

The conference duly opened on 19 October 1943, an hour late at 4pm following a bibulous luncheon hosted by Molotov. All the meetings took place in the splendid Spiridonovka Palace.[88] The Soviet team was led by Molotov and included his deputy Vyshinski, Litvinov, and Marshall Voroshilov for the military. Apart from Hull and Harriman, the other chief American figures were Green Hackworth, the legal adviser, and Lt. Gen. Deane. It became clear that the Soviets' main aim for the conference was merely final and binding agreement on a date for a cross-Channel invasion. Even at this late date, Churchill was trying to delay, [89] and telegraphed Eden repeatedly during the conference urging caution and imprecision on the matter. Although some provisos were aired, it was made evident to Molotov at an early stage that there would indeed be a cross-Channel invasion in 1944. Clark Kerr himself, although keen to see a second front, was not happy to see Britain lead on the Soviets again only to disappoint them later. If no guarantee could be given, he would have preferred no promise at all, however vague, to be made. As Ambassador, he did not savour the idea of having to rebuild relations which would be wrecked by any failure to deliver, once the conference was over. [90] Nonetheless, the Soviet side was reassured on the matter and thereafter the conference went remarkably well. Paradoxically, the Soviet successes in the field were now so great that some Soviet analysts were less insistent on a second front, preferring some breathing-space to allow the Red Army to reoccupy Poland and secure Soviet borders and territorial ambitions before the Allies gained a foothold on the Continent.[91] In fact, although it was not realised until too late, the second front was now more in the West's interests than the Soviet Union's.

The convivial atmosphere allowed many important decisions to be agreed, particularly in the field of Allied co-operation. There was the establishment of the Advisory Council for Italy, on which the Soviets had a seat; the Allied Control Commission; and Eden's baby, the European Advisory Commission (EAC), to make plans for the armistice and its enforcement; there was Hull's Declaration on General Security, which pledged fighting the war to the end; and an agreement about holding discussions on Roosevelt's 'World Organisation'. The position of China took up much time, the US keen to see them recognised as a counter to Japan; time was also given over to general ideas about the future of Europe, with the USSR piously rejecting the idea of 'spheres of influence!'[92] As can be appreciated, one reason for the amicable atmosphere was the general avoidance of talk on any thorny issue such as Poland, the future of Germany, and Eastern Europe. These were, perhaps, the most pressing matters, but at least some mechanisms, such as the EAC, had been created which might resolve these matters later. Hull's preoccupations can be judged by the fact that when an aide raised the parlous state of USSR-Polish relations and the inherent dangers, Hull replied 'I don't want to deal with piddling little things. We must deal with the main issues.'[93]

The American preoccupation with gaining agreement about China's inclusion in the leadership of the new world organisation left them impatient and uninterested in many detailed European matters. Molotov, hindered by an inability to initiate anything without Stalin's agreement, was also unable to propose much of novelty, and so it was left to Anthony Eden to lead many of the discussions, raise most suggestions, and counter Molotov effectively. Hull seemed both unprepared and unable to contribute. Indeed Oliver Harvey, Eden's Private Secretary, noted in his diary of 22 October 1943: 'A.E. does practically all. We are carrying the American delegation'.[94]

The conference, therefore, was something of a personal triumph for Eden. Clark Kerr had been an admirer for some time, but by now he did in fact find cause to reassess his opinion, becoming inclined to the view that Eden was too absorbed in the progress of his own career to be a true statesman.[95] However, there was no denying Eden's success: he had been the dynamo and had created a situation in which Britain became, during the course of the conference at least, the key world power. Britain guided the three major countries in the anti-Nazi alliance through the conference and directed the future agenda of the free world. Probably at no point in her twentieth-century history, and rarely before, had Britain been in such a pre-eminent position of political power; yet it was a position now based ironically on a diminishing economy and waning might. The empire was about to crumble, the bank balance about to disappear, but for one brief and final moment, Britain headed the top table. Never again would the Americans play such a subordinate role; never again would the Soviet Union let the expediency of military necessity overrule her political objectives; never again would Britain be in a position to command the respect of the two superpowers and have them attend to her own agenda.

It had been a hectic twelve days for Clark Kerr. Quite apart from the demands of the plenary sessions, there had been a full round of other bilateral talks and all the social trappings of luncheons, dinners and parties. On the twenty-eighth Clark Kerr had hosted a dinner at the embassy for Molotov, for example, and on the thirtieth had held a cocktail party for diplomatic and prominent Soviet guests such as Ilya Ehrenberg and the writer Alexei Tolstoi. Later that night saw a grand dinner in the Kremlin to toast the success of the conference. Stalin, the host, sat with Cordell Hull on his right and Clark Kerr on his left: it was a fitting tribute to his role in keeping relations with the Soviet Union so smooth over the 18 months of his labours.

Back in London, Eden was generous in his praise of Clark Kerr's contribution to the success of the conference. In his report to the House of Commons on Thursday 11 November 1943, Eden said, 'I must pay a special tribute to the work of Sir Archibald Clark Kerr. Much of the preparatory laying of the ground that is necessary for such a conference fell to him, and he has rendered already remarkable services to Anglo-Soviet understanding.'[96] Clark Kerr's full recognition would be his elevation to the Privy Council in the New Year's Honours List.

The Moscow Conference and its absence of rancour created something akin to euphoria in its wake. There was a general belief that the hopes of extending the wartime coalition into a lasting peacetime alliance were actually within reach. Few were prepared to spoil the party by mentioning the many unburied skeletons still capable of reappearing to haunt the feast. Indeed, in that same Commons debate, only Jimmy Maxton, the old ILP warrior, had the necessary equilibrium to judge things more calmly. He bluntly told Eden that he simply did not believe that he had 'laid down the machinery of permanent peace or even a machine that would continue very long after the cessation of this war... He did not believe that Soviet Russia, large-scale capitalist America, and conservative Britain represented political, economic or social philosophies which could enable them to continue as companions on an extended journey.'[97] In some ways the situation mirrored events in China, where wartime exigencies created for a time an alliance between communist and nationalist, but it was a superficial union which merely masked temporarily the deep and unbridgeable divisions which would reappear all the more starkly once the adhesive of a common enemy had been removed.

What was important in November 1943, however, was the element of surprise: after a year of so many bitter recriminations, it was such a pleasant shock to find an amicable atmosphere in Moscow that it was quite understandable to dismiss Maxton as a 'killjoy'. At last it looked as if the adhesive could be made to last.

Soviet pleasure at the Conference was even more marked. On the night of 7 November, Molotov threw a lavish party at the Spiridonovka Palace to celebrate both the 1917 Revolution and the recent events in Moscow. Earlier in the day, in his annual speech to the nation, Stalin had even praised fulsomely the contribution of the western allies to the war effort.[98] Molotov and the other foreign ministry officials all turned up in their splendid new uniforms, significantly reminiscent of old Tsarist garb. Few foreign diplomats had brought their formal wear to Moscow but Clark Kerr, following Britain's triumph at the conference, felt it his duty to appear well turned out. He managed to scrape together a full formal rig-out, to which he added a great red and blue sash and a variety of medals. As such, he was the only one of the visiting diplomats to come close to the splendour of the Russian hosts. Even many of the previously hidden Politburo wives appeared, as did numerous writers, artists and musicians, such as Shostakovich.

From an early stage, it became clear that both Harriman and Clark Kerr were the targets for the customary intoxication exercise. This task was entrusted mainly to Mikoyan, the Kremlin drinking champion. Clark Kerr was honest enough to report on the booze-up to Eden.

> After a short and sprightly concert Molotov led me to a secluded supper room and planted me at a table in the corner with Cherbakov, Mikoyan, and Korniechuk, who hemmed me in, the three toughest drinkers in the union. Everything but sheer vodka and a bowl of apples was excluded from the table. They would not allow me to eat 'because it would spoil the vodka'. I knew I was in for it and I was... Molotov clucked round us now and then like a hen worried about the welfare of one of her chickens. Meanwhile the temperature rose and so did the fumes of vodka and brotherly love began to manifest itself in a cascade of kisses from Korniechuk and the party boomed on. So did my head.

A moderate drinker of claret and an occasional tippler of whisky, Clark Kerr struggled to cope. Harriman, meanwhile, was only barely surviving the endless round of toasts, which ranged from the politically correct to the drunkenly ludicrous. Harriman had the advantage of the company of his daughter Kathleen, however. About midnight, when she noticed that Clark Kerr was rising to the toasts with increasing difficulty and that Harriman's expression was growing more and more fixed, she took her father by the arm and led him out, mostly under his own steam, to the car.[99] The Japanese had left long before, snubbed by the Americans and cold-shouldered by everybody else; they were followed by a succession of casualties, vodka-soaked emissaries carried out feet first to their waiting chauffeurs; all this much to the boyish amusement of the Soviet underlings whose job was to transport the fallen bodies.

Clark Kerr was soldiering on, his rather macho self-image forcing him to see the escapade through to the end, however predictable the certain conclusion. In the midst of the vodka and camaraderie a significant diplomatic row broke out, as he later informed Eden:

> ...Molotov came back from one of his excursions amongst his other guests. With him was the Swedish minister and Vyshinski. Heads and blood seem to have been hot (I say 'seem' because truly I do not remember). But they tell me that Vyshinski began by telling the Swede that he did not much like neutrals. Then Molotov chipped in and gave him a sharp homily about people who keep themselves in mean neutrality. Somehow or other even the patient Swiss were dragged in. The unhappy Swede's arguments were roughly brushed aside. By this time Mikoyan had fled. Korniechuk had been taken away and Cherbakov was dozing in his corner.[100]

At some hazy hour thereafter, while the Swedish row rumbled on, Clark Kerr rose grandly from his corner to attempt one last great toast. All around, the cream of the diplomatic corps lay sprawled, drowsy and defeated. Sir Archibald Clark Kerr, GCMG, His Britannic Majesty's Ambassador Extraordinary and Plenipotentiary, teetered speechlessly in all his glittering regalia for one brief but splendid moment, before falling with an almighty crash onto the table in front.[101] There he lay for a dishevelled instant amongst the wine glasses and emptied bottles before he managed to extricate himself with what enfeebled dignity he could and resume his position. There was a cut on his forehead but otherwise he was smilingly unscathed. There was, in fact, something grimly symbolic about Clark Kerr's collapse: coming so soon after the British triumph at the Conference it seemed to encapsulate neatly the false position of pre-eminence which Britain now held in the free world. She could sit quite easily at the top table but there was something unmistakably rickety about her chair: it was well-padded and ornate but there was no telling when the legs might give way underneath. The Empire was crumbling and time was running out.

Clark Kerr quickly recovered what composure he could in the circumstances:

> Someone decided that it was time to go and we moved, or were moved, all of us, into the passage ... the altercation with the Swede pursuing us as we went. There were long halts in the passage and at one of these Molotov, comparing me with the Swede and addressing himself to the Swede, thumped me in the chest and said 'Kerr is all right. He's the sort of chap we like!' Then at the next halt came another thump and: 'If he was one of us, he would be a partisan'.
>
> '... They tell me that I left under my own steam, which I find hard to believe, and that Molotov had to be propelled by a large group of his followers. Next morning the Swedish minister sent his secretary round to find out what happened for his master could not remember. Averell had to spend the day in bed. The Canadian had to send for the doctor. I had to go to the Kremlin to talk to Molotov about... Turkey. I felt like an empty eggshell – all the yolk scooped out and the top cracked, but my face was as red as ever. Molotov looked nacreous but claimed to be as frisch and munter as ever. He said that it was a pity we could not have parties like that more often – we should keep ourselves in training.[102]

Clark Kerr had in fact woken that morning to find himself still fully clothed in his study, lying with his head in the grate. His butler was dozing in his chair nearby. When he inquired of the footman how he had come to be lying in the grate while the butler was in the comfort of the seat, the poor man had to reply, 'Because, Your Excellency, you insisted'.

By this stage, arrangements had finally been made for a Big Three meeting to be held at Teheran, the furthest from base which Stalin would venture. Churchill was keen to arrange a tête-à-tête with Roosevelt prior to this, both to iron out the military situation and to consult on tactics for the conference. His plans were thwarted, however, by Roosevelt, who did not want to be seen to be 'ganging up' on Stalin. He insisted that a Russian observer be present at these talks to be held in Cairo. As a result of this, Clark Kerr was also instructed to be present, and this was judged even more important when Roosevelt also arranged for Chiang Kai-shek to attend. The net effect of this, however, was to scare off Stalin, who did not want to antagonise the Japanese by being seen to confer with the Chinese. Molotov was therefore instructed not to proceed to Cairo.

Clark Kerr left for Cairo on 18 November 1943 on a flight with Harriman, General Deane, General Martel and the British and American interpreters, Birse and Bohlen. Because of engine failure, the flight was aborted at Stalingrad, where they had to remain overnight until repairs could be effected. After a tour of the war damage, the party was entertained to an impromptu Russian banquet with the dreaded vodka toasts. Clark Kerr and his company were overwhelmed by the hospitality, particularly given the desperate state of the city and the poverty of its supplies. After much drinking, dancing and singing, the party finally broke up in the early hours. Harriman, whose chaperone daughter was absent, and so was somewhat tired and emotional by this point, brought the evening to a close with a warbling rendition of 'Show Me the Way to Go Home'. Clark Kerr told him that he had never heard the song sung with such genuine feeling: a cry from the heart after a Russian night out.[103]

Roused at five to resume their flight, the party was presented with a further challenge: a Stalingrad breakfast after the night before. It consisted of steak, mutton chops, bacon and eggs, caviare, a choice of fish, vodka, red wine and white wine. The very sight of the groaning tables sent a few more fragile members of the party scurrying out wildly into the outdoor chill.[104]

With the war in Africa over and Molotov absent, the few days in Cairo were something of a pleasant break for Clark Kerr, and offered a good opportunity to renew old friendships. On Sunday the twenty-first, after a brief visit to see Chiang and his wife, Clark Kerr was able to meet his old colleagues Robin Furness and Gerald Delaney, acquaintances from those heady Allenby days. Throughout the week, Clark Kerr had a pleasant round of social engagements and the occasional political discussion, but generally the conference was concerned with matters military. To Churchill's annoyance, a good deal of time was taken up with Far Eastern questions, to the extent that by the time of departure on the twenty-seventh nothing much had been decided on in terms of a joint British-American position for the Teheran talks.

Clark Kerr arrived with part of the British delegation in the Persian capital in mid-afternoon on the 27th. It was an arrival of some mixed emotions, recalling all the contrary memories of times nearly thirty years before. As soon as he arrived, he was thrown into action. He and Harriman had first to call on Molotov to deliver a copy of the Cairo communiqué agreed with the Chinese.[105] Harriman was asked by Molotov to provide a draft agenda and details of the US delegation, but he declined on the grounds that Roosevelt wished for something much less formal. Whether or not Clark Kerr knew of Harriman's position is unclear, but when he called privately on Molotov later he fell in with Molotov's request.[106] It is possible that he thought it a good opportunity for Britain to regain the initiative after the frustrations at Cairo. However, Harriman paid a visit to the British delegation later that evening to discover Eden and Clark Kerr in flagrante, trying to draw up a formal agenda. That Harriman was annoyed at the detail involved in their plan seems to support the idea that the Americans were far less organised in preparation and merely seeking to smooth the President's personal relationship with Stalin rather than concern themselves with specifics. Roosevelt had again changed his team, with Harry Hopkins having replaced the elderly Hull. After a heated argument, Eden acceded to some of Harriman's objections and simplified the proposed agenda.

After midnight, Clark Kerr was roused from his much-needed slumbers to make an urgent return visit to Molotov. There he was joined by Harriman, and Molotov spun them a vague tale of a suspected plot against the American delegation, urging them to move into quarters in the Soviet legation. Although neither Harriman nor Clark Kerr believed Molotov's story, there was nothing to be gained by refusing and, accordingly, Roosevelt and his entourage flitted to the Soviet compound on the following day. Quite why Stalin was so keen to have the Americans close by is not obvious, but long before the assassination rumour was concocted he had been lobbying for the American delegation to be billeted in the Soviet quarters and had cabled thus to Roosevelt when he was in Cairo.[107] It is certainly possible that these buildings were bugged, but it is also possible that Stalin felt that proximity would improve his chances of winning over Roosevelt in preparation for one of Churchill's wobbles on the proposed Normandy invasion – Operation Overlord. Stalin's blandishments were almost superfluous, as Roosevelt was determined to be as amenable and chummy to Stalin as possible, while keeping Churchill at arm's length. Sir Alec Cadogan certainly saw it in that light. He thought the US party was 'in Stalin's pocket' from day one, and was appalled by the lack of professionalism in their delegation's haphazard approach.[108]

Stalin and Roosevelt did have their first ever talk together prior to the opening plenary session, which commenced at 4pm on Sunday 28 November. As it was mainly concerned with military affairs, neither Clark Kerr nor Cadogan was present. With Cadogan, the Permanent Under-Secretary at the Foreign Office, in the British delegation, Clark Kerr's role was less exalted than it had been at the conference of foreign ministers in Moscow. Nevertheless as the senior 'field' diplomat present, and with his good relations with Stalin, he was a vital member of Churchill's team. For all that, Clark Kerr's ready humour and lack of seriousness occasionally irked the Prime Minister. At a lunchtime delegation talk on the twenty-eighth for example, Clark Kerr could not resist a chuckle when the flatulence of one member of the party momentarily, and rather noisily, interrupted proceedings. Churchill turned on him. 'Do not,' he chided, 'let the heat imparted by someone else's buttocks detract you from the discipline of a solemn matter.'

Following the first plenary session, at whose drift Churchill was most displeased,[109] there was a dinner at Roosevelt's villa. There were just 11 guests: Roosevelt, Churchill, Stalin, Hopkins, Eden, Molotov, Harriman, Clark Kerr and the interpreters Bohlen, Birse and Pavlov. Talk was generally light-hearted to begin with. Roosevelt took an early interest in Clark Kerr: 'Well, well, it's about time I knew all about you'. Churchill told Roosevelt that Clark Kerr was a 'tough' and to watch him. The talk then moved on to the topic of France and Germany and their respective demerits, much of the conversation verging on the racist. After Roosevelt left, looking ill, Churchill tried to draw Stalin on the Polish question and raised the idea, to which the Marshall did not object, of moving Poland *en masse* westwards to provide land for Russia in the east and to punish Germany in the west. Following the close of the meal, Clark Kerr was invited up to Churchill's apartment for drinks and a general chat with his senior advisers. The mood was rather flat because of the inconstant behaviour of the Americans. Churchill managed to cheer the company, however, by reminding them that the thirtieth would be his sixty-ninth birthday and declaring that they would all get 'blotto'.

The 29th was marked by the presentation of the Stalingrad Sword of Honour. This was made on behalf of King George VI to mark the great Russian victory in the city. It proved to be a moving ceremony but, despite it all, did not serve to improve the Soviet mood at the second plenary session. Clark Kerr was present on this occasion, and found the experience depressing. Churchill and his military advisers were constantly pressed on the Overlord question, on which they were tending to shilly-shally. Churchill spoke too much, which further riled Stalin and the Americans, who supported the Soviet demand for a definite date to be fixed. At dinner that night, hosted by Stalin for the same limited guest-list, Churchill was baited relentlessly by Stalin. There was a large number of toasts, led off by Molotov, but the constant bickering and play-acting simply annoyed Clark Kerr, who got very bored with it, as did Eden. At one point when heckled by Stalin on the question of Overlord, Churchill confirmed that it would indeed take place, 'with God's will'.

'God is on your side?' retorted Stalin. 'Is he a conservative? The devil's on my side. He's a good communist!'[110]

Churchill took it all in his stride until Stalin proposed that, on the German question, it would be necessary to shoot 50,000 officers to prevent Germany rising again in the future as a military threat. Churchill said that could not be tolerated and, when Stalin pressed the point, declared that he would rather be shot himself that be a party to such infamy. Roosevelt tried to defuse the situation by lightheartedly suggesting that a compromise of 49,000 shootings could be considered. At this Churchill made to walk out, only to be coaxed back by Stalin and Molotov, who declared that it had all been a joke. It may have been, but it certainly shed new light on the Katyn dispute. There was more drink, a bibulous reconciliation and hugs all round.

Roosevelt slumped in Clark Kerr's respect that evening at dinner. Clark Kerr thought his conversation commonplace, riddled with clichés and his whole demeanour lacking in honesty, as if he were play-acting continuously. After the dinner, Churchill, Eden and Clark Kerr had a few drinks together, during which Churchill waxed lyrical on the future of warfare and the crucial factor of air supremacy.

30 November marked the high point of the conference. Stalin's undertaking to come in against Japan once Germany was repulsed was sufficiently appealing for a deal to be struck on a date for Overlord: May 1944. Stalin had got his way and all the clouds vanished. Apart from a slight disagreement between the

CIGS, Alan Brooke, and Stalin, who distrusted him greatly, the dinner was a cordial affair with much drink taken. Even Harriman had told Clark Kerr that he was 'scared to death' of Brooke's attitudes, particularly his total antipathy to the idea of Overlord.[111]

Churchill called it in his memoirs one of the most memorable occasions of his life, and it was indeed a remarkable event: the leaders of Great Britain, the USA and the USSR sitting down to sup together, wholly at one. The party did not break up until midnight after a great many toasts, Churchill even toasting the proletarian masses and Stalin the Conservative Party.[112] At one point Stalin asked if he could call Mr Churchill 'my good friend'. 'You may call me Winston' was the reply. The extraordinary relationship Clark Kerr had cultivated with Stalin was evidenced at one point, and had shocked Churchill. Stalin had been smoking and went to light another cigarette. Clark Kerr turned to him and suddenly said: 'It's cissy to smoke cigarettes'. While Churchill sat quaking at the likely response, Stalin rather sheepishly stubbed out his cigarette and fumblingly lit up his pipe.[113]

The following day was taken up with the major political issues which had largely been overshadowed by the military matters requiring decisions at the conference. These included attempts to persuade Turkey to join the allies; the future of Germany; and the ever-present Polish question. This last was partly alleviated by concentrating on the border issue rather than Stalin's rift with the London Poles. Stalin plainly showed that he had no intention of seeking reconciliation with the Polish Government-in-exile, many of whose members he believed were pro-German. That matter was left unresolved, but Churchill and Stalin, without consulting any Polish opinion, did agree that the old Curzon line should mark Poland's eastern border and the Oder river her western frontier. On this general outline the two leaders agreed.

The conference therefore ended in a great blaze of optimism. The mercurial relations which had dogged Clark Kerr during his lonely struggle in Moscow over the past two years had miraculously been all but forgotten during these last four days. It was therefore in a happy frame of mind that he joined Churchill for the return flight to Cairo on 2 December.

After a few days of more talks with the Americans and Chinese, Clark Kerr was able to have a few free days in Cairo. Then on the twelfth he flew to Algiers and on the sixteenth arrived in Puerto Rico, bound for the United States on a private visit. Its sole purpose was to attempt some kind of reconciliation with Tita, then living in New York City, and whom he had not seen for nearly three years. The visit was a shattering experience: Tita at first refused to meet him at all, and only finally agreed to see him in the presence of another man. Clark Kerr was heartbroken by it all and returned to Moscow in late January 1944 like a 'nervous wreck' according to his colleague Tom Barman.[114]

The early months of 1944 were largely concentrated on the Polish issue, which was indeed why Clark Kerr had returned before his leave was officially over. In London, the British were trying to get Mikolajczyk, the leader of the

Government-in-exile, to restructure his cabinet to make it more appealing to Stalin. In Moscow, Clark Kerr's main task was in trying to get Stalin to agree to reopen links with the London Poles, and stress the attempts being made in London to root out the most anti-Soviet Poles from the Cabinet. It was a slow and frustrating business. Indeed, after the euphoria of Teheran, British-Soviet relations resumed their tempestuous normality: in mid-January *Pravda* had seen fit to publish a story that British and German officials were conducting 'peace' talks in Spain; then later in the month Stalin sent an offensive reply to Churchill over the quality and quantity of the ships proposed for Russia following the carve-up of the Italian fleet.

As may have been expected, the Polish Cabinet in London refused to accept the Curzon line, on the understandable grounds that some four million Poles would thus be abandoned to the Soviet Union. Churchill, however, was adamant that the Poles had to accept the deal as the price of peace with the Soviet Union, and that without that peace Poland could never be 'independent' in any secure sense. In any case, as Orme Sargent acknowledged on 24 January, the Soviet army was bound to reach Warsaw sooner or later, and unless the London Poles made a deal with Stalin before then, they would effectively lose Poland altogether to whomsoever Stalin appointed.[115]

On 28 January Churchill warned Stalin that the creation of any Soviet-sponsored alternative government for Poland would have grave consequences for the Alliance.[116] When Clark Kerr saw Stalin on 2 February, his first meeting following his return, he had to suffer some two hours of Stalin be rating the London Poles for their failure to accept the Curzon line and their pro-German bias.[117] Despite that, it was a pleasant enough talk, Clark Kerr bringing back from London presents of tobacco and a pipe for Stalin. Stalin was pampered enough to give an oral pledge on the future independence of Poland, but still demanded the removal from the Polish Government of three senior figures: Sosnkowski, Kot and Kukiel. Churchill, oddly enough, fully supported the Russian territorial demands, and was out of patience with the Poles' refusal to agree.[118] On the other hand he was angry at the intransigence of Stalin, who seemed unwilling to deal with the emigré Government on any terms.[119]

Throughout February British-Soviet relations were very strained over the Polish question. Churchill continued to urge Stalin to move on the matter of recognising the London Poles, promising in return to seek to have their Cabinet rid of any professed anti-Soviet elements, and to push them to accept this. Despite that assurance, Stalin was immoveable: at the end of the month Clark Kerr had another fruitless audience. 'It was not a pleasant talk,' he recorded. 'He attempted to dismiss with a snigger the position of the Polish government... It was a dreary and exasperating conversation.'[120] Things were so hopeless that Clark Kerr suggested that it was time to reconsider British support of the London Poles. Churchill was outraged at this, noting on the report of Clark Kerr's suggestion: 'I don't much like this stuff. He would give up everything to appease Stalin.'

In response, Churchill sent a long telegram on 7 March to Stalin regretting the latter's inability to make up with the London Poles, whom Churchill and the Cabinet would continue to support solidly. The affair was casting a shadow over the alliance. Clark Kerr was unhappy at the veiled threat, and urged Churchill to make some changes in the tone of the message.

> Any remark by myself about the casting of a shadow over the coming operations would, I fear, suggest to Stalin's suspicious mind that we were not going to live up to our promises made at Teheran.

Instead, Clark Kerr wanted Churchill to emphasise that the door was still open for agreement over Poland. Churchill was in no mood for such compromise. Stalin's reply would determine whether or not the door was still open, and as for the rest of the message, it was to be delivered as it stood.[121]

As Clark Kerr had feared, Stalin's reply was violent, accusing the British and the Ambassador, in particular, of threatening the Soviet Union. 'Stalin's lamentable message' so depressed Clark Kerr that he cabled Cadogan at the end of the month raising the possibility of being recalled from Moscow as a token of British unhappiness.[122]

In fact, at this the Cabinet decided to back off and let things lie.[123] In any event, Churchill was now much more concerned with Soviet intrigue in the Balkans and Italy, and in early May he considered recalling Clark Kerr as a protest about that instead.[124] Despite Clark Kerr's front-line position in this acrimonious dispute, some in the Foreign Office were unhappy at his attitude to the whole Polish question. Frank Roberts, head of the Foreign Office's Central Department, complained on 21 April 1944 that Sir Archibald Clark Kerr seemed 'to take the whole question of recognition and our obligations towards Poland very lightheartedly'.[125] Roberts's misgivings stemmed from Clark Kerr's odd suggestion made earlier that the Polish Government-in-exile be broadened by adding to its ranks one Wanda Wasilewska. Quite apart from her nymphomaniac reputation, she was also married to the Ukrainian Foreign Minister, whose Government laid claim to a huge chunk of Polish territory. Roberts dismissed Clark Kerr's notion as ludicrous.[126]

Generally, the first half of 1944 was dominated by the questions of Poland, Italy, Rumania, Greece and Yugoslavia. There was a continuous guessing-game to predict Soviet intentions in those areas and so co-ordinate responsive policy. In fact, it ended up in the pragmatic arrangement touted by Eden that the USSR could organise activities in Rumania, provided Britain were given a free hand in Greece. The Soviets pushed for a formal arrangement, sanctioned by the US, but at this the British baulked, knowing full well the US's hatred of this sort of imperialist carve-up and 'spheres of influence'. Indeed, so great were the concerns over Soviet designs in Eastern Europe, and so great the Red Army's own advances, that what should have been the great highlight of Clark Kerr's time in Moscow, the D-Day landings of 6 June, turned out to be something of an anticlimax. However, at least the Soviets had been given their second front, and so great was the air of anticipation in the Kremlin that Clark Kerr was able to send merely a four-word note to Stalin on the day of the Normandy invasion: 'We are off tonight'. For a while, British-Soviet relations blossomed in the after-glow of the second front.

All too soon, Soviet intrigue in eastern Europe brought matters back to nervous suspicion. On 23 July Soviet troops reoccupied Lublin and 'made contact' with a group of Poles known as the Polish Committee of National Liberation. Stalin told Churchill that he had hopes of this serving as the nucleus of a provisional government.[127] As the Soviet troops neared Warsaw, time was short and Churchill therefore sent off Mikolajczyk and two colleagues to Moscow to negotiate with Stalin over the status of the London Poles. In the meantime, heeding a call from Moscow Radio and sensing the weakening of the German occupation, the Polish Home Army rose in rebellion against their Nazi overlords. Much has been written of this tragic event, but there is no doubt that had the Soviet Union any desire to aid the Poles they could have done so. Instead, they sat and waited while the rebellion was brutally crushed: Poland would be liberated on Soviet terms by Soviet soldiers, and not before.

Both Harriman and Clark Kerr pressed the Kremlin to aid the uprising, and to allow Allied planes to land in Soviet territory and so fly in supplies to the resistance. Stalin had promised Mikolajczyk on 9 August that aid would be forthcoming. On August 15 Vyshinski told the two ambassadors that there would be no involvement in the irresponsible Polish 'adventure'. Clark Kerr and Harriman demanded to see Molotov, who met them the following evening but again stonewalled until Stalin himself, on the twentieth, dismissed the uprising as the actions of 'power-seeking criminals'.[128] In September, some aid was dropped to the Polish resistance but by then it was too late and the defeated Polish fighters finally surrendered to the Germans on 4 October 1944. For the London Poles it was also a crippling defeat, the beginning of the end of their official reign as the 'Government-in-exile'.

The Polish debacle merely heightened fears over Soviet activities in liberated Europe. Churchill decided that another meeting with Stalin was vital: the Russian armies had now occupied Bulgaria and Rumania, were rolling through Poland, and were advancing into Hungary and Yugoslavia. Prior to Churchill's visit, Clark Kerr penned a lengthy memorandum on Soviet policy.[129] Dated 31 August 1944, it presents a rather depressing view of the Soviet political machine and its conduct of foreign policy. Perhaps for the first time, Clark Kerr gave voice to deep-seated concerns about the prospects for a lasting postwar alliance with the Soviet Union. Clark Kerr identified three likely results of the war: the removal of any immediate threat to Soviet security; the consolidation of Stalin's dominant position in Soviet society; the use of Communist parties abroad to serve the interests of 'Russia as a state as distinct from Russia as a revolutionary notion'. However, trying to guess resulting Soviet policy was almost impossible because of the Soviet regime's 'complete freedom of manoeuvre in foreign affairs'. There were no restraints – political, ideological and practical – on its capacity to alter course at will. Allied to this, Clark Kerr identified an 'obstinate blend of pride and sensitiveness to criticism' which further complicated attempts to deal with the Soviet Government. The only good point that could be made about their capacity for about-turns was that 'the knowledge that a foreign power is tenaciously abiding by its objective may induce them to alter course wherever the balance of advantage points to the need for readjustment'.

From this analysis, Clark Kerr could only reach the sobering conclusion:

> A Soviet foreign policy divorced from the restraining influence of enlightened public opinion and hypersensitive in all matters affecting national prestige is likely to offer serious impediments to the development of postwar inter-allied relations in an atmosphere free from recurring tension.

This document is therefore instructive for those who contend that Clark Kerr became a sentimental pro-Bolshevik during his time in Moscow, and failed to appreciate the realities of the Stalinist regime and its implications for post-war international relations. The only hope that he could identify was that the Soviet Union's new superpower status might instil a more amenable spirit in the conduct of her affairs and develop an awareness that her interests would be better served 'by methods of compromise and tact than by a boorish display of rigidity and brusqueness'.

Clark Kerr's rather pessimistic views about the prospects of a lasting alliance were echoed in September by George Kennan, a senior figure in the US Moscow Embassy. In a 29-page telegram (not to be confused with his 'long' telegram of 1946!) he expressed grave doubts about the ability of Western governments, particularly that of the USA, to understand Russia.

> The apprehension of what is valid in the Russian world is unsettling and displeasing to the American mind. He who would undertake this apprehension will not find his satisfaction in the achievement of anything practical for his people, still less in any official or public appreciation of his efforts. The best he can look forward to is the lonely pleasure of one who stands at long last on a chilly and inhospitable mountain top where few have been before, where few can follow, and where few will consent to believe that he has been.[130]

In this rather sombre atmosphere, Churchill arrived for his second wartime visit to Moscow. It was of a significantly different nature to the 1942 visit, when the main issue was that of placating Stalin over the second front. Now, the relationship was seriously altered: with final victory more likely, the main aim was to achieve some agreement with Stalin over post-war arrangements, particularly in Poland and Eastern Europe. Britain had little or no leverage on the matter, other than the weight of moral argument. In these circumstances, and perhaps influenced by Clark Kerr's call for total realism in conducting negotiations,[131] Churchill adopted a hard-headed business-like attitude to these talks. Fears over a UK-USSR bargain which might perpetuate imperial divisions in world politics influenced Roosevelt to despatch Harriman to attend the talks as an observer. Despite all the problems throughout the year, the Polish rising and the inconclusive nature of the UN preparatory talks at the Dumbarton Oaks conference, Clark Kerr was optimistic about the chances of reaching agreement in Moscow. 'The iron stands hot for the striking,' he told Churchill.[122]

Churchill and his large party, including Eden, arrived in Moscow on 9 October 1944. They proceeded straight to the Kremlin that night for talks. This first meeting was the occasion of Churchill's notorious 'naughty document', as Clark Kerr described it. During a discussion on Eastern Europe, Churchill passed to Stalin a paper in which he outlined a proposed plan for British-Soviet influence in the Balkans. Expressed in crude percentages, it gave the USSR 90% influence in Rumania; 75% in Bulgaria; Yugoslavia and Hungary were to be 50-50; in Greece, Churchill wanted a 90% British stake. Stalin calmly changed Bulgaria to 90%, ticked the paper and handed it back. This incredible performance by Churchill, sanctioned neither by Parliament nor Cabinet, far less the governments and peoples of South-eastern Europe, has been the subject of endless speculation and debate. Given Britain's impotence in Europe, it could be said to be simple realism. If Stalin would agree, then there would be seen at last a path through the post-war woods. On the other hand, it does seem extraordinary that Churchill should so dispassionately condemn so much of Eastern Europe to total Soviet domination without the merest mention of democracy or free parliaments. In one moment, he gave the green light to Soviet manipulation and exposed both British impotence and lack of interest in the fate of many millions of Europe's 'liberated' people. For all that, neither Eden nor Clark Kerr seemed to demur, and Eden returned the following night to hammer out the further details of this carve-up. In any event, no one seemed even to question what '10% influence' or '20% influence' in any particular country might actually mean in practical terms. One wonders what historians would have made of this deal had it been hatched by someone other than Churchill. It was fortunate for Archie Clark Kerr and his reputation, for example, that he was not the prime motivator; it would have been judged a very different 'deal' had it been his work.

Clark Kerr was present at both meetings and seemed delighted, like all in the British party, with the progress and atmosphere. The main event of 10 October as far as Clark Kerr was concerned was a private talk with Eden about his own future. After his customary complaint about his dissatisfaction with the Moscow post, Clark Kerr expressed himself fit and enthusiastic to continue in the Foreign Service. Eden did not miss his cue: when a suitable time came, Washington would be Clark Kerr's. It was an emotional moment: after nearly 40 years in diplomacy, the plum post in the British Foreign Service was within his grasp. For a marvellous moment all the loneliness and frustration of the Moscow posting were swept away, and the glittering prize of the Washington Embassy, the elevation to the peerage, and the final professional triumph shone before him like the Holy Grail.

The only contentious issue to surface at Moscow was the continuing dispute over Poland, its territory and future government. Anxious to settle a deal, Churchill had cabled Mikolajczyk to come to Moscow to join the talks. Earlier in the year, Clark Kerr and his team had managed to gain access to the pro-Soviet Lublin Committee of Poles. In late July they had been invited to the Embassy for talks and to allow Clark Kerr a chance to assess them. Despite his determination to be fair and even sympathetic to them, he could not but be unimpressed by the obnoxious pro-Soviet pleadings of the Lublin Poles – Bierut, Osobka-Morawski and Minc. After a lengthy presentation of their credentials, plans, and hopes, talk turned to their request for aid to reconstruct Poland. When Clark Kerr asked for specific shortages, Minc bizarrely answered that, for example, Polish medical schools were short of skeletons. 'Dear me,' murmured Clark Kerr, 'I should have thought there was no shortage of skeletons in Poland. All they need is a spade or two.'[133]

Before there was a chance for Churchill to meet the Lublin Poles for himself, there was the small matter of a function at the British embassy on the night of 11 October. This proved to be the highlight of Churchill's visit and an outstanding achievement for Clark Kerr. For the first time ever, Stalin had been persuaded to enter a foreign embassy for dinner. The evening was a great success, with the Soviet leader remaining in convivial mood until his departure at four in the morning.

The following day, the London Poles arrived for talks. There were three of them led by Mikolajczyk – Sosnkowski, the most anti-Soviet of the Cabinet having been dismissed in late September. Little progress was made at this first conference, owing to the Poles' refusal to countenance any loss of territory. However, the following evening gave Churchill and his party the opportunity to hear from the Lublin Poles. The meeting was a depressing revelation: the Lublin Poles showed themselves to be a group of treacherous stooges whose outspokenly pro-Soviet pronouncements even provoked Stalin to embarrassed laughter.[134]

On the morning of the fourteenth, Churchill desperately tried to persuade the London Poles, for whom he had even greater sympathy after his encounter with the Lublin puppets, to accept the Curzon line as the only basis for becoming involved in the post-war Polish Government. A raging argument ensued, during which Churchill stormed out. It was all to no avail: the Poles would not budge on the border issue.

These talks rumbled on ineffectually for the next few days: their frustrating, inconclusive and bad-tempered nature is summed up in Clark Kerr's brief diary entry for 15 October: ' Mik: Christ god damn fuck and bugger'. Finally, Mikolajczyk accepted the Curzon line as a 'line of demarcation' and agreed to return to London to attempt to persuade his colleagues. Clark Kerr was optimistic, since the two Polish sides had been brought together, and expected that Mikolajczyk would return in the promised ten days and help form a government. Mikolajczyk never returned. On 24 November, having failed to win over his colleagues, he resigned. Clark Kerr was bitterly disappointed and felt now that the time had come to abandon the London Poles altogether. Churchill was not yet prepared for this.[135]

Despite the Polish problem, the conference ended on a high note with another lavish Kremlin banquet on 18 October. It was another liquid affair: Jock Balfour, Clark Kerr's most senior colleague, had a hangover which lasted for a fortnight. Churchill left in high spirits, judging that the relations between the two countries were closer than they had ever been.[136]

Following the conference, Clark Kerr set out his views on Soviet policy in another lengthy dispatch to the Foreign Office.[137] He felt that the Russians viewed solid enmity to Germany as the touchstone for the prospects of the new alliance. Clark Kerr suggested that the Soviet Union would not object to the idea of an alliance of Western European governments provided it were directed against Germany. This would merely match, as he pointed out, the Soviet Union's own plans 'to organise a continental orbit of power in regions adjacent to their borders'. Clark Kerr also warned that unless Britain moved towards 'a closer association' with her European neighbours there would be the temptation for left-wing elements in these war-weary nations to push for closer reliance on Soviet power. Similarly, the Soviet Government, in the absence of any rivals, would be tempted to flex its newly-acquired muscles to exploit the power vacuum. In this Clark Kerr was absolutely correct and, indeed, it was because of this very situation that the Marshall Plan was to be initiated in 1947.

With the conference completed and UK-Soviet relations smoothed once more, Clark Kerr was able to take some welcome home leave, arriving in London on 10 December 1944. His six weeks at home followed the usual pattern: briefings and meetings at the Foreign Office; a snatched period of peace at Inverchapel; a visit to Windsor, and then a hectic swirl of social engagements and further talks in London. Generally speaking it was a rather low period for him. Dissatisfaction with the isolation in Moscow was increased by the reluctant acceptance of the finality of Tita's desertion. There was no prospect of winning her back, and so he set in motion a formal appeal for divorce during his few days in Scotland. The divorce was subsequently granted in February. Despite the finality of this legal move, Clark Kerr clearly had never lost his love for Tita. He made no attempt, for example, to alter his will, in which she was the main beneficiary, and indeed he rejected any idea of doing so when the subject was broached by his legal advisers. As far as he was concerned, she was still his wife.

With matters in the Soviet Union so delicately poised there was no possibility of a move in the foreseeable future. Indeed, during Clark Kerr's leave events moved on apace, with the Soviet Union on 7 January formally recognising the Lublin Poles as the Government-in-waiting. The Foreign Office was naturally concerned and, at a meeting on 23 January, decided to push for the dissolution of both the London and Lublin groupings in the hope of starting afresh with something more generally acceptable.[138] As the urgent Big Three conference approached, however, it became clear that the more realistic hope was that the Lublin Government could be expanded to include some of the more moderate elements in the London bloc.

Despite the ominous reports filtering out of Poland under Soviet occupation, Clark Kerr returned in an optimistic frame of mind to Moscow via Stockholm on 28 January 1945. There he had only time to deposit his luggage before setting off for the Crimea, arriving in Yalta on 2 February. Along with the chief members of the British party, Clark Kerr was based in the Vorontzov Palace, a large villa about five miles from Roosevelt's base at the Livadia Palace where all the plenary sessions were held. This arrangement was to prevent any inconvenience for the ailing President, whose gaunt appearance at Yalta shocked even his most intimate acquaintances.[139] Roosevelt's illness had seriously impaired his preparation for the conference, and he seemed to have trouble concentrating for long periods. For all Churchill's energetic perkiness he too had lately been showing signs that his seventy years were beginning to take their toll: for some time now his associates had been increasingly exasperated by his lack of preparation for meetings, his longwindedness, and irrelevant deviations. In these circumstances, Stalin's sharpness and mental acuity quickly impressed even the most cynical of Foreign Office observers.[140] Sir Alec Cadogan, not the most tolerant of diplomats, judged that Roosevelt simply didn't know what was going on most of the time. Churchill's performance, on the other hand, infuriated him:

> How have we conducted this war, with the PM spending hours of his own and other people's time simply drivelling, welcoming red herring so as only to have the pleasure of more irrelevant, redundant talk.[141]

As the first session was not held until late on 5 February, Clark Kerr had some time to kill, and the opportunity to do a little posing, ostentatiously immersing himself in tomes of Confucian philosophy during the morning briefings.[142] Generally speaking, the conference was conducted in a spirit of good humour and friendliness. The war was going well and the Nazis were everywhere on the run. Clark Kerr was present at all the main sessions with Churchill, Eden, Cadogan, Sir Edward Bridges and Birse, the interpreter. Initial talk on Germany was inconclusive, but agreement was at last reached on the arrangements for the proposed 'World Organisation'. On 6 February, talk turned to the Polish *imbroglio*: in fact, over the next few days a fair degree of agreement was reached, but the key issues were generally postponed. An ad hoc committee of Molotov, Harriman and Clark Kerr was formed with the purpose of bringing together a more representative provisional Polish Government, pledged to hold free elections as early as possible. There was a great deal of nice debate on the exact wording of the Polish agreement, but with Roosevelt unable or lacking the interest to contribute effectively, Stalin and Molotov were able to pad away much of the British team's concerns about the independent future of Poland.

The conference, of course, had its round of grand dinners and endless toasts. On 8 February Stalin had hosted a huge reception which abounded in good humour and a general closeness between the Big Three. After the usual toasts, Clark Kerr, perhaps emboldened by the occasion or the vodka, rose to toast his neighbour the awful Beria, head of the secret police. After all the toasts to goodwill, friendship and comradeship, Clark Kerr said he now wished to toast the man 'who looked after our bodies': Beria, boss of the soldiers guarding the conference. Churchill reacted sharply, leaning forward quickly. 'No, none of that. Be careful, Archie, be careful.'[143] Clark Kerr was untroubled by the rebuff: he and Beria managed to get along, although quite why their dinner conversation centred on the sex life of fish is something of a puzzle. As with many social events in Russia, the answer may have lain in the presence of vodka which, Clark Kerr averred, was the only spirit which went 'straight to the middle and then round the waist'.[144]

The conference ended on an upbeat note, and Churchill, on his return to the Commons on 27 February, was lavish in his praise of the Soviet Union. 'I know of no government,' he declared, 'which stands to its obligations, even in its own despite, more solidly than the Russian Soviet government'.[145] Although there is no doubt that Churchill was being a little wishful in his thinking, and hoping to flatter Stalin into fidelity, the mood generally was one of optimism about the future of the alliance. The only reservation remained that of Stalin's behaviour re Poland.

Back in Moscow, to which Clark Kerr returned on 18 February, meetings about the Polish Government, as planned at Yalta, began immediately. Clark Kerr, however, was incapacitated for a time by painful eye trouble, which eventually involved having to enter hospital in early March for attention to ingrowing eyelashes which seemed to be the root cause.

Once talks resumed, Molotov, predictably, proved less accommodating than Yalta had suggested. He demanded that the pro-Soviet Polish committee now installed in Warsaw ought to have a veto over additions to their number. After a strong protest from Clark Kerr and Harriman, Molotov amended his position to the Warsaw Government merely having the right to express an opinion on the matter. However, when eight names were suggested as desirable for absorption into the Polish cabinet, all but one were rejected by Molotov and Warsaw. Incredibly, even the name of the admirable Mikolajczyk was dismissed as unacceptable. Clark Kerr was astounded, declaring that, as far as he and his government were concerned, Mikolajczyk was a 'sine qua non'.[145] Clark Kerr insisted that in these circumstances he could not possibly yet meet a delegation from the Warsaw group, and also complained that no reliable information could be gleaned from inside Poland in any case. Molotov blithely agreed that observers could be sent, only to withdraw the invitation two days later on the delicate grounds of not wishing to insult the Warsaw Poles by suggesting anything untoward was happening behind the Allies' backs.

By now it was becoming clear that the spirit of Yalta had simply vanished. On the very night Churchill had spoken so warmly of Russian good faith, Vyshinski had arrived in Bucharest determined to reconstruct the Rumanian Government on pro-Soviet lines. When King Michael refused to bow to pressure, Vyshinski stormed out in such a violent rage that his door-slamming brought plaster crashing down about the young King's ears. Backed by Soviet tanks and troops, a pro-Soviet Government took office on 6 March.

By then, well-documented reports of mass arrests and deportations in Cracow, the centre of non-communist power in Poland, were reaching the Foreign Office.[147] The terror that was Russia was spreading throughout Eastern Europe.

Eventually, Molotov's intransigence forced the UK and US Governments to present identical memos, drafted initially by Clark Kerr himself, to Molotov on 19 March repudiating the idea of a Warsaw veto over government membership, insisting that Mikolajczyk be invited to the discussions, demanding access for Allied observers into Poland, and an end to the purges. Over the next weeks, Molotov continued to stall, thereby allowing ample time for his cronies in Warsaw to consolidate their position. By the beginning of April, Clark Kerr and Harriman felt they were at 'breaking-point'.

Stalin had by this stage informed the Allies that Molotov would not be attending the UN opening conference in San Francisco and, on 7 April, blamed Clark Kerr and Harriman for the failure of the Polish negotiations. The death of Roosevelt on 12 April ended this unhappy period of deadlock on the Polish question.

Despite an honest assessment of the unpleasant nature of Soviet action since Yalta, Clark Kerr still persisted in trying to remain hopeful about the future. In a long submission to the Foreign Office on 27 March, he fully endorsed the view that there had to be 'fresh anxieties about future Russian intentions and the possibility of continued collaboration between the Soviet Union and the West'.[148] Nevertheless, he sought to paint a realistic picture of Soviet attitudes, pointing out that following the notorious percentages agreement of October 1944, they assumed that they would have a free hand in Rumania and Bulgaria provided they left Greece alone. On these matters, Clark Kerr felt that there was no point straining the alliance by objecting, since vital British interests were not threatened. On Poland, Clark Kerr interpreted the position in a similarly pragmatic way:

> They are chiefly bent upon getting a comfortable neighbour. To them this is a matter of the first importance. To us, who are more concerned with decencies, it is not.

Clark Kerr did contend, however, that:

> the Polish question is, and must remain, one of the utmost consequence, for upon its satisfactory solution rests a great part of our hope and belief in the possibility of a real and cordial understanding between the Soviet people and our own.

Despite that, Clark Kerr did not believe that it was an issue which 'need prevent the maintenance of an alliance'. It would not be the great alliance once hoped for, but he did not believe that the Polish question was one for which it was worth sacrificing relations with the Soviet Union. In his typically playful, if slightly sentimental and patronising, way, he likened the behaviour of the

Soviet Union in its present victorious buoyancy to that of 'a wet retriever in someone else's drawing-room'. From this 'puppydom' he was hopeful she would emerge.

Nonetheless, he also called for franker criticism of Soviet policy and an end to the 'gush of propaganda' in Britain about the Soviet war effort and political system. Clark Kerr rightly claimed that the hard-headed realists in the Kremlin took such nonsense as an indication of British 'fear and inferiority'. Clark Kerr's final message was for Britain to restrict its quarrels with the Russians to issues on which Britain was prepared to stand its ground, and on which it could both sound strong and, as importantly, look strong. In the dynamocratic atmosphere of Stalinist Russia it was power, not principle, which counted. Clark Kerr did not believe recent problems ought to create fears for the worst. He still felt that the alliance with Russia was:

> ... one of the flashes of genius which from time to time light our foreign policy. In this view I remain unshaken, for I am convinced that the alliance will serve us well and pay a steady, though not spectacular, dividend.

All considered, this memorandum was a coolly perceptive and calculated analysis of Soviet policy and motivation. Yet it clearly erred badly on the side of optimism in the gloss put on Soviet actions. On the one hand Clark Kerr baldly presented Soviet failings, aggression and anti-democratic and destabilising measures in Eastern Europe, while still calmly holding out hope of some kind of happy accommodation with the USSR notwithstanding this way of conducting foreign affairs. If Clark Kerr did have a failing, it was his tendency to give opponents the benefit of the doubt, to believe the best of them. For years he had been preaching the need to treat the Soviet Union as an equal, to trust her. Unfortunately, now that she had been trusted, it was difficult to accept that she could abuse that trust so quickly and so completely. Part of the problem was Clark Kerr's great respect and admiration for Stalin – understandable given the extent to which Stalin shone among his commonplace associates. However, it did make Clark Kerr reluctant to criticise Stalin on any but marginal issues. Oddly enough, this was the very flaw in his approach identified by Tom Driberg, of all people, in an otherwise glowing portrait published just the previous month. 'If he has a fault,' wrote Driberg, 'it is not a bad fault in a diplomat – a tendency to hero-worship some of the great men to whom he has been accredited.' Driberg did not indicate this of Stalin but gave instead the example of Chiang Kai-shek whose 'nobility and significance' he claimed Clark Kerr had overestimated.[149]

The other point to remember is that these despatches were not wholly Clark Kerr's views.[150] They had tended to be composed in collaboration with Jock Balfour and Tom Barman, both of whom shared a much less rosy vision of the future of UK-USSR relations. By this stage, Balfour had gone to Washington, to be replaced by Frank Roberts who held strong views on the failings of Soviet behaviour. It is therefore easy to see that the apparent contradictions in the despatch are a result of an attempt to marry Clark Kerr's optimism with the others' grim realism, Clark Kerr's hopes with the others' fears. Certainly, for example, when Harriman in the US gave a rather harsh and outspoken view of Soviet policy, Clark Kerr aired strong disagreement to the Foreign Office, criticising Harriman's lack of 'balance'.[151] In fact, as Harriman proved, in an astute telegram in early April, whatever his failings as a diplomat, he was better able to identify Soviet foreign policy objectives in a dispassionate and blunt style, free of Clark Kerr's varnish.[152]

Even without the death of Roosevelt, the protracted talking on Poland would have been interrupted by the inaugural meeting of the 'world organisation', planned for San Francisco in April. The death of Roosevelt did create an unexpected improvement in allied relations as Stalin finally allowed Molotov to attend the conference as a gesture of conciliation to the new Truman administration. As a result of this *volte face*, Clark Kerr was also required to be in attendance at the Conference.

By this stage, mid-April 1945, the Foreign Office was in some confusion of attitude towards the Soviet Union. The developments since Yalta had given many advisers a considerable jolt, and there was much talk about the need for a showdown with the Russians sooner rather than later. Senior figures such as Cadogan and Orme Sargent tended to back away from such apocalyptic analyses, pointing to the lack of wholehearted American support as the chief weakness of such a policy aim. Even at Yalta, Roosevelt had indicated his desire to see a rapid withdrawal of US forces from Europe once Germany had been defeated, and there was certainly no desire to see US forces remain to lend succour to British policy, highly suspect as it was held to be in America. British action in Greece to uphold the monarchy was already being criticized and, on the whole, Americans were unhappy about being used to support Churchill's imperial vision. For some time Clark Kerr had been uneasy at Churchill's insistence on seeing the British Empire emerge unaltered from the war,[153] and particularly disconcerted by his outspoken imperialist speeches and pronouncements at the big conferences. These only served to alarm the Americans, as Clark Kerr's acquaintances in the States soon informed him.[154]

Apart from the American desire to withdraw from Europe – a policy ill-advisedly communicated to Stalin at Yalta – there was also the problem of a new administration in the White House. Truman, like most politicians, viewed the maintenance of the *status quo* in any policy area as some kind of slight on his political manhood, and decided to despatch two special envoys in an attempt to solve at a stroke Polish and other problems: Harry Hopkins was to fly to Moscow in late May, while Joe Davies was to fly to London.

Meanwhile, representatives of the free world, or at least the non-Nazi world, began to arrive in San Francisco. Clark Kerr left Moscow very early on 17 April 1945 accompanied by his interpreter, Birse, and Averell Harriman. It was a long and exhausting journey by way of Italy, Morocco and the Azores, which took them to Washington at midnight the following day.

Eden was already in the US capital hoping to resume talks on Poland with the US Secretary of State, Stettinius, and Molotov. On the twenty-second

Clark Kerr joined them for the first talks on Poland. These proved so unhappy that Eden was all for postponing the San Francisco Conference until some better atmosphere emerged concerning the Polish question. The main issue continued to be the failure to enlarge the provisional government to include more representative members. Further tension had been created by the USSR's recent unilateral decision to conclude a mutual aid treaty with this Polish 'government.' Further talks on the twenty-third found Molotov as immoveable as ever, but the focus moved after all to San Francisco when Molotov agreed to wire Stalin on the US-UK proposals to break the deadlock.[155]

The following day Clark Kerr flew to New Mexico before reaching San Francisco on the twenty-fifth. There he would remain for over a fortnight, largely free of the Polish incubus, the deadlock having reached such an impossible state that even Churchill despaired of any hope until another Big Three conference could be arranged.[156] The conference began with a series of wrangles and proceeded slowly in a frustrating legalistic atmosphere. Although Clark Kerr had a role to play as a senior and influential member of the British delegation, the hiatus in Polish talks meant that he had a good deal of free time and the chance to enjoy some well-earned socialising after his spartan Moscow existence. Clark Kerr particularly impressed the conference fringe with both the breadth of his interests and the depth of his knowledge – 'Moscow's saving grace, a totally cultivated man', as one journalist described him.[157]

7 May proved to be particularly memorable and exciting: in Rheims, Germany's surrender at last brought six years of bloody war in Europe to an end. Immediately thereafter, Clark Kerr flew to Washington for a few days before reaching London on 16 May. On the eighteenth he was with the Churchills for lunch, and Gusev was also present. After lunch Churchill gave the Soviet Ambassador a private talking-to, chiding the Soviet Government in very strong language for 'dropping an iron screen across Europe from Lubeck to Trieste'. Because of this and the failure to consult the allies on what was happening behind this screen, Churchill said that the demobilisation of the RAF had been delayed as a precaution.[158] Clark Kerr felt, when informed, that Churchill had overdone things in his threats, and informed the Foreign Office that, while he accepted that much of what the Soviet Union was doing was regrettable and unilateral, the main aim was to secure her borders against any future German aggression. In this regard, therefore, her actions should not be 'interpreted as a sign of hostility to the west or as a danger signal for the future'.[159] Clark Kerr was consistent throughout 1945 in his belief that Soviet interference in her neighbours' affairs sprang from justifiable fear of invasion, and that understandable concerns over security motivated the Soviet Union's actions and not any desire to dominate. There was no cause to fear for the future of the alliance with the West. Clark Kerr had, after all, seen many dark and difficult days in his three years in Moscow, and peace and harmony had always returned. The bitterness over the second front and the cancelling of convoys had been dispiriting for a while, but had eventually passed. Clark Kerr firmly believed that the same would be true of the current crisis.

On 21 May Clark Kerr was a guest of the royal family at Windsor, and after the usual round of meetings at the Foreign Office he returned to Moscow on the twenty-eighth. The most urgent matter was to try to keep tabs on Truman's representative, Harry Hopkins, who had arrived in Moscow to seek a final settlement of the Polish dispute. This had been further complicated by the Soviet arrest, in dubious circumstances, of 16 leading members of the Polish underground army in March. Only in early May did Molotov finally admit that they were being held in Moscow awaiting trial on vague charges relating to 'diversionary tactics' against the Red Army. Perhaps simply because the Russians had by now consolidated *de facto* control in Poland, Stalin proved to be more accommodating on the Polish question, suggesting that some four of the twenty cabinet posts could be given to other parties' representatives, and that Mikolajczyk would now be acceptable. Although he refused to release the arrested Poles, many of whom Clark Kerr felt were fascists anyway, this was a concession which broke the deadlock. In June, invited Polish leaders met to reorganise the Government and by 5 July it was sufficiently broad-based to be recognised officially by the British and US Governments. There still remained grave doubts, but in the circumstances of Soviet occupation and a lack of willingness to push the issue to war, the US and the UK simply agreed, although still holding out for free elections.

Meanwhile arrangements had been finalised for a Big Three conference to be held in Potsdam, near Berlin, in mid-July to decide on the post-war map of Europe. In the weeks running up to the summit there was some anxiety about Soviet actions, and Clark Kerr was involved in repeated representations to the Soviet authorities: dissatisfaction with the proposed administration of the Polish elections; concern about Soviet pressure on Turkey for bases in the Straits; worries about rumours of wholesale looting by the Red Army in occupied territories; unhappiness at the Soviet-Czech treaty of 29 June which transferred territory to the Ukraine and was concluded without consulting the US or the UK despite the agreement that all territorial issues be left to the final conference; and disputes about the area around Trieste. Despite his repeatedly expressed hopes for the future of the alliance, Clark Kerr did not flinch from criticising Soviet action. On 9 July he cabled London encouraging criticism in the British press of Soviet behaviour, as he felt it might prove salutary. The 'underlying pattern of developments throughout the area under Soviet influence' needed to be exposed and criticised, he wrote.[160]

Summing up the position of Soviet policy before the Potsdam Conference, Clark Kerr sent an expansive review to Eden on 10 July. Looking at recent developments, he was upbeat about the resolution of so many problem areas in relations with the Soviet Union and happy that, at last, the Soviet Union seemed to be 'gradually substituting the technique of international negotiation for that of unilateral action'. For all that, he had to recognise that in none of the major sticking-points thus resolved had the Soviet Government 'given way substantially on any issue affecting their vital interests'.

Significantly, the lesson Clark Kerr drew was that since the USSR seemed to conciliate the USA more than the UK, American backing was essential on any question likely to involve trouble with the Russians, but also that Truman's military threat over Trieste had been particularly successful in halting Soviet intrigue. Soviet behaviour he attributed to youthful zest springing from her military successes and a desire to flex her new-found muscles. For Potsdam, Clark Kerr called for a forthright expression of British foreign policy, to leave the Russians in no doubt about what Britain considered to be her vital national interests. At the same time, to allay deep-seated Soviet fears, there had to be a firm commitment to 'the task of uprooting fascism and punishing war criminals' in Europe. In conclusion, he argued strongly that whatever concessions might be made to the Soviet Union in foreign policy, there should be no such compromise on political philosophy:

> At the same time we may base our policy in all tranquillity upon our own conception of democracy without too nice a regard for what to us may seem to be inadmissible Soviet susceptibilities. And, in doing this, it would be prudent to... enlighten our own public opinion... about what is distasteful to us in some aspects of Russian democracy.[161]

This despatch was particularly well received in the Foreign Office, although it was not given attention until the Potsdam Conference was under way. Considered beside earlier reports on Soviet policy in 1945, it is distinguished by its certainty of tone. There is a clear line running throughout, and there is also a noticeable absence of the kind of wishful varnish which characterised many of Clark Kerr's previous reports. This can be attributed both to a growing anxiety about Soviet activity and to the growing influence of Frank Roberts in the Moscow Embassy. Roberts was not a simple Russophobe but a highly capable young diplomat who, in his two years as Head of the Foreign Office's Central Department, had formed a very clear and informed perception of Soviet intentions. The report circulated to favourable reviews from both Bevin and Sargent, who recommended that it be given King and Cabinet distribution.[162]

En route to Potsdam, Clark Kerr spent a day in Warsaw to apprise himself of the situation on the ground, and he was gratified to find that Mikolajczyk was not too downhearted about the prospects.[163] Having been briefed, Clark Kerr set off once more and arrived in Potsdam on 14 July. With a few days to spare there was ample time for pre-Conference consultations, principally with Eden and Sir Alec Cadogan. On the sixteenth he lunched with Churchill, and later in the afternoon they went into Berlin to tour the rubble of the Third Reich.

The conference proper commenced on 17 July in the Cecilienhof, the former royal palace. With the need for a military alliance having vanished, political agreement became less likely to be achieved with any degree of ease. In addition, both Truman and his Secretary of State, James Byrnes, were new to international dealings, while Churchill and Eden were fresh from an election on 5 July and their continuance in power was by no means certain. With the war in Europe over, domestic issues had become much more crucial in Britain, particularly because of the parlous state of the economy. British aims for the conference involved the hope that Americans would be more generous with their lend-lease provisions, and that the Russians would provide more from their zone in eastern Germany in the way of foodstuffs for the population in the British zone of occupation.[164] British foreign policy options were therefore considerably weakened by economic stringency.

Clark Kerr was present as part of the British delegation at all the plenary sessions. The first commenced at 5pm on 17 July and the list of subjects proposed for discussion by each of the delegations provides a revealing insight and tends to back up Clark Kerr's views on the nature of Soviet foreign policy objectives. Britain wanted discussions on the procedure for a general European settlement; application of the Yalta Declaration on liberated Europe; permission for the press to function freely in eastern Europe; and policy agreement on the treatment of Germany. The Americans wanted to concentrate on a Council of Foreign Ministers formed to draft and settle the peace treaties; policy with regard to Germany; and the Yalta Declaration on liberated Europe. For their part, the Soviet Union presented the following list of their priorities: the future of, and proposed break-up of, the German fleet and merchant navy; reparations; and territories to be placed under trusteeship.[165] Her main aims were to get what she could in coldly practical terms, and fight for them on the basis of power politics.

Over the next few days, the conference got under way and, for his sins, Clark Kerr was appointed to a drafting committee on Poland. It was due to report on 21 July, but failed to do so because of a predictable disagreement, principally on the issue of free elections. Meanwhile the main sessions also became bogged down on the Polish question, a divergence appearing on the definition of her western borders. While at Yalta there had been provisional acceptance of the Rivers Oder and Neisse as the western frontier, no decision had been made on which of the tributaries of the Neisse, western or eastern, was to mark the border. Several thousand square miles were at stake. In addition, various late night meetings with Mikolajczyk revealed the true nature of life in Poland and the likelihood of a communist one-party state emerging. Clark Kerr rather wearied of the territorial issue, judging it not worth the argument, as it involved taking a bite out of Germany.[166]

In the middle of all this, Churchill and Eden flew home for the election result. They would not return. On 28 July the new Prime Minister Clement Attlee, who had been at Potsdam since the opening session, returned with his new Foreign Secretary, Ernest Bevin. The following morning there was an urgent staff conference to discuss, primarily, the Polish issue. Clark Kerr laid his cards firmly on the table: there was no point pushing the Neisse river question since the Soviet army occupied the disputed territory and a *fait accompli* would be the eventual outcome, regardless of British opinion. Once more he was adhering to diplomatic principles he had formed 25 years earlier: there is no point trying to argue for, and hold a line on, what is either unnecessary or impossible to enforce. Attlee disagreed strongly, and the final outcome was that expert advice was to be sought regarding the disputed region and its population.[167]

Clark Kerr was on stronger ground than Attlee, and the fact became more obvious from a talk with Mikolajczyk the following day. While Churchill's defeat had been a great shock, Stalin was astute enough to realise, as he informed Mikolajczyk, that the result meant that the British people were more interested now in the domestic, and weary of war. Stalin judged the time ripe to push his own greed further, sensing a weakening in British interest in defending democratic rights in Eastern Europe.[168] Given that reality, the issue of the Western Neisse was better conceded graciously than argued for and lost, as it inevitably would be. Clark Kerr, however, could not resist some mischief-making over the British election results. To Molotov at lunch he said: 'Your folk – the Communists – have done well. They've doubled their representation in Parliament.'

'Really,' said an excited Molotov. 'How many seats have they got?'

'Two,' replied Clark Kerr, straight-faced.

Following further consultation, a draft memo on the Polish border question was prepared by W.D. Allen of the Foreign Office. A concluding paragraph reasserted the supreme authority in this matter of the Allied Control Authority in Germany – a joint US-UK-USSR board. This paragraph was dropped at the insistence of Clark Kerr, who pointed out correctly that such an arrangement would merely allow further Soviet interference in Polish affairs.[169] Again this displayed his basic political and diplomatic outlook: stick to essentials and avoid needless pitfalls and concessions.

At the end of July agreement was finally reached on the Polish question, linking it to a compromise on German reparations. Many other matters were simply passed to the newly created Council of Foreign Ministers scheduled to meet in London in September. On 2 August Clark Kerr returned to Moscow.

Although he was by now a supporter of the Labour Party, the Conservative defeat did present some professional difficulties for Clark Kerr. From Eden he had been given the promise of the Washington job, the only real diplomatic ambition he had left. Now with the new administration, there was no certainty of that. Indeed, given the hostility of many in the Labour ranks to the Oxbridge influence in the Foreign Office, and their impression of its right-wing bias, there was every possibility of a radical shake-up in the whole basis of the Diplomatic Service. Career diplomats like Archie Clark Kerr might well be viewed with suspicion and mistrust.

Probably the most important event of the Potsdam Conference was Truman's revelation about the successful testing of an atomic bomb. Although history would show that Stalin had been aware of these developments anyway through espionage, it did cause a flurry of Soviet diplomatic activity. At Yalta the Americans, keen to have Soviet support to crush the Japanese, promised to back Soviet territorial claims in Asia, largely at the expense of China, provided the Soviets declared war on Japan at the appropriate moment. Now, with the atomic bomb on their side, the Americans had less need of the Soviet

Union. Stalin, however, was determined not to forfeit gains in the east and, following the shattering news of the attack on Hiroshima, Clark Kerr and Harriman were called late to the Kremlin to be told of the Soviet declaration of war on Japan.[170] Two days later, facing atomic annihilation, Japan surrendered. It is symptomatic of Soviet diplomatic style that, despite having been at war for only two days, Molotov at first demanded a major role in accepting the Japanese surrender.

Clark Kerr only had a month in Moscow before leaving again for England in early September to attend the first meeting of the Potsdam-agreed Conference of Foreign Ministers. Before departing, he drew up another analysis of Soviet policy for Foreign Office consumption.[171] Uncertain of Bevin but enthusiastic about Washington, Clark Kerr determined to impress the new Foreign Secretary both with his political acumen and with a display of youthful dynamism and hard work.

He presented a not-too-pessimistic picture of the state of current relations. He felt that the atomic bomb had served to circumscribe Soviet action. However, he did also suggest that, in fact, the Soviet Union had largely achieved most of her immediate aims in both Europe and the Far East. Clark Kerr identified the Near and Middle East as areas of potential conflict but felt that Britain was now in a stronger position in Europe to follow her own policy objectives. The Soviet Union might not like the idea of Britain seeking to strengthen her ties with her Western European neighbours, particularly France, but Clark Kerr still felt that the British should continue to pursue these reasonable aims and 'need not allow ourselves to be deflected from them by the gusts and cross-currents which will no doubt come our way from Moscow'.[172]

Clark Kerr arrived back in Britain on Saturday 8 September 1945. The conference began on the Tuesday, and so there were two busy days of meetings and preparation at the Foreign Office first. Throughout the conference Clark Kerr enjoyed the company of London 'society', dining regularly with the important hostesses of the day, Lady Colefax and Lady Cunard. It was to be a long and difficult conference, consisting of no less than 33 formal meetings before it broke up inconclusively on 2 October. In addition to the three 'great powers', Chinese and French delegates were also in attendance.

The conference made painfully slow progress in its task of preparing peace treaties with Italy, Rumania, Bulgaria, Hungary and Finland. Molotov was particularly obstinate and pedantic and on 21 September actually proposed that France and China be removed from the discussions as they had not actually signed any original surrender terms. Matters became very heated the following day when a remark by Bevin was interpreted by Molotov as likening him to a 'Nazi'. The near walk-out which resulted led Bevin to take stock of the whole situation, which was approaching irretrievable breakdown.

On the following day Bevin took Clark Kerr alone with him to the Soviet embassy for a heart-to-heart with Molotov in an attempt to reach a compromise. Warned by the Embassy in Moscow about Soviet suspicions, Bevin sought to allay Molotov's fears about an alliance with France and a Western

European 'bloc'. Although the meeting ended cordially enough, there was little evidence of a breakthrough.[173]

Finally, on 1 October in an attempt to avert a breakdown, a meeting of Bevin's advisers was held at which Clark Kerr drew up a ten-point plan, marking a fresh approach to Molotov. This was enthusiastically agreed and forwarded to the Americans.[174] Byrnes indicated his general agreement, subject to some alterations on the conditions for recognising the Rumanian and Bulgarian Governments. That night, talks with the Russians went on late but broke up acrimoniously, as Clark Kerr officially recorded: 'On leaving Mr Molotov, the Secretary of State said that he regretted so little progress had been made. M. Molotov made some incomprehensible noise in reply.'[175] After two more days of wrangling the conference broke up without agreeing on a protocol.

With the Soviet Union effectively having isolated herself at the conference, Clark Kerr tended to agree with Bevin that no independent approach should now be made to resolve the differences between Britain and the Soviet Union.[176] Indeed, there was a feeling in the Foreign Office, after the initial dismay, that the inconclusiveness of the conference might at least have brought home to the Soviet Union Britain's determination to stand by her principles and protect her vital interests.

After the conference, a weary and somewhat disillusioned Clark Kerr was able to escape to Inverchapel for some peace. The wartime cohesion had gone, and real and potentially damaging strains were beginning to appear. For the first time a major intergovernmental conference of the Big Three had failed to reach agreement, and there was no prospect of any immediate improvement.

In personal terms, the Conference had been quite successful for Clark Kerr: his energy and intelligent advice had impressed Bevin. Just after the close of the conference, while the memory was fresh, he wrote to Bevin about his position. A new world was developing and it was time, he felt, for a change. His wartime role in papering over the cracks in Moscow had now been overtaken by events, and a fresh start was required. Yet, as he sought to remind Bevin, he was not finished.[177] It is 'no attempt to run out on you,' he declared, but, after suffering three and a half years of Molotov, he requested, '... if, as I expect, there is no other job for me, that I should be allowed to disappear into the Highlands'.

Just in case Bevin should unfortunately agree, Clark Kerr quickly reassured him:

> I cannot claim the easy refuge of many – illhealth, for my health is good, nor indeed fatigue, for I am not tired, but I can suggest, with all sincerity, that the time has come for a fresh mind in Moscow. Mine is weary of Molotov and is therefore of diminishing value... The chiefest of my duties has been to smooth over rough places while the war was going on. Now we shall have to face up to these rough places and it seems to me that this would be better done by some other man than myself, against whom the past would always be quoted.

Personally, it was a necessary note: Bevin was already under some pressure from his backbenchers to make Foreign Office changes and there were rumours of a 'clearout'.[178]

Clark Kerr remained at Inverchapel for three weeks, the longest he had spent there for years, and his first real break from work since 1930. However fit he may have been for a man of sixty-three, it was a much needed rest. On 28 October he left the hills of his beloved Argyll once more, and on 6 November arrived back in wintry Moscow. In late November, in an effort to break the Soviet suspicion of an Anglo-American bloc, Byrnes instructed Harriman to approach Molotov about a meeting of the three Foreign Ministers in Moscow. Bevin was not informed of this move, and only learned of it when Clark Kerr cabled him on 24 November about Harriman's activities.[179] Bevin was not at all pleased, not simply because of the lack of consultation, but because he felt that Byrnes had made a tactical error. Bevin's view was that the Soviet Union had been taken aback when the London conference broke down, and ought to have been left to manoeuvre themselves out of their own corner. Byrnes had thrown them a lifeline.

The British attitude towards the conference was one of foreboding, and Bevin only agreed to go reluctantly. The extent of the apparent split with the Americans can be gauged by the fact that Byrnes proposed to blame Bevin for the delay in opening the conference, planning to inform Stalin of this and claiming that Bevin was unwilling to attend. In the event, Harriman refused to pass on this message to Stalin, and instead informed Clark Kerr of its contents.[180] In fact the delay came about from a conflict between Byrnes, Truman and leading senators who felt left out by Byrnes's independent policy-making style.[181]

In all, the conference lasted for eleven days, including Christmas Day itself, and long, late-night sessions. Although Byrnes tried to be as accommodating as he could, progress was slow, although there was agreement reached on the issue of atomic energy control. Some advance was made on enlarging the Rumanian and Bulgarian Governments to allow the US and the UK to recognise them formally. As far as Rumania was concerned, it was agreed that a tripartite commission of Vyshinski, Harriman and Clark Kerr be established, and travel to Bucharest to oversee the restructuring of the Rumanian Government.

The main British team at the conference consisted of Bevin, Clark Kerr and Cadogan. Many of the complaints which the British and Americans made about Soviet activities in Rumania, Bulgaria, and Turkey were simply countered by Molotov citing British interference in Greece. These matters mirrored rather closely the 'percentages' agreement by Churchill during the previous year, and there was some feeling in the British camp that the fight for Rumanian and Bulgarian democracy should not be pursued too vigorously if Greece could be saved instead. As far as Turkey was concerned, Clark Kerr's position had hardened from earlier in the year when he had been criticised for not being strenuous in his representations.[182] He now hoped for a robust Anglo-Turco-American front to force the Russians to back down, and for a decision to be reached about whether or not they were 'ready to meet force with force'.[183]

The feeling in Moscow generally was that the British were being troublesome obstacles at the conference. The conference itself ended in farce in the early hours of 28 December when a communiqué, omitting reference to Bulgaria on which nothing had been agreed, was to be signed. English texts were circulated, but when the Russian text finally appeared, Molotov explained that a typist had 'accidentally included' sections on Bulgaria, but suggested that these could be signed anyway. In such bizarre ways did the Soviets exercise their diplomacy. Needless to say Bevin and Byrnes refused to sign, and the original communiqué was finally endorsed at 3.30am.[184] The long, tetchy meetings took their physical and emotional toll on Bevin. At one meeting his private secretary informed Clark Kerr that Bevin was afraid he was developing corns on his bottom. Clark Kerr blithely commented that he had himself sat on these same chairs for seven hours at a stretch. In any case, he said, referring to Bevin's largish posterior, 'What's the use of being nice and round, when it still hurts?'[185]

The conference did allow Clark Kerr to impress Bevin, and the two worked together well, Clark Kerr's earthy style being suited to Bevin's approach. Washington was not mentioned, but the hints had been left. Immediately after the conference, however, Clark Kerr was off to Rumania to try to secure a reorganisation of the Government to allow Western recognition to proceed. Along with Vyshinski and Harriman, he left by train for Bucharest on 28 December.

The situation in Rumania was one of political stalemate, with the King virtually on strike after he had asked the Communist Government, who lacked public support, to resign. They refused to do so and into this *impasse* the commission was propelled. Clark Kerr's room for manoeuvre was limited: the British Government was reluctant to jeopardise Greece by pushing the Russians too hard in Rumania, about which Churchill had already signalled limited concern in his October 1944 agreement. Furthermore, Bevin at Moscow had acceded to Russian demands that Maniu – head of the Peasant party, Bratianu – head of the Liberal Party, and another popular non-communist, Lupu, should not be allowed into the Government. This existing Government, led by two communists Dr Petru Groza and Gheorghe Tatarescu, had continued in office, backed by the Soviet Union, despite King Michael's refusal to recognise them.

The Moscow delegation arrived on 31 December and began talks immediately. The main aim was to add one member of the National Peasant Party and one member of the Liberal Party to the Government, and that this reorganisation should be followed by free and unfettered elections. Generally speaking, the non-communist opposition parties were suspicious about the whole exercise and dubious about the chance of fair elections ever taking place. Despite lobbying strenuously for them to co-operate, Clark Kerr was hard put to it to allay their fears. 'Indeed I cherish a good many myself,' he confessed.

By 3 January 1946, however, it was agreed that Ion Mihalache would be the Peasants' nominee and Bebe Bratianu the Liberals'. This took much persuasion from both Clark Kerr and Harriman, and so their peremptory rejection by Vyshinski and the Government the next day came as something of a shock. Clark Kerr called this meeting 'a sickening business', during which Groza launched a violent attack on Mihalache, accusing him of having been in the fascist forces under the pro-Nazi Antonescu regime. This was a rich accusation indeed, considering that many of the current government had similarly served, including Tatarescu himself! Bratianu's nomination was also rejected. Clark Kerr was taken aback at this reaction, particularly as earlier in the day Groza had appeared satisfied with the two candidates. To the Foreign Office he cabled:

> I confess that I formed the worst possible impression of the Government and of their intentions, and indeed of the part that Vyshinski seems to be playing behind the scenes.[186]

The next day, Harriman was able to produce documents refuting the charges made against Bratianu and Mihalache. In the circumstances, however, it was agreed that the Peasants and Liberals should forward a list of names which the commission and Government could discuss. It was not a pleasant business, but there is no doubt that Vyshinski had outwitted the two ambassadors at an early stage. Representing that the main stumbling-block was the refusal of non-communists to join the government, Vyshinski had suggested that both Clark Kerr and Harriman should deal with this aspect while he, Vyshinski, should liaise with the government. In fact it became clear that Vyshinski's role was a crucial one of keeping the Rumanian Government in line with Soviet policy. The division of tasks thus agreed kept Clark Kerr and Harriman away from the government and any influence. They were placed instead in the position of supplicants, pleading the case of powerless, albeit popular, opposition politicians. Vyshinski was in the position of strength, and he made full use of it.

During one heated exchange the pressure told, and he ended up shouting and roaring at Clark Kerr, whose quiet logic annoyed him. The rage was such that it provoked Clark Kerr's one loss of temper in all his trying Soviet years. Slamming his fist on the table, he shouted back at Vyshinski: 'Don't yell at me as if I were Trotsky!' Harriman sat terrified, but Vyshinski was stopped in his tracks. After a pregnant pause, he sat back in his chair and laughed. 'You win' he conceded.[187]

To the Foreign Office Clark Kerr revealed all his genuine concerns about the Rumanian situation. Groza and Tatarescu he described as:

> uncommon rogues (one of whom is desperate), in whose good faith it would be most imprudent to put any confidence. Groza is a genial fool. He is also a mountebank... Tatarescu is steeped to the lips in deceit and treachery.

His experiences had even led Clark Kerr to reassess his whole approach and attitude towards the Soviet Union.

> You will remember that from out of the darkness of Moscow I have tended to give the Russians here and there the benefit of the doubt in matters of good faith. But my visit to the Balkans has allowed me a peep, as it were, under the skirts of Soviet policy as it manifests itself on the fringes of the Russian sphere of influence. This has not been edifying and it would be disingenuous in me if I were not to admit that I am somewhat shaken.[188]

After further talks it was finally agreed that Emil Hatieganu of the Peasants and Mihai Romniceanu of the Liberals be added to the Government. Both, however, came into the Cabinet without portfolios, and their influence was severely restricted.

Following this agreement, the party moved on to Sinaia in the Carpathian Mountains, where the King and his mother were in residence. King Michael, although only 25 years old, greatly impressed Harriman and Clark Kerr, and in turn was grateful for their efforts, although he recognised the limits to their power, given their Governments' positions. The political agreement was duly signed and Clark Kerr had the chance of a few hours chat with the Queen Mother, formerly Princess Helen of Greece, whom he had known in his young days.

Following these talks, Clark Kerr returned to Bucharest to press Groza further on his commitment to free and fair elections, to be held as soon as possible. The experience left him depressed:

> a melancholy business, but I do not see what more we can do, unless you consider that, without breaking faith with the Russians, you can make recognition conditional on the holding of early elections.[189]

He left Bucharest on 12 January. By February both the US and UK Governments recognised the Groza regime; in November 1946 came the elections, in which Groza took an improbable 89% of the 'vote'; by the end of 1947 the King had been deposed and banished, and the communist stranglehold was complete.

Although King Michael felt himself let down by the US and UK Governments following the departure of the diplomatic mission, he attached no blame to either Clark Kerr or Harriman. Both, he felt, were merely following their government's orders, which urged that arguing for democracy in Rumania was not worth the potential upset it might create for wider relations with the USSR.[190] Although back in Moscow Clark Kerr did make some rather flippant remarks to Molotov regarding Rumanian independence this was no more than diplomatic banter, and cannot mask the strong representations he did make while in Bucharest.[191]

After arriving back in Moscow, he flew at once to Berlin and then to London, arriving at noon on 16 January 1946. That evening he was to meet Bevin at 5.30. Bevin got straight down to business: he was going to propose Sir Archibald Clark Kerr's name for the post of Ambassador to the United States of America. Not surprisingly Clark Kerr broke into a broad smile. Bevin leaned back in his chair and laughed: 'Ah, Archie, I know you want the job, but you needn't think you're the best man for it. What you are is a member of the union and I'm the General Secretary. So you're going to get it!'[192] Despite backbench pressure, Bevin had decided that it was good union practice to make his diplomatic appointments from within the service itself. In those closed shop circumstances, Archie Clark Kerr was the obvious and outstanding candidate.

Not only was the job the premier one in the Diplomatic Service, but in those days it was considered to be of such status that all appointees were automatically raised to the peerage. Bevin therefore confirmed that a barony would be conferred upon Clark Kerr. Clark Kerr had no hesitation in choosing his title: he would be Lord Inverchapel, just as he had fantasised as a boy. Although not to be gazetted until May, he would become the 1st Baron Inverchapel of Loch Eck in the County of Argyll. His dreams of more than forty years were all but fully realized, and the finest post in the service was his.

CHAPTER 8

Pinnacle 1946–48

The transfer to Washington was not scheduled to take place until May. Before then, Bevin wanted Clark Kerr to undertake a special mission as mediator in the negotiations over the dispute between the Dutch Government and Indonesian nationalists in the Dutch East Indies. It was hoped that Clark Kerr might be able to broker a deal within three or four months. In fact, that proved far too optimistic and, although Clark Kerr put in a hectic schedule and managed to force a conference, no settlement resulted.

On 27 January 1946, after nearly four years, Archie Clark Kerr left Moscow for the last time. Reviewing his performance, most observers' opinions have been coloured by the distorting fogs of the Cold War. His former deputy, Sir John Balfour, for example, considered his period as ambassador in Moscow only a success 'on balance'. Another view, clearly glossing over the fact that Britain and the USSR were allies during his time, saw him as having been too much the mouth-piece of Moscow and having avoided challenging Stalin when required.[1] Others have been more fulsome. His relations with Stalin and Molotov could not have been bettered, and few diplomats were as able as Clark Kerr in dealing with the sinister Vyshinski. Through many difficult and potentially disastrous crises, Clark Kerr managed to maintain the alliance with the Soviet Union, and preserved the united anti-Nazi front. It was not simply his shared earthy sense of humour and unorthodox approach which enabled him to create such a cordial and effective relationship with the Politburo, but also his obvious fairness, integrity, willingness to listen and desire to understand and appreciate the Soviet point of view. If, following the defeat of Germany, tensions arose it was only natural, a return to peacetime normality. Just as in China, where an odd alliance could be maintained against a common enemy, so in Europe the capitalist-communist alliance only held as long as the Third Reich remained. Once it had collapsed and the Soviet Union emerged so powerful that there could be little hope of a smooth relationship continuing. Perhaps those who hunt for the origins of the Cold War are in error: the Cold War was merely a return to the normality which existed, albeit less threateningly, prior to the war. The two systems were not compatible, could only appear to be so if one or both were suppressed, as in wartime, and could only clash and conflict in the post-war years. That they had not done so from 1941 was a tribute to the many diplomats and politicians, amongst whom Clark Kerr was prominent, who had sufficient vision and statesmanship to realise that necessity demanded co-operation. Undoubtedly, his judgement failed on certain matters, and he did perhaps praise and admire Stalin too highly. Certainly in the obituary he prepared for the BBC in 1950 he was still prepared to play down Stalin's internal butchery at the expense of his wartime role. That is understandable, given Clark Kerr's perspective. He was honest about the situation generally, however. At Potsdam, when Churchill inquired what he made of the Russians, Clark Kerr could only shake his head and say, 'Sir, I have no idea'.

Following his short weeks in the Dutch East Indies, where Clark Kerr enjoyed his status as something of a diplomatic trouble-shooter followed around by a voracious, and largely adoring, media circus – he was roundly feted as 'the greatest diplomat in the world' – he returned at last to London. His role had been the subject of much conjecture: the Americans, ever suspicious of Britain's colonial past, judged that he was playing some game to gain Britain imperial advantage; others, more in tune with the real Clark Kerr and not the British diplomat of stereotype, accurately suspected that he was in fact pro-Indonesian; but even they never knew that he was so much inclined towards the forces of national liberation that he virtually prepared their case for them and coached them on negotiating technique. However, he was too keen to see an early settlement, and although he brought the parties to Europe for a treaty, it never transpired.

On 10 April, his duties over, Sir Archibald Clark Kerr went to Buckingham Palace for the official ceremony, being created 1st Baron Inverchapel. A short break at Inverchapel was snatched thereafter, during which he travelled over to Glasgow to accept an honorary doctorate from the University. In the course of his acceptance speech he reviewed and assessed his career, particularly the many uncomfortable and difficult postings which had fallen to his lot. 'There is a myth in Downing Street,' he told his listeners,' which all my life I have failed to kill. Its legend is: "Archie likes these funny places".' Of Foreign Office policy, he continued in similar vein. 'When there is a difficult job to do they nearly always turn to a Scot. This is probably prudent in them. But they also tend to demand from a Scot a willingness to be bucketed here and there and everywhere about the world where things seem to need tidying up.'

After the degree ceremony, Inverchapel (as we must now refer to him) headed for London to consult with authorities about his new coat of arms, but more importantly for a reunion with Tita, who had just arrived from America. On 1 May they had both lunch and dinner together before Inverchapel returned north in a mood of some optimism. In Edinburgh to consult with the Lord Lyon, Inverchapel also dined with his old friend Bob Boothby. According to Boothby, he claims that he advised Inverchapel not to take the Washington job but to retire while he was at his peak. Boothby may well have done, but it could hardly have been at this point, as Inverchapel had accepted the post months earlier.[2]

In fact, Inverchapel's heraldic discussions with the Lord Lyon must have raised a few eyebrows. Although his choice of arms was basically conventional, an amalgam of the Clark and the Kerr coats, he did add one or two embellishments of his own. Supporting the arms on either side, he added two naked male athletes, complete with obvious genitalia: one athlete holding a quill, to represent Lord Inverchapel's literary tastes and its place in the history of the family; the other holding a discus, representing his callisthenic tastes. Inverchapel included part of the Clark motto – 'Blast' – and a form of the Kerr motto, 'Late but Hungry'; but the main motto was 'Concussus Surgo' ('Having been shaken, I rise'). Given the context of male genitalia, the motto's amusing *double entendre* can only be assumed to have been accidental. *Burke's Peerage*, however, took fright: in their 1950 edition, the athletes were each demurely provided with a pair of underpants.

From Edinburgh, Inverchapel returned to his Loch Eck home for another fortnight. The late spring weather was glorious, and he spent most of the time bare-chested working away in his gardens. It was the first time since he had cultivated the area in 1922 that he had been able to enjoy for himself the great splash of hillside daffodils in their spring-time blossom. There was always time for fly-fishing, but also for learning more about the herding of flocks and the sowing of seed in preparation for his post-diplomatic days.

In mid-May he left finally for London for serious talks about UK-US relations, and also to be introduced into the House of Lords. At last, on 23 May he set sail on the *Queen Mary* to face his last, supreme challenge.

Although Washington had always been his greatest goal, and the peerage a once impossible dream, now that they were within his grasp, Inverchapel experienced considerable and uncharacteristic self-doubt during the four-day voyage. His chief fears were over his uneasiness with, and hatred of, public speaking, the likelihood of having to grace countless pompous ceremonies, and of having to deal with an inquisitive and critical free press. Washington would be the first democracy he had served in as Ambassador and the first post where the media were off the leash. Another anxiety was about his own personality: to overcome his natural shyness he had long since become addicted to making controversial and shocking remarks, which usually served to break the ice, but which he acknowledged might not go down too well in American high society. In fact, after 40 years of suffering fools and pomposity gladly, he had become rather less tolerant of the sort of social niceties and small-talk which the post of Ambassador seemed to attract. These, however, were mostly minor irritations: he already knew most of the key players in the US administration, and must have been confident of his ability to represent the British case effectively amongst them.

Two other points, however, are worth making. The successful conclusion of the war against Hitler meant that Inverchapel's approach to Washington was less intense and dynamic than to any post he had held since Iraq in the mid-1930s, and that was inauspicious, especially for someone of sixty-four with half an eye on retirement. And, in fact, with economic woe and the infancy of the Cold War, the post would demand as much if not more than he had ever given. A second point is that Inverchapel's acceptance of the post had been coloured by two decisive factors, neither of which ought to have been, objectively, so compelling. Firstly, the post, long held – and still so regarded – as the jewel in the diplomatic crown, could not be resisted on purely egotistical grounds; secondly, Tita's choice of the USA as her adopted home gave the ever-hopeful Inverchapel an incentive to be there, and so much the better in an exalted role.

A significant factor in his Atlantic depression must have been his recognition that economic issues were growing ominously in importance in Britain's international relations. Economics were not only a complete bore to Lord Inverchapel but they utterly bamboozled him. He had no desire to have anything to do with them.

Of necessity, economics had come to the fore. The ravages of war had been disastrous for the British economy. Churchill's beloved empire had certainly been saved, but Britain had spent so much to do so that it now could not afford to run it. Indeed, the country could barely afford to run itself. Britain had lost almost one quarter of its pre-war wealth, its merchant marine had been devastated, its manufacturing base worn out by the war effort, its exports down by nearly 40%, as was its income from foreign investments. On the other side of the equation, imports were up by 50% and overseas debts had increased seven-fold.[3] Britain was now the world's largest debtor nation: a grim reward for the country which had stood alone, at one point, against Nazi Germany.

Truman's sudden and unexpected decision to halt America's vital lend-lease supplies to Britain immediately following the surrender of Japan brought matters to crisis-point. Facing bankruptcy, the Labour Government had no alternative to seeking a loan from the US to see Britain out of the economic slough of victory. The Americans were determined to exact some leverage with their economic superiority. The Americans pushed Britain to open up the Commonwealth trading bloc and to accept the convertibility of sterling. Generally speaking, as part-payment of a loan, the US demanded British acceptance and support of the American aim for a world free from trade barriers and tariffs. There was no little unease in the Labour Cabinet over the terms of the loan, but economic necessity demanded acceptance, and in late December 1945 it passed through parliament, although the US Congress still had to approve the measure.

There was no guarantee that the passage would be calm. Many Americans, still hopeful about the prospects of alliance with the Soviet Union, did not want to be seen to be 'ganging up' with the Brits. Others, too, were unhappy about granting loans to a country whose government was embarked on an ambitious socialist programme. Yet again, the involvement of British troops in Greece supporting a right-wing Government was viewed in some American quarters as old-fashioned imperialism which the US ought to abhor.

If there were such underlying tensions in UK-US relations, they were of much less prominence that those generated by the situation in Palestine. For various reasons, Britain was keen to retain a favourable position in the Middle East, particularly at a time when Soviet eyes seemed to be turning enviously in that direction. Since the end of the First War, the mandate for Palestine had been in British hands, and the Chiefs of Staff were especially keen to see Britain remain in a position of influence in the region. The main reason was its strategic importance in imperial communications and its proximity to the vital Suez Canal, but of increasing relevance became the presence of the area's oil reserves. Bevin hoped to improve relations with Arab nations and keep Britain in a favoured position in the Middle East.

In the wake of the Holocaust, and with the colossal problem caused by refugees in Europe, there was considerable agitation for an increase in Jewish immigration into Palestine. Zionist calls for a Palestine Jewish homeland were long-standing, bolstered by the Balfour Declaration of 1917 and supported by the Labour Party Conference in May 1945, and now increased in both volume and persuasiveness. The British Government, unwilling to antagonise the Arabs, to whom many wartime pledges had been given, resisted the pressure. Many British officials, including Bevin, were of the view that were it not for Zionist propaganda, most Jews would prefer Europe or the USA to migration to Palestine. The main public relations success of the Zionists was in the United States, where an effective lobby, representing the country's Jewish millions, succeeded in exerting massive pressure on Congress and Truman throughout the summer of 1945. The chief rallying-call was for the British to allow 100,000 European Jews to settle immediately in Palestine.

Britain was unwilling to accede to what it judged would be disastrous for relations in the Middle East. Truman had privately argued for the admission of the 100,000 at Potsdam, but in late September, despite pleas from Attlee to the contrary, he went public and backed the Jewish Agency's demands. His main reason for doing so was to placate the Jewish lobby in the run-up to the congressional elections. Yet again, Britain's foreign policy was undermined by the perceived requirements of an American election campaign. Willkie's demands for a second front; Elliot Roosevelt's claim that F.D.R. smoothed friction between Churchill and Stalin at Teheran; and now Truman's call for the entry of the 100,000 were all done purely with an eye to the American polls. Each instance damaged Britain: Inverchapel had been particularly annoyed at Elliot Roosevelt's picture of relations at Teheran, and believed that it was done purely with the purpose of aiding Roosevelt's 1944 campaign. 'I saw no sign of friction,' Inverchapel later said. 'It was sheer nonsense to suggest it.'[4]

Indeed Truman's tendency to tailor policy to match floating public opinion rather than fixed principle was beginning to irritate British officials generally. Halifax, the outgoing Ambassador in the USA, warned that the Truman administration seemed to chart its course 'in the manner best calculated to propitiate... the prevailing sentiments of Congress and... pressure groups'.[5] This was not necessarily anything new: Roosevelt's concerns in Eastern Europe often seemed designed merely to satisfy emigré groups in the US, not based on any real commitment to the rights of small nations or democratic principles. If Palestinian Arabs had been blessed with a large and monied emigré lobby in the United States the history of the Middle East would have taken a very different course.

However, the damage had been done, and the Attlee Government was placed on the defensive. In response, the Cabinet agreed to set up a joint US-UK commission of inquiry into Palestine as an attempt to head off Zionist demands. Just prior to Inverchapel's departure, the commission had reported. Truman, without consulting Bevin or Attlee, renewed his call for the admission of the 100,000, to which the commission had given qualified backing, while stopping short of partition or the notion of a Jewish state. There is no doubt that the US administration's persistence on this issue was a source of great irritation to British policy-makers, charged with administering justice in Palestine. The task of refereeing a fierce local derby is rarely made easier by the blinkered contributions of partisan spectators.

This irritation was matched by a degree of disappointment in the British camp at apparent American apostasy regarding control of atomic weapons. At the tail end of 1945, Attlee had travelled to the United States, returning with an understanding that the wartime collaboration and control would continue, pending the establishment of an effective international body to oversee the atomic energy issue. By early 1946, however, there were clear signs that the US was becoming less willing to co-operate freely: British officials in Washington, for example, found access to information becoming increasingly restricted and difficult. Partly this was out of fear of antagonising the Soviet Union with too obvious a British-American bloc; partly from pro-UN pressure in the US not to secrete information for only US or UK eyes; and partly from isolationist pressure not to continue open collaboration with a weakened but still imperial Britain. These disparate strands in American political life combined to dash British optimism. A further complication had arisen in the defection to the West in September 1945 of a Soviet agent in Canada, Igor Gouzenko. He revealed the presence of a major Soviet spy ring operating in Canada, whose particular interest was nuclear. As a result of Gouzenko's revelations, 16 people were arrested in February 1946, one of whom was a senior British scientist, Dr Allan Nunn May. After a swift investigation, he was sentenced to ten years' imprisonment on 1 May 1946.

While the Canadian spy scandal had decreased American willingness to share its atomic research, it did tend to firm up both British and American distrust of Soviet intentions worldwide. Early hopes that the wartime alliance could be sustained were being severely strained by Soviet pressure on both Turkey and Iran, her intrigues in Greece, and fears over the growth of communism in both Italy and France, where the de Gaulle Government had fallen in February.

In Paris for the Council of Foreign Ministers in April–May 1946, there was a significant change in the American approach to the USSR, involving a more aggressive attitude. Partly this had been inspired by Churchill's famous speech at Fulton, Missouri, on 5 March 1946, in which he spoke forcefully of Russia's Iron Curtain having come down across Europe 'from Stettin in the Baltic to Trieste in the Adriatic'. Writing from Moscow in February on similar lines, George Kennan, the influential US Charge d'Affaires, had painted a picture of the basic incompatibility between the West and the Soviet Union in his famous 'Long Telegram'. There was a clear policy shift evolving, from collaboration to containment. American policy was on the move. This is not to say that it had full public backing: many Americans were suspicious of Churchill's motives in his speech. There was a widely-held belief that the 'wily Brits' too often inveigled America into helping Britain out of difficulties.

Despite their many differences and areas of tension, therefore, the British and American Governments were being brought closer together in foreign policy, at least, through their common distrust of Soviet intentions and their common concern for the future of Europe and democracy.

That is not to say that the British Government was wholly taken up with the desire to align the US with herself. There was still a strong desire to maintain an independent foreign policy, made more conscious a goal by the recognition that the proposed dollar loan seriously undermined British economic independence. Bevin, although enthusiastic about eliciting an American commitment to European economic revival and military security, did not yet see Britain as part of a full alliance. Rather he viewed Britain as a key player between the two superpowers:

> In the European scene... we are the last bastion of social democracy. It may be said that this represents our way of life against the red tooth and claw of American capitalism and the Communist dictatorship of Soviet Russia.[6]

This was the very point which Inverchapel made years before about the situation in China, and one of the reasons for his support for the Labour Party. He viewed their general political outlook, if not all their policies, as both far more fair than those of the Tories but also as essential to prevent those sickened with class division and social inequity being lured by communism. The Labour Party offered an acceptable alternative which was why it was so loathed by Stalin: in the aftermath of a ruinous war, all he wanted to offer Europe was chaos or communism. Social democracy was an unwanted intruder.

On 27 May 1946, the *Queen Mary* docked in Halifax, Nova Scotia and Lord Inverchapel set foot on the American continent as the senior British figure at a critical moment of history. His appointment had attracted an unprecedented number of rave reviews in the American press: most national journals carried lengthy profiles, some of which repeated the description of him as 'the greatest diplomat in the world'. Much was made of his colourful past, his eccentricities and unorthodox style, his eleven languages, his piper, as well as glowing tributes to his skills and ability.[7] Inverchapel was rather embarrassed by it all, and to Bevin he wrote, 'They have put me on a kind of pinnacle from which I am bound to topple'.[8]

Inverchapel's mid-Atlantic misgivings proved immediately well-founded. His public relations performance on arrival in the United States was as bizarre and controversial as could have been feared. He succeeded in annoying the Canadians, upsetting the English, confusing and puzzling the Americans, and alarming his prospective colleagues all within two days. Generally his flippancy and humour were lost on a press corps used to the viceregal Halifax and absorbed in the serious matters of growing international tension and fear. When asked what comment he had for the American public, he replied 'Just tell them I have a red face and a big nose. They always say that about me.' As he had disembarked with 2000 war brides and numerous babies, he also opined to the waiting newsmen that British babies were lovely: it was only when they got older that they became so ugly.[9] In a desperate attempt to evoke some vaguely political response, a reporter asked him what he felt about the current debate on the Canadian flag. Inverchapel stated boldly that he hoped that the Union Jack would remain part of it. For this he was roundly condemned in the Canadian parliament and press, being accused of interfering in Canada's internal affairs.[10] While in Halifax, en route to New York, he also informed the press that he was looking forward to watching some baseball, as he thought that cricket was 'the dullest game ever invented'. As far as cricket was concerned, he would rather watch 'spillikins'. No one knew what this was so his Press secretary had to return later to explain that it was a bar-room game related to skittles.

Once arrived in New York, where he was met by Sir Alec Cadogan, now UK representative at the UN, he held a disastrous press conference on the quay. The intended site for the conference was locked, so the press gathered under a pier shed where they had to strain to hear his quiet comments. They were also lectured about taking photos of him unaware: self-conscious about his new false teeth, he reacted angrily to any snaps taken of him with his mouth open. Unconvincingly, he sought to correct the report of his cricket comments, claiming rather pedantically that he had not at all said it was 'the dullest game ever invented' but only that it was 'dull'. In an effort to deflect attention and surprise the press he made reference to the fact that he had in Yevgeny Yost, his footman, 'a Russian slave given to me by Stalin', but this only served to confuse matters further. After all that, his officials were relieved finally to have him closeted in the Washington embassy on 29 May. Perhaps it all ought to have been treated as a good laugh, as Inverchapel intended, but it was a different world, less ready to chuckle.

As can be expected, most of the US press were puzzled and unsure of what to make of the new ambassador.[11] Others were more favourable, taking the cricket jibe in the spirit it was made. The *New Yorker*, for example, enjoyed the joke, remarking that 'Americans have very reason to believe that this is the beginning of a beautiful friendship'.[12] *Newsweek*'s profile of the new ambassador described him quite accurately as 'a shrewd Rabelaisian humanist'.[13]

In actual fact, it was in Britain that any attacks appeared, solely over his cricket comments, which were rather touchily viewed as amounting to treason. Inverchapel's tongue-in-cheek tone was utterly missed by even *The Times*, to which Sir Pelham Warner, grand old man of English cricket, was moved to pen a blimpish rebuff to Inverchapel. Of all the column-inches battered out on angry typewriters, it was probably the *Yorkshire Post* which made the most astute political comment. The policy of decrying one's own culture and institutions in favour of those of one's host country the paper termed 'dangerously transparent'. Uttering feelings close to most Britons' minds at the time, it continued: 'There is moreover a limit to self-abasement even in the promotion of Anglo-American relations'. Lord Inverchapel, it felt, had 'conceded too much' already.

With this unfortunate opening behind him, Inverchapel set about becoming acquainted with his new surroundings. The Embassy was now a massive operation, made even more so by the continued presence of numerous British wartime missions, which were also ostensibly under the control of the Ambassador. When Inverchapel had last been in Washington as a diplomat in the days before the Great War there had been a staff of nine diplomats; now there were 483. Fortunately, he was assisted by a clutch of distinguished British diplomats in senior roles in the embassy. Among those were Sir John Balfour, Sir George Sansom, Sir Gordon Munro, Sir John Magowan, and among the more lowly First Secretaries were diplomatic 'notables' of the future: Paul Gore-Booth and Donald Maclean.

Washington itself had also changed: the almost rural rhythms of life in the rather romantic pre-war capital Inverchapel had known thirty years before had long gone. There had now developed a harder, less forgiving city, absorbed with the importance of its own hectic business as the emerging centre of a distraught world. The unruffled ease of old diplomatic life had given way to a new world, more impatient and less understanding, where the urgent demands of the omnipotent grey technocrat far outweighed diplomatic convention. This tougher, utilitarian lifestyle was one to which Inverchapel struggled to adapt, found increasingly unpleasant and disagreeable, and from which he eventually simply withdrew. Diplomacy had suddenly become hard-nosed bargaining, based on crude economic realities and commercial considerations; the days of the personal approach, the building of mutual trust, and political manoeuvring, in which Inverchapel had so excelled, seemed to be passing.

In this more calculating atmosphere, the perception of Britain's diminishing stature also assumed far greater significance for those entrusted with representing her interests in the United States. In Washington now, diplomats of a military power could count on being respected; those of an economic power on being courted; but those from a waning power merely on being tolerated. Inverchapel quickly found that in seeking to carry out his onerous and vital duties, Britain simply no longer had the clout to demand attention.

The marked change in Britain's status was not lost on some of the more experienced observers in Washington. It was noted, albeit *en passant*, that Inverchapel's arrival in the capital had been attended by only a fairly minor State Department official. This was contrasted unfavourably with the arrival of Lord Halifax as Ambassador in 1941 when Roosevelt had travelled to Annapolis to meet him, boarded his ship to welcome him personally, and then driven back with him in style to Washington.[14]

Nevertheless, Inverchapel quickly got down to his duties. On 5 June he presented his credentials formally to President Truman at the White House. To waiting newsmen he expressed the hope for UK-US relations 'that the spirit which inspired their joint struggles on the battlefield would crown with success their common efforts to make a solid and lasting peace'.[15] Over the next few days he met some of the more prominent political commentators in the States: Joe Alsop, Walter Lippmann and Scotty Reston. Lippmann, a highly respected and influential journalist, had lately come to doubt the prospects of lasting peace with the Soviet Union,[16] as had the American and British Governments generally, following the breakdown of the Paris Conference. Inverchapel was not yet prepared to abandon hope, however, and in an address to the National Press Club on 10 June he expressed the view, then beginning to lose credibility, that the differences were not so fundamental that they did not admit of solution.[17]

In his first weekly political summary to Bevin, Inverchapel had admitted that many in the United States now considered the main barrier to good relations with Russia as a 'basic philosophical divergence'. Inverchapel also, however, considered that US secrecy over the atom bomb had not helped matters. Although no longer promoting his earlier belief that Soviet Russia just wanted to 'join the Club', and needed a more welcoming approach from the Western Allies, he continued on another longheld notion. 'Whereas the United States has now emerged from the adolescent stage,' he rather condescendingly observed, 'the behaviour of the Soviet Union is still that of an unruly youth who requires to be disciplined like a High School student by the patient firmness of its elders'.[18] The problem now, however, as Bevin and Byrnes had come to realise, was that the Soviet Union had outgrown this form of parental discipline, to which it neither now wished, nor needed, to submit itself.

The first weeks of Inverchapel's time in Washington were dominated by the loan debate in the House of Representatives, the measure having squeezed through the Senate in May after four months' deliberation. Apart from traditional isolationist arguments put forward against aid to Britain, two other issues dominated the proceedings: Britain's imperial record, and action in Palestine. Inverchapel wired in early July that the position was 'touch and go', and there was constant fretting about British actions which might prejudice the smooth passage of the Loan Bill. Despite Britain's urgent need for food supplies – bread rationing came in July – a treaty regarding wheat which had been agreed with Canada had to be delayed in case it would give the wrong impression in the Senate: that Britain did not now need so much cash, or that she was cosying up to her old Colonies.[19] However, the most serious obstacle remained Palestine, and matters were not helped by the general impression in the United States that Bevin was being unnecessarily obstructive to Zionist aspirations. Bevin's remarks at Bournemouth on 12 June, where he had been quoted as saying that Americans were keen on Zionist demands because they 'didn't want too many Jews in New York'[20] had caused an understandable furore, and the Truman administration was especially worried that it might even provoke Sol Bloom, the key Chairman of the House Foreign Affairs Committee, to speak against the loan. Inverchapel argued strongly that every effort be made to explain British action in Palestine and counter the claims of the Jewish Agency. However, his own Zionist sympathies did not help matters, particularly as the American press were aware of them and were not averse to referring to them to diminish the force of British arguments.[21] Inverchapel did not push the Zionist case too strongly with Whitehall – that was not his place – but he did point out to Bevin the benefits which would accrue in place of the difficult rearguard action being waged with unequal forces by British diplomats in the United States. Instead of this, things could be much simpler 'if HMG were ready to make any precise and positive advance... in regard to... the report of the Anglo-American Commission'.[22]

An attempt to sweeten US opinion by offering bases to the US military on British territory across the globe was gradually reduced in importance for fear of being interpreted – correctly – as a straight bribe.[23] Instead, Inverchapel pushed the more persuasive, if venal, line that the loan was essential to rebuild world trade, and, by implication, American corporate profits.[24]

None of the British efforts succeeded in swinging much American political opinion. Instead, it was growing anxiety over the Soviet Union, particularly in the wake of the unpleasant Paris Conference of Foreign Ministers, which began to move support behind the loan, as a means of countering Soviet influence in Europe. A tough memo to Congressmen from Truman stressed the serious repercussions in Britain which would result from the refusal to agree to the loan. The picture was painted of a Britain whose economy might well collapse and either lay the country open to Soviet pressure or, indeed, see its people turn to communism as the only alternative. Truman's warnings struck a chord with many already anxious about Soviet intentions. Accordingly, the Loan Bill was passed in mid-July by a comfortable 219 to 155 votes with some 61 Republicans fearful enough of the Soviet threat to vote with the Democrats. Considering how many Republicans had actually voted against lend-lease at the outset of the war, the shift in opinion was seen by many commentators as a landmark on the road from isolationism. Such was the climate of concern that even the Rabbi of New York's Central Synagogue joined in support of the loan, as did Sol Bloom, as it happened.[25]

On 15 July 1946, Inverchapel travelled to the White House to witness Truman's signature to the dollar loan. Given the insecurity which riddled UK-US relations at this point, it was a moment of considerable satisfaction and relief. Nevertheless, Inverchapel's role in achieving the passage of the bill could not be said to have amounted to much: indeed, it had almost been counterproductive. His own Zionist sympathies, about which he had been characteristically honest, tended to undermine British arguments as expressed in the United States.[26] Furthermore, his forceful pronouncements of optimism regarding relations with the Soviet Union cut right across the Truman line which had actually proved decisive in securing the Loan Bill victory.

Problems in countering Zionist propaganda in the United States tended to focus attention on the publicity side of embassy activities at this point. Herbert Morrison, the Lord President, who had recently visited the States, presented a paper to the Labour Cabinet in which he stated, 'In Washington I received the impression that we are missing many American publicity opportunities... I hope we can take the initiative and clear away bogies such as British Imperialism.'[27]

The *Daily Mail* correspondent made a similar point on 10 July, expressing frustration at the lack of public promotion of the British position: 'No one has stated our case – not the British Ambassador, not the British Information Service, not a single minister, or spokesman'. There was a degree of accuracy in these points, although Bevin's dislike of Morrison meant that his comments were treated more as the pompous interferences of a busybody.

Considering the perceptive views, which had been given quite an airing in Embassy despatches, about Truman's tendency to tailor policy to meet current public and press opinion, little organised attempt was made to counter that influence directly in the press. Instead, other channels were used in an attempt merely to offset the power of the media. No doubt this was Inverchapel's chosen policy, but even in the time of his successor, Sir Oliver Franks, the same complaints surfaced.

Inverchapel judged that his most important task was to try to influence congress rather than the press, since he believed it mightier. 'My first and supreme duty,' he told Bevin, 'must be to do my utmost to nobble members of the Senate and the House alike. No easy job this and it is here that I want you to give me a hand.' Inverchapel's plan was for Bevin to make a 'fullblown' visit to Washington and for him to 'sweep a joint session of Congress off its feet with a thumping speech'. Perhaps influenced by the impact of Churchill's visits to Moscow, and indeed to North America, during the war, Inverchapel hoped that this personal approach by Bevin would boost Britain's status and increase American understanding of the British viewpoint. He told Bevin quite frankly, '... the few weeks I have been here have been enough to persuade me that you have not got yourself across the American footlights in such a way as to be able to sway opinion here on important questions'.[28]

Despite that, Bevin was not impressed by Inverchapel's suggestion. At the end of July he dismissed it in a rather boorish way:

> I frankly don't believe that addressing Congress will make any difference in their attitude to this country – Churchill has done it, Attlee has repeated it, but notwithstanding all they have said it makes no difference... I would prefer not to do it. In the carrying out of foreign policy I do not believe this method of exhibitionism has any effect at all.[29]

Bevin's reluctance was a mistake. Inverchapel was not advocating any special mission, but merely to use the opportunity of his scheduled visit to the United States later in the year to the best effect. Instead of presenting a favourable image, Bevin continued to be something of a bogeyman to Zionists and others in the United States. This poor image, based on hearsay, could have been dispelled by an appearance in congress. For all that, there was insufficient recognition on the Embassy's behalf of the extent of the influence of the press on congressmen: an American politician, no matter how charmed by Inverchapel's personal touch, even to the length of being 'nobbled', would always seek to appease the press first in any potential clash. That is not to say the media were ignored by the Embassy: far from it. Inverchapel enjoyed good private relations, but they certainly were not fully exploited.

Inverchapel, with his dislike of public speaking and grand functions, was not the ideal person to make up for these deficiencies in the British public relations approach. His first public speech at the Ladies' Dinner in Chicago in late June 1946 had not been very auspicious: a markedly brief oration read inaudibly without raising his head from his notes did little to win friends or influence people. Frustratingly, in private afterwards he would be his charming self, impressing and delighting the small groups with whom he came in contact. It has to be said, however, that key opportunities to influence public opinion were not fully taken advantage of because of Inverchapel's oratorial limitations. He was much happier chatting to State Department officials, or politicians informally rather than in these grand public appearances. His lack of experience of working in a democracy with a free press was also a major influence: after 40 years of practising his profession it was difficult to reform his *modus operandi*. In all his major posts, the press did as the government dictated: if an ambassador could influence the government, the rest fell into place unaided. In America it was a much more intricate and impenetrable nexus.

Press publicity within the Embassy was far from the art such affairs have now become. Publicity about Inverchapel's actions, audiences and speeches was sent out in a rather innocent way with no obvious effort to tailor the message to suit sub-editors or slant it in any marked way. For example, if Inverchapel spoke in New York on the subject of the Palestine question, then the Embassy would inform the media by means of a press release. This generally would be headed simply 'Lord Inverchapel Speaks in New York' and would consist of the full text of his speech. There was no attempt to highlight the political message felt to be most important; as a result it was left to subeditors to pick and choose what to highlight. This is no criticism of Inverchapel, of course: British efforts at influencing the media were very much in their infancy, but their failures certainly did him, reserved and quiet as he was, no favours.

Where Inverchapel did score heavily was in the fact that he was personally committed to the principles of the Labour Government. If his Zionist sympathies and Grand Alliance optimism put him out of line with Bevin and British foreign policy generally, then his political alignment with the Labour Party was a vital factor in UK-US relations at the time. Throughout his period in Washington, Inverchapel stoutly and astutely defended the Labour Government's ideas and record. This was not done in any slavish way but in a reasoned and persuasive manner. Whatever criticisms may be levelled at his performance as Ambassador, it is difficult to believe that the Labour Party could have chosen any other career diplomat who could give such commitment to their cause. British difficulties with US relations were great enough, but Inverchapel's skilful presentation of Labour Party policy to the American administration and people certainly helped allay many of the fears which lay just beneath the surface, and could have proved to be highly damaging otherwise. For example, Inverchapel defended vigorously against the common charge in the US that Labour's nationalisation programme was similar to what a communist dictator might implement. He was not so foolish, however, as to seek at one stroke to win over American capitalists to belief in socialist philosophy. Instead, he made much of the damage caused to the British economy in fighting for the free world against tyranny, of the hardships endured by her courageous people, and that nationalisation was a necessary, and limited tool – 80% of industry was still in private hands – to enable the British economy to be put back to work. It was not the whole truth, of course, but it was very cleverly suited to American audiences. For example, to the St Louis Chamber of Commerce on 26 October 1946 he explained:

> We did not fight the dictators for six years with the idea of copying them when it was all over. To return to the old days of wholesale competition with all the hazards of booms and slumps would not be accepted by our people today and would be politically impossible, even if it were economically desirable.

The summer of 1946 brought greater economic pressure on Britain, where the necessity to keep their German zone fed was proving both financially crippling and politically unacceptable: while the British people were facing bread rationing, tons of wheat had to be sent to the German zone secretly for fear of causing social unrest at home. The Americans were initially dubious about British claims of difficulty in this matter, believing that the Canadian deal meant that Britain had ample supplies. However, as the year progressed, and in the wake of the Soviet amalgamation of the Social Democrats and the Communists in their zone, the Americans began to accept the need for greater unity between the US and UK zones.

Similarly, the two countries came closer together on the issue of reciprocal use of military bases worldwide, and by October an 'understanding' had been reached on naval bases.[30]

The main issue of contention remained that of Palestine: if anything, Zionist outrages such as the bombing of the King David Hotel served only to stiffen Bevin's resolve not to be forced into partition. In late July, Truman sent an official to London to seek out a compromise but had himself to back down owing to continuing Zionist pressure in Washington.[31] Bevin and Attlee were hoping to organise a Jewish-Arab conference in London, and were particularly keen that Truman should not jeopardise the chances of a level playing-field for any talks. Despite Attlee's pleas, Jewish pressure was more persuasive, and on 4 October 1946, Truman backed the Zionist call for partition and for the 100,000 refugees to be admitted at once.[32] British officials were bitterly disappointed at Truman's response and the US government's indulgent attitude towards Zionist groups in America who openly backed illegal immigration into Palestine and terrorist methods. Particularly galling was the fact that many Zionist organisations were able to claim back the cost of anti-British advertising from their income tax under US fiscal leniency.[33]

British unhappiness was compounded by the passing of the McMahon Act on 1 August 1946 which severely restricted the dissemination of atomic information 'to the nationals of other countries'. Again Attlee's protests were to no avail, and this rebuff effectively led the British government to embark on an independent atomic project of its own. Part of the motivation was the clear belief that the possession of atomic weapons might well greatly enhance Britain's status in power politics, so gravely undermined by economic hardship.[34]

In late August, Inverchapel set off for a tour to the West Coast. Generally speaking, it was tiring but quite successful in getting the British point of view across to the people of Colorado, Utah, Idaho, Oregon and Washington state. The visits received prominent attention on the front pages of the local press. Here and there his visits prompted Zionist protests,[35] but the very fact that he had travelled from Washington at all tended to give him a favourable reception. However, the failure again to tailor press releases to specific needs meant that some common prejudices were not dispelled. For example, a forceful defence of Britain's policy of giving up her empire in favour of a new commonwealth of independent states was reported in one local paper under the headline, 'England Trying to Hold Empire, Envoy Says'.[36] However, these trips enabled Inverchapel to meet ordinary Americans, and with them he was both more at home and far more influential than amongst the primness of high society functions in Washington.

In September Inverchapel was host to Hugh Dalton, the Chancellor of the Exchequer, and various other officials in preparation for Bevin's visit at the end of the year. He was also often entertaining Tita, with whom he was becoming closer once more. With official affairs under the able control of so many colleagues, Inverchapel was not a little bored with life in Washington.

In particular, he lacked stimulating intellectual company: Washington tittle-tattle and grand parties tended simply to bore him. In late October, in an attempt to get to know the real America, he spent three days on an Iowa farm, away from it all. He enjoyed the privacy and peace of the Newburn farm in Eagle Grove, and when it was over was able to enjoy numerous plaudits from the US press for his efforts to probe below the surface of 'official' America. It was not all successful: the family with whom he lodged were strictly teetotal; Inverchapel's gift of a quart of Scotch and a quart of peppermint Schnapps created something of an embarrassed stir. Inverchapel also met with some predictable criticism from the *Chicago Tribune*, then under the control of the notorious Colonel Robert R. McCormick, whose isolationist anti-British viewpoint was heavily promoted through its editorials. While not slow to pick faults, mostly petty, even the *Tribune* had to admit that Inverchapel deserved praise for his manner and efforts to acquaint himself with real America and to influence opinion. The paper quoted a local man, not surprisingly said to be in sympathy with its own editorial outlook, who said of Inverchapel's visit:

> I've always had a sneaking hunch England was taking us for a bunch of suckers. And I ain't changed much. But if she is, I've met one of the reasons why. He's quite a guy![37]

Immediately following his return from the sticks, Inverchapel had to travel to New York to meet Bevin who, was scheduled to arrive from England. Not only was Bevin due to attend the Council of Foreign Ministers which ran from November to mid-December, but the United Nations was also meeting in full session. Bevin's chief aim was to conclude finally the Italian and other peace treaties. Inverchapel's main involvement concerned the Palestine issue and final attempts to negotiate an acceptable framework, favourable to all sides. These opening days of November saw some crucial political changes: in the US mid-term elections, Truman's Democrats lost control of both the Senate and the House of Representatives; in the French elections, the Communists emerged the largest single party, contributing to a period of considerable uncertainty for the whole of Western Europe; in London nearly 60 Labour MPs backed a motion of censure on Bevin's conduct of foreign affairs. Despite these brakes on policy, the US and UK Foreign Ministers were able to come to a reasonable, if cagey, settlement with Molotov on many thorny issues.

As the world's attention turned to New York, Inverchapel was also busy speech-making, partly no doubt to impress Bevin. In late October was his robust, reasoned defence of Labour's programme made in St Louis, and also at the end of the month he gave a lengthy interview on US radio explaining British policy regarding Indian independence. During the early days of Bevin's stay, he addressed the Pilgrims Society in New York, again on nationalisation. This, he sought to reassure his sceptical audience, was restricted to certain basic industries and essential services.

Palestine, however, continued to dominate. Bevin's arrival on the *Aquitania* in November was met by placard-carrying Zionist protesters; dockers refused to handle his baggage; and 2000 police were needed to protect Bevin's open-topped New York welcome. Throughout November Inverchapel shuttled from meetings with British advisers, to talks with Jewish leaders, to chats with State Department officials. Hardline Jewish activists whose propaganda campaign was very finely tuned were pushing for an autonomous Jewish state; others such as the more moderate Dr Weizmann were prepared to agree to partition as a solution. The British Government felt there were only three options remaining at this point: partition; the 'Morrison-Grady' canton plan; or simply a surrender of the mandate by Britain to the UN.[38] Bevin was wary of partition for fear that, having granted that, the Zionists would push then for the whole of Palestine; the US administration had not favoured the Morrison-Grady plan when it was first announced the previous summer; and both sides regarded the surrender of the mandate as a possible prelude to increased violence and disorder and an invitation to Soviet interference at the UN.

In his isolated position, Bevin was keen to secure US support for whatever plan he might be able to achieve at the forthcoming Palestine Conference due soon in London. Inverchapel was therefore involved in a number of high-level discussions aimed at achieving US support. With the US Secretary of State, James Byrnes, in New York for the Council of Foreign Ministers talks, Inverchapel's chief American contact was the Assistant Secretary, Dean Acheson. From November 1946 to February 1947 Inverchapel and he had numerous talks on the Palestine question. From Acheson's own memoirs, it seems clear that he was not always certain about Inverchapel's approaches, what their purpose was, and just how fully he was representing British policy and opinion.[39] Certainly Inverchapel was following Bevin's line in trying to nail down the US to specific pledges of support on specific plans for Palestine. Inverchapel was, however, a pro-Zionist of long-standing and an acquaintance of Chaim Weizmann since 1919. He had even once been offered a job by the Zionists. From the tone of these meetings, it appears likely that Inverchapel's own preference, like Weizmann's, was for partition, that he wished to extract an American pledge of support for this policy, and so convince Bevin that partition was the solution to aim for. In that sense Inverchapel was following an independent diplomatic initiative by which he certainly hoped to aid Bevin, but only by having Bevin fall in with Inverchapel's own preferred position.

In talks in New York with Bevin and Rabbi Silver on 20 November, Inverchapel had extracted from Silver a willingness to accept partition if the alternative were the chaos likely to ensue from the surrendering of the mandate, which Bevin bluntly told Silver was a genuine possibility. With that grudging acquiescence extracted, Inverchapel called on Acheson on 22 November to sound out US opinion on partition, using Silver's comments in support. Acheson gave only a very tentative reply that, in the absence of anything else and with the prospect of British abandonment of the mandate, the Truman Government would probably 'go along with' a partition plan.[40]

With another unwilling recruit to the cause, Inverchapel quickly transmitted his rather massaged findings to London.[41] On 8 December he accompanied

Bevin to dinner with Truman at the White House, where Bevin expressed himself as still interested in pursuing the Morrison-Grady plan rather than partition.[42] A few days later Bevin embarked for Britain, the issue still unresolved.

1946 ended with a growing awareness in the United States that the balance of power was clearly shifting, and that increasingly the United States, because of its wealth and power, was expected to provide a lead to the Western democracies, of which Britain was now viewed as just another ailing member. Opinion was hardening against the Soviet Union, but there was nothing apocalyptic about the matter yet.[43] However, amongst senior figures in the Truman administration the prevailing tone was one of pessimism about reaching any satisfactory post-war accord with the Soviet Union. In this regard, there was a wide gulf emerging between the predominant State Department opinion and Inverchapel, who still held somewhat stubbornly to the view that if the West would be flexible enough an arrangement with the Soviet Union could happily be made. In particular he was opposed by James Forrestal, the Navy Secretary and soon to be first US Defence Secretary, who thought Inverchapel far too 'soft' on the Russians.[44] Inverchapel's similarly candid view of the likelihood of communist victory in China enraged others on the American right with whom he came in contact. Henry Luce, influential editor of *Time* magazine, was one who was particularly outraged by his views on China.[45] The fact that Inverchapel continued to employ a Russian valet, about whom he boasted and deliberately made considerable fuss, only confirmed the view that the British Ambassador was a curious maverick with oddly romantic and optimistic views of future relations with the Soviet Union.[46]

Despite serious misgivings, which US officials had harboured at the time of Churchill's Fulton speech, that Britain was trying to entangle the United States in anti-Soviet moves designed to preserve the integrity of the British empire, by the end of the year they had come so far as to be concerned that Britain might contemplate unilateral action aimed at reaching agreement with the USSR. American concern at this was apparently so great that in early February 1947 Inverchapel felt it necessary to present a statement to the State Department, dismissing any suggestion that 'the British government are weakening in any way in their desire for the closest Anglo-American cooperation'.[47] Part of the US worry centred on Labour back-bench criticism of Bevin, and the publication of a pamphlet 'Keep Left', which argued for a distancing of Britain from the US.

However concerned US officials may have been to present a common front, this did not entail a desire for full co-operation with Britain as far as atomic energy was concerned. Bevin's belief that international power would depend on ownership of atomic weaponry, and the full implications of the McMahon Act now being made manifest, led to an increasingly frantic lobbying of the US administration to share atomic intelligence.

In early 1947, Inverchapel had talks with the US Secretary of State about the possibility of making public the wartime deal on the issue. Clearly Britain hoped to promote the idea that the US was morally obliged to share the technology, and that the McMahon Act had breached an earlier undertaking.[48] The Americans were having none of it, and when Roger Makins, the Embassy official responsible, called again on the matter he was politely rebuffed. The head of the US Atomic Energy Commission, David Lilienthal, told him bluntly that the wartime agreement should be considered as terminated and that the divulging of information was now illegal under the McMahon Act.[49] Britain had by this point decided, albeit secretly at Cabinet level only, to press ahead with an independent weapons programme. Information was vital. Makins, who was due to leave for a senior post in the Foreign Office, quickly tried again, surely raising US suspicions of Britain's motives with the intensity of his pleading. In an ingenious gambit, he attempted to persuade Acheson that, since the McMahon Act did not become law until the autumn of 1946, all research and technology developed prior to that date ought to be made freely available to British scientists. The sophistry was to no avail.[50]

Despite the American resistance to sharing information, the bodies which had co-ordinated allied atomic development in wartime continued to meet. Inverchapel had been formally installed as the chief UK member serving on the Combined Policy Committee (CPC) the previous summer.[51] His role was mainly titular, with the executive functions carried out by Roger Makins, Field Marshal Maitland Wilson and Gordon Munro. There was also a sub-committee charged with carrying out specific tasks – mainly in materials acquirement – for the policy committee, the Combined Development Trust. Although these committees now met only intermittently, they were still privy to highly sensitive material. The committees were serviced by a small secretariat, on which the British representative was one Donald Maclean. If, as Inverchapel averred,[52] the US's nervousness about divulging atomic material had been triggered by the treason of Allan Nunn May, particularly since his fidelity had been strongly endorsed by the British Government, it is little wonder that Maclean's later defection was so catastrophic for trust in UK-US relations. Just how helpful Maclean could have been to the Soviet Union on the atomic question is a debatable point. He would have been able to indicate at least what materials the West possessed, and where in the world they were extracting and purchasing them, which would have been of immense political, but limited scientific, interest to the Soviet Union. Nevertheless, his status as a member of the CPC could have given him access to a range of secret material, which would have been granted him unquestioned, given his role. Inverchapel's delegation of important work to Maclean was merely the result of abiding by the universal opinion that Maclean was an excellent, conscientious and highly reliable diplomat.

1947 dawned with a significant reshuffle in the State Department. James Byrnes, whose difficulties with Truman had led to his tendering his resignation the previous summer, finally left office. There was no mourning in the British camp: Bevin had never really trusted, nor warmed to, him. In his place, Truman appointed General George Marshall, already 66 years old, who had been Chief of the US General Staff during the war, and thereafter special envoy to China.

In Britain, 1947 opened with a serious slump in her already depressed economic fortunes. The worst winter of the century combined with declining coal stocks dealt a savage double blow to the economy. Power cuts resulted in much of industry going on short-time, while the continuing blizzards virtually brought the rest of the country to a standstill. By mid-February, the Government officially cut power to many areas of the country; unemployment rocketed from 2.1% in December 1946 to 15.5%, 2.3 million. The chances of any imminent economic recovery simply evaporated, and the effect the financial crisis would have on Britain's foreign commitments became the major talking-point in diplomatic and press circles. The *Economic Survey* for 1947 which appeared in mid-February was described by *The Times* as 'the most disturbing statement ever made by a British Government'.[53] The beleaguered Chancellor, Hugh Dalton, had pointed to the need to reduce drastically Britain's foreign commitments, particularly in terms of the cost of troops stationed across the globe, in order to tackle the economic disaster at home. To all informed observers it seemed clear that Britain could no longer afford the stake required to stay in the game of international politics.

The most obvious candidates for cut-backs were the costs involved in the thankless administration of Palestine and the expensive but unrewarding British involvement in Greece and Turkey. On 18 February, after fruitless talks in London between Jewish and Arab leaders, Bevin announced to the Commons his intention of referring the Palestinian problem to the United Nations. This did not wholly solve the problem with the USA: Truman's repetition of the call for the entry of 100,000 Jewish immigrants brought a sharp response from Bevin, who complained that Truman's earlier intervention had badly undermined British efforts to produce a settlement. The British surrender of the mandate and the simultaneous announcement of the commitment to Indian independence brought many American commentators to the conclusion that Britain was on the ropes, perhaps for the final time. In a way it was most unfortunate: however much Inverchapel expounded the analysis that the declaration on India was a proof of the end of the old empire and the birth of the new democratic Commonwealth, Americans preferred to see it not as a symptom of social democratic principles in action, but as evidence of the economic frailty of Britain and the end of her major international role.

However, the real blow fell on 21 February 1947. On that day, Britain finally decided to intimate to the Americans that she could no longer maintain her commitments to Greece and Turkey. Marshall had already left for the weekend by the time Inverchapel phoned for an urgent appointment that Friday. Therefore, a secretary, Herbert Sichel, was sent from the embassy to deliver the British notes on the subject to the State Department. Britain could no longer afford the cost of the aid, and wanted to elicit US opinion on what could be done instead, to prevent these vitally strategic nations falling under the Soviet aegis. Britain intended to terminate aid on 31 March, a demonstration of her desperate economic plight. A meeting was arranged for 9am at the State Department on Monday morning, 24 February.

The meeting went ahead as planned: Marshall and Loy Henderson, whom Inverchapel had known in Moscow and was now Director of Near Eastern and African Affairs at the State Department, listened carefully to Inverchapel's presentation of the British position.[54] There was little to add to the notes of Friday, and the meeting was something of an anti-climax. For all that, none of the participants could fail to sense its historic significance: in one moment, Britain was signalling its withdrawal from its supreme international role and, in communicating this to the State Department, was effectively passing the torch of leadership from her own ailing grip to the younger, surer grasp of the United States of America. Less than four years earlier, at the first Moscow Conference in October 1943, Inverchapel had assisted Eden in representing the free nations of the world, and had been a vital member of the British team who had set the agenda, led the discussion, and finally charted the course of the post-war future of the world. Now, in a small side-room in Washington, he was signing Britain's letter of resignation, marking her departure from office as a leading world power.

As Inverchapel departed for a pleasant, if rather liquid, evening as guest of the students of Yale, the State Department, recognising the gravity of the problem which had landed in its lap, moved into top gear. That afternoon a special committee met to discuss assistance to Greece and Turkey. Loy Henderson summarised for the meeting the British difficulty as being no isolated problem, but as part of a general trend: the move was 'in line with recent British moves' and Britain 'seemed to feel unable to maintain its imperial structure on the same scale as in the past'.[55]

The US administration would take some time, and have to experience a major change in outlook, before it could contemplate taking on fully the British commitment to Greece and Turkey. A rather worried Dean Acheson, the US Under-Secretary of State, therefore sent off a memo to the British Embassy on 1 March, requesting that the British guarantee to continue aid, pending the start of US aid.[56] The Americans were very conscious that this was part of a trend, and that continued British retrenchment would entail much greater and persistent calls on US support in the future. Acheson's note stated that 'the maintenance of Greek and Turkish independence and territorial integrity is closely related to problems of common concern involving other countries in Europe and Asia'. Inverchapel was intrigued and heartened by this wider reference, and Acheson's suggestion that he would welcome 'informal conversations' with regard to these 'problems'. He immediately telephoned Acheson for clarification, which Acheson provided in a written memo later that day.[57] The hectic consultation in American circles which the notes of 21 February precipitated had led the State Department to the view, most forcefully put by Acheson at a meeting with Truman and influential politicians on 27 February, that the Soviet Union was poised, in the absence of US action, to take advantage of numerous countries in Europe and Asia who had been similarly been weakened and divided by the war. Without US action now, communism was threatening to exploit the economic chaos. Greece and Turkey were only the first and most urgent of many.[58]

In response to Acheson's request of 1 March, Inverchapel replied three days later that Britain intended to reduce military involvement to one brigade in Greece by 31 March and to end all involvement by the summer. Britain would not be able to continue aid of £2m a month beyond June, and thereafter hoped that US aid to Greece would enable the Greek Government to reimburse loans due to Britain.[59] Naturally, the US were opposed to this last idea, but appreciation of the gravity of the situation was certainly reinforced.

Accordingly, on 12 March 1947, President Truman made his historic speech to a joint session of Congress. 'The Truman Doctrine', as it became known, committed the United States not just to aiding Greece and Turkey, but supporting democracy and 'free peoples' everywhere. While it is undeniable that many in the Truman administration saw this as a principled stand against the threat of totalitarianism and communism, it is also true that a decisive factor in Truman's far more wide-ranging and generalized response to Britain's notes of 21 February was a conscious desire to prevent his being accused of 'picking up the tab' for Britain, or 'pulling British chestnuts out of the fire'. Truman's record shows that his foreign policy was guided principally by an urge to placate and match public opinion within the US rather that by any internationalist or political vision of his own. In order to convince public opinion in the United States, which had swung away from him in the mid-term elections, that American action in Greece and Turkey was justified, Truman had to paint a frightening picture of the world, on the brink of political collapse, looking to the United States to hold the line of freedom. It was thus no matter of a mere hiccup in the economic affairs of two distant and rather backward Mediterranean countries, but part of an incipient ideological struggle. Further to justify American action, Truman similarly had to persuade Americans that Britain was exhausted utterly, no longer capable of lending a hand. Only if this were true would Americans accept the need for action. Truman largely succeeded in convincing America and winning his people round to their new world role.

Although Bevin and the British Government were relieved to have drawn the US Government into Europe and a wider international role, the manner in which it was done did create difficulties. First of all, opinion in the US quickly concluded that Britain was 'finished'; secondly, with the ideological seeds of a communist threat now implanted, the programme of state socialism as favoured by the Labour Government began to evoke fear and suspicion in American minds. Inverchapel was presented with the problem of countering these impressions in the face of the whole drift of Truman policy and propaganda. Inverchapel had always viewed the Soviet threat not as ideological, but as much more to do with 'spheres of influence'. If compromise could be reached on Soviet borders and security, then the free and communists worlds could co-exist. Inverchapel's view was unsatisfactory given the scale of Soviet intriguing abroad, but it did have something in its favour: the potential for agreement and peace. The picture which was sketched out by the Truman administration over the succeeding months was that of good versus evil, a stark Manichean view of a fallen world. In such a conflict, there could be no compromise: good would have to be seen to triumph, no matter how long the struggle. If the seeds of the Cold War were planted by Stalin in the woods of Katyn, they reached full ripeness in the Truman doctrine. In neither case, however, was there much conscious awareness of the full implications of each set of actions.

Throughout 1947, Inverchapel was called upon, therefore, to make countless public speeches designed to counter these unfavourable views of Britain. He was not a good orator, and detested the task, but despite that and his sixty-five years he set about the job with energy if not enthusiasm. Although viewed with disfavour by many on the American right, and suspiciously by the Washington social establishment, who disliked his informal manner, quiet lifestyle, and the lack of respect he paid them,[60] he was still admired by a significant section of American political life. Lew Douglas, the new US Ambassador to Britain, told him that he was 'the most popular man in the western hemisphere'. Inverchapel got on well with Marshall, Acheson, Henderson and Jack Hickerson, Head of the State Department's European section, and he had his own circle of senator friends, particularly liberals such as Senator Fulbright.

Immediately after the Truman speech, Inverchapel spoke out strongly, rejecting the view that British power had ended. In a speech to the English Speaking Union in Richmond, Virginia, which was widely reported on both sides of the Atlantic, he paid tribute to the British people's 'guts': they were down but not out. The *Daily Mirror* devoted an editorial to his speech, warmly commending his approach:

> Lord Inverchapel talks exactly as British Ambassadors abroad should be talking these days. He tells Americans, gloating over the prospect that they may be gravediggers at the funeral of the British Empire, that the corpse just won't turn up.[61]

The week before, addressing New York University Law alumni, with a typical eyebrow-raising flourish, he quoted Trotsky in warning Americans that it was 'a mistake to judge the strength of a country from the temporary condition of its technical apparatus'. Given the growth of Russophobia, the invoking of Trotsky on Britain's behalf was not the most judicious of moves, particularly since he was often at pains to stress the Labour Government's Fabian, evolutionary principles, in contrast to those of communism. Before his departure on leave in late June, Inverchapel delivered more than a score of major speeches across the length and breadth of the United States. His travels and speeches took him through nearly two dozen states, stressing the same themes in Britain's defence and promotion. Even the *Daily Mail*, whose US diarist Don Iddons had earlier been stridently critical of the lack of publicity on Britain's behalf in the USA, had to acknowledge the strenuous efforts Inverchapel made on his nationwide tour.[62]

Depending on the circumstances, Inverchapel's speeches tended to follow the same broad pattern. While accepting Britain's economic plight, he was at pains to show that this was merely temporary and, in any event, had largely been brought about by Britain's self-sacrifice in the war against the dictators. The country was not done, the spirit of the people was undaunted, and recovery was on the way. As far as the Labour Government was concerned, its social democratic values were wholly opposed to communist principles, springing instead from Britain's own evolutionary, Fabian tradition. The economic conditions caused by the wartime effort demanded a programme of nationalisation but, in any case, 80% of the economy remained in private hands. On the international front, the myth of the British Empire and her exploitation of her colonial subjects had long since been overtaken by events. The aim now was a commonwealth: India and the other nations were being encouraged to seek self-determination. Britain was not foregoing her international role, and had high hopes of the United Nations, being fully at one with the United States in her hopes for the future of that body. The seriousness of the job of image-making for Britain did not wholly eclipse Inverchapel's sense of humour: appealing for American tourists to spend their holidays and dollars in Britain, he acknowledged the state of the British economy by recommending Britain particularly for tourists 'who wanted to slim'.

The truth about the British Empire was a topic of great interest to republican America. On 12 April, Inverchapel appeared on NBC's 'University of the Air' to discuss the changing role of the Empire. It was an able performance, but the level of questioning tended to stress the depth of US misconceptions about what 'Commonwealth' meant. Inverchapel's interview style had always involved regular pedantic quibbling about the phrasing of questions, usually done in a light-hearted way, but with the serious aim of both putting the interviewer on the defensive and emphasising his own sharpness. As would befit someone who employed a personal piper to skirl a reveille each day, Inverchapel was scrupulous about challenging the common American error of referring to the United Kingdom of Great Britain and Northern Ireland as 'England'. The interview that night was peppered with interruptions from Inverchapel to correct his host's repeated misuse of the term 'England'. During the talk, however, Inverchapel was anxious to hail the implications of the Truman doctrine and the United States' new role as international 'watchdog'.[63]

Despite his robust defence of Britain and repeated declarations that recovery was just around the corner, the reality in Britain was that economic problems were simply multiplying. In early March, Dalton had told Bevin that Britain could do with another $1 billion from the US, but that the situation was not such as to merit Bevin formally approaching Marshall at Moscow (where they both were for another conference) about delaying sterling convertibility, planned for late summer. Three weeks later Dalton was speaking of 'alarm' at the rapid exhaustion of the dollar loan. By early April, Bevin was mandated to tell Marshall that the 'burden' of Britain's international commitments, particularly aid to the Germans, was 'proving almost more than we can bear'.[64]

During the lengthy conference in Moscow it seems that Marshall had already formed his own opinions about the economic state of Western Europe. Certainly his team in the State Department were moving in a logical direction from the hints given in that March memo from Acheson to Inverchapel, and the implications of the Truman speech. The piecemeal approach, and the likelihood of repeated appeals from myriad quarters for more dollar assistance, were beginning to concentrate American minds on a more organised, co-ordinated scheme for the recovery of Europe.

With Inverchapel on tour for most of the period from late April until June, including another stay on the farm in Iowa, the Embassy and UK-US relations at this crucial point were very much left in the hands of his able deputies, Sir John Balfour and others. Speaking in Mississippi in early May, Under-Secretary Acheson gave clear signals of the way in which American minds were turning.[65] Not only was a weakened Europe needing US aid simply to survive, but if the US economy was going to continue to enjoy its present health and prosperity, the nations of Europe and the rest of the world had to be in a state of economic stability and fitness to be able to buy the goods the US had to sell. Over dinner with British officials on 22 May, Acheson elaborated on this theme, setting out clearly the plans Marshall had for European recovery.[66] In many ways, the drift of American policy and the needs of the Truman Government to pursue certain lines to gain public backing left Inverchapel and his colleagues in a quandary. Just as Inverchapel was travelling the continent promoting Britain as still strong, vibrant and recovering rapidly, so American politicians were telling of the economic disaster zone that was Europe. Only by portraying Britain and Europe as in economic chaos – which, indeed, was close to the truth – could Truman and Marshall hope to get any package of foreign aid through congress and supported nationally. That aid was vital, but Inverchapel's duty was to promote Britain, and that he had to do, even when it was not, paradoxically, in Britain's financial interests.

There has been no little debate about the British response to the programme Marshall was to outline on 5 June 1947. What is certain is that the responsibility for this lay with Inverchapel's assistants, as he himself was still in the mid-West when Marshall made his speech.

From the perspective of the Foreign Office and political analysts in Britain, it would seem that the Washington Embassy failed to register the significance of what was being announced, and so failed to alert London. However, as one might expect, the Embassy position is very different, and it does seem to be overstating the case to say that the Foreign Office were told nothing. It may well be that not enough stress was laid on what was transpiring in US policy, but Bevin could not have responded so quickly had he not been given a good deal of detail and guidance from the Embassy in Washington. The Embassy version of events is that following Acheson's briefing, Inverchapel called a meeting of his senior advisers to discuss the American proposals. Balfour's report on the forthcoming US aid package reached Bevin's desk on the very day, 5 June, on which General Marshall announced his dramatic programme of colossal financial aid to Europe. Marshall was careful to offer aid to all areas of Europe, not just the Western democracies, but he also indicated that some kind of joint European response was expected. This was in line not only with the views of US economists closely involved in the European scene, but also chimed nicely with the views of many American politicians, who favoured political union at regional and global level as part of their vision of world peace. Marshall's views also matched those in the European Movement, like Churchill, who were calling for unity as a way to avoid future war.

Britain was in a very good position to respond to Marshall's speech. Not only had Bevin been well-briefed in advance[67] but, having agreed the Treaty of Dunkirk in March with the French, had already sent the right kind of signals of internationalist co-operation to the US administration. Britain was keen to be seen to be reacting in a leadership role, and Bevin immediately set off to Paris to consult the French on a united response. Inverchapel's report to Marshall on Bevin's trip was markedly upbeat, and on 17 June he told him of Britain's hopes that Bevin's trip would 'be the first step in a speedy and concerted response to your inspiring lead'. Mention was made of Bevin heading on to the Netherlands and Belgium to co-ordinate a united European response, and that even the USSR had been asked for their observations. Inverchapel did add, however, that this was 'mere courtesy' and not designed to elicit any serious participation on the issue.[68]

The very next day, however, Inverchapel was back at the State Department to deliver a memo on the grave state of the British economy, which it was intended that the influential US Under-Secretary for Economic Affairs, William Clayton, should study before his forthcoming talks in London.[69] Oddly enough, despite the honest assessment of the critical position of Britain's finances, when Clayton arrived in London he was pressed strongly by Bevin and Dalton about Britain being treated as a partner in the Marshall Plan rather than being simply lumped in with the rest of Europe. Agreement on the way forward for the Marshall Plan was finally reached; fruitless talks with the Soviets began before the end of June; on 12 July the Conference on European Reconstruction opened in Paris with all but the Soviet satellites represented.

At the end of June, with the Marshall Plan launched successfully, Inverchapel returned to Britain for his annual leave. With him came Tita, with whom he had become very close again over the past months; also on board was Yevgeni Yost, whose presence as a Russian in Washington had been a source of constant anxiety to the FBI and embassy staff alike, and who had now been informally asked to go.

Inverchapel and his party arrived in Southampton on 7 July, and after an audience of the King and Queen headed north to Loch Eck. Although Inverchapel needed the rest more than ever, it proved to be a very busy furlough. He had experienced some heart problems over recent months, resulting in some discomfort and fluid difficulties. At Inverchapel Lodge there was much to be done preparing for his transformation, at some coming point, into gentleman farmer. Inverchapel was excited at the prospect, not least because a

Clark would be returning to farm the area after an absence of nearly 50 years and resuming a link between family and land which had lasted for centuries. Yevgeni, having variously been a footman, masseur, butler and clerk, was now to be given an introduction to farming in the hope that he could oversee the estate and livestock when Inverchapel and Tita returned to the States.

The main, and surprising, event of the leave took place on 19 August, when Inverchapel and Tita slipped quietly through to Edinburgh to be remarried, after only two years of divorce. Despite secrecy, the press had got hold of the story, and when he and Tita emerged from Registrars' House in Hunter Square, they were besieged by a large crowd of cameramen and assorted hacks. In a world where divorce was less common and remarriage a rarity, the story naturally attracted attention, particularly when the groom was not only British Ambassador to the United States but, at sixty-five, nearly 30 years older than his bride. As she was a glamorous blonde, it was too good a story to pass up. After a rather undignified chase through Edinburgh streets, they managed a quiet lunch before spending their first afternoon of new married life, none too romantically, inspecting a Scottish Tourist Board exhibition as guests of Tom Johnston, Secretary of State for Scotland.

From Edinburgh they headed straight back to Loch Eck, and head-first into Britain's economic crisis. Things were so severe that at any moment Inverchapel might be ordered back to Washington. To this end, telephone engineers had descended on his home, laying a cable so that Inverchapel could be reached by Downing Street whenever necessary. It was hardly the ideal start to (re)married life.

The economic crisis had been brewing for over a month. The problems originated in the terms of the US dollar loan of 1946. One of the American conditions attached was that sterling should become convertible on 15 July 1947. Even before then, the promised recovery had not materialised, causing excessive drawings on the dollar loan. The convertibility clause meant that following the agreed date, Britain would start to 'unfreeze' her war debts to other nations, allowing them to go shopping in the US for necessary goods, and have Britain pay the bill in dollars from the American loan. By the end of July matters had reached such a head that there was even talk of a move to replace Attlee, and for a major change in Labour policy. On 1 August the Cabinet agreed to an austerity programme, but within a fortnight it was clear that this was not enough to tackle the gravity of the situation. On 17 August, Dalton, the Chancellor, reported that in the five days to 15 August there had been a run on Britain's dollar resources to the extent of $176m. As there was only $700m dollars of the loan left unspent, the chances were that all would be gone within the month. In the circumstances, the Cabinet decided that sterling convertibility would have to be suspended, and further cuts and rationing imposed.

Inverchapel was ordered back to Washington to oversee new negotiations to sort out Britain's economy and American aid. There was no time to allow for a leisurely Atlantic cruise: Inverchapel and his new bride arrived in New

York by plane on 24 August and proceeded straight to Washington. That Autumn, Washington was the venue for a series of high-level talks, the most prominent of which were those, led by Oliver Franks, of the Conference on European Economic Cooperation, regarding the framework for the Marshall Plan. The Americans had not been entirely happy with the initial direction of the European talks, and were sceptical about Britain's real commitment to an integrated European programme of recovery.[70] At the same time Britain was sternly resisting US pressure at the GATT talks in Geneva to end the system of imperial preference, and there were continued talks in Washington about the future of the economy of Bizone, the joint US-UK area of Germany.

Ever since Inverchapel's vacation, economic matters had come to dominate diplomatic activity in Washington. Inverchapel, uninterested and lacking the motivation to become learned on these arcane topics, delegated all this to his advisers. As a result, he became more bored that ever with life in Washington. Apart from a very few acquaintances, such as Felix Frankfurter, he never really found much congenial company. He didn't enjoy grand functions and so threw as few of them as possible. Washington society was disappointed: hopes that remarriage might have kindled a new desire for socialising proved premature. There were a few quiet dinners, and evenings with select invited guests, such as the Kennedy clan on one occasion, but generally speaking things were reserved.[71] Some British observers praised the Inverchapels for their regard to the austerity regime in Britain, and felt that to throw lavish receptions would have been unseemly in Britain's straitened circumstances.[72] This was not the whole picture, however: even when guests at others' functions, Inverchapel and Tita tended to leave early, when observing austerity was hardly an excuse. After the excitement of their remarriage, many colleagues found it strange, also, that Inverchapel paid Tita so little attention. He still preferred male company, particularly young, intellectually energetic talkers.

Although he took little active part in the continuing negotiations on a whole range of economic issues, he was soon back on the lecture trail. Opposition to aid for Britain came from a number of US sources, but the most common complaint was that Americans were being expected to underwrite the Labour Party's socialist experiment. Others even suggested that it amounted, in effect, to Marxism. Again and again Inverchapel argued the point: stressing Labour's Fabian roots, he explained that evolution and not revolution was the *modus operandi*, and that far from approximating communism, the Labour Party model actually gave a clear alternative to the people of Europe who might be tempted otherwise by the Stalinist approach.

Although the Foreign Office was appreciative of Inverchapel's efforts,[73] there must have been a concern that his lack of familiarity with economic theory, and his evident uneasiness with financial facts and figures – he added and omitted noughts at will from his briefed material – was hampering his ability to communicate effectively the British case to the American administration. At the end of October, Bevin sent a lengthy telegram on the matter. 'Things are getting tough here,' he cautioned, 'and I want you to know how much my colleagues and I are relying on you to put things across in Washington to the utmost of your ability.' Rather revealing of the Foreign Office concern then, Bevin continued:

> Is there any material or guidance I could give you which would help? You are already doing a fine job with the American public with your speeches, but what I am thinking of now is how we can help you to influence the minds of the important people in the administration. I want you to be fully in the picture of all our difficulties and plans here and of our determination to win through. Then you can go in with a fighting spirit and push our various requirements with maximum effect.[74]

Inverchapel replied quickly in determined fashion:

> You may of course count upon all of us here to do our utmost. We never stop hammering away... We are in very close, personal, and friendly touch with them [the administration] all down the line.

Inverchapel did confess that it was a 'hard, plodding business' seeking to 'nobble' politicians without appearing to lobby, and that the many absences of Marshall had been a drawback.[75] In fact, very often Inverchapel was unable to get to Marshall when directed to by London. Instead of admitting it, he resorted to a terminological ruse to keep the Foreign Office satisfied: Jack Hickerson, the State Department's European Director, was a native of Marshall, Texas. Whenever General Marshall could not be contacted, Inverchapel would collar Hickerson instead, deliver whatever message he had to, and then report to London 'Marshall connection made', or some other such ambiguity.[76]

Although Inverchapel had established a good relationship with Marshall's new deputy, Bob Lovett, it was not altogether satisfactory, as he told Bevin: 'Lovett suffers from a hampering, but diminishing over-caution... a much shyer bird'. As far as Bevin's offer of help was concerned, Inverchapel did ask to be kept fully in the picture as only in this way could he hope to take the Americans completely into his confidence, and this was Inverchapel's much preferred way of operating. He did advise the Foreign Secretary, however, that Bevin could help by making more kind references to friends in the US who were seeking to help; by reiterating as vigorously as possible his detestation of communism; and by avoiding casual public remarks which the press would pounce on.[77]

By this point, October 1947, rumours had started in the British press that Inverchapel was about to retire as Ambassador to the United States. These were automatically denied by the Foreign Office, but the fact that the story was picked up by several papers would tend to suggest that there was some basis to it. Inverchapel himself clearly had felt insecure in Washington, conscious that his performance was the subject of debate.[78] The rumours certainly did his credibility no good, and nor did they aid his already very difficult task. Clearly, however, the issue had been discussed, and Inverchapel was by no means desperate to remain in Washington anyway. His aim was still to turn his hand to farming at some point, as he had told an American Farmers Convention in Kansas the previous month. At the end of October, however, he was involved in the dramatic resignation of someone else instead.

The problem arose over British reluctance to end the imperial preference – a system by which Britain was in a favoured trading position with the nations of the Empire – until in a more healthy economic condition. The chief US negotiator on this matter, William Clayton, had indicated privately to some British officials that Marshall aid might be jeopardised if Britain did not cut sufficiently the imperial preference. It seems certain that this was a personal initiative on Clayton's part, but it was one to which the British took strong exception. Inverchapel was instructed to approach Marshall to lodge a complaint. When he did so, and Marshall indicated sympathy, Clayton tendered his resignation. All of this was not revealed, however, and instead the cause was said to be the ill-health of Clayton's wife.[79] Some papers did identify Inverchapel as the root cause, however, but in the aftermath a new compromise tariff arrangement was successfully settled.

As 1947 drew to a close, Bevin and his advisers, particularly Gladwyn Jebb, a rising assistant Under-Secretary who had a low opinion of Inverchapel's suitability for Washington, finalised their plans for his replacement. Inverchapel was only too glad to fall in with the plan, as he told Bevin on 21 December. He stated that he was keen to go: '... for, as I told you in Moscow [1945], I am anxious to turn my hand to farming while there is still time.

> I should be glad to stay here long enough to see the Marshall Plan through and if, as is probable, this takes until the middle of 1948 I shall by then have rounded off about the toughest two years I have ever had. It will then be logical, proper and decent that I should be packed away in the museum among the mothballs whose fragrance becomes more and more alluring to me. So please let us aim at June which would suit me splendidly.[80]

Bevin had decided to revert to a non-career diplomat for the Washington job. His choice of Oliver Franks, then heading the Marshall Plan negotiations, shows clearly the stress being placed on economic matters and also the desire to have Britain represented by a much more youthful figure.

Even in the midst of these decisions about his retirement, Inverchapel continued to hammer away at the American public. The sterling crisis of the late summer had reinforced the prevailing view in America that Britain was 'finished' as an international force. On 22 December in Detroit he came up with a phrase which the press on both sides of the Atlantic picked up as capturing accurately Britain's perception of her own condition. Rejecting the idea that economic weakness was irreversible, Inverchapel declared that recovery was on the way and that the British people, to whose dogged spirit he often paid tribute, had 'left Bleak House and were on their way to Great Expectations'. While many Americans were still reluctant to have their aid used to support the Labour Government's social programme and economic reforms, growing unease at the events unfolding in Eastern Europe meant that these reservations loomed less large. The breakdown of the London Conference of Foreign Ministers at the end of the year and the Soviet rejection of the Marshall Plan were only parts of the equation: the withdrawal of Poland and Czechoslovakia from the Marshall programme under Soviet duress; the communist seizures of power in Poland and Rumania; and the Cominform-inspired strikes in France and Italy all set alarm-bells ringing in American minds. The decisive factor in swinging US opinion behind the European Recovery Programme, and conclusively against the Soviet Union, would be the communist coup in Czechoslovakia in February 1948.

An interesting indication of the change of mood in US opinion is the voting record in congress on a selection of key foreign policy issues over the years to 1948. A clear trend emerges, matching closely the dramatic changes in public perception which took place during Inverchapel's two momentous years in Washington. The British Loan of 1946, for example, passed through the House of Representatives on a 219-155 vote; aid to Greece and Turkey in 1947 on a 287-107 vote; and the Marshall Aid Programme was passed in 1948 on a 317-75 vote. The pattern in the Senate is no less clear on these three litmus votes: 46-34 on the British Loan, 67-23 on Greece and Turkey, the Marshall Aid Programme being passed by acclamation without the need for a vote. Amongst Republican congressmen, the shift from isolationist suspicion was the most significant: a mere 15% of Republican congressmen supported lend-lease in 1941; only 33% backed the British Loan of 1946; 58% supported aid to Greece and Turkey in 1947; and finally, a whopping 73% backed Marshall Aid in 1948.[81] These shifts represent one of the most decisive changes in twentieth century international politics. The United States, despite its initial reluctance, had entered the world stage as the key player.

However, in late 1947, before the crucial events in Czechoslovakia, full US support could not be guaranteed. It was true that the US wanted close European co-operation through an economic recovery programme, and it also became clear that as the Soviet bloc solidified only a close alliance amongst the other European powers could prevent them being picked off, one by one. Bevin grasped these two facts, and in a persuasive paper, presented to Cabinet on 8 January 1948 argued that 'some form of union in Western Europe', with the backing of the Americans, was the only road forward.[82] The paper was approved by Cabinet, and Inverchapel presented an outline of Bevin's plan to Marshall on 13 January 1948. While the State Department was enthusiastic, it were less favourably inclined towards the series of mutual defence treaties which were the proposed means of cementing the 'union'.[83] An early attempt, communicated by Inverchapel to Lovett in late January, to have a US commitment in advance to underpin the Western union was rejected. The US administration much preferred to see definite agreement among the European powers before being pressed to contribute themselves. Inverchapel was not so easily rebuffed: on 6 February he returned to Lovett, arguing that Britain would not be able to persuade the other European countries to collaborate fully without the promise of US backing. Britain, alone, could not give the necessary defence guarantee to underpin the union. The following day, Lovett and Hickerson met again with Inverchapel, and told him in a rather exasperated way: 'You are asking us to pour concrete before we see the blueprints'.[84]

Following this clear signal, there was a lull in British lobbying of the US on the Western alliance. At the beginning of March, however, anxieties expressed by Norway that the Soviet Union was touting for a pact raised a wholly new fear that the Soviet Union was now seeking a toe-hold on the Atlantic itself. In the wake of the communist coup in Czechoslovakia, and having learnt a lesson from his earlier approach to the US, Bevin now came up first with a clear plan of action to meet the new situation. Inverchapel delivered these views to Marshall on 11 March, which included a 'scheme of Atlantic security', as one of its concrete proposals. The very next day Marshall informed Inverchapel that the US was 'ready to proceed at once in the joint discussions on the establishment of an Atlantic security system'.[85] So NATO was born.

A week later the Brussels Treaty joined Britain, France, and Benelux in a mutual defence treaty, while at the same time Gladwyn Jebb flew amidst great secrecy to Washington to begin talks on the Atlantic alliance. There is something blackly comic about the elaborate measures taken to screen the true purpose of Jebb's visit to the US: sitting sphinx-like through it all was Donald Maclean.[86]

After the signing of the Brussels Treaty and Truman's endorsement of its aims, Inverchapel aired his own strong belief in the idea of Western union and an eventual United States of Europe. This, he said, was 'now within the reach of practical politics for the first time, for under the impulsion of apprehension man becomes gregarious'.[87] He declared himself all in favour: 'I feel sure that you will see a United States of Europe in your time, perhaps in mine'.[88] On the Brussels Treaty itself, Inverchapel believed it was 'a landmark. It reveals our determination – and determination is a very strong word – to prevent the spread to these countries of imposed totalitarianism.'[89]

However, Inverchapel well recognised that only economic improvements could guarantee that the countries of Europe would not slip into communism. In a speech in Chicago in April, which almost did not proceed until pickets agreed to withdraw from the venue to allow Inverchapel to enter, conscience clean, without having to cross a picket-line, he welcomed the passing of the Marshall Bill through Congress.

> In solving the economic problems we shall go a very long way toward checking the spread of communism, which has its roots in poverty, want, confusion, and a sense of insecurity.

He again portrayed the Labour Party in its real colours, free of right-wing prejudice:

> It is nothing new or terrible. It is old and mellow. It grew out of the liberal human-itarian and revivalist movements of the early 19th century and it categorically rejected the doctrines of Marx and Engels. It has sought and it still seeks to build

what it conceives to be a fairer society upon the principles of Christian and classical society which have always inspired our political progress.[90]

By this time, Inverchapel's retirement had been officially intimated. US support, through the Marshall Aid programme and negotiations on Atlantic security, had been elicited, and his task was over. It had been a very trying two years, disappointing ones in many respects: Archie Inverchapel's lively hope for a continuation of the wartime alliance had not materialised, and in its place had come suspicion, fear and new conflicts. His hopes for a grand climax to his career had similarly not come true: he had simply lacked the energy and motivation to come to terms with a brash, and often shallow, new America, and at sixty-six was rather glad to be escaping from its hectic lifestyle to the gentler foothills of Argyll.

In one of a number of farewell speeches, he reviewed his American years to a meeting of the St George's Society in New York, which he had last addressed as a nervous junior diplomat 35 years before. The speech was a very emotional one, and at times he was almost overcome. He began first with a personal confession, which was illuminating in the sense that it revealed a perception of a weakness in himself that he was by nature vulnerable to let-down and disappointment simply through his open, trusting nature. 'I have to confess,' he told his listeners, 'to a vast natural capacity for love. It has always been my trouble and here and there it has got me into trouble.'

Of his time in Washington he was equally frank.

> They are the last two years of a long, and perhaps an overlong, practice of my profession. They have been two uncommonly lively years, brawly, ugly years, with some shining exceptions. A multitude of unhappy events have scarred and disfigured them. The hopes for a new world of harmony, brotherhood and peace which were high in our hearts, have been sadly pushed about and jostled. If we have been disillusioned and frustrated we have at any rate learned a lot, and so long as we keep our heads and our patience, our firmness unshaken, I refuse to admit that the peace we want is beyond our reach...

The result had at least been a new sense of harmony between the US and the UK: 'St George and St Andrew have now been hitched to St Samuel (Uncle Sam)' and, he continued, '... if we pull together, as of course we shall, we shall bring safely and joyfully home that heavy load called peace'.

The reaction in the American press to his departure was quite mixed. The Henry Luce stable, who scorned his liberal views and friendships, were dismissive of his performance and achievements. *Time* led the attack:

> Few ambassadors ever came to Washington with the spectacular advance notices of Great Britain's tweedy, impassive Lord Inverchapel. His glittering reputation spanned more than 40 years... But once in the US, Inverchapel became known as 'the invisible ambassador'. He studiously avoided the press, ducked official parties, made no effort to cement all-important friendships on Capitol Hill.[91]

This jaundiced view, born of a bitter disagreement over US policy in China and the nature of Chiang's regime, cannot be taken as anything other than partial. That is not to say Luce's views were unique: another society columnist ascribed Inverchapel's departure to the fact that he was 'doddering way past retirement age and in very poor health'.[92] These personal attacks hurt him very much, although he knew well their root cause. Even other members of his staff were quoted as being 'bloody sore' about the criticisms of Inverchapel's alleged failings.[93] An official who worked at the embassy recalls going in to see him to offer his sympathy at his removal, and being met with a furious response at the Foreign Office's handling of the announcement of his retiral. Given Inverchapel's enthusiasm at the end of 1947 to be retired, it seems more likely that this anger was directed towards the press.[94]

While *Time*'s comments were excessive, there is no doubt that Inverchapel had, at least latterly, given the impression that he was 'not up to' the job of ambassador. For many it was simply a lack of energy and the toll of old age; for others, even in the Embassy, it was an impression that he was too quiet and unassuming to succeed in the onerous task of influencing the movers and shakers in American society. It is difficult in these matters to cite an objective view. Perhaps the nearest to it would be the attitude of David Lilienthal, Chairman of the US Atomic Energy Commission. On his first meeting with Oliver Franks, Inverchapel's successor, he noted in his diary: '... a considerable improvement, from my point of view, over old Inverchapel, who was through and done'.[95]

It must therefore be conceded that he had displayed obvious symptoms that his heart was no longer in the work, and that even if it had been, he lacked the capacity to fulfil it adequately. After so many years of outstanding, loyal service, where supererogation had simply become Inverchapel's norm – to the extent that on his departure from Washington he was owed over two years in holiday entitlement – there is something almost tragic in the outcome of these Washington years. In many ways, it was the failure of the wartime alliance to continue much beyond the armistice which was the key to his loss of interest and enthusiasm. And in Washington the growing anti-communist hysteria simply set the seal on a depressing shift in international relations. At the same time there was the keen disappointment that the Stalin with whom he had joked and caroused was now the tyrant wreaking havoc throughout Eastern Europe. In a sense, he took it personally that his vouching for Soviet goodwill had been proved so badly misplaced.

It would be quite wrong, however, to jump to the conclusion that Inverchapel's period in Washington was some kind of 'disaster'. That is certainly the impression given by some commentators, but it cannot be upheld by a close examination of the events of the time. For example, in its summative assessment of Inverchapel's time in Washington, the *Chicago Daily News* – notoriously anti-British – commented:

> The function of an ambassador is to promote the interests of his country and Lord Inverchapel... has done so with conspicuous success... He has a persuasive salesmanship that glides over the flaws in his article, makes a disarming admission of

both self-interest and past errors, and presents the whole as something that no good American could do without.'[96]

Inverchapel certainly did manage to foster good relations with many of the key players in the administration and congress, and through them to weave his 'persuasive salesmanship'. Sir Nicholas Henderson, the distinguished diplomat who served as a First Secretary under Lord Inverchapel in Washington, has supported the view that Inverchapel's private diplomacy was a highly significant factor during these years and difficult times. Inverchapel was often able by his winning charm to get 'something for nothing', and cannot be dismissed as a failure, nor anything like it.[97] The fact is that Britain was on the slide and no amount of diplomacy could conceal such a painful truth. As the figure who represented Britain in America, Inverchapel therefore came to be associated with this impression of decline, but he was not the cause, merely the messenger. As for an alleged lack of zeal in courting the press and media, and the general disinclination to indulge in bare-faced public relations exercises, these were not Inverchapel's failings alone but a British failing which continued during Sir Oliver Franks's time.[98]

The positive aspects of Inverchapel's spell in Washington are far more impressive than appear at first sight. If one considers the difficulties which had arisen in UK-US relations at the point when Inverchapel first arrived in Washington, they make grave reading. There was the unilateral termination of lend-lease by Truman and the subsequent squabbling over the loan arrangements; US suspicion of British motives in Greece and elsewhere; US distaste of the British Empire and its restrictive trading practices; the McMahon Act and the end of atomic co-operation; Palestine and the Zionist dispute; US desire not to 'gang up' on the Soviets; US suspicion of the Labour Government and its socialist philosophy. There were numerous other instances in the early days of Inverchapel's term of office which would suggest a far from rosy future and they, coupled with the unhappy development of Soviet policy, were fuelling the Embassy's difficulties.

Yet by the end of his two years, the two countries were acting almost everywhere in unison, and were on the threshold of a military alliance, the first in US history. Similarly, if one looks at Bevin's policy aims for relations with the USA at the time of Inverchapel's despatch to Washington, it is clear that they had largely been met by the time of his return.

Whatever Lord Inverchapel may be accused of, he certainly did oversee the emergence of the remarkable rapprochement in UK-US relations. According to those who worked with Bevin while he was Foreign Secretary, the main priorities were to keep the US involved in European affairs, particularly militarily, and to revive the European economy.[99] By the Marshall Aid Programme and the budding NATO talks, these two aims were achieved by May 1948. In addition, and this is a factor few have recognised as being important, Inverchapel's own sympathy with Labour Party principles and policy, and his astute method of presenting these to the American people, meant that a crucial area of vulnerability in Britain's armour in the United States during his years was well-guarded.

Of course, as the passing of the Loan Bill proved, in the American mind fear of the Soviet Union counted for much more in the final analysis than did suspicion of Labour policy. Nevertheless, without Inverchapel's vigilance in supporting and explaining Labour policy and actions, there could easily have been serious problems in UK-US relations.

In fact there is a clear hint of political undertones in the criticism of his performance in Washington. His outspokenly leftish comments and attitudes, his ability to dispense with the snobbish conventions of diplomatic life, and his impatience with reactionary views, angered many on the right who were only too glad to criticise when the chance arose.

From the vantage-point of 50 years hindsight, there are perhaps other aspects of his work which may have contributed to his 'old and done' image. Although he prided himself on keeping abreast of modern developments, particularly in the fields of art and literature, there is a sense in which, during his time in Washington, the twentieth century caught up with him with a vengeance. The acquired gentle rhythms of his lifestyle, developed during 42 years of diplomacy, must have been violently upset by the post-war bustle of Washington. There must have been times when he looked around himself in the embassy and shuddered at an unfamiliar world; there must have been those in contact with his operational routine who felt the unmistakeable air of other days around them. At the most basic level, for example, his continued use of a quill, with which he wrote his reports long-hand on stiff foolscap, was not only almost perversely old-fashioned but also unnecessarily time-consuming and inefficient. His dislike of the telephone – which he used as little as possible – was another example of a professional failure to make use of developing instruments of communication. Other elements of a vanishing world, such as his dated conversation topics, his preference for 'at homes' and other remnants of the Victorian and Edwardian eras, were not in line with developing society in America. None of these could be cited by observers as individually responsible, but taken together they did present an outdated image of Britain to the American public. At the same time such formality was additionally puzzling because it did not seem to fit in with his looks, manner and personality. In spite of the upper-class formalities of the right, he looked like an ex-boxer who still trained in the sun, could talk like one, and canvassed on behalf of the left. Though a doyen of His Britannic Majesty's Diplomatic Service, he was given to outrageous pronouncements, on a wide variety of subjects including sex, and possessed an overall roguish manner.

On the other hand, it must also be acknowledged that the Washington of those years disappointed Inverchapel. The American characteristics which he most admired and had enjoyed in the company of US newsmen over the years – their hard-drinking, irreverent, open-minded ways – and which he looked forward to experiencing once more were simply absent from Washington society.

Social attitudes were small-town, the atmosphere cliqueish and regimented by protocol, and he very soon became disillusioned and bored with it.

The chief reason, however, why Inverchapel's term in Washington has been considered by some as a period of 'disaster' is that he happened to preside over an Embassy in which one of his junior staff, Donald Maclean, systematically fed to the Soviet Union every secret available to his privileged hands. There is no sense, however, in which Inverchapel can be blamed for either not knowing about it or not preventing it. With a staff of nearly 500, it was impossible for him to know well any but a few close associates. Maclean was a mere First Secretary, and Inverchapel had no call to know any more about him other than that he was a very industrious, efficient and able subordinate.

Over the years, further unfounded allegations have surfaced to the effect that not only was Maclean a Soviet agent but so was the Ambassador. They rest on taking Inverchapel's success in having established a close relationship with Stalin and a very real regard for Stalin's ability and tenacity against the Nazis, not as evidence of diplomatic success but as evidence of treachery and betrayal.

These baseless smears are invariably encountered in the more sensational and hysterical outpourings of right-wing molehunters, whose methods too often involve exaggeration and misrepresentation.

The allegation that Inverchapel may have been a Soviet agent rests, albeit precariously, on idle speculation hung loosely on the vague evidence of one, Walter Krivitsky. Walter Krivitsky, also known as Samuel Ginsberg, had been a senior figure in first Soviet Military Intelligence (GRU) and then the NKVD in the 1930s. Fearing that a recall to Moscow in October 1937 would result in his 'liquidation', Krivitsky defected in France. He later surfaced in the USA, where he struggled to gain credibility. However, he did manage to convince the American journalist, Isaac Don Levine, and through him began to be taken more seriously. He identified for the British authorities a Soviet agent, Captain J. H. King, in the Communications Department of the Foreign Office. Despite their haughty scepticism, King was presented with the accusation; he promptly confessed and received a ten year prison sentence.[100]

With this surprising success to his credit, Krivitsky was brought to Britain by MI5 for further interview. During the course of his interrogation, Krivitsky mentioned another Soviet agent in the Foreign Office, of whom he had second-hand knowledge. He described him as 'a Scotsman of good family, educated at Eton and Oxford, and an idealist who worked for the Russians without payment'. He 'occasionally wore a cape and dabbled in artistic circles'.[101] He also said he had been recruited in Europe in the mid-thirties and had 'bohemian tastes'. As far as his post went, he was unsure but he had access to the minutes of the Committee on Imperial Defence.[102]

When later interviewed by Gladwyn Jebb of the Foreign Office, Krivitsky was unable to supply any further information except that the agent was 'a young Scotsman' and 'had a prominent father'.[103] Krivitsky's information was insufficiently specific for Jebb to take matters much further. He judged that the details could vaguely have fitted about 20 Foreign Office staff. Krivitsky, however, was too dangerous a source as far as the NKVD was concerned. Despite FBI surveillance, Krivitsky was found dead in a Washington hotel room, in suspicious circumstances, early in 1941.

Despite their obvious weaknesses, and their relevance to Maclean, the son of a cabinet minister, these details have been used to identify none other than Inverchapel. Even some serious analysts have been tempted by this canard.[104] Inverchapel quite simply does not fit the bill: he was not an old Etonian and at the time of Krivitsky's defection in 1937 was already 55 years old and Ambassador in Baghdad. The description, although perhaps contaminated by elements which seem to refer to John Cairncross – certainly Scottish, a spy, and with bohemian tastes – does clearly indicate Donald Maclean, who at 24 in 1937 was 'a Scotsman', as his name indicates, and 'of good family' with a father, Sir Donald Maclean, who was an MP, cabinet minister, and Chairman of the Liberal Party.

In fact when one considers the evidence, there are only two 'facts' which do not exactly fit Donald Maclean: he was at a Public School other than Eton, and at Cambridge, not Oxford. However, the conclusive evidence is still to emerge. The agent who recruited Donald Maclean in the mid-thirties at Cambridge University, and who induced him to apply for work with the Foreign Office in the first place was one Theodore Maly.[105] In the summer of 1937, two years after Maclean had begun life in the Foreign Office, Maly travelled to Paris to consult with other Soviet agents about the 'purge' currently being murderously executed by Stalin against his own agents. One of the colleagues with whom Maly considered the future was Krivitsky himself.[106] In the autumn of 1937 Krivitsky defected; Maly returned to Moscow and death.

This presents clear evidence of how Krivitsky could have come to know details of the mysterious Foreign Office mole. Krivitsky knew simply because he knew Maly, who was Maclean's 'control'. The evidence against Lord Inverchapel is laughably weak; the evidence against Maclean is overwhelming.

Even though Inverchapel's spell in Washington was not all it could have been and after 42 years of service, he had reached the point where suffering fools and pomposity gladly had become too much of a strain, and he could have found favour in more circles, he succeeded in presenting Britain to America in the most positive light. The atmosphere in which he departed, as far as UK-US relations were concerned, was brighter than it had been for years. Opposed to those disappointed in him, there were far more ordinary Americans with whom he had come in contact who could testify to his wisdom, kindness and integrity.[107]

CHAPTER 9

Cairn
1948–51

Lord and Lady Inverchapel bade farewell to the United States on 22 May 1948. However desirous of returning to Loch Eck he may have been, Inverchapel still had some professional activities to perform. Back in February he had been recommended to Viscount Portal of the Olympic Committee for a post as contact and host for the many foreign dignitaries expected to attend the Olympic Games in London that summer. The games were held during the first fortnight of August, and only when they were concluded were he and Tita able to head north to Inverchapel and peace.

Lord Inverchapel had every intention of retiring completely from public life. His main aim was to immerse himself in the life of a gentleman farmer able to return to the home of his Clark ancestors which had passed out of the family following the death of his namesake in 1900.

As can be imagined, the return to Inverchapel was as much a quest as a retirement. It was an attempt to recreate the past, to re-establish a link that fate had broken, and to restore the family name to the family home. It was also an attempt to rediscover the world of his childhood holidays, the place where the future had opened to him with that first tantalising foretaste of success and greatness. In his heart, however, he knew that it was a vain endeavour: Inverchapel the place had been confused with Inverchapel the memory – of happiness, of freedom, of hope, of family, of sadness, and wistful regret – but it was a place beyond recovery. He knew from Proust, his favourite author, that 'Remembrance of a particular form is but regret for a particular moment; and houses, roads, avenues are as fugitive, alas, as the years'.[1]

Inverchapel was lucky to have the able service of John Webster, the factor at Benmore, the Youngers' botanical garden next door, because the property he had bought included not just the farmhouse and buildings at Inverchapel and Coylet, but 1,700 acres of inbye and hill, the inns at Whistlefield and Coylet, and the important asset of the salmon fishings at the mouth of Loch Eck.

He and Tita were initially only to enjoy a very brief period of relaxation at their lodge by the loch. On 7 November 1948, Attlee wrote to Inverchapel inviting him to join the British delegation to the newly-constituted Committee on European Unity, created the previous month by the Brussels Treaty powers. The inaugural meeting was due to open in Paris on the fifteenth. Inverchapel accepted with little hesitation: he was enthusiastic about European unity, and attracted by the tightly structured nature of the task. The work was for a limited time only, and a specific purpose. The chief reason for his invitation was that one of his fans, Hugh Dalton, was to lead the British delegation and had requested Lord Inverchapel's inclusion. Dalton greatly admired Inverchapel's abilities, but was also a confirmed busybody and gossip, and loved Archie Inverchapel's social company, particularly now that Inverchapel seemed to be in his anecdotage.[2]

Britain's involvement in the whole idea of a scheme for European unity was hardly wholehearted. While some in government favoured closer ties with Europe, the main impetus came from America, where some senators, such as Inverchapel's friend James Fulbright, were indicating that they might not support the European Recovery Programme unless Europe federated.

Bevin viewed federalist ideas as 'dangerous', and was determined to prevent them coming to fruition. What he had in mind was a 'Council of Ministers of Western Europe', consisting of government delegations and their advisers, meeting perhaps twice a year and serviced by a permanent secretariat. This was hardly what the Hague Congress or US politicians had in mind, and was some way also from the French plan which pushed for political and economic union. Bevin's position was wholly expedient: he had no desire to relinquish power to a European body, but needs must when the dollar drives. The British Labour Party was generally unsympathetic to calls for a federal Europe. In an odd precursor of Tory arguments of 50 years later, they argued that their domestic political programme would be altered and impeded by a politically contrary Europe. In fact, the stated position did not present the fundamental antipathy: with an empire and new commonwealth, and English-speaking nations elsewhere to be considered, Britain never really felt part of Europe, but felt separate and superior. Another key factor was that Churchill's outspoken support for European union at The Hague put Bevin in an awkward position with his backbenchers, many of whom would have seen any similar enthusiasm as further damning evidence of his following a 'Tory' foreign policy.

Dalton presented Britain's 'Council of Europe' plan on 26 November. The French scheme, as opposed to Britain's inter-governmental idea, was parliamentarian, with individual members voting, rather than just heads of delegation. The French scheme pointed towards a European parliament with all its functions and paraphernalia. Bevin and Dalton were determined to avoid a scheme whereby decision-making would be devolved from Cabinet level to any such body.

Throughout December intense negotiations took place in a series of sub-committees in which Inverchapel was heavily involved. Quite apart from the American hints about aid being dependent on European unity, Inverchapel was quickly enthused by the arguments of the federalists. He saw in their vision of the future, something exciting, progressive and secure.

Dalton, however, remained adamant, and by the time of the final plenary session on 18 January 1949 an attempt had to be made simply to marry the two principal rival ideas. What emerged was a rather unwieldy structure for a Council of Europe which brought together a Committee of Ministers, whose members would cast the votes, and a merely consultative parliamentary assembly. The seeds for future conflict were predictably sown, and Inverchapel was deeply disappointed at the British Government's failure to budge on the real issue of union.

On 20 January 1949 Inverchapel wrote a very strong letter to Bevin in which he effectively resigned from further involvement on the Government's behalf. He stated that he had been 'greatly distressed' at the final document tabled by Dalton:

> ... the effect of your present plan would be to call into question the sincerity of His Majesty's Government, to muzzle the freedom of speech (particularly in regard to the manner of voting you propose) and thus to dash the very real and high hopes that have been set upon the Union of Europe.

Instead, Inverchapel thought the Government should have been much more enthusiastic. He conceded that the European ideal demanded an 'act of faith' and would 'inevitably involve the taking of risks' but, he declared, this was a risk 'from which I feel strongly that we should not flinch'. Bevin's reply was less than convincing, and confirmed in its tone the lack of sincerity of interest which Inverchapel had earlier detected.[3]

At the same time, the press were airing rumours about a political role for Inverchapel in the House of Lords as a part of the Labour team. He was quoted as a potential successor to Lord Listowel as Colonial Minister, the latest in a long line of rumours about his political future.[4] According to another newspaper, Inverchapel was named as a possible replacement for Lord Henderson, the Under-Secretary for Foreign Affairs.[5] There is no evidence to support these claims, and it is possible they simply resulted from wrong conclusions reached by imaginative journalists aware of his current work with Hugh Dalton. Although Lord Inverchapel travelled quite often to London from Argyll to meet old friends, there is no record of his ever having voted in the Lords, never mind spoken. He was by now adamant in his description of himself as 'farmer' and not as ex-diplomat or anything else. He had no intention of a permanent return to the political stage.

The first winter in Inverchapel had been something of a shock for Tita. She had been prepared for the cold and even the dark, but the incessant rain took her aback. As soon as was practicable she headed back to the States, and Inverchapel was left alone with only Yevgeni Yost and a few farm and forest workers for company. Some friends found it hard to imagine that one who relished select congenial company, warm climates and constant movement was now exiled in the wilds of Argyll, alone in the long dark winter nights with wind and rain lashing the house. Harold Nicolson even feared that he might take to the bottle in his desolation.⁶ In fact he appears to have loved it all: perhaps the very contrast with what he always thought was the unreal and slightly absurd world of diplomacy was the attraction. He was determined to make a personal success of the farming, and for that purpose had terminated the lease of Inverchapel farm so that he could take it on himself. He engaged assistance, but did as much farming and shepherding as his sixty-seven years would allow. For someone who had led quite a sedentary life, 1700 acres of rough land, 600 sheep, lack of electricity and arrears of maintenance were quite an undertaking.

Despite the preoccupations with the development of the estate, he maintained some of his other interests. In April he took part in a radio discussion on the Scottish Home Service with T.M. Knox, Professor of Philosophy at St Andrews University. The programme was one of those rather serious academic drawing-room chats which seemed to fill the BBC schedules of the time, and later provided so much rich material for 1960s satirists. It did, however, provide an invaluable insight into Inverchapel's motivation, his beliefs, and his approach to people and diplomacy. In an honest expression of his own character and attitudes, he stated his strong preference for the practical over the theoretical, the active over the philosophical. 'I've shunned philosophy,' he told Knox, 'as I've shunned other... to me... uncomfortable things... like science, mathematics, machinery, and so on, largely because I've been afraid of them'. Inverchapel then went on to show how his practical approach had affected his style of diplomacy.

> In dealings with my fellow men, whatever be their nationality, I've tried first to be honest and frank. Tolerant and patient... The first duty of a diplomatist [He hated the word 'diplomat'] is to establish himself in the confidence of the man or men with whom he is dealing. The only way he can do this is by following the four simple... principles of honesty, frankness, tolerance, and patience... the greatest call is made upon patience.

While frankness had to be relative to the circumstances, he did believe that 'you must be frank in essentials'.

Later, talk turned to current affairs. On the Soviet Union, Inverchapel thought that they had always had tyrants and secret police, so that Bolshevik terror was nothing new to them. The Russians 'hate the system', said Inverchapel, 'but they submit to it' because of that history. He did not say much about his own beliefs except for his 'supreme and undying faith in the British people'.

In early June 1949, Lady Inverchapel was due to return from the States to spend the summer at Loch Eck. Yevgeni Yost, now adding the role of chauffeur to his repertoire, drove Inverchapel up to Glasgow in their left-hand drive Pontiac station wagon. After collecting Tita from Plantation Quay where she had disembarked from a transatlantic liner, the party set off for the long return road trip to Loch Eck. Just outside Glasgow, Yevgeni lost control of the car at a crossroads: the car roared through a red light and slewed across the junction, before slamming into the side of a five-ton lorry which, in trying to avoid the collision, shed its load of sand and rubble on top of the Pontiac. All three were trapped inside. Yevgeni freed himself and managed to drag Lord Inverchapel clear, but Tita was trapped for quite some time. Yevgeni was unscathed, but Lord and Lady Inverchapel were both removed to Glasgow's Western Infirmary. He had cuts to his hands and was suffering badly from shock; she was worse off, with a bad wound to her forehead and numerous other cuts.

After three nights in hospital, during which the Palace was among the many who phoned their good wishes, Inverchapel was discharged. Tita, however, spent a week in hospital. For someone of Inverchapel's age, and with his heart difficulties, it proved to be a considerable blow to his health, and he was never as strong thereafter. The accident put paid to a planned US lecture tour, recuperation at Inverchapel being required instead.

Life soon returned to its relatively quiet normality, and Inverchapel was more than happy with his new role on the land. The growing international tension in Europe, the Communist triumph in China and the McCarthyite panic in America may have been disappointments, but they all seemed so distant and remote now. His experience in China, however, did attract the attention of the BBC, and in October he travelled to Glasgow to record a talk entitled 'Communism in the Far East'. Inverchapel first explained why he had originally been so sanguine about Chinese communism:

> In many a long talk Chou En-lai confessed to me the aims and hopes of his party which reduced themselves to this: escape from the cold tyranny of landlordism, from the crippling usury of which the peasantry was victim, eventual escape too from the weight of the capitalism of the foreigner. All this seemed to be blameless enough. It was certainly lulling. But time showed that Chou En-lai's modesty had been mistaken.

Now, Inverchapel felt, the Chinese communists had 'sold their souls to the Kremlin'.

Of the future of Asia, he was fearful. He raised the possibility of communism spreading from China to Tibet, Vietnam, Burma, and Malaya. History proved him to be not much mistaken. As far as the West was concerned in Asia, there had to be a new approach now. 'The age of colonialism is dead... we westerners must understand that we cannot now recapture the past.' What was needed, Inverchapel believed, was a fresh political start offering 'something less barren and less dismal than the wares of Moscow'. With that new liberal outlook there might still be a future for the West in Asia.

Over the next year or so, Inverchapel made several contributions to the BBC, the most notable of which were his profiles of General Marshall, Truman and Stalin. These were produced by Gerald Priestland, and were basically intended to be obituaries, ghoulishly but practically, recorded before the death of the subject for subsequent, more appropriate, transmission. His 'obituary' of Stalin could only be described as glowing, and it badly misjudged the verdict of history. Inverchapel, biased by his wartime experiences, felt that the memory of Stalin's purges and tyranny would fade in the minds of Russians when set beside his role as a military hero. In fact, the opposite is true, but then history is always changing, and it may be that the future will bring with it views more in line with those Inverchapel held.

This talk provided a headache for the producer: senior management at the BBC took exception to the tone of Inverchapel's opening remarks and requested an alteration. Despite Priestland's cajoling, Inverchapel refused to budge. The obituary would begin as he had scripted it: 'So Uncle Joe has died on us at last'. In the international atmosphere of late 1950, with a showdown in Korea imminent, such chummy flippancy seemed wholly misplaced. However, Inverchapel was clearly revising his opinions. In the summer of 1950 he was commissioned by the *New York Times* to write an article entitled 'Stalin As I Knew Him'. It was never actually published, but it provides interesting reading. Inverchapel had by now abandoned any hope for Soviet friendship, and fully supported the Cold War strategy of the West:

> ... a shocked world... has heard the sickening preaching of democracy and peace and has seen a mockery made of the one and the deliberate blocking of the road to the other. It has totted up the lamentable list of broken promises and recoiled in disgust from all that the Soviet Government stands for. It is now gathering itself together in a balanced self-defence in order to escape the aggression of a perverse ideology.

He did defend the wartime friendship and his own role in its maintenance, although he conceded that the green shoots of future problems were always present.

> We were allies. Nevertheless as such we had often to exercise a patience and a forbearance that taxed us high. Our best efforts in the common cause and our scrupulously honest intentions were constantly misinterpreted and frustrated to the point of exasperation.

Inverchapel now fully believed, however regrettable he felt it to be, that Stalin himself was behind the Soviet Union's 'reiterated acts of bad faith'. Reality in the form of a brutal Soviet dictator had dashed Inverchapel's hopes of a world of peaceful coexistence.

Having failed to find the necessary time and motivation to begin his own memoirs, Inverchapel did pen a few fictional stories in addition to political jottings and book reviews during the long periods of solitude at Inverchapel. He sold several of these, part of a planned series of Scottish ghost stories, to the *Atlantic Monthly* and at $300 a time this proved a rewarding exercise. With Tita's long absences, the home at Inverchapel could be a lonely place, particularly in winter. On the long, dark evenings, with the rain rampaging with the wind up the loch, there was nothing much else to do but snuggle up to the fire with whisky, pipe and quill and let the imagination take its course.

In the autumn of 1950, however, Lord Inverchapel was surprisingly recalled to the public stage. It was the year of Glasgow University's rectorial election, and he was approached by a group of students who wished to nominate him. Inverchapel readily agreed and a campaign was organised. As the term of office would coincide with the University's quincentenary, it was expected to be much more high profile than usual.

The office of Lord Rector, unique to the old Scottish universities, is ostensibly the highest office in the university. Elected by the students, the Lord Rector chairs the University Court and can have a major influence on the affairs of the institution. In practice, however, the person elected tended to be a well-known public figure who rarely had the time or inclination to attend to the duties of the post. As a result, the office was usually titular, the election merely an opportunity for students to indicate their support for, or dislike of, the political figures or parties of the day.

Lord Inverchapel had been proposed by a non-political group representing students at the university's halls of residence. Inverchapel indicated his assent and assured them that he had the time and interest to be a 'working rector'. This tag became the main plank of the Inverchapel campaign and, as it was the first time that slogan had been used in a rectorial election, it proved to be persuasive. Traditionally, the rectorial candidates do not campaign themselves, and instead have prominent supporters speak for them. Inverchapel's friends Bob Boothby and Harold Nicolson both travelled to the university to speak, and messages of support were elicited from some of his international acquaintances, including Eisenhower. As one would expect, the election campaign was more high jinks than serious politics. However, Inverchapel and his team were determined.

The other candidates were backed by student political groups: for the Tory students, Sir David Maxwell Fyfe, the Conservative MP and later Lord Chancellor; for the Labour students, George Macleod of Fuinary; for the student nationalists, John MacCormick of the Scottish Covenant and Home Rule campaign. There was also a joke candidate, Rosamund John, nominated by the Filmgoers Club.

The Inverchapel campaign showed early signs of success, but in the end the appeal of John MacCormick and Home Rule proved too much. MacCormick seemed to capture the mood of the age: after all, only two months later it would be Glasgow University students who would daringly remove the Stone of Destiny, ancient symbol of Scottish nationhood, from Westminster Abbey.

In those circumstances, Inverchapel's narrow defeat 661-636 was a very creditable performance. Although disappointed not to have won, Inverchapel did greatly enjoy coming higher in the polls than either the Tory or the Labour candidate. He made much of this among his political friends, especially those who had spoken at Glasgow in favour of their party's candidate.

The rectorial campaign was essentially Lord Inverchapel's public swansong. The rest of his life was spent in quiet seclusion by Loch Eck, tending his flocks, looking after his garden, writing a little, and enjoying the peace and natural beauty of his beloved surroundings.

His final political activity tends to confirm that he had by now given up all hope of the USSR being brought into amicable alliance, and had indeed decided that strength and containment were the only answers. In January 1951, the British-China Association approached him about adding his name to an open letter they were proposing to release, criticising the policy of General McArthur in the Far East. Inverchapel, however, refused to have anything to do with it. He felt that it was wholly inappropriate to criticise American policy and so 'cause offence to people whose friendship is essential for our survival'.

If the world he had hoped for had faded, and the trust he had placed in Stalin's word had been cruelly abused, it was as nothing to the shocks still to come. On 7 June 1951, the *Daily Express* broke the sensational story of the disappearance of two Foreign Office diplomats, Donald Maclean and Guy Burgess. To those for whom that story is now old and well-worn, it is hard to imagine just how dreadful a shock that story was for those who had worked with and trusted Burgess and Maclean. For some, indeed, it was too much to bear: Philip Jordan, Attlee's press secretary, who had known Maclean in Washington and had been told that the story was going to break, collapsed and died of a heart attack, at 48, that very night. For Lord Inverchapel the news was similarly traumatic, and he never fully recovered from it. Throughout June as the story was pieced together and analysed in the press, to the sense of shock was added a deep sense of personal betrayal. Men whom Inverchapel had openly trusted had wholly deceived him, and to the physical upset was added mental grief and emotional hurt. Maclean's treachery had cast a dark shadow over the whole of Inverchapel's later career, and he felt bitterly let down and disappointed. Maclean's actions first took away Lord Inverchapel's peace of mind, then his life, and later threatened his reputation.

In early July, Lord Inverchapel experienced such physical discomfort from his heart condition that he was removed to hospital in Greenock, across the Firth of Clyde. It was too late, however. On the afternoon of Thursday 5 July 1951 he died. He was only sixty-nine.

The funeral, the following Monday, was from the beautiful church of St Munn's on the Holy Loch. After the service, the cortege, led by a piper, made its way back to Inverchapel and Archibald John Kerr Clark Kerr, PC, GCMG, 1st Baron Inverchapel of Loch Eck was laid to rest in the family plot he himself had planned and laid out. So passed on the last of the Clarks of Inverchapel, and the greatest of them.

A few weeks later a memorial service was held at St Margaret's Westminster to enable his diplomatic and political friends to pay their last respects.

The King and Queen were represented, as were Sir Winston Churchill, Ernest Bevin and Anthony Eden.

Tita, Lady Inverchapel, who had never settled in Argyll, left Inverchapel in August 1951, returning eventually to the United States. In 1960 she married an elderly American business magnate, Ross Tresseder, and following his death she returned to Santiago, where she died in 1987. Yevgeni Yost, armed with a legacy from Lord Inverchapel, moved a little south to Rothesay on the Isle of Bute, where he built up a very successful catering business.

The immediate family made considerable efforts to see the estate maintained, letting out the property, home farm and fishings, and carefully overseeing the general management. Only after a few years, when it became clear that none of the family was in a position to take on the estate on a permanent basis, was the property relinquished and an end made to the Clark connection with the area.

As the years pass, so too the memory and significance of Archie Inverchapel's career has faded. His death marked not just the passing of an attractive personality, but also the end of a noble brand of diplomacy. Developments in telecommunications and transport have greatly reduced the political role of diplomacy. Leaders can now chat easily down a hotline, can be in each others homes in a matter of hours, have little need to depend on others to do their talking. Inverchapel was one of the last of the great political diplomatists, meeting leaders, conducting negotiations, personally representing premiers and foreign ministers. It was a role in which he excelled, and in executing it so ably during the wartime years he rendered invaluable service not just to Britain but to the free world. That would have been something he would most have treasured: to be credited with having served not just his country, but mankind. For if, as a stoutly pragmatic individual, he did have any firm, unshakeable beliefs they were in the dignity of all human life, in the essential equality of every human, regardless of background, wealth or rank. It was that passion, openly demonstrated in his words and actions, which enabled him to function so successfully in the many corners of the globe to which he was posted, and it was that love of mankind which drove him on through the many disappointments and setbacks which he inevitably experienced.

Of his own personal contribution to world affairs it can fairly be stated that, given his wartime service in China and the Soviet Union, and in the United States, and his presence at the great meetings at Teheran, Yalta and Potsdam, he was easily the most influential Scotsman in international politics of the century. That, too, would have been something of which he would have been hugely proud. To have served his country was his duty, to have been of service to humanity was something infinitely better, but to have done so as a Scot was a matter of the greatest pride. For all his work in the highest councils of international affairs, as important to him was a small spot of rural Argyllshire which he owned and loved: the home towards which his thoughts were always turning.

Where one is born, where one lives, where one labours, where one dies, are all simply physical, often accidental, sometimes undesired. Home is something infinitely greater: it is the place where we choose to centre our being, the single point where we unite the self with the material world. It is that commitment, that willingness of the heart, which transforms a mere place and imbues it with the vital sense of belonging.

The words of the great poet of modern New South Wales, Les Murray, writing of the pull of home and the importance of belonging, could also be used of that older son of New South Wales, Archibald Clark Kerr, who found his spiritual home on the far side of the earth, by the shores of Loch Eck in the shadow of Highland hills:

> Though I myself run to the cities, I will forever
> be coming back here to walk, knee-deep in ferns,
> up and away from this metropolitan century,
> to remember my ancestors, axemen, dairy-men, horse-breakers,
> now coffined in silence...
> ... Though I go to the cities, turning my back on these hills,
> for the talk and dazzle of cities, for the sake of belonging
> for months and years at a time to the twentieth century,
> the city will never quite hold me. I will always be
> coming back here on the up-train, peering, leaning
> out of the window to see, on far-off ridges,
> the sky between the trees, and over the racket
> of the rails to hear the echo and silence.'

Notes on the Text

The principal source for this book is the Inverchapel Deposit held in the Modern Papers Reading Room of the Bodleian Library, Oxford. These private and political papers of Lord Inverchapel have been placed there on loan by the Executors of Lord Inverchapel's Estate. All quotations in this book, except where otherwise credited, are derived from this excellent source. Sir William ('Tony') and Lady Lewthwaite also gave me access to further private papers which they retained.

Lady Boothby kindly allowed me to see and use a number of letters from Lord Inverchapel to her late husband, and these are credited in the notes.

Other useful sources are in the Public Record Office, Kew, particularly the Inverchapel Papers at FO 800/298-303. Other helpful material is in the general Foreign Office files FO 371. Useful material, especially on wartime policy, can be found in the CAB files, and the PREM files. Crown copyright material in the Public Record Office is reproduced by permission of the Controller of Her Majesty's Stationery Office.

All papers, correspondence, and background material for this book have also been deposited in the Bodleian Library, Oxford, so that as much Inverchapel material as possible can be available to scholars at the one site.

A separate bibliography has not been provided: texts which were found to be most useful are credited in the notes below.

CHAPTER 1 – SHORE 1882-1900

1 Information on James Clark of Crossbasket came principally from two sources:
   i *James Finlay & Company Ltd 1750-1950* (Glasgow, Jackson & Co., 1951), Foreword by A.H. McGrigor;
   ii *The Memoirs and Portraits of One Hundred Glasgow Men* (Glasgow, James MacLehose and Sons, 1886).
   Although biographical notes on James Clark, as published in the works noted above, state that he graduated from Edinburgh University in 1835, there is no mention of his name in the graduation lists.
2 Information on John Kerr from James Watt Memorial Library, Greenock. I could find no grave of Margaret Kerr Clark in west Scotland, but research in Newfoundland proved that she died in Greenock, following the family's return from Canada.
3 Serle, Geoffrey, and Ward, Russel (eds), *Australian Dictionary of Biography* vol. 6, 1851-1890, R-Z (Melbourne, Melbourne University Press, 1976) p 39.
4 *Ibid.*, p 40.
5 Serle, Ward (eds), *op. cit.* p 40.
6 *The Bathonian*, March 1900, p 13 (Bath City Library).

CHAPTER 2 – UPLAND 1900–1915

1. Sir Nevile Henderson, (1882–1942) later served with Clark Kerr in Egypt (see Chapter 4); he ended his career, notoriously, as Ambassador to Germany 1937–39.

   Gerald Villiers had a fairly undistinguished Foreign Office career but was awarded the CMG for his work at the Tangier Conference in 1923. He left the service in 1929 but returned to work in the war years. He died in 1953.

   Gerald Tyrrwhitt-Wilson (1883–1950) became 14th Lord Berners in 1918, at which point he left the Foreign Service. He achieved some fame as a composer and artist.

   Lord Gerald Wellesley, (1885–1972) later 7th Duke of Wellington, left the Foreign Service in 1922. He later achieved some distinction as an architect. Clark Kerr employed him to draw up the ambitious plans for the mansion at Inverchapel, which was never actually built.

   Francis Gerald Agar-Robartes (1888–1966), later Viscount Clifden, served in numerous capacities without reaching the higher Foreign Office posts.

   The Hon. Henry Lygon (1884–1936) son of the 7th Earl Beauchamp, was President of the Oxford Union and later a local politician with extreme right-wing views.

   Sir Reginald (Rex) Hoare was latterly Minister at Bucharest 1935–41. He died in 1954.

   Reginald Bridgeman (1884–1968) left the Diplomatic Service in 1923 and spent a remarkable life as a hard left activist in various organisations. See entry in Joyce Bellamy and John Saville (eds), *Dictionary of Labour Biography* vol. VII (London, Macmillan, 1984) pp 26–50.

   Sir Miles Lampson, later 1st Baron Killearn, (1880–1964) served in Egypt from 1933, first as High Commisioner, and then Ambassador. His final two years were as special commissioner to South-East Asia, taking over from Lord Inverchapel in the negotiations over Indonesian independence.

2. For another picture of Eustace Percy see the portrait by his nephew, Gavin Maxwell, in *The House of Elrig* (London, Longmans Green & Co., 1965); Percy's own memoirs of Washington are general and remarkably impersonal: *Lord Eustace Percy, Some Memories* (London, Eyre & Spottiswoode, 1958); a little of the life of the Washington embassy is given in Ivar Campbell, *Poems by Ivar Campbell with Memoir by Guy Ridley* (London, Humphreys, 1917). Another sidelight on Washington life of the time is in Archibald W. Butt, *The Letters of Archie Butt*, ed. Lawrence F. Abbott (Garden City, Doubleday, Page, 1924). Butt was a Presidential aide, and sometime flatmate of Clark Kerr's, before his tragic death on the *Titanic*.

3. Felix Frankfurter's notes to *The Times* obituary, 19 June 1951.

4. Gavin Maxwell, *Raven Seek Thy Brother* (London, Longmans Green & Co., 1968), p 102–3; Douglas Botting, *Gavin Maxwell: A Life* (London, HarperCollins, 1993), p 39.

5. James Rennell Rodd, *Social and Diplomatic Memoirs* vol. III (London, E. Arnold, 1925), p 221–2.

6. Letter from Archie Clark Kerr to Bob Boothby, 18 January 1919 (Boothby Papers).

NOTES ON THE TEXT

CHAPTER 3 – FOOTHILLS 1915–1922

1   John Buchan, *Greenmantle* (London, Hodder & Stoughton, 1916), p 10–11.
2   An excellent history of the war in Persia is given in *Operations in Persia 1914–1919* (Imperial War Museum, HMSO 1987).
3   Theodore H. White notes (Bodleian); see also Sir Robert V. Rhodes James, *Boothby* (London, Hodder & Stoughton, 1991).
4   Sir Robert V. Rhodes James, *op. cit.*
5   Letter to the author from Captain D.J. Archibald, Assistant Regimental Adjutant, Scots Guards, 19 July 1990.
6   Rom Landau, *Moroccan Drama 1900–1955* (San Francisco, The American Academy of Asian Studies, 1956), p 174–5.
7   Ivone Kirkpatrick, *The Inner Circle* (London, Macmillan, 1959), p 35.

CHAPTER 4 – OUTCROP 1922–1925

1   *Great Britain and Egypt 1914–1951* (Information papers no. 19, Royal Institute of International Affairs, Second Edition, 1952), p 2 (hereafter referred to as RIIA).
2   Amine Youssef Bey, *Independent Egypt* (London, J. Murray, 1940), p 57.
3   A.P. Wavell, *Allenby in Egypt* (London, Harrap, 1943), p 41. Although Archie is not credited with having assisted Wavell in this production, a draft copy of the introduction to this book is in the files in the Bodleian Library. The style of the introduction is not inconsistent with Archie's own, and he may thus have penned it, or at least edited it, for Wavell. That he receives no credit is perhaps explained by the fact that he was a career diplomat and so restricted in public comment on British policy.
4   *Ibid.*, p 44.
5   RIIA, *op. cit.*, p 6.
6   Wavell, *op. cit.*, p 78; see also Lord Hardinge, *Old Diplomacy* (London, J. Murray, 1947), p 233–4.
7   Wavell, *op. cit.*, p 78.
8   RIIA, p 8.
9   Youssef, *op. cit.*, p 89.
10   Wavell, *op. cit.*, p 86.
11   Youssef, *op. cit.*, p 104–5.
12   This section was prepared by Sir William Lewthwaite.
13   Youssef, *op. cit.*, p 115.
14   Wavell, *op. cit.*, p 83.
15.   *Ibid.*, p 102–3.
16   Letter from Ingram to Archibald Clark Kerr, 24 January 1924 (Bodleian Files).
17   George Glasgow, *MacDonald as Diplomatist* (London, Jonathan Cape, 1924), p 224.
18   Youssef, *op. cit.*, p 115.
19   *Ibid.*, p 129–139.
20   FO Record [No.168 E 1284/22/16], 15 February 1924.
21   Wavell, *op. cit.*, p 103.
22   *Ibid.*, p 105.
23   Glasgow, *op. cit.*, p 216.
24   RIIA, p 10.

25 *The Times*, 18 August 1924.
26 E 8669/368/16.
27 Youssef, *op. cit.*, p 121.
28 Wavell, *op. cit.*, p 108.
29 *The Times*, 20 November 1924. Another account of the Sirdar's death is in T. Russell, *Egyptian Service* (London, J. Murray, 1949), pp 219–221.
30 Allenby to Foreign Office, 19 November 1924, nos. 361, 362, 363.
31 Allenby to Foreign Office, 20 November 1924, no. 368.
32 Allenby to Foreign Office, 20 November 1924, no. 369.
33 Foreign Office to Allenby, 22 November 1924, no. 228.
34 Referred to in letter to his mother 15 December 1924 (Bodleian Files).
35 Allenby to Foreign Office, 21 November 1924, no. 380.
36 FO 800/256/326.
37 Allenby to Foreign Office, 22 November 1924, no. 383.
38 Wavell, *op. cit.*, p 111.
39 E 11296/368/16.
40 *The Times*, 24 November 1924.
41 Youssef, *op. cit.*, p 127.
42 Allenby to Foreign Office, 23 November 1924, no. 391.
43 Lord Boothby, *Recollections of a Rebel* (London, Hutchinson, 1978), p 27.
44 Allenby to Foreign Office, 23 November 1924, no. 390.
45 Wavell, *op. cit.*, p 115.
46 Foreign Office to Allenby, 24 November 1924, no. 239.
47 Martin Gilbert, *Winston S. Churchill* vol. V (Companion) 1922–29 (London, Heinemann, 1979), p 256.
48 Letter to his mother, 28 November 1924 (Bodleian).
49 Allenby to Foreign Office, 7 December 1924, E/11296/368/16.
50 Austen Chamberlain to Allenby, 22 December 1924.
51 *The Times*, 29 November 1924.
52 FO 800/256/148.
53 Austen Chamberlain to Allenby, 24 November 1924.
54 Wavell, *op. cit.*, p 122; FO 800/256/326; FO 800/256/246; Sir Nevile Henderson, *Water Under the Bridges* (London, Hodder & Stoughton 1945), p 135. Here he protests too much about the extent of the briefings he received which, even on his account, still seem inadequate.
55 FO 800/256/167.
56 FO 800/256/169.
57 FO 800/256/174.
58 Martin Gilbert, *op. cit.*, p 275.
59 FO 800/256/245.
60 Allenby to Austen Chamberlain, 28.11.24.
61 FO 800/256/255.
62 *The Times*, November 27th 1924.
63 FO 800/256/326; also in FO 800/264.
64 FO 800/256/156; FO 800/257/1.
65 Sir Nevile Henderson, *op. cit.*, pp 136–39. The fact that he fails in his book even to acknowledge the presence in Egypt of Clark Kerr, an acquaintance from Scoon's 20 years before, adds strength to the view that it is Clark Kerr he holds as behind the antagonism he sensed.
66 Allenby to Austen Chamberlain, 26 April 1925, J 1257/29/1.

NOTES ON THE TEXT

CHAPTER 5 – CORRIE 1925–1937

1 Ben Pimlott, (ed.) *The Second World War Diary of Hugh Dalton 1940–45* (London, Cape, 1986), p 567–8.
2 Theodore H. White notes (Bodleian).
3 Ben Pimlott, *op. cit.*
4 *Ibid.* Also, Frank Giles, *Sundry Times* (London, Murray, 1983), p 51.
5 Although Maria Theresa was always quoted as having been born in 1911, Sir William Lewthwaite has pointed out that her death certificate gives her date of birth as 1907.
6 Information to author from colleague in Sweden.
7 Lord Boothby, *op. cit.*
8 Robert Payne, *Chungking Diary* (London, Heinemann, 1945), p 34
9 Nigel Nicolson (ed.), *The Letters of Virginia Woolf* vol. 5 1932–1935, *The Sickle Side of the Moon* (London, Hogarth Press, 1979).
10 *The Times*, 16 January 1935.
11 Gavin Maxwell, *op. cit.* [2:4], pp 102–3
12 FO 800/298/45–47.
13 FO 800/298/214.
14 P.W. Ireland, *Iraq: A Study in Political Development* (London, Cape, 1937), p 426–7.

CHAPTER 6 – RIDGE 1938–1942

1 FO 371/20995.
2 A. Cave Brown, *Bodyguard of Lies* (London, W.H. Allen, 1976), p 392–3; Sir Berkeley Gage, *It's Been A Marvellous Party* (London, Privately published, 1989), p 69.

Despite appearances, Sir Hughe Montgomery Knatchbull-Hugessen did not boast the finest moniker in public service. His double-barrelled effort was no match for that of the Admiral who led the British military talks in Moscow in 1939: Admiral the Honourable Sir Reginald Aylmer Ranfurly Plunkett-Ernle-Erle-Drax.

Documents on British Foreign Policy, Second Series, vol. XXI (1984), p 266.
3 Aron Shai, *Origins of the War in the East* (London, Croom Helm, 1976), p 44.
4 Bradford A. Lee, *Britain and the Sino-Japanese War 1937–1939* (Stanford University Press, 1973), p 40.
5 *Ibid.*, p 87.
6 FO 371 20958.
7 Speech at University of Glasgow, April 1946.
8 FO 800/299/14.
9 FO 800/299/2–3.
10 Letter from R.G. Howe to Sir Archibald Clark Kerr, 7 February 1938 (Bodleian Files).
11 Nicholas R. Clifford, *Retreat From China: British Policy in the Far East 1937–1941* (London, Longmans, 1967), p 47f.
12 Lee, *op. cit.*, p 114.
13 *The Times*, 30 April 1938.
14 FO 800/299/36.

15 Gage, *op. cit.*, p 65.
16 FO 800/299/55.
17 FO 371 22108.
18 Shai, *op. cit.*, p 189f.
19 FO 4969/84/10.
20 Lee, *op. cit.*, p 132–3.
21 M. Oksenberg and R.B. Oxnam, *Dragon and Eagle, US-China Relations: Past and Future* (New York, Basic Books, 1973), p 145; Edgar Snow, *Journey to the Beginning* (London, Gollancz, 1959), p 200ff.
22 W. Burchett and R. Alley, *China: The Quality of Life* (London, Penguin Books, 1976), p 51ff.
23 E. Snow, *op. cit.*, p 200.
24 Burchett, Alley, *op. cit.*, p 62.
25 Helen F. Snow, *My China Years* (London, Harrap, 1984), p 305; Burchett, Alley, *op. cit.*, p 64.
26 Burchett, Alley, *op. cit.*, p 67.
27 E. Snow, *op. cit.*, p 203, 206.
28 Agnes Smedley, *China Correspondent* (London, Pandora Press, 1984), p 146 (first published as *Battle Hymn of China* [London, Gollancz, 1943]).
29 K.E. Shewmaker, *Americans and Chinese Communists 1927–1945* (Ithaca, Cornell University Press, 1971), p 90.
30 See Anthony Glees, *Secrets of the Service* (London, Cape, 1987); Chapman Pincher, *Too Secret Too Long* (London, Sidgwick & Jackson, 1984); Richard Deacon (1), *The British Connection* (London, Hamish Hamilton, 1979); (2) *Spyclopaedia* (London, Futura, 1988); Christopher Dobson and Ronald Payne, *A Dictionary of Espionage* (London, Harrap, 1984).
31 Smedley, *op. cit.*, p 149.
32 James Bertram, *The Shadow of a War* (London, Gollancz, 1947), p 79.
33 William G. Hayter, *A Double Life* (London, Hamish Hamilton, 1974); Alaric Jacob, *A Window in Moscow* (London, Collins, 1946), p 104.
34 David Dilks (ed.), *The Diaries of Sir Alexander Cadogan 1938–1945* (London, Cassell, 1971), p 86.
35 J. Harvey (ed.), (1) *The Diplomatic Diaries of Oliver Harvey 1937–40* (London, Collins, 1970), p 160.
36 Documents on British Foreign Policy, Third Series, vol. VIII (1955), p 4 (hereafter DBFP).
37 *Ibid.*, pp 7, 8.
38 Clifford, *op. cit.*, p 82.
39 Shai, *op. cit.*, p 163.
40 F.S.G. Piggott, *Broken Thread* (Aldershot, Gale & Polden, 1950), pp 300–302.
41 DBFP, pp 10–19.
42 *Ibid.*, p 2.
43 *Ibid.*, p 19.
44 *Ibid.*, p 30.
45 *Ibid.*, p 50.
46 *Ibid.*, p 122.
47 *Ibid.*, p 142.
48 Shai, *op. cit.*, p 210ff.
49 DBFP, p 156.
50 FO 371 22149.

51 Lee, *op. cit.*, p 122.
52 DBFP, p 195.
53 Lee, *op. cit.*, p 153; DBFP, pp 249, 283.
54 Lee, *op. cit.*, pp 128–9.
55 Clifford, *op. cit.*, pp 89–90.
56 DBFP, pp 308.
57 Clifford, *op. cit.*, p 99.
58 FO 371 23409.
59 DBFP, p 332.
60 *Ibid.*, p 342.
61 Shai, *op. cit.*, p 195.
62 FO 371 23409.
63 *Ibid.*
64 DBFP, p 409.
65 Clifford, *op. cit.*, p 103.
66 FO 371 23396.
67 FO 371 22398.
68 Hayter, *op. cit.*, p 55.
69 J. Harvey (ed.), (2) *The War Diaries of Oliver Harvey 1941–1945* (London, Collins, 1978), p 274.
70 Documents on British Foreign Policy 1919–39, Third Series, vol. IX 1939, p 19 (hereafter DBFP [IX]).
71 *Ibid.*, p 33.
72 *Ibid.*, p 34.
73 *Ibid.*, p 55.
74 *Ibid.*, p 66.
75 FO 371 23397.
76 DBFP (IX), p 82.
77 *Ibid.*, p 106.
78 *Ibid.*, p 111.
79 *Ibid.*, p 116.
80 *Ibid.*, p 123.
81 *Ibid.*, p 139.
82 *Ibid.*, p 152.
83 FO 800/299/134.
84 *Ibid.*, pp 132–152 passim.
85 Lee, *op. cit.*, p 186–7.
86 DBFP (IX), p 177.
87 *Ibid.*, p 190.
88 *Ibid.*, p 216.
89 P. Lowe, *Great Britain and the Origins of the Pacific War* (Oxford, Clarendon Press, 1977), pp 79–80, 88–89.
90 Letter in Bodleian papers.
91 FO 800/299/149.
92 J. Harvey (ed.), (1) *op. cit.*, p 299; Harold Nicolson, *Diaries and Letters 1930–39* (London, Collins, 1966), p 391.
93 DBFP (IX), pp 307, 316, 341, 343.
94 David Dilks (ed.), *op. cit.*
95 Lee, *op. cit.*, pp 193–4.
96 Shai, *op. cit.*, p 230.

97 Bertram, *op. cit.*, p 13.
98 Clifford, *op. cit.*, p 128.
99 FO 371 24708.
100 Clifford, *op. cit.*, p 128.
101 J. Bertram, *op. cit.*, p 46.
102 H. Abend, *My Life in China 1926–41* (London, Lane, 1944), p 33.
103 FO 371 24666.
104 FO 371 23407.
105 P. Lowe, *op. cit.*, p 142.
106 A. Smedley, *op. cit.*, p 347.
107 D. Dilks (ed.), *op. cit.*, p 311ff.
108 J. Harvey (ed.), (1) *op. cit.*, p 352.
109 J. Bertram, *op. cit.*, p 87.
110 Ben Pimlott, (ed.), *op. cit.*, p 121.
111 Michael Lindsay, *The Unknown War, North China 1937–45* (London, Bergstrom & Boyle, 1975).
112 Gunther Stein, *The Challenge of Red China* (London, Pilot Press, 1945), p 15.
113 Martin Kitchen, *British Policy Towards the Soviet Union During The Second World War* (Basingstoke, Macmillan, 1986).
114 Bertram, *op. cit.*, p 95.
115 *The Times*, 20 January 1942.
116 J. Bertram, *op. cit.*, p 97.
117 *The Times*, 4 February 1942.
118 *Ibid.* 3 February 1942.
119 *Ibid.*, 4 February 1942.
120 F 4531/113/10, February 3 1942.
121 *The Leader*, 3 February 1945.
122 Joseph W. Alsop, *I've Seen the Best of It* (New York, Norton, 1992), p 151ff.
123 Shewmaker, *op. cit.*
124 *Ibid.*, p 143; E. Snow, *op. cit.*, p 229.
125 Shewmaker, *op. cit.*, p 260ff.
126 C. Thorne, *Allies of A Kind* (London, Hamish Hamilton, 1978), p 42.
127 *China Weekly Review* XCI, 13 January 1940.
128 Theodore H. White, *In Search of History* (London, Cape, 1978), p 104.
129 See J. Costello, *Mask of Treachery* (London, Collins 1988); A. Glees, *op. cit.*; R. Deacon, *op. cit.* (1), pp 196–208; C. Pincher, *Their Trade is Treachery* (London, Sidgwick & Jackson, 1981) and *op. cit.*; Rebecca West, *The New Meaning of Treason* (New York, Viking Press, 1964), p 245.
130 J. Costello, *op. cit.*, p 291.
131 *Ibid.*; also Gordon Prange, Donald Goldstein, Katherine Dillon and Target Tokyo, *The Story of the Sorge Spy Ring* (London, Hodder & Stoughton, 1986); Robert Whymant, *Stalin's Spy* (London, I.B.Tauris, 1997).
132 Shewmaker, *op. cit.*, *passim*; *Der Spiegl*, 18 July 1951.
133 Prange *et.al.*, *op. cit.*, p 103ff.
134 Michael Schaller, *The US Crusade in China 1938–45* (New York, Columbia University Press, 1979), p 44.
135 FO 800/300/39-40.

NOTES ON THE TEXT

CHAPTER 7 – MOUNTAIN TOP 1942–1946

1 Martin Kitchen, *op. cit.*, p 59ff.
2 *Ibid.*, p 50–51.
3 *Ibid.*, p 101.
4 Graham Ross, *The Foreign Office and Kremlin* (Cambridge, Cambridge University Press, 1984), pp 79–80. This is an excellent text which provides a detailed survey of relations between Britain and the Soviet Union.
5 FO 371 32876.
6 FO 800/300/34.
7 FO 800/300/9.
8 FO 800/300/184.
9 FO 800/300/22.
10 FO 800/300/23.
11 FO 800/300/24.
12 FO 800/300/9.
13 *Ibid.*, p 13.
14 *Ibid.*, p 20.
15 *Ibid.*, p 9.
16 *Ibid.*, p 11.
17 *Ibid.*, p 14.
18 *Ibid.*, p 21.
19 W. Churchill, *The Hinge of Fate* (London, Cassell, 1951), p 305.
20 FO 371 32909.
21 PREM 3, 76/1, 5 July 1942.
22 PREM 3/76A/1, 28 July 1942.
23 Churchill, *op. cit.*, p 241–2.
24 FO 371 329/1.
25 F.L. Loewenheim, H.D. Langley and M. Jonas (eds), *Roosevelt and Churchill, Their Secret Wartime Alliance* (London, Barrie & Jackson, 1975), p 231.
26 Churchill, *op. cit.*
27 FO 800/300.
28 FO 800/300/121. For Clark Kerr's certainty of victory and personal success see Gavin Maxwell, *op. cit.* [2:4], p 102–3.
29 *Ibid.*
30 FO 800/300/50.
31 *Ibid.*, p 123.
32 *Ibid.*
33 *Ibid.*
34 *Ibid.*, p 125.
35 *Ibid.*, p 126.
36 *Saturday Evening Post* (Pa.), 28 September 1946.
37 FO 800/300/128.
38 FO 800/300/138-145; see also G. Ross, 'Operation Bracelet: Churchill in Moscow 1942' in D. Dilks (ed.), (2) *Retreat From Power*, vol. 2 (London, Macmillan, 1981). This article provides a very full report of Churchill's visit.
39 *Ibid.*, p 147.
40 Alexander Werth, *Russia At War 1941–1945* (London, Barrie & Rockliffe, 1964), p 481.
41 FO 800/300/155.

42   PREM 3/76A/10 Folio 7.
43   PREM 3/76A/11 Folio 15.
44   FO 800/300/198.
45   *Ibid.*, p 172.
46   FO 800/300/232; David Dilks (ed.), *op. cit.*, p 479.
47   FO 800/300/200; E. Barnard and Wendell Willkie, *Fighter For Freedom* (Michigan, Michigan University Press, 1966), p 359.
48   Ben Pimlott, *op. cit.*, p 550.
49   A.Werth, *op. cit.*, p 492.
50   FO 371 35338.
51   *Ibid.*
52   CAB Paper 79/87 no. 346.
53   M. Kitchen, *op. cit.*, p 146.
54   K. Young (ed.), *The Diaries of Sir Robert Bruce Lockhart 1939–1965* (London, Macmillan, 1980), p 221.
55   FO 800/300/159.
56   *The Times*, 8 February 8 1943.
57   Ben Pimlott (ed.), (2) *The Political Diary of Hugh Dalton 1945–60* (London, Jonathan Cape, 1986), p 446.
58   FO 371 33154; FO 371 35388.
59   FO 800/301/15.
60   FO 800/301/12
61   J. Lehmann, *I am My Brother, Autobiography II* (London, Longman, 1960), p 151.
62   FO 800/301/48.
63   *Ibid.*, p 25.
64   PREM 3, 354–8.
65   J. Harvey (ed.), (2) *op. cit.*, entry for 10 February 1943.
66   A. Werth, *op. cit.*, p 627.
67   FO 800/301/33.
68   W.A. Harriman and E. Abel, *Special Envoy to Churchill and Stalin 1941–46* (London, Hutchinson, 1976), p 213.
69   FO 371 36925.
70   FO 800/301/117.
71   FO 954 25B.
72   D. Dilks (ed.), *op. cit.*, p 545, p 534.
73   FO 800/301/94.
74   FO 800/301/102.
75   *Ibid.*, p 104.
76   PREM 3, 237–11.
77   FO 36956/4630.
78   Herbert Feis, *Churchill, Roosevelt, Stalin* (Princeton University Press, 1957), p 170.
79   FO 800/301/110.
80   FO 800/301/92.
81   Harriman, Abel, *op. cit.*, p 225.
82   Werth, *op. cit.*, p 747.
83   D.Dilks (ed.), *op. cit.*, p 565.
84   *Ibid.*, p 564.
85   FO 800/301/127.

86   PREM 3, 237–11.
87   Ted Morgan, *FDR* (London, Grafton Books, 1986), p 677ff.
88   Numerous sources for reports of this conference. For a US perspective see FRUS and memoirs such as J.R. Deane, *The Strange Alliance* (London, Murray, 1947).
89   W. Churchill, *Closing the Ring* (London, Cassell, 1952), p 256.
90   Harriman, Abel, *op. cit.*, p 238.
91   Werth, *op. cit.*, p 747.
92   Kitchen, *op. cit.*, p 168.
93   W.A. Harriman and E. Abel, *op. cit.*, p 236.
94   J. Harvey, ed., (2) *op. cit.*, entry for 22 October 1943.
95   J. Lehmann, *op. cit.*, p 150.
96   *The Times*, 12 November 1943.
97   *Ibid.*
98   Abel Harriman, *op. cit.*, p 254.
99   *Ibid.*, p 255.
100 FO 800/301/250ff.
101 Hugh de Santis, *The Diplomacy of Silence* (University of Chicago Press, 1979), p 103; A. Werth, *op. cit.*, p 753.
102 FO 800/301/250.
103 Harriman, Abel, *op. cit.*, p 256.
104 Arthur Birse, *Memoirs of an Interpreter* (London, Michael Joseph, 1967), p 151–2.
105 Sir Archibald Clark Kerr's diary suggests that this may have been a.m. on 28 November (Bodleian Files).
106 Abel Harriman, *op. cit.*, p 263.
107 *Ibid.*, p 262.
108 David Dilks (ed.), *op. cit.*, p 586.
109 Lord Moran, *Churchill – The Struggle For Survival, 1940–65* (London, Constable, 1968), p 135.
110 Entry in diary of Sir Archibald Clark Kerr (Bodleian Files)
111 FO 800/301/240.
112 Moran, *op. cit.*, p 143.
113 Lord Boothby, *op. cit.*, p 28.
114 K. Young (ed.), *op. cit.*, p 394.
115 FO 371 39386.
116 PREM 3, 355–8.
117 *Ibid.*
118 Kitchen, *op. cit.*, p 182.
119 Loewenheim, Langley and Jonas (eds), *op. cit.*, p 461.
120 PREM 3, 355–9.
121 *Ibid.*
122 FO 800/302/36.
123 Dilks (ed.), *op. cit.*, p 613.
124 M. Gilbert, *Winston S. Churchill* vol. 7, *Road To Victory 1941–1945* (London, Heinemann, 1986), p 754.
125 FO 43408/2340.
126 Victor Rothwell, *Britain and the Cold War 1941–47* (London, Jonathan Cape, 1982), p 170.
127 Loewenheim, Langley and Jonas, (eds), *op. cit.*, p 556.
128 Abel Harriman, *op. cit.*, p 343.
129 FO 371 43306.

130 FO 800/302/192ff.
131 FO 371/43336 para. 12.
132 W. Churchill, *Triumph and Tragedy* (London, Cassell, 1954), p 190.
133 Tom Barman, *Diplomatic Correspondent* (London, Hamish Hamilton, 1968), p 172.
134 V. Rothwell, *op. cit.*, p 172.
135 M. Gilbert, *op. cit.*, p 1072; Werth, *op. cit.*, p 91.
136 W. Churchill, *op. cit.* [7:132], p 211.
137 FO 371 40725.
138 D. Dilks (ed.), *op. cit.*, p 698.
139 Harriman, Abel, *op. cit.*, p 388.
140 D. Dilks (ed.) *op. cit.*, p 705ff.
141 *Ibid.*, p 720.
142 Joan Bright Astley, *The Inner Circle* (London, Hutchinson, 1971), p 196.
143 Harriman, Abel, *op. cit.*, p 416; Charles Bohlen, *Witness to History* (London, Weidenfeld, 1973), p 354–5.
144 Astley, *op. cit.*, p 162.
145 W. Churchill, *op. cit.* [7:132], p 351.
146 Harriman, Abel, *op. cit.*, p 427.
147 M. Gilbert, *op. cit.*, p 1242.
148 FO 371 47941.
149 *The Leader*, 3 February 1945.
150 K. Young (ed.), *op. cit.*, p 377.
151 FO 800/303/151.
152 FO 800/303/43.
153 *Chicago Tribune*, 1 November 1946.
154 Letter from Felix Frankfurter to Richard Casey, 8 January 1943 (Bodleian Files).
155 H. Feis, *op. cit.*, p 578.
156 W. Churchill, *op. cit.*, [7:132], p 439.
157 Sir Berkeley Gage, *op. cit.*, p 128; Hugh Thomas, *Armed Truce* (London, Sceptre Paperbacks, 1986), p 301.
158 PREM 3, 396–12.
159 FO 371 47076.
160 Documents on British Policy Overseas, ed. R. Butler, Series I, vol. I (1984), p 79.
161 FO 371 47883.
162 DBPO, *op. cit.*, p 142–148.
163 *Ibid.*, p 769.
164 W.H. MacNeill, *America, Britain, and Russia 1941–1946* (London, Oxford University Press, 1953), p 613.
165 DBPO, p 345–6.
166 *Ibid.*, p 499.
167 *Ibid.*, p 968.
168 *Ibid.*
169 *Ibid.*, p 1049.
170 Abel Harriman, *op. cit.*, p 495ff.
171 FO 371 47883.
172 *Ibid.*
173 A. Bullock, *Ernest Bevin, Foreign Secretary 1945–51* (London, Heinemann, 1985), p 132–3; *Documents on British Foreign Policy Overseas*, ed. Butler, Series I, vol. II (1985), p 316.

174 Bullock, *op. cit.*, p 134; DBPO (II), p 447ff.
175 DBPO(II), p 449f.
176 G. Ross, *op. cit.*, p 259.
177 FO 800/303/173ff.
178 Bullock, *op. cit.*, p 72–3.
179 FO 800/446/CONF/45/4.
180 FO 800/303/183.
181 FO 800/303/187.
182 DBPO (I), p 151.
183 DBPO (II), p 669.
184 *Ibid.*, p 903–4.
185 P. Dixon, *Double Diploma: The Life of Sir Pierson Dixon* (London, Hutchinson, 1968), p 203.
186 1946 Files (Bodleian) no. 16, 5 January 1946.
187 Letter to author from Walter Bell, CMG.
188 FO 59095/505.
189 1946 Files (Bodleian) no. 59, 11 January 1946.
190 Letter to author from King Michael of Rumania, 6 March 1990.
191 FO 181/1022.20.46.
192 A. Bullock, *op. cit.*, p 100.

CHAPTER 8 – PINNACLE 1942–1946

1 John Balfour, *Not Too Correct An Aureole* (London, Michael Russell, 1983), p 104; K. Young (ed.), *op. cit.*
2 See Lord Boothby, *op. cit.*; Sir Robert V. Rhodes James, *op. cit.*; see also Randolph Churchill in the *Daily Telegraph*, 11 December 1945.
3 Paul Kennedy, *The Realities Behind Diplomacy* (London, Allen & Unwin, 1981), p 317–8; R.M. Hathaway, *Ambiguous Partnership: Britain and America 1944–47* (New York, Columbia University Press, 1981), p 23–5; R. Eatwell, *The 1945–51 Labour Governments* (London, Batsford Academic, 1979), p 70.
4 Radio broadcast, BBC 1950.
5 R.M. Hathaway, *op. cit.*, p 225.
6 PRO CO(46) 40 CAB 131/2.
7 The *Sunday Star* (Washington), 5 May 1946; *St Louis Post-Despatch*, 23 June 1946; *New York Times Magazine*, 23 June 1946; *New Yorker*, 8 June 1946; *Newsweek*, 8 July 1946; *Saturday Evening Post* (Pa.), 28 September 1946; *Collier's Magazine*, 25 May 1946.
8 FO 800/513/161.
9 *Evening Standard*, 30 May 1946.
10 *New York Herald-Tribune*, 30 May 1946.
11 *Washington Evening Star*, 30 May 1946; the full story of Yevgeni Yost is well told by Frank Giles in *The Sunday Times*, 6 January 1980.
12 *New Yorker*, 8 June 1946.
13 *Newsweek*, 8 July 1946.
14 *The Times*, 30 May 1946.
15 *Ibid.*, 6 June 1946.
16 *Washington Post*, 16 May 1946.
17 *New York Daily News*, 11 June 1946.

18 Documents on British Policy Overseas (hereafter DBPO), Series I, vol. IV (1987), p 326.
19 Ibid., p 366.
20 Ibid., p 367.
21 Newsweek, 8 July 1946.
22 DBPO (IV), p 367.
23 Ibid., p 279.
24 New York Times, 14 July 1946.
25 DBPO (IV), p 388.
26 Dean Acheson, *Present at the Creation* (London, Hamish Hamilton, 1969), p 178.
27 FO 800/513/172.
28 FO 800/513/179.
29 FO 800/513/183.
30 FO 800/513/234.
31 FO 371 52546.
32 FO 371 52560.
33 Hathaway, *op. cit.*, p 288.
34 A. Bullock, *op. cit.*, p 352.
35 *Seattle Post Intelligencer*, 12 September 1946.
36 *Salt Lake Tribune*, 31 August 1946.
37 *Chicago Tribune*, 1 November 1946.
38 FRUS (1947) vol. 5, p 1008–11.
39 Acheson, *op. cit.*, p 178ff.
40 FRUS (1946) vol. 7, p 723.
41 FO 800/475/ME/46/21.
42 FO 800/513/255; Bullock, *op. cit.*, p 344.
43 Balfour, *op. cit.*, p 111.
44 Telephone conversation with Sir Nicholas Henderson, 9 May 1990; Forrestal developed Cold War-induced paranoia, and met a tragic end: see Daniel Yergin, *Shattered Peace* (Boston, Houghton Mifflin, 1977), pp 206–8.
45 Letter to author from Walter Bell, CMG.
46 *Times Herald*, 2 February 1947.
47 FRUS (1947) vol. 4, p 528.
48 FRUS (1947) vol. 1, p 781–3.
49. Ibid., p 784.
50 Ibid., p 785.
51 FRUS (1946) vol. 1, p 1256.
52 FO 115/4335.
53 *The Times*, 22 February 1947.
54 FRUS (1947) vol. 5, p 43–6.
55 Ibid., p 45.
56 Ibid., p 71.
57 Ibid., pp 71, 73.
58 J.M. Jones, *The Fifteen Weeks* (New York, Viking Press, 1956), p 138ff.
59 FRUS (1947) vol. 5, pp 79, 105.
60 *Philadelphia Inquirer*, 18 May 1947.
61 *Daily Mirror*, 19 March 1947.
62 *Daily Mail*, 12 March, 22 March, 17 May 1947.
63 *New York Times*, 13 April 1947.
64 FO 800/514/14ff.

65 Jones, *op. cit.*, p 274.
66 Balfour, *op. cit.*, p 118.
67 This according to J. Balfour, *op. cit.* Inverchapel's diary for 1947 is not available but press reports indicate he was in the mid-west during this time. He gave speeches in Nebraska on 28 and 29 May, and spoke in Des Moines, Iowa, on 1 June. He followed this by a second visit to Eagle Grove Iowa and the Newburn farm. On 5 June itself he may well have been entrained returning east. He gave a speech at Lansdowne High School in Pennsylvania on 6 June. This is within easy reach of Washington and so he could have returned to the Embassy just before this date or immediately afterwards.

Most historical works dispute Balfour's account. For example, see John Dickie, *Special No More* (London, Weidenfeld & Nicolson, 1993), p 23.
68 FRUS (1947) vol. 3, pp 253, 256.
69 FRUS (1947) vol. 3, p 17.
70 Bullock, *op. cit.*, p 458.
71 N. Henderson, *The Private Office* (London, Weidenfeld & Nicolson, 1984), p 49.
72 *Glasgow Bulletin*, 12 December 1947.
73 FO 800/514/108.
74 *Ibid.*, p 116.
75 *Ibid.*, p 119.
76 Verne Newton, *The Butcher's Embrace: The Philby Conspirators in Washington* (London, Macdonald, 1991), p 394.
77 FO 800/514/119.
78 *Tribune*, 10 October 1947; *Evening Standard*, 10 October 1947; K. Young (ed.), *op. cit.*
79 *News Review*, 23 October 1947.
80 FO 800/514/167.
81 C. Rossiter, *Parties and Politics in America* (Ithaca, Cornell University Press, 1960), pp 125–6.
82 Bullock, *op. cit.*, pp 516–7.
83 FRUS (1948) vol. 3, p 3; p 9ff.
84 *Ibid.* p 19.
85 *Ibid.* p 48.
86 *Ibid.* p 59ff.
87 *Christian Science Monitor*, 17 March 1948.
88 *Boston Trawler*, 17 March 1948.
89 *Boston Evening Globe*, 17 March 1948.
90 *Chicago Sun Times*, 9 April 1948.
91 *Time*, 23 February 1948.
92 *St Louis Post-Despatch*, 13 January 1948.
93 *Washington Evening News*, 24 February 1948.
94 Telephone conversation with W.P.N. Edwards, 13 February 1990.
95 *The Journals of David E. Lilienthal* vol. II, *The Atomic Energy Years 1945–50* (New York, Harper & Row, 1964), p 381.
96 *Chicago Daily News*, 12 April 1948.
97 Henderson, *op. cit.*, pp 48–9; also conversation with author.
98 Conversations with Sir Nicholas Henderson and Bill Edwards.
99 Sir Frank Roberts, 'Ernest Bevin as Foreign Secretary' in R. Ovendale (ed.), *The Foreign Policy of the British Labour Governments 1945–51* (Leicester, Leicester

University Press, 1984), pp 24, 27; Michael Charlton, *The Price of Victory* (London, BBC, 1983), p 48–9.
100 Robert Cecil, *A Divided Life: A Biography of Donald Maclean* (London, The Bodley Head, 1988), p 93.
101 *Ibid.*, p 105.
102 John Costello, *op. cit.*
103 V. Newton, *op. cit.*, p 17.
104 Costello, *op. cit.*; see A. Glees, *op. cit.*, p 271 for rebuttal.
105 Cecil, *op. cit.*, p 68.
106 *Ibid.*, p 83.
107 Felix Frankfurter in *The Times*, 24 July 1951.

CHAPTER 9 – CAIRN 1948–1951

1 Marcel Proust, *Remembrance of Things Past*, vol. 2: *Swann's Way* 'Place Names' trans. C.K. Scott Moncrieff (London, Chatto & Windus, 1943), p 287.
2 Ben Pimlott (ed.), *op. cit.*
3 Letter from Lord Inverchapel (Bodleian); FO 800/303/242.
4 *West Africa*, 1 January 1949; *Sunday Despatch*, 17 February 1946.
5 *Evening News*, 21 December 1948.
6 See Sir Robert V. Rhodes James, *op. cit.*
7 From 'Noonday Axeman' in Les Murray, *Collected Poems* (Manchester, Carcanet Press, 1991), pp 6–7. Reproduced with kind permission.

Index

Abbas Hilmi (Khedive) 32, 49, 50, 60
Abdin Palace 61
Abyssinia 83, 86
Acheson, Dean 197, 199, 201, 202, 203; on European recovery programme (1947) 205f
Aden 33
Adly Pasha 33, 34
Adriatic 187
Afghanistan 20, 146
Afifi 54
Agar-Robartes, Francis Gerald 'Greg' *see* Clifden, Viscount
Alexander, Prince, of Greece 16
Alexander, John 93
Alexandria 36, 41 46, 50, 52, 58, 61, 68
Algiers 156
Allen, W.D. 173
Allenby, Lord 32, 33, 35, 36, 37, 39, 41, 43, 44, 45, 46, 47, 48, 50; Clark Kerr's view of 35, 37, 65; drink problems 37, 56; and 1924 talks 48; in London 49, 51; and MacDonald 52; returns to Egypt 55; and death of Sirdar 37, 56; response 56–60; goes to Egyptian Parliament 59; ignores FO cable 59; response to FO 63; to Zaghlul 59–60 ; FO reaction 61–62; disputes Henderson's appointment 63–64; tenders resignation 64; 65–66; 68; 72; 153
Alley, Rewi 93–94, 114
Alnwick 28
Alsop, Joe 114, 190
Amine Youssef Bey 36
Amos, Sir Maurice Sheldon 35, 38, 47, 56, 66
Ampelisca 6
Anders, Gen. Wladyslaw 136
Anglo-Soviet Treaty (1942) 123–4, 127, 128, 143
Angus 39
Annapolis 190
Antonescu, Ion 178
Archangel 137
Argentina 14, 15, 16
Argyll, Duke of 25, 28, 180
Argyllshire 1, 111, 176, 213, 221, 222, 227
Asia 87, 88, 99, 173, 223

Asquith, Herbert 55, 62
Astor, J.J., MP 48, 72
Astor, Nancy 72
Atbara 50
Athens 11, 12, 16, 78
Atlantic 48, 188, 207, 210, 212, 213
Atlantic Charter (1941) 123–4, 147
Atlantic Monthly 225
Attlee, Clement 124; becomes PM 172; at Potsdam 172–4; 185–6; and atomic weapons 186, 195; 207, 220, 226
Australia 1, 3, 5–6, 7, 14, 70–71, 118
Axis 20, 24
Azores 168

Bagallay, Lacy 123, 146
Baghdad 80–84, 118, 218
Bakr Sidqi, Gen. 84
Baldwin, Stanley 43; returns to power 55
Balfour, Sir John (Jock) 146, 163, 167, 181, 189, 205
Balfour, Arthur, Lord 24, 25, 26; 'Declaration' 185
Balkans 16, 138–9, 158, 161, 179
Balniel, Lord David (later Earl of Crawford and Balcarres) 72
Balmoral 11
Baltic states 123–24, 138
'Barbarossa' (German invasion of USSR, June 1941) 116, 117, 120–22
Barclay, Agnes 2, 14
Barclay Clarks 3, 5, 8–9
Barman, Tom 117; to Moscow Embassy staff 146; 156, 167
Barrington, Eric 22
Bath 5
Bath College 6, 8, 70
BBC 140, 182, 222, 223, 224
Beauchamp, Earl 7
Beaverbrook, Lord mission to USSR 121; resigns 124; 140
Bee, HMS 89
Belgium 206, 212
Benelux 212
Benmore 219
Bergen 18
Beria, Lavrenti 164–65
Berlin 10ff, 23, 103, 170, 179
Berliner Tageblatt 117

Berners, Lord (Gerald Tyrrwhitt-Wilson) 10
Bertram, James 114, 115
Bessarabia 138
Bevin, Ernest 171; appointed Foreign Secretary 172; at Potsdam 172; 174, 174–75, 175–76; in Moscow 176–77, 179–80, 181, 188; and Palestine 185–86, 191; 190, 192, 195; rejects US tour 192–93; in US 196–98; 199; Palestine mandate 200–1; 202, 204; response to Marshall Plan 205ff; 208–9, 210; and 'Western Union' 211; and NATO 212; 215; and European unity 220–21; 227
Bias Bay, China 98
Bierut, Boleslaw 162
Birkenhead, Lord 63
Birse, Arthur 136, 153, 154, 164, 168
Blackburn, Sir Arthur 92, 113
Blairmore 1
Blenheim Palace 25
Bloom, Sol 191, 192
Boers 8
Boggabri, N.S.W. 3, 5
Bohlen, Charles E. 'Chip' 153, 154
Bolshevik(s) 53, 141, 222
Bolshoi ballet 124
Bonn University 70
Boothby, Robert, Lord 18, 25, 35, 36, 72, 74, 80, 81, 84, 88, 108, 183, 225
Bournemouth 191
Bow (Essex) 3
Bowes-Lyon, Elizabeth *see* Elizabeth, HM Queen
Bratianu, Constantin 177–78
Brenan, Sir John 102, 109
Bridgeman, Reginald 10
Bridges, Sir Edward 164
British-China Association 226
British Merchants Morocco Association 28
British Petroleum 81
Brooke, Sir Alan 132, 139, 140, 156
Brown, G.H. 'Harry' 5
Brussels Conference (1938) 88
Brussels Treaty (1948) 212, 220

245

Bryce, James, Lord 15
Buchan, John 59, 73
Bucharest 16, 165–66, 176, 177
Buckingham Palace 182, 223
Bucks Club 28
Budyenni, Marshal Semyon 137
Buenos Aires 14
Bulgaria 138, 159, 161, 166, 174–75, 176, 177
Burgess, Guy 140, 226
Burke's Peerage 71, 183
Burma 96, 100, 112, 223
Burma Road 96, 100; closure 109; 110; reopens 110; 113
Bushey, Guards Training Camp 25
Bute 28, 227
Bute, Marquis of 25, 29
Byrnes, James 171, 175, 176–77, 190, 197, 198

Cadogan family 40
Cadogan, Sir Alec 95, 123–24, 130, 131, 132, 133, 136, 137, 154, 158; exasperation with Churchill 164; 168, 171, 176; at UN 188
Cairncross, John 145, 218
Cairo 29; Chapter 4 passim; 72, 73, 81, 129, 130, 137, 152–53, 156
Calder, Ritchie 140
Cambridge 218
Campbell (ADC to Sir Lee Stack) 55–56
Campbell, Ian 25, 28
Canada 186–87, 188, 191, 194
Canton 90; captured 98; 99, 100
'Carlton-Browne of the FO' 28
Carol, King of Rumania 16
Casablanca 139
Castle Toward 2
Castro, Zaghlul's Press Officer 51
Caucasus 139
Cavendish-Bentinck, William (Duke of Portland) 79
Cecil, Lord Robert 24
Cecilienhof 171
Chamberlain, Austen 33, 55; and response to Sirdar's death 58, 61; and Allenby 33, 62ff; 67, 69, 72, 77, 79
Chamberlain, Neville 85, 87, 88, 89; blocks aid to China 95; 96, 103, 106, 109, 118
Changsa 98, 99
Cheng Lien-shih 103–4
Cherbakov 151

Cherbourg 139
Chialing River 111
Chiang Kai-shek 86, 91, 93, 93, 95, 96, 97, 98, 99, 99–100, 101, 104, 109–10, 111, 114, 115–16, 118; in Cairo 152–53; 167; political outlook 91, 115–16, 214
Chiang, Madame 89, 91, 94, 104, 153
Chicago 193, 212
Chicago Daily News 214–15
Chicago Tribune 195
Chile 13, 40, 74–77, 103, 118
China 34, 72, 84; Chapter 6 passim; 120, 122, 124, 132, 148, 150, 173, 181–82, 198, 200, 214, 223, 227
China Association 88–89, 106
China Department (Foreign Office) 10, 90
Chou En-lai 112, 115, 223
Christian Science Monitor 117
Chungking 86, 90, 103; description 103; bombing 104–5; 108, 110–11, 112, 113, 115, 116, 120
Churchill, George 21, 31
Churchill, Winston 18, 25, 33, 37; defects to Tories 53; 63, 71–72, 73, 74, 85; becomes PM 109; 110, 111, 114; aid to USSR 120–21; on USSR 122; 123, 124; Second Front 128–29; 130; visit to Moscow (1942) 129–37; 139, 141; on imperialism 147; on Katyn 142–43; in Quebec 144–45; 147, 148, 152; in Cairo 153; at Teheran 153–156; on Polish question 157–159; presses for Stalin meeting 159; visit to Moscow (1944) 160–63; at Yalta 164–65; effusive on USSR 165; 169; at Potsdam 171; election defeat 172; 182, 184, 185; 'Iron Curtain' speech 187, 198; 193, 206, 220, 227
Civil Service Commission 22
Clark family 1, 13, 74, 76, 77, 207, 219, 226, 227
Clark, Archibald (1819–1900) 1, 5, 219
Clark, Lady Beatrice Kerr (nee Moore) 23, 24
Clark, Duncan 3
Clark, Gwladys (Mrs Prickett) (sister) 5
Clark, James (grandfather) 1–3, 6, 14

Clark, John Kerr (father) 1, 2ff, 5–6, 8, 9; death 14; 71, 74
Clark, Kate (Mrs Astley) (sister) 5
Clark, Kate Louisa Robertson Kerr (mother) 1, 3, 4–5, 6–7, 14, 16, 18, 21, 22, 23, 26, 35, 40, 43; visits Egypt 44; 53, 65, 67, 68; to Guatemala 73; death 40, 73–74; 76
Clark, Lois Mairi Kerr (Lady Lewthwaite) 23
Clark, Mairi (Mrs Vickers) (sister) 5, 22, 74
Clark, Margaret (Mrs G.H. Brown) (sister) 5, 14, 22
Clark, Muriel (sister) 5, 11, 14, 15, 22, 65; death 67; 73, 74
Clark, Struan Robertson Kerr ('Robin') (brother) 5, 7, 16–17, 22; killed 23; 24
Clark Kerr, Sir Archibald John Kerr *see* Inverchapel, 1st Baron
Clark Kerr, Maria-Theresa 'Tita' (nee Diaz Salas) *see* Inverchapel, Lady
Clayton, William 206; resignation 209
Clifden, Viscount 10
'Clovelly' 1, 5
Clyde, River 75, 76, 226
Cold War 122, 181–82, 184, 203, 224
Colefax, Lady 174
Colorado 195
Comintern 143
Commercial Department (FO) 23–25
Communism in China 92, 93, 100, 112, 114–18; New Fourth Army clash 112; 122–23; general 122, 159, 173, 181–82; in France 187, 196; postwar 187, 194, 211, 212, 223
Conference (Council) of Foreign Ministers: Moscow 1943 146–50, 154, 201; London 1945 173, 174–75, 176; Moscow 1945 176; Paris 1946 187, 190, 191; New York 1946 196ff; London 1947 211
Confucius 111, 164
Conservative Party *see also* Tory Party 44, 46; 1924 landslide 55; 88; Stalin toasts 156; 1945 defeat 173
Constantine, King of Greece 11, 16
Constantinople 67

INDEX

Cossacks 23
Cowal 2
Coylet 220
Cracow 166
Craigie, Sir Robert 88, 96, 97, 98, 100, 102; talks in Shanghai 103; 104, 106; talks with Japanese 107; 'Craigie-Arita formula' 108; 108–9
Crimea 164
Cripps, Sir Stafford 110, 113, 121; return from USSR 122; 124, 126, 127
Crossbasket House 2, 3, 71
Crossman, Richard 140
Crowe, Sir Eyre 66
Cunard, Lady 174
Cunninghame Graham, R.B. 73
Curzon, Lord 25, 33, 48
Curzon Line 156, 157, 162
Czechoslovakia 125, 143, 144, 146, 170, 211; Communist coup (1948) 211, 212

Daily Express 43; and Ramsay MacDonald 51; 226
Daily Mail 192, 203
Daily Mirror 203
Dalton, Hugh 77, 78, 81; visits US 195; 200, 204, 206, 207; European union talks 220–21
Davies, Joe 143, 168
Davies, Margaret E. 3
Dawson, Geoffrey 80
de Gaulle, Charles 187
Deane, Lt-Gen. John 148, 153
Delaney, Gerald 35, 37, 43, 44, 47; plan to defeat Zaghlul 53; 60, 61, 65, 68–69, 153
Detroit 210
Diaz Salas, Maria Theresa 'Tita' *see* Inverchapel, Lady
Diplomatic Service 6–7, 8, 9, 10, 22, 173, 180, 216
Don River (USSR) 129
Douglas, Lew 203
Driberg, Tom 114, 167
Drogheda, Earl of 24
Drummond, Air-Marshal 139
Dryburgh 76
Dumbarton Oaks Conference (Washington 1944) 161
Dunkirk, Treaty of (1947) 206
Dunlop, John 131, 136
Dutch East Indies 112, 181, 182

Eagle Grove (Iowa) 195
Eastern Department, FO 25, 31
Eck, Loch 1, 24, 74, 77, 180, 183, 207, 219, 220, 223, 226, 228

Eden, Anthony 81, 84, 85, 87; resignation (1938) 90; appointed Foreign Secretary 111; 113; in Moscow 1941 122–23; 124, 126, 129, 130, 136, 139; on postwar reconstruction 141; 144; at CFM (1943) 146–50; commanding role 149; Clark Kerr's opinion of 149; praises Clark Kerr 50; 151; at Teheran 153–56; 158; in Moscow (1944) 161–63; at Yalta 164–65; in Washington and San Francisco (1945) 168–69; at Potsdam 171; election defeat 172; 227
Edinburgh 71, 76, 183, 207
Edinburgh, University of 2
Edmont's Hotel 5
Edward VIII, HM King (Duke of Windsor) 39; in Sweden 79, 81
Egypt Chapter 4 passim; 68, 69, 71, 73, 77, 81, 88
Ehrenberg, Ilya 149
Eisenhower, Gen. Dwight D. 225
Elisabeth of Rumania, Princess 16
Elizabeth, HM Queen, the Queen Mother 28, 39–40, 75, 206, 227
Elizabeth II, HM Queen 40
Engels, Friedrich 145, 212
England 5, 10, 21, 67, 77, 139, 140, 174, 204
Essex 3
Eton 25, 77, 217, 218
Etter 23
European Advisory Commission (EAC) 144, 148, 149
Evening Standard 77

Faisal, King of Iraq 82
FBI 206
Fierlinger, Dr Z. 125, 143
Finland 121, 174
Finlay, James and Co. 2, 3
Finlay, Kirkman 2
Fleming, Peter 96
Foreign Office 8, 9–10, 16, 17, 18–19, 21, 22, 23, 24, 25, 31, 32, 37, 41, 42, 47, 48, 51, 52, 53, 55, 69, 74, 77, 80, 82; and World War I 16–20, 22, 23–25; working practices 9–10, 28; response to death of Sirdar 56–66, 72; and Allenby 33, 56–64; and China 87, 88, 90, 95, 96, 98, 100, 102, 106, 107, 109,
111, 113, 115, 116, 118; and Japan 88, 97, 107, 110; and Cripps 121–22; and USSR 122–24, 125, 127, 128, 136, 138–40, 141, 142; rethink 144–45; 145, 147, 154; and Polish issue 158, 163, 164; 166, 168, 169, 170–71, 173, 174, 175, 176, 178, 182, 198; and Marshall Plan 205ff; 208–9, 213; and Soviet agents 217–18
Forfar 39
Forrestal, James F. 198
France 8, 48, 76; and Tangier 26–29; and China 97, 100, 102; fall of (1940) 121; 128–29, 136, 154, 174–75, 187, 196, 206, 211, 212, 217
Franco 85
Frankfurter, Felix 15, 208
Franks, Sir Oliver 192, 208, 210, 213, 215
Franz Ferdinand, Archduke 16
Frederick III, Kaiser 11
French North Africa 128, 131
Friedrichsdof 11
Fuad, Sultan (King of Egypt) 32, 34, 36, 37, 38–39, 40, 41, 43, 44, 61, 66
Fulbright, James W. 203, 220
Fulton, Missouri 187, 198
Furness, Robin 38, 48, 153

Gallipoli 129
GATT 208
General Strike (1926) 74
Geneva 71, 208
George, Prince of Greece 16
George V, HM King 64, 81, 82
George VI, HM King 39–40, 154, 171, 206, 227
Germany *see also* Nazis 8, 10ff, 20, 107, 108, 109, 110, 120–21, 122, 129, 137, 139, 140, 141, 149, 154, 155, 156, 159, 163, 164, 168; surrender (1945) 169; 172, 173, 181, 184, 194, 204, 208
Gezira 57ff
Ghazi, King of Iraq 82–84
Ghoolendaadi 3, 4, 7, 9, 14
Gibraltar 26, 33, 41
Ginsberg, Samuel *see* Krivitsky, Walter
Glamis Castle 28, 39–40
Glasgow 2, 76, 182, 223, 226
Glasgow, University of 2, 182, 225–26

Gore-Booth, Paul 189
Goschen, Sir Edward 11
Gouzenko, Igor 186
Greece 11, 16, 77, 158, 166, 168, 176, 185, 187; surrender of mandate (1947) 200–202, 211, 215
Greenock 2, 226
Grenadier Guards 17
Groza, Dr Petru 177–79
The Guardian 117
Guatemala 71, 73–74
Gusev F. (USSR ambassador) 143–44, 147, 169
Gustav, Prince of Sweden 79

Hackworth, Green 148
The Hague 220
Haking, Gen. 52
Halifax, Lord 90, 92, 95, 97, 99, 100; and Tientsin crisis (1939) 104, 105, 106, 107; to Washington 111; 124, 125, 128, 148, 186, 190
Halifax (Nova Scotia) 188
Hamilton 5, 71
Hankow 86, 90, 91, 94, 95, 96, 97; captured 98; 100
Hannay, Richard 20
Hardinge, Lord 24
Harriman, W. Averell 121; with Churchill in Moscow (1942) 130, 131, 132; offered Moscow post 143; 147–48, 151, 152, 153; in Teheran 153–56, 159; Polish talks 160–61, 164–65; 168, 174, 176; in Romania 177–79
Harriman, Kathleen 151, 153
Harris, Walter 26f
Hatieganu, Emil 179
Harvey, Sir Oliver 95, 142, 149
Helena, Princess of Greece (later Queen of Rumania) 16, 179
Hemingway, Ernest 111
Henderson, Lord 221
Henderson, Loy 201, 203
Henderson, Nevile 10; appointed to Egypt 62–67; 103
Henderson, Sir Nicholas 215
Hersey, John 111
Hess, Rudolph 121–22
Hickerson, Jack 203, 208, 212
High Blantyre 2
Hiroshima 174
Hitler, Adolf 87, 103, 116, 120, 137, 139, 142, 184
Hoare, Rex 10
Hodge (Lord Inverchapel's pet alsatian) 74, 76, 111; death 118–19
Holy Loch 226
Honduras 71, 73
Hong Kong 89, 90, 94, 95, 98, 99, 104, 105, 110
Hopkins, Harry 154, 168, 170
House of Commons 33, 35, 48, 72, 135, 150, 165, 200
House of Lords 49, 183, 221
Howe, R.G. 89
Hull, Cordell at Moscow Conference (1943) 147–49; 154
Hungary 159, 161, 174
Hunter River 3

Ibrahim Yehia 39, 41, 66
Ichang 91
Idaho 195
Iddons, Don 203
India 2, 21, 30, 81, 118, 196, 200, 204
Indochina 112
Indonesia *see* Dutch East Indies
Indusco 94, 100
Inverchapel, Loch Eck 1, 5, 8–9, 13, 23, 24, 25, 36, 39, 42, 48, 69, 71, 74, 76, 77, 98, 163, 175, 176, 182, 206–7, 219, 220, 224, 225
Inverchapel, Sir Archibald John Kerr Clark Kerr, 1st Baron, of Loch Eck ancestry 1–4; birth 1,5; childhood in Australia 5; school in Bath 6; Diplomatic Service preparations 8; visits France 8; holidays in Scotland 8; early interests and attitudes 8; at Scoon's 8; at Inverchapel 9; fails exam for Diplomatic Service 1905 9; passes exam 1906 9; starts in Foreign Office 9; social life 1906 9–10; posted to Berlin (1906) 10; friendship with Princess Sophie 11–12; relationship with Louvima Knollys 11; promoted to Third Secretary 11; meets Kaiser 12; desires Rome 13; meets Harold Nicolson 13; leaves Berlin 13; reviews Berlin years 13; character 13–14; posted to Buenos Aires (1910) 14; trip to Paraguay 14; death of father 14; in London 14; posted to Washington (1911) 14; changes name 14–15; attitude to Lord Bryce 15;
friendship with Lord Eustace Percy 15; end of Knollys relationship 15; offer of Teheran 15–16; FO attitude 16; posted to Rome (1913) 16; reaction 16; lack of promotion 16; Mediterranean Cruise 16; reunion with Princess Sophie 16; tries to enlist 16–17; lobbies Ambassador Rodd 17; FO blocks enlistment 17; threatens resignation 17; posted to Teheran (late 1914) 17–18; secures Churchill's help 18; travels to Persia 18–19; worry at Townleys' departure 21; unhappy at Mission's performance 21; attitude to Charles Marling 21; attitude to George Churchill 21; language progress 21; goes native 22; death of brother 23; becomes Commercial Secretary 23; joins Cossacks 23; eye trouble 23; sent home 23; visits Scotland 23; joins Commercial Department at FO (1917) 23; object of whispering campaign 24; approaches Hardinge 24; obtains letter of explanation 24; tries to enlist 24; appeal rejected 24; new scheme to enlist 24–25; joins Scots Guards (1918) 25; at Bushey training camp 25; meets Robert Boothby 25; back at FO (1919) 25; at Blenheim 25; meets Churchill 25; in Eastern Department FO 26; and Zionism 26; offer of post in Palestine 26; promotion to First Secretary 26; posted to Tangier (1919) 26; promotion to Consul-General 26; situation ideal 27; attitude to International Zone 27; attitude to Times correspondent 27; efforts to influence press 28; leave in Scotland 28; arranges letter to Times 28–29; posted to Cairo (1922) 29; status of post in Egypt 30; resume of experience 31; arrival in Cairo 35; attitude to Allenby 35; friendship with Gerald Delaney 35; home leave 36; attitude to Egyptian situation

248

INDEX

36–37; attitude to rise of Labour Party 37; delight at Churchill's defeat 37; bullies Tewfik Nessim 38; awareness of Allenby's limitations 38; plan to reduce King's powers 38; success of plan 38–39 relationship with Elizabeth Bowes-Lyon (HM Queen Mother) 39–40; reaction to her engagement to Duke of York 40; new house 41; persuades Allenby to lift exile of nationalists 41; sympathy with nationalists 41; bribery 41; personal involvement in Egyptian affairs 42; political outlook 42; visits Inverchapel 42; London meetings 42–43; Acting Counsellor 43; attitude to Labour government 42, 43–44; mother visits 44; meets Zaghlul in secret 44; reaction to Egyptian election 45; meets Zaghlul re amnesty 46–47; FO's happiness with work 47; surprise at stubborn FO attitude to Egypt 47–48; London leave 1924 48; meetings in London 48; holiday 48; as Charge d'Affaires 49; rebukes Egyptian Premier 50; and Ramsay MacDonald 'error' 51; considers resignation 51; lobbies London to be more conciliatory 51; disappointed at failure of talks (Oct. 1924) 52; attitude to Ramsay MacDonald 52–53; non-imperialist outlook 53; strategy to sideline Zaghlul 53–54; change of British government 55; shooting of Sirdar 55–56; reaction to shooting 56; plans response with Allenby 56–57; disappointed FO line 57; presses FO strongly 58; ignores FO cable 58–59; reaction to situation 59 supports Allenby's hard line 60–61; fury at posting of Nevile Henderson 63; aware of likely punishment 65–66; opprobrium from FO 66; Sir Eyre Crowe's anger 66; death of sister 67; posting to Japan 68; leaves Egypt 68; reflections on Egypt years 68–69; worry at FO reaction 69; at Inverchapel 69; decides to leave Diplomatic Service 69; fails to find work 69; falsifies *Who's Who* entry 69–70; Scottish identity 70–71; plans for Inverchapel 71; appointed Minister to Guatemala (1925) 71; meets Churchill at Waverley 71–72; meets Austen Chamberlain 72; trouble with FO smoothed 72; contacts at Westminster 72–73; takes mother to Central America 73; butterflies for Mr. Churchill 73; accredited to Honduras, Nicaragua, Salvador 73; attitude to USA 73; death of mother 73–74; boredom 74; anxiety over new posting 74; appointed to Chile (1928) 74; speech in Valparaiso 75; Scottishness 75–76; meets Maria Theresa Diaz Salas 76; marriage 77; to Britain 77; leaves Chile 77; looks forward to fatherhood 77; Maria Theresa's illness 77; death of child 77–78; appointed to Sweden (1931) 78; boredom 78; portrait by Virginia Woolf 78–79; Prince of Wales visit 79; contemplates resignation 79; offered Mexico 79; FO view of him 80; attitude to marriage 80; hint of Moscow 80; diplomatic 'cockteasing' 80; appointed Ambassador to Iraq (1935) 80; knighthood conferred 80; review of Swedish years 80; knighted 80; journey to Iraq 81; convinced of own future success 81; reports on Iraqi king 82–83; appointed Ambassador to China (late 1937) 84; delight at recognition 84; unease over Chamberlain 85; view of Sino-Japanese conflict 85; China brief 88; audience with Chamberlain 88; meets China Association Committee 88–89; leaves for China 89; arrives in Hong Kong 89; meets T.V. Soong 89; visits bomb sites 90; travels to Chungking 90; presents credentials 90; to Hankow 91; meets Chiang Kai-shek 91; returns to Shanghai 91; argues for aid to China 92; backs Indusco scheme 93; meets Edgar Snow 92–93; visits Mme Sun Yat-sen 94; prods Kung for funds 94; poses as socialist 95; meets Agnes Smedley 95; disappointed at Cabinet refusal of aid 95; meets Chiang in Hankow 96; invites Craigie to Shanghai 96; lobbies FO re peace initiative 97; depression at Munich agreement 97; meets Chiang in Changsa 99; respect for Chiang 99–100; warns FO over aid inaction 100; dismisses Wang's defection 100; tribute from journalists 100–1; worry over Chinese action on loans 101; visits Tientsin 102; resists Japanese pressure 102; talks with Craigie 103; considered for Berlin post 103; life in Chungking 103; refuses to cooperate re Tientsin assassination 104; warns Chiang on terrorism 104; backs internment as answer 104; refuses to sanction handing over suspects 104; blocks Jamieson's plans 104; assassination threat 105; bullet-proof protection 106; rows with Craigie 106; worried over Craigie-Japanese talks 107; 'Far Eastern Munich' 107; fears action will push USSR and Germany together 107; reaction to expulsion of suspects 107; hopes for US support against Japan 108; seeks informal contact with Japanese regime 109; disappointed at Burma Road closure 110; relieved at reopening 110; refuses to move Embassy 111; sneers at Hemingway's machismo 111; life in Chungking house 111; quoted for Washington post 111; US journalists' backing 111; admiration for Chou 112; talks in Singapore 112; Tita deserts 112; reaction 112–13; letters to Tita 113; announces Burma Road remaining open 113; refuses to move Embassy 113; awarded GCMG 113; appointed Ambassador to

USSR (1942) 113; farewell to China 114; review of China years 114; assessment of communist power 115; awareness of likely Mao victory 116; friendship with Gunther Stein 117; travels to India 118; arrives in Kuibyshev 119; atmosphere in Kuibyshev 120, 124–5; views on occupation of Baltic states 124; delight at 1942 Treaty 124; work with Vyshinski 124; frustration in Kuibyshev 124–25; dislike of diplomatic circle 125; travels to Moscow 125; meeting with Stalin 125–26; analyses rapport with Stalin 126; view of Molotov 126; attitude to Soviet atrocities 126; seeks leave 127; Vyshinski party 127; importance of relation with Stalin 127–28; routine in Kuibyshev 128; interview with Molotov re Second Front 128; raises Churchill visit 129; describes Churchill's arrival 130; makes Washington ambition known 130; tribute to Churchill's abilities 131; accompanies Churchill to Kremlin 131; annoyance at Harriman 131; rouses Churchill's wrath 131–32; dislike of Alan Brooke 132; dropped by Churchill for second Kremlin visit 132; refuses to valet Churchill 132; disappointed at Churchill's behaviour 133; crucial talk with Churchill in garden 133ff; Churchill's triumphant return from Kremlin 136; tribute from Churchill 136–37; reviews Churchill's visit 137; party during Willkie's visit 137–38; jokes with tommy-gun 138; rapport with Stalin 138; responds to Second Front criticism 138; on leave in London 138; summative report on USSR (1942) 138–39; addresses Chiefs of Staff 139; viewed as pro-Soviet 139; meets Churchill and Eden 139–40; unhappy at FO attitudes 140; proposes Beaverbrook as new ambassador 140; meets young Left 140; literary contacts 140; meets Guy Burgess 140; broadcasts on BBC 140; quizzes Churchill on line to be taken 141; raises issue of postwar settlement 141; judged to have erred 141; status in FO 142; view of Katyn 142; rejects Churchill's draft response 142; views Joe Davies film 143; admiration for Standley 143; rationale for Maisky's recall 143; impression of Gusev 143; pained at FO approach to USSR 144; justifies Soviet attitude 144; keeps Stalin informed on Quebec talks 145; notes reappearanbce of Tsarist icons 145; presented with tommy-gun 146; distaste for diplomatic set 146; prospects for Conference for Foreign Ministers (1943) 147; role in British delegation 148; view of Eden 149; hosts dinner 149; guest-of-honour at Kremlin 149; tribute from Eden 150; joins Privy Council 150; party at Spiridonovka Palace 150ff; row with Swedes 151; collapses during toast 151–52; wakes in grate 152; morning after with Molotov 152; attends Cairo talks 153; at Stalingrad 153; at Teheran Conference 153ff; arranges agenda 153; meets Roosevelt 154; opinion of Roosevelt 155; calls Stalin a 'cissy' 156; to Cairo 156; visits USA 156; meeting with Tita 156; returns to USSR 156; sees Stalin re Polish issue 157; finds Stalin intransigent on Poland 157; suggests abandoning London Poles 157; unhappy at Churchill's threats 158; proved correct 158; suggests recall to London 158; FO view of Clark Kerr and Poland 158; informs Kremlin of D-Day 158–59; presses Stalin to aid Polish resistance 159; memorandum of August 1944 159–60; pessimism over alliance 160; Churchill's 1944 visit 160–61; Churchill's naughty document 161; delighted at progress 161; Eden promises Washington job 161; unimpressed by Lublin Poles 162; hosts Stalin's visit to Embassy 162; frustration at Mikolajczyk 162; post-conference despatch 163; leave in London 163; files for divorce 163; to Yalta 164; on Polish Committee 164; toasts Beria 165; warned by Churchill 165; assessment of vodka 165; eye trouble 165; failure of Polish Committee 166; remains optimistic 166–67; Driberg's opinion of Clark Kerr 167; method of composing memoranda 167–68; criticism of Harriman 168; in Washington 168; talks with Eden 169; at San Francisco UN meeting 169; defends USSR re borders 169; at Windsor 170; review of Soviet policy pre-Potsdam 170–71; in Warsaw 171; at Potsdam 171; on Polish drafting committee 172; presses for acceptance of Polish borders 172; disagreement with Attlee 172–73; humours Molotov 173; rejects part of Polish agreement 173; returns to Moscow 173; problem for career of Labour victory 173; attends CFM in London (Sept. 1945) 174; social life 174; accompanies Bevin in talks with Molotov 174–75; draws up plan for USSR agreement 175; at Inverchapel 175–76; approaches Bevin re his future 175–76; returns to Moscow 176; CFM talks (Moscow Dec. 1945) 176; appointed to Rumania Committee 176; toughens approach to USSR 176; impresses Bevin 177; travels to Romania 177; unimpressed by Soviet manoeuvring 178; shouts at Vyshinski 178; sees dark side of Soviet policy 179; visits King Michael and Queen Mother 179; returns to London 179; Bevin offers Washington 179–80;

INDEX

appointed Ambassador to USA (1946) 180; choice of title 180; mission to Dutch East Indies 181; Moscow farewells 181; review of Moscow years 181–82; returns from East Indies 182; at Buckingham Palace 182; at Inverchapel 182; Honorary degree ceremony at Glasgow 182; reunion with Tita 183; meets Boothby 183; chooses coat-of-arms 183; at Inverchapel 183; enters House of Lords 183; sails for USA 183; dislike of economics 184; annoyance at Elliot Roosevelt's memoirs 185–86; arrival in US 188; press conference and comment 188; attitude to Washington society 189–90; meets Truman 190; addresses National Press Club 190; Zionist sympathies 191; pressure for loan 191; at White House signing 192; criticism of public relations role 192; outlines own task 192; lobbies Bevin to visit 192; public speaking 193–94; commitment to Labour philosophy 194; tours Western USA 195; visit of Dalton 195; boredom 195–96; visits Iowa farm 196; meets Bevin in New York 196; relations with Acheson 197; talks on Palestine 197–98; at White House with Bevin 198; clashes with US Right 198; talks on atomic cooperation 198–99; on Combined Policy Committee 199; delegation of work to Donald Maclean 199; to State Department re Greece and Turkey 200; opinion of Truman doctrine 201–202; status in US 203; defends Britain 203; analysis of speeches 204; appears on NBC 204; tours US 205; reports Bevin's reaction to Marshall speech 206; reports UK economic plight 206; on leave in Britain 206; heart problems 206; at Inverchapel 206–207; re-marriage to Tita 207; leave cut short 207; economic talks in Washington 208; social life 208; explains Labour policy 208; distaste for economics 208; FO offers of support 208–209; relations with Marshall 209; rumours about retirement quashed 209–10; involvement in Clayton's resignation 210; agrees retirement plan 210; plans for Western defence union 211–12; involvement in birth of NATO 212; favours European union 212; retirement announced (1948) 213; farewell speeches 213; reaction to Washington years 213–14; analysis of success and failures 214ff; relation with Donald Maclean 217–18; leaves US 219; in London 219; involvement in Olympic Games 219; retires to Inverchapel 219–20; accepts role in European union talks 220; in Paris 220; criticises stance of British government 221; resigns 221; press rumours of political role 221; estate management 222; Tita's departure 222; radio broadcast 222; car crash 223; broadcast on China 223; row over Stalin obituary 224; publishes stories 224–25; candidacy for University of Glasgow rectorship 225–26; backs US in Korea 206; reaction to defection of Burgess and Maclean 226; death 226; funeral 226; retrospect 227–28.

APPEARANCE 10; goes 'native' 22; 70, 77, 79, 138, 188, 216.

ATTITUDES AND BELIEFS to Chamberlain government/appeasement 84, 85, 97, 103, 107, 107, 118; to Communism 53, 94–95, 115, 116, 117–18, 186–87, 191, 198, 213, 223, 224; to fascism/dictators 83–84, 85, 87, 103, 140; to diplomacy 12, 18–19, 30–31, 35, 53, 80, 81, 93, 124, 133, 137, 143, 144, 159–60, 166–67, 173, 181–82, 183, 189–90, 192, 195, 213, 214f, 218–19, 221, 222, 227; to European union 163, 212, 220–21; (anti-)imperialism 27, 36–37,42, 51, 81–82, 88, 92–93, 100, 168, 182, 200, 204, 223; to Labour Party 37, 42, 53, 68–69, 173, 187–88, 194, 264, 208, 213; liberal ideas 27, 35, 36, 41–42, 53, 68, 81, 91, 94, 148, 187, 191, 213, 224; to marriage 76, 77, 78, 80, 112, 125; to national self-determination 36, 41, 42, 81, 98, 100, 107, 182; politics (early attitudes) 8,42; pragmatism/realism 13, 32, 36, 42,45, 49, 68, 92–93, 109, 117, 123, 126, 160, 166, 173, 223; to public duty 19, 80, 105, 113, 126–27, 184; public speaking (dislike of) 74, 184, 192, 193, 203; to school 36, 70; Scottish identity 6, 9, 13, 15, 37, 70–71, 73, 75–76, 176, 204, 219; sex 13, 25, 82, 125, 138, 146, 164, 183–84; to socialism 42, 87–88, 94–95, 140, 187, 194, 213; to Spanish Civil War 83, 85; to Tory party 8, 37, 42, 53, 74, 88, 187; values 13, 32, 35, 42, 49, 94, 143, 187, 223, 227; to World War I 16–19, 22, 25; to the young 77–78, 140, 209; Zionism 26, 191, 194, 197.

ASPECTS OF CHARACTER ambition 8, 9, 16, 22, 69, 79, 81, 130, 162, 176, 180, 184, 211; charm 13–14, 35, 80, 112, 119, 170, 193, 195, 214, 215; confidence13, 74, 91, 81, 85, 87; diffidence 13, 40, 184, 193, 213–14; disappointment/pessimism 11, 12, 13, 15, 36, 40, 78, 79, 80, 108, 119, 124, 126, 146, 157, 160, 175; early character 13–14; energy 79, 91, 113, 174, 177, 203, 209, 213; fairness 15, 42, 45, 52, 53, 82, 93, 108, 126, 152, 182; grievance (sense of) 17–18, 22, 42, 80; honesty 13, 31, 53, 118, 131, 133, 133–34, 139, 144, 182, 223; humour 8, 13, 75, 112, 129, 130, 138, 141, 143, 154, 159, 162, 173, 177, 182, 183; informality 13, 79, 81, 95, 100, 103, 127, 129, 130,

251

145, 159, 177, 182, 187, 224; integrity 45, 52–3, 100, 105, 219; loyalty 80, 163, 207, 213, 223, 226; outspokenness 13, 14, 40, 78, 79, 95, 133f, 139, 184, 188; personal involvement 29, 41, 43–44, 65, 67, 197; political skill 23, 27, 29, 35, 43, 45, 80, 81, 100, 111, 119, 133f,182, 189, 191; popularity 30, 47, 68, 74, 81, 96, 111, 114, 142, 170, 187, 203; pride/vanity 3, 22, 40, 49, 69–70, 78, 84, 85, 87, 96, 111, 113, 120, 164, 188; resilience 22, 74, 183; sensitivity 24, 69; sentimentality 13, 75–76, 160, 207, 219; shrewdness 31, 43, 80, 92–93, 119, 128, 133f, 153, 175, 188; sympathy 14, 27, 42, 90, 100, 104, 167, 213; toughness/courage 55, 100, 102, 107, 111, 113, 119, 127, 133, 139, 183; writing skill 74, 127, 216, 224.

HEALTH Burgess/Maclean defection, effect of 226; car crash, effect of 223; death 226; eye trouble 24, 165; false teeth 188; fitness 70; heart trouble 206, 213, 226; hospital 223, 226.

HONOURS KCMG 80; GCMG 113; PC 150; Barony 180; Honorary degree (Glasgow) 183; House of Lords 184; also, Honorary degree from Johns Hopkins University, USA; Chinese Order of the Jade; Swedish Grand Cordon; Order of Merit (Chile).

MARRIAGE meets Tita 76; marriage 77; leaves Chile 77; death of child 77–78; boredom in Sweden 78; FO view of marriage 80; difficulties in Iraq 83, 84; problems in China 91; strains 98, 103; Tita deserts 112; Clark Kerr's reaction 112–13, 119, 128; attempted reconciliation 156; divorce 163; faithfulness 163; reunion 182, 184; new closeness 195, 206; remarriage 207; 208, 222; 225.

RELATIONSHIPS (PERSONAL AND PROFESSIONAL) Dean Acheson 197; Lord Allenby 35, 37, 56–66; Ernest Bevin 174–75, 177, 179–80, 192–93, 196–7, 220–21; Robert, Lord Boothby 18, 25, 35, 72, 74, 80, 88, 108, 183, 225; James (Lord) Bryce 15; Austen Chamberlain 63–66, 69, 72, 79; Chiang Kai-shek 92, 100, 114; Winston Churchill 18, 25, 33, 37, 53, 71–72, 73, 109, 130ff; fallout 132; talk in garden 133ff; 137, 141, 147, 154–5, 156, 160–63, 165, 169; Sir Robert Craigie 97, 102–103, 106 ; Hugh Dalton 78, 81, 195, 220–21; Gerald Delaney 35, 47, 53; father 8, 9, 14; Sir Anthony Eden 81, 84, 85,·113, 149, 162, 172; Elizabeth, HM the Queen Mother 28, 39–40, 75, 170; with Foreign Office 16–19, 22, 25, 42, 47, 57, 64, 66, 69, 72, 74, 80, 103, 111, 127, 139, 142, 158, 170, 208, 210, 213; W. Averell Harriman 132, 151–2, 153, 159, 165, 168, 176; Walter Harris 26; Louvima Knollys 11, 14, 15; Ramsay MacDonald 52–53, 62, 72; Donald Maclean 198, 217–18, 226; V. M. Molotov 126, 128–29, 138, 146, 147, 151, 152, 166, 173, 181; mother 8, 14, 22, 26, 67, 73–74, 76; Muriel, sister 67; Harold Nicolson 13–14, 28, 51, 77, 78, 79–80, 88, 225; Lord Eustace Percy 15, 28, 72, 74; Franklin D. Roosevelt 154–55, 164, 190; Princess Sophie 11–12, 16; Joseph Stalin first meeting 125–26, 127–28, 138, 141, 143–44; 'cissy' 156; 158, 159, 181, 182, 214, 217, 224; Gunther Stein 114, 117; Sir William Tyrrell 16–19, 25, 69, 72; Andrei Vyshinski 124, 126, 177; shouting-match 178; 181. SPEECHES Valparaiso (1928) 75–76; leaving China (1942) 114; to Chiefs of Staff (Dec. 1942) 134; BBC broadcast(1943) 140; University of Glasgow (1946) 182; National Press Club (Washington,1946) 190; St Louis Chamber of Commerce (Oct. 1946) 194; Pilgrims (Nov. 1946) 197; ESU (Richmond.Va., March 1947) 202; on American 'tour' 264; on NBC (April 1947) 204; Chicago (April 1948) 213; St George's Society of New York (May 1948) 213; Scottish radio (April 1949) 222; BBC talk on China (Oct. 1949) 223; BBC 'obituary' of Stalin 224.

TASTES acting 8; alcohol 75, 127, 152, 165, 201, 222, 225; art/painting 79, 111, 216; botany 73; Confucianism 111, 164; erotica 13, 25; farming 25, 183, 207, 209, 211, 219, 221, 226; fishing 8, 48, 75, 183; fitness 69, 127, 137; gardening 25, 183, 226; interests 48, 170; languages 21, 27, 69, 141, 187; literature 18, 75, 78, 140, 216; skiing 78; smoking (pipe) 111, 125, 138, 141, 157, 225; sport 8, 29, 75, 76; sunbathing 76, 111, 137; swimming 111, 127; writing 22, 127, 216, 225

Inverchapel, Lady Maria Theresa Clark Kerr, (nee Diaz Salas) background 76; appearance 76; marriage 76; in England 77; leaves Chile 77; pregnancy 77; loss of child 77–78; status in Sweden 78; returns to London 78; bored in Sweden 78; of Iraq 80; becomes Lady 80; leaves Sweden 80; on leave from Iraq 83; discontent in Baghdad 84; to China 84, 89; to Chungking 90; returns to Shanghai 91; social life 91; strain of life in China 91, 98, 103; holiday in Chile 103; deserts to US 112; 119, 128, 146, 156, 163; reunion with Archie 183, 184; new closeness 195; holiday in Scotland 206–207; remarriage 207; 208, 219, 220; dislike of Argyll 221; revisits US 222; returns 223; car crash 223; injuries 223, 225; later history 227
Inverchapple see also Inverchapel 1
Invermark Lodge 39
Iowa 195, 205
Iran see also Persia 187
Iraq 15, 34, 80–84

INDEX

Irish nationalism 8
Iron Curtain 169, 187
Islington, Lady 39
Ismay, Gen. Hastings 148
Italy 8, 10, 16, 83, 86, 110, 139, 145, 148, 157, 158, 168, 174, 187, 211

Jamieson, E.D. 98–99; Tientsin crisis 104–107
Japan 68, 69, 84, 148, 151, 155, 173–74; and China policy pre-1938 86; Chapter 6 passim; surrender 174, 184
Jebb, Gladwyn 210, 212, 217–18
Jewish Agency 185, 191
John, Rosamund 225
Johnson, Nelson 94
Johnston, Tom 207
Jordan, Philip 226

Kalinin, Mikhail, President of USSR 125
Kames Castle 28
Kansas 210
Karachi 146
Katyn 142–43, 155, 203
Kennan, George F. 160, 187
Kennedys 208
Kent, Prince George, Duke of 40
Kent, P.B.H. 106–107
Keown-Boyd 38
Kerr, Archibald John Kerr Clark *see* Inverchapel, 1st Baron
Kerr, John 2
Kerr, Margaret 2, 14
Kerr Clark family *see* under Clark
Kerrs & McBride 2
Khartoum 40, 48, 64
Khedive *see* Abbas Hilmi
Killearn, Lord (Miles Lampson) 22
Kilmun 9
Kindersley, Hugh 25
King, J.H. 217
King David Hotel 195
Kitchener, Lord 32
Knatchbull-Hugessen, Sir Hughe Montgomery shot 87; 89, 91
Knollys, Lady 11
Knollys, Louvima 11, 14, 15
Knox, Prof. T.M. 222
Korea 224
Korniechuk 151
Kot 157
Kowloon 98

Kremlin 124, 130ff, 138, 141, 143, 146, 149, 151, 152, 158, 161, 163, 167, 174, 223
Krivitsky, Walter 217–18
Kuibyshev 118, 120, 123; description 124–25; 127, 128, 137; Foreign Ministry returns to Moscow 146
Kukiel 157
Kung, H.H. 92, 93, 94
Kung, Mme 94
Kunt, Mustapha 146
Kuomintang (Chinese Nationalist Government) 86, 91, 92, 93; and Indusco 93–94; 99, 100; military strategy 101; 109, 110; clash with communists 112, 115, 118
Kurds 83
Kursk 145
Kutuzov, M.I., Prince of Smolensk 145

Labour Government (1945) 184, 194, 202, 203, 204, 207, 210, 215, 216
Labour Party 25, 37, 42–43; 1924 govt. 43, 44; foreign policy 45, 46; 1924 govt falls 52; 53, 55, 68, 72; 1929 victory 77; 173; 1945 Conference 185; 187, 194, 196, 198, 208, 212–13, 215; and Europe 220–21; 225
Ladybird, HMS 89
Lampson, Miles *see* Killearn, Lord
Lascelles, Sir Frank 10, 79
Lauder, Harry 75
Lauterbach, Richard 111
Lawrence, William H. 111
League of Nations 61, 81, 86
Lehmann, John 140, 141–42
Leningrad 131
Levine, Isaac Don 217
Lewthwaite, Lady *see* Clark, Lois Mairi Kerr
Liberal Party 8, 15, 44, 46, 53, 55, 218
Lilienthal, David E. 199, 213
Lippmann, Walter 190
Listowel, Lord 221
Litvinov, M. 148
Livadia Palace, Yalta 164
Liverpool Plains 3
Lloyd George, David 33, 53, 72
Loch Eck *see* Eck
London 8, 12, 18, 23, 24, 33, 36, 42, 47, 48, 49, 50, 51; 1924 Egypt talks 52; 54, 71, 78, 79, 80, 81, 83, 85, 88, 91, 124, 128, 138, 143, 150,

156, 159, 163, 168, 170, 173, 179, 182, 183, 196, 197, 211, 219, 221
Loos, Battle of (1915) 23
Lothian, Marquis of 111
Lovett, Robert E. 208, 211, 212
Lubeck 169
Lublin 159; 'Lublin Poles' 162, 164
Luce, Henry 198, 213–14
Lupu 177
Luxembourg 212
Lygon, Henry 10
Lyon, Lord 183

MacCormick, John M. 225
MacDonald, Ramsay 43, 44; brakes on freedom 45–46; 47, 48, 49, 50; 1924 Egypt talks 51, 52; accuses Zaghlul 51; repudiates press report 51; Clark Kerr's view of 52–53; criticises Allenby 62; 72, 77
Maclean, Donald 189, 198, 212, 217–18; defects 226
Maclean, Sir Donald 218
Macleod, George 225
Maddox, Arthur 118
Madrid 79, 80, 83
Magowan, Sir John 189
Mahdi 31, 48
Mahmoud 54
Maisky, I. 143–44
Makins, Roger (later Lord Sherfield) 199
Malaya 112, 223
Malta 32, 50
Maly, Theodore 218
Manchuria 86, 89, 99
Maniu 177
Mao Tse-tung 34, 86, 93, 100, 112, 114, 117, 118, 122–23
Marling, Charles (Sir) 21, 23, 31
Marsh, Eddie 18
Marshall, Gen. George C. 199–200, 201, 203, 204, 205–206, 209, 210, 211; and NATO 212; 224
Marshall Plan 163, 205–206, 208, 209, 211, 212, 213, 215, 220; and Congress 211, 213
Marshall, Texas 208
Martel, Gen. 142, 153
Marx, Karl 145, 212
Marxism 122–23, 208
Mason-Macfarlane, Gen. 121
Maxton, James, MP 150
Maxwell, Gavin 15, 81, 130–31

253

Maxwell Fyfe, Sir David 225
Mazloum 54
McArthur, Gen. 226
McCarthyism 114, 223
McCormick, Col. R.R. 195
McHugh, James 117
McMahon Act 195, 198–99, 215
Mediterranean 16, 26, 45, 202
Melrose 76
Mesopotamia 23, 24
Mexico 79–80
MI5 217–18
Michael, King of Rumania 165–66, 177–79
Mihalache, Ion 178
Mikolajczyk, S. 156–57, 159, 162, 165, 166, 170, 171, 172–73
Mikoyan, A. 151
Milner, Lord 32
Minc, Hilary 162
Mississippi 205
Missouri 187
Mohammed Said 50, 51, 54
Molotov, V.M. 124; remains in Moscow 124; 125, 126; and Second Front 28; 130, 131, 132, 137, 138, 141, 142, 146, 147, 148, 149, 150, 151, 152, 153; at Teheran 153–56; Polish talks 159; 164, 165–66; in Washington 168–69; 170, 173, 174; in London (1945) 174–75; 179, 181, 196
Molotov-Ribbentrop pact (1939) 107, 110, 112, 142
Moore, Lady Beatrice see Clark
Moore-Brabazon, Col. 122
Moran, Lord (Sir Charles Wilson) 132, 133
Morocco 26–29, 168
'Morocco' 30
Morrison, Herbert 192
Morrison-Grady Plan 197–98
Moscow 80, 84, 113, 116, 118; Chapter 7 passim; 181, 187, 192, 201, 204, 205, 217, 218, 223
Munich agreement (1938) 97, 98, 99, 107, 120
Munro, Sir Gordon 189, 198
Murray, Jack (FO) 48, 55, 69
Murray, Les 228
Mussolini, B. 87, 145

Namoi, river 3–4
Nanking 86
National Party of Scotland 73
NATO 212, 215

Nazis see also Germany 83, 112, 120–21, 122, 124, 143, 145, 149, 164, 168, 217
Neisse, River see Oder
Netherlands 181, 206, 212
New Fourth Army (China) 112
New Mexico 169
'New Order' (Japan) 99, 100, 108
New South Wales 1, 3, 4, 7, 228
New York City 14, 112, 156, 188, 191, 192, 193, 195, 196ff, 203, 207–208
New York Times 224
The New Yorker 189
New Zealand 93
Newburn family (Iowa) 195, 205
Newcastle 18
Newfoundland 2
News Chronicle 117
Newsweek 189
Nicaragua 71, 73
Nicolson, Harold 13–14, 28, 51, 68, 77, 78, 79–80, 88, 222, 225
NKVD 124, 218
Normandy 154, 158–59
North Africa 26, 29, 129, 138, 139, 153
Northcliffe, Lord 28
Northumberland, Duke of 15
Norway 212
Nova Scotia 188
Nunn May, Dr Allan 186, 198
Nuri es-Said 83

Oberammergau 11
Oder-Neisse, River 156; Polish border issue 172–73
Olympic Games (1948) 219
Orabi revolt 31
Oregon 195
Osobka-Morawski, Edward 162
'Overlord' 154, 155, 156, 158–59
Oxford 6, 217, 218

Palestine 25, 52, 185–86, 191, 193, 195, 196; Nov.1946 talks 197–98; 200, 215
Panay, USS 89
Paraguay 14
Paris 28, 32, 187, 190, 206, 218, 220
Parker, Ralph 140
Parmoor, Lord 49
Patterson, Sir Reginald 35, 52, 56

Pavlov (Soviet translator) 131, 154
Pearl Harbour 113
Peking 86; Japanese puppet government installed 87; 101
Percy, Lord Eustace 15, 28, 72, 74
Persia see also Iran 16, 18–19, 20–23, 24, 25, 31, 34, 42
Piccadilly 40
Piggott, Maj.-Gen. 96, 102–104
Plautus 6
Poland 108, 123–24, 138, 141; Katyn issue 142–43; 144, 148, 149, 154, 156; Clark Kerr's negotiations with Stalin (1944) 157–58; 159; 1944 talks 160–63, 164–65, 166–67, 168, 169, 170; Clark Kerr in 171; Potsdam talks 172–73; 211
Politburo 128, 137, 143, 150, 181
Port Talbot 62
Portal, Admiral 139, 219
Potsdam Conference (1945) 170–74, 182, 185, 227
Powell, J.B. 93
Pravda 136, 157
Priestland, Gerald 224
Proust, Marcel 219
Puerto Rico 156
PWE (Political Warfare Executive) 146

Quebec Conference (1943) 144f, 146
Queen Mary, RMS 183, 188

RAF 48, 82, 139, 169
Red Army 145, 149, 159, 170
Red Cross 142
Red Sea 48
Reston, James 'Scotty' 190
Reuters 35, 37, 43, 47, 51
Rheims 169
Ribbentrop-Molotov Treaty (1939) 107, 110, 112, 142
Richmond, Va. 203
Robartes, Greg see Clifden, Viscount
Roberts, Sir Frank 158, 167, 171
Robertson, Sir John 3–5
Robertson, Kate Louisa see Clark, Mrs John Kerr
Robson, Dr Newby 37–38
Rodd, Sir James Rennell 17–18
Rome 13, 16–18
Romniceanu, Mihai 179
Ronald, Nigel 66

INDEX

Roosevelt, Elliot 185–86
Roosevelt, Franklin Delano 108, 123–24; Second Front 128; 129, 130, 139, 143; at Quebec 145; 147, 148, 152; at Teheran 153–56; 160; at Yalta 164–65; death 166; 168, 185–86, 190
Rostov 129
Rothesay 227
'Rudens' (Plautus) 6
Ruhr 46
Rumania 16, 158, 159, 161, 165, 166, 175, 176; Tripartite Commission (1945–46) 176, 177–79; 211
Russia see also USSR 18, 20, 40, 46

St Andrews 76, 222
St Andrew's Society, Valparaiso 75
St George's Society of New York 213
St Louis 194, 197
St Margaret's Church (Westminster) 226–27
St Munn's Church (Kilmun) 226
St Petersburg 13
Sackville-West, Vita 78–79
Salvador 71, 73
San Bernardino 14
San Francisco (UN Conference 1945) 166, 168–69
Sandringham 81
Sansom, Sir George 108, 189
Santiago 75, 76, 227
Sargent, Sir Orme ('Moley') 141, 157, 168, 171
Sarwat Pasha 34, 36, 37
Saxe-Weimar 2
Scoon's 8, 10, 62
Scotland 8, 14; politics 37; 39, 70–71, 75–76, 163, 225
Scots Guards 25
Scott, Sir Basil 28
Scott, Hon. E.S. 35, 38, 43,
Scottish Labour Party 73
Seaforth Highlanders 16, 23
Second Front 121, 124, 128–29, 131ff, 139, 140, 143, 148, 160, 169
Selby, Walford 47, 48, 67, 69, 71, 78
Seychelles 33
Shah of Persia 34
Shanghai 87, 89, 90; scene in 91; 92, 96, 97, 98, 103; Craigie talks 103; 105, 109, 110, 117
Shi'ites 83

Shostakovich 150
Sichel, Herbert 200
Sidky Pasha 66
Silver, Rabbi 197
Simon, Sir John 92, 95
Sinaia (Rumania) 179
Singapore 112, 113; fall of 118; 119
Sirdar see Stack, Sir Lee
Smedley, Agnes 93, 95, 114, 115, 116
Smolensk 142
Snow, Edgar 92f, 105, 115, 118
SOE (Special Operations Executive) 118
Soong, T.V. 89, 92
Sophie, Princess (of Greece) 11–12, 16
Sorge, Richard 117
Sosnkowski, Gen. 157, 162
South America 14, 15
Southampton 206
Soviet Union see USSR
Spa Hotel, Bath 6
Spain and Tangier 26–29; 83, 85, 95, 157
The Spectator 28
Spiridonovka Palace 148, 150
Spoor, Ben, MP 42–43, 48
Ssu Ching-wu 98–99, 102, 107
Stack, Lady 56
Stack, Sir Lee (the Sirdar) 38, 49, 50, 52; shot 55–56; dies 57; funeral 58; 60, 81
Stalin, Joseph 16, 107, 120; presses for aid 121; view of Cripps 121–22; deal with Hitler 120, 123; 124; remains in Moscow 124; Clark Kerr's first impression 125–26, 127–28; and Second Front 128–29; meets Churchill (1942) 131–37; tommy gun 'joke' 138; and E.Europe 138–39; 140, 141; and Katyn 142–43; 143–44; and Quebec talks 145–46; 149, 150; at Teheran 152, 153–56; and Poland 157–59; and Churchill's visit (1944) 160–63; at Yalta 164–65; Clark Kerr's opinion 167; 168, 169, 173; pressure on China 173; 176, 181; Clark Kerr's judgement 182; 185, 187, 188, 202, 214, 217, 218, 224, 226
Stalingrad 137, 139; German surrender at 141; 153, 159
Standley, Admiral 125, 32, 136, 143, 145, 148

Stein, Gunther 105; connection with Clark Kerr 114, 117
Stettinius, Edward 168
Stettin 187
Stockholm 78ff, 164
Stone of Destiny 225
Strachey, St John 28
Strachur 28
Strang, Sir William 148
Stuart, Lord Colum 24, 25, 28, 72
Sudan 32, 33, 34, 38, 39, 44, 45, 46, 47, 48, 49, 50–51, 51–52; assassination of Stack 55–56; water supply 57ff
Suez Canal 30, 33, 34, 37, 45, 46, 47, 48; and Sept. 1924 talks 51–52; 185
Sun Yat-sen 86
Sun Yat-sen, Mme 89, 93–94
Suvorov, Count Alexander 145
Sweden 18, 78–80, 83, 117, 146, 151
Switzerland 78, 82, 151
Sydney 1, 3, 4, 14, 118

Tangier 26–29, 30, 31, 42
Tasmania 4
Tatarescu, Gheorghe 177–78
Taunus mountains 11
Tegucigalpa 73
Teheran 15, 18–19, 118, 130, 152
Teheran Conference (1943) 153–56, 157, 158, 185–86, 227
Tewfik Nessim 36, 38, 39, 54
Texas 208
Thomson, Lord 52
Tibet 223
Tientsin 86, 98, 102; 1939 crisis 103–107, 108
Time 198, 213, 214
The Times 26, 28; on Egypt 43; 48; shooting of Sirdar 56, 59–60; on Nevile Henderson's appointment 64; 80, 107, 140, 189, 200
Tobruk 129
Tokyo 68, 88, 96, 97, 98, 103, 107, 109, 117
Tolstoy, Alexei 149
Tong, Hollington K. 112
Tory Party see also Conservative Party 8, 33, 42, 53, 74, 187; and Europe 220–21; 225
Townley, Sir Walter 15–16, 21
Tresseder, Ross 227
Trieste 169, 170, 171, 187
Trotsky 178, 203

Truman, President Harry S. 168, 170, 171; at Potsdam 171–73; 176; political style 168, 186, 202; and Loan 184, 190, 191–92; and Palestine 185, 195, 196, 197, 198, 199, 200; and Truman Doctrine 202–203, 204, 205; 215, 224
Tsar(ism) 20, 122, 145–46, 150
Turkey 20–21, 31, 49, 146, 156, 170, 176, 187; and surrender of UK mandate 200–202; 211
Tweed, River 76
Tweedy, O.M. 43
Tyrrell, Sir William 16, 17–19, 25, 69, 72, 79
Tyrrwhitt-Wilson, Gerald 'Newt' see Berners, Lord

Ukraine 158, 170
Union of Soviet Socialist Republics (USSR) 95, 104, 107, 113, 116–17; Clark Kerr arrives in 118–19; Chapter 7 passim; 181–82, 185, 186; US fears over 187, 190, 191, 201; German zone 194; 198; and Marshall Plan 206, 211; 212, 215, 216; and British spies 145, 199, 217–18; 200, 202–203, 222, 224, 226, 227
United Nations (UN) 161, 166, 186, 188, 196, 197, 200, 204; 'World Organisation' 147, 148, 164, 168
United States of America (USA) Clark Kerr in 14–15; 73, 90, 91, 97, 100, 101, 109, 111, 112, 113, 121, 129, 138, 141, 143, 144, 156; policy change on Japan 101, 108, 111; policy in China 114, 115; and CFM 147; Clark Kerr in (1943) 156; US view of British Empire 137, 168, 158, 215; 166, 168, 171, 173–74; Clark Kerr appointed ambassador 179–80; Chapter 8 passim; 219, 222, 223, 227
Utah 195

Valparaiso 75
Venice 36, 78
Victoria, HM Queen 5, 8, 11
Vietnam 223
Villiers, Gerald 10

Virginia 203
Volga 118
von Bulow 11, 12
Vorontzov Palace, Yalta 164
Voroshilov, Marshal Klimenti 131, 137–38, 148
Vyshinski, Andrei 124, 126; hosts party 127; 148, 151, 159; in Romania 165–66, 176, 177–79; 181

'Wafd' 32, 44, 46, 49, 54
Wales, HRH Prince of see Edward VII, Edward VIII
Wales, Nym (Mrs Edgar Snow) 93
Wang Ching-wei 100
War Office 17
Warner, Christopher 127
Warner, Sir Pelham 189
Warsaw 159, 165, 166, 171
Washington, DC 14–15, 81, 111, 124, 125, 128, 130, 143, 144, 148, 161, 167, 168, 173, 174, 177, 179–80; Chapter 8 passim; 226
Washington State 195
Wasilewska, Wanda 158
Wassef Bey Ghali 60
Watson's Bay 1
Wavell, Field-Marshal Viscount 132
Waverley Station 71
Webster, John 219
Webster's Dictionary 15
Weizmann, Chaim 25, 197
Welles, Sumner 147–48
Wellesley, Lord Gerald see Wellington, Duke of
Wellington, 7th Duke of 10
Westminster Abbey 5, 225
Whistlefield 220
White, Sir Herbert 26
White House 168, 190, 192, 198
Whitehall 9, 16, 17, 18, 66, 73, 87, 97, 99, 118, 143
Who's Who 69ff
Wiggin, Arthur 43
Willhelm II, Kaiser 11, 12, 23
Willkie, Wendell 137–38, 146, 185
Wilson, Sir Charles see Moran, Lord
Wilson, Geoffrey 144
Wilson, Field-Marshal Maitland 198
Wilson, President Woodrow 32
Windsor 40, 163, 170
Windsor, Duke of see Edward VIII, HM King

Woolf, Virginia 78–79
Wuhu 89

Yale 201
Yalta Conference (1945) 164–65, 166, 168, 172, 173, 227
Yangtze 86, 91, 98, 100, 103, 110–111, 112, 113
Yenan 86
York, HRH Duke and Duchess of see George VI, HM King; Elizabeth, HM (the Queen Mother)
Yorke Faussett, Mrs 22
The Yorkshire Post 189
Yost, Yevgeni 188, 198, 206, 207, 222; car crash 223; 227
Younger (Benmore) 219
Yugoslavia 146, 158, 159, 161

Zaghlul, Sa'ad Pasha (Egyptian nationalist leader) 32, 33, 34, 35, 36, 42, 44, 47, 48, 55; in exile 32, 33, 34, 35; returns from exile 43; election victory 44–45; and Ramsay MacDonald 45–46; party problems 46, 49; shot at 49, 50; calls off talks 51; reinvited 51; in London 52; no compromise 52; returns to Egypt 53; plan to oust him 54–55; shooting of Sirdar 56; rumour of resignation 58; given ultimatum 59; reaction 59–60; resigns 61, 62; returned as PM 66; 72
Zamalek 40
Zinoviev letter 53
Zionism 25, 185–86, 191, 192, 193, 194, 195, 196, 197, 215
Ziwar Pasha 54; becomes PM 61; 64, 66

1. RIGHT. Archibald Clark Kerr, schoolboy, *c.* 1898

2. BELOW. Crossbasket House, 1908

3. LEFT. Archibald Clark Kerr, young attaché, Foreign Office, 1906

4. BELOW. Archibald Clark Kerr with the Princes of Wales (later Edward VIII) and Kent, Stockholm 1932

5. ABOVE. Sir Archibald Clark Kerr and Lady Clark Kerr arriving at Shanghai, February 1938
6. BELOW. Sir Archibald Clark Kerr following the presentation of his credentials, China 1938

7. LEFT. Dining with Gen
and Madame Chiang Kai
1939

8. BELOW. With General
Madame Chiang Kai-she
General Sir Archibald W
and officers, China 1941

9. RIGHT. Sir Archibald Clark Kerr, Molotov and Stalin await Churchill, Moscow 1942

10. BELOW. Churchill's arrival in Moscow, 1942

11. ABOVE. Churchill and Stalin meeting in Moscow, 1942

12. BELOW. Sir Archibald Clark Kerr (facing camera) with the Big Three at the Yalta Conference

13. ABOVE. Sir Archibald Clark Kerr with Vyshinski, Harriman and the Romanian Queen Mother, Romania, December 1945

14. RIGHT. Lord Inverchapel in 1946

15. Lord and Lady Inverchapel in Washington, 1947

16. Lord Inverchapel, 1947

Printed in Great Britain
by Amazon